World communication report

World communication report

The media and the challenge of the new technologies

UNESCO Publishing

General Editor: **Alain Modoux**
Author: **Lotfi Maherzi**
Statistical tables and charts: **My von Euler**

About the author

Lotfi Maherzi holds a Ph.D. in Political Science (University of Paris) and a degree of Bachelor of Law from the University of Algiers and received training in cinematography at the Institute of Advanced Cinematographic Studies (Paris). He has conducted research in the fields of communication and the new technologies, which he also taught at the Universities of Algiers, Tunis and Versailles/Saint-Quentin (France). In the course of his university career the author published a study of the Algerian cinema and dozens of specialized articles relating to information and communication. He was Rector of the Algiers University of Continuing Education from 1989 to 1995.

Cover photo: Thierry Petillot/SIPA Image
Layout by Jean-Francis Chériez
Text composed by Éditions du Mouflon, 94270 Le Kremlin-Bicêtre (France)
Printed by Imprimerie Darantière, 21800 Quetigny (France)

Published in 1997 by the United Nations Educational,
Scientific and Cultural Organization
7 Place de Fontenoy, 75352 Paris 07 SP (France)

ISBN: 92-3-103428-6

Preface

When the founding states adopted UNESCO's Constitution in 1945, they chartered the course of its future action, which included the task of promoting 'the free flow of ideas by word and image' (Article I). The Preamble stated the purpose of UNESCO, namely, to construct the defences of peace 'in the minds of men' through education, culture and co-operation in science. But the founders were aware that there was only one key to achieving this ambition: free communication, or the free flow of information.

UNESCO's 'new communication strategy' – adopted by consensus in 1989 by its Member States – has three objectives: to encourage the free flow of information at both national and international level; to promote a wider and more balanced dissemination of information, without any obstacle to freedom of expression; and to strengthen the communication capacities of the developing countries, in particular through the International Programme for the Development of Communication.

The adoption of democratic terms and of the principles of press freedom led directly to action – to concrete programmes and results. UNESCO became, firstly, an organization actively committed to the defence of fundamental freedoms – especially freedom of the press – and, secondly, an effective body engaged in promoting the development of communication, giving priority to the needs of the new democracies both in the East and in the South.

There can be no doubt that the future of the new democracies will depend in part on the development and strengthening of free, independent and pluralist media in both the public and private sectors, since the spread of knowledge and values is impossible without freedom of communication. The importance of this principle in democratic societies is undeniable: free communication enables ordinary citizens to express themselves and make their voices heard and, as a result, to influence the events that shape their daily lives.

It is in this context that UNESCO is paying close attention to the progress of digital technologies and their applications throughout the world. The emergence of a society of mass communication, of a 'programmed' society in which information technology, information and communication are all combined, is overturning our preconceptions of culture, science, education and development and, indeed, of life itself. But the change that has been set in motion is also full of promise: it should lead us to a civilization of knowledge.

The traditional media, for their part, need to effect their own revolution. New services, new modes of communication and new audiences are within reach, thanks to considerable expansion in the flow of communications, interactivity and the possibilities of combining text and images. Nevertheless, these media must find a way to achieve their metamorphosis.

The purpose of producing a second edition of the *World Communication Report* was pragmatic: the aim was to provide a reference work for decision-makers, planners, researchers, students, media professionals and the general public. In view of the scope of the subjects covered and the rapid outdating of certain features, this Report makes no attempt to be exhaustive, but brings out the convergence between information technology, information and communication and their applications in the various media (written press, news agencies, radio and television) and provides statistics on the changes observed in this field. It also attempts to highlight the major problems connected with the development of new information and communication technologies, such as the regulation of networks, media attitudes to violence and access of women to the media.

The question that lies at the heart of this Report may be summed up as follows: how are we to reinvent our patterns of thought and knowledge in the context of the technological multimedia revolution, which is proving both profound and irreversible?

It is my hope that this Report will encourage the international community to join in a debate on all these complex issues, which call for a variety of approaches. I urge all those concerned to search for common solutions, so that information and communication technologies may be placed in the service of human progress while at the same time guaranteeing a real choice that respects the dignity and freedom of each individual, and so that they may benefit as many people as possible, in both the North and the South, and within each country.

It is in situations of tension, even of crisis, that each of us can create, invent, give, and give of ourselves. Real changes occur far from the point of balance. Creative tension yields unexpected treasures and opens up new paths.

Reinventing often means rediscovering the original source. Let us dare sow the seed again in the field of our common future, whose harvest will be meaningful only to the extent that it is shared.

Federico Mayor
Director-General of UNESCO

Acknowledgements

The World Communication Report is appearing thanks to
Professor Lotfi Maherzi, a researcher in communications,
Associate Professor at the University of Versailles (France), and
former Rector of the University of Continuing Education
in Algiers (Algeria).

I wish to express my sincere appreciation of his excellent
research, his unflinching and even-handed approach and
his inexhaustible energy. May these few words convey my deep
respect for his flawless approach to the accomplishment
of a most exacting analysis.

I also seize this opportunity to warmly thank
My Von Euler, a sociologist and statistician who graduated
from the University of Stockholm (Sweden) and The Open
University (United Kingdom), and whose task it was
to gather and update the data assembled here from a number
of national and international sources.

Alain Modoux
Director of the Communication Division,
UNESCO

Contents

Introduction
Information, knowledge and development – the new challenges

Since the publication of the first *World Communication Report* in 1989, the world has changed. These profound transformations have been political, economic and technological, and have modified frontiers, created new cultures and markets, and raised hopes as well as concerns.

A disoriented world

In geopolitical terms, the world has become a hybrid: liberated, and yet at the same time elusive. The fall of the Berlin Wall in 1989 and the collapse of the Communist states of Europe have had a huge impact on world public opinion, intensified by images that have circled the globe via satellites. In the same period, live radio and television, as well as other media, have enabled audiences to experience the birth of new democracies in the countries of Central Europe and other regions of the world. These new societies seem less prone to conflict, more dynamic, and founded on greater democratic participation – although there are still widespread scattered attacks on fundamental human rights, especially the right to freedom of expression. Ideological rivalries have given way to greater economic interdependence and cultural interaction, which have blurred the old divisions of the world, when they have not rendered them obsolete.

In the vast Southern hemisphere, numerous countries have emerged from an almost uniformly poor Third World to make up a more differentiated South. The traditional distinction between industrialized countries and the developing world now seems less and less clear-cut. New countries in Asia, Latin America and Central and Eastern Europe have made economic breakthroughs and have even managed to compete with the industrialized countries in a number of areas. These new growth opportunities cannot mask significant economic inequalities, however, both between the industrialized countries and the developing world, and within the group now benefiting from increased growth.

As regards communications, the world has also become more complex, as a multitude of interconnected technological, political, cultural, economic and regulatory problems have emerged. Analysis of these problems is made all the more difficult since the new information and communications technologies have been integrated into unified, interconnected networks which have profoundly changed the conditions and means of production, forms of distribution, and society's ways of consuming and functioning.

Society breaks with the past

According to the experts, these changes are going to prove as significant as those brought on by the Industrial Revolution of the nineteenth century. They are the signs of a new civilization based on information and knowledge. They signal a break with the past and the opening of a new phase of economic, social and cultural development that is fundamentally different from its predecessors.

A number of authors and researchers agree that a new information age is in the process of rapidly replacing the industrial era.[1] They refer to the three major stages that Western civilization has passed through. The first is said to be the agrarian phase, whose economic activity was marked by an ample material base, but with little knowledge. The second phase, now coming to an end, began with the Industrial Revolution, with its mass-production methods. The decisive strategic factor in this second phase was energy. Lastly, the third era is the age of information and new technologies. In this new phase, science and knowledge are becoming the critical vectors of the so-called 'value-added' economy. Global networks are no longer mere pathways for information, but generate new knowledge which has a part to play in the processing of products. This underscores the importance of non-material resources such as software, computer applications, programmes and services: these become the new raw materials and the real wealth of the knowledge-based society.

With the arrival of this third phase, the hierarchy of economic, political and cultural values is shattered. The world of communications is gradually changing from an economy of scarcity and government-structured controls to a free economy oriented towards abundant supply and diversity. This change quickens the pace of the elimination of monopolies in the delivery and distribution of information, in both telecommunications and the audiovisual field.

Concurrently, information itself and high value-added products are vying for supremacy in global industry. For the first time in the history of humanity, non-material transfer constitutes the heart of the global exchanges of capital, ideas and images which make up the new economy. In these circumstances, where the non-material infiltrates production, the underlying framework of human activity is transformed and the function of states, national boundaries and cultural foundations is called into question. In addition to the geopolitical transformations, the new information society gives rise to a number of challenges which bring both tremendous hopes and a certain number of risks. Let us pause and consider briefly three challenges which have a crucial bearing on the creation of this new society: development, access to information and globalization.

The new technologies and development

The new information and communications technologies are first of all considered as factors in

---

1.　The notion that the West has experienced three major phases of civilization has been shared by a number of authors, such as Alvin Toffler, Peter Drucker, Régis Debray, Marshall McLuhan and Joël de Rosnay. Although the way of conceiving the three stages of social evolution differs in each case, there is agreement on the typology of the phases in terms of the manner of production: agrarian, industrial and informational. For a fuller presentation of the concept of a break with the past, see M. Cartier, *Les inforoutes, mythes et réalité* [Information Highways: Myths and Reality], Montreal, 1995.

development in the fields of education, health and other sectors of economic activity. The surge in multimedia, video-conferencing and artificial intelligence is resulting in an expanded ability to transform information, thereby increasing the possibilities for spreading and sharing knowledge. In the world of education and training, these new possibilities are changing methods of learning and enlarging the sphere of dissemination. Distance no longer matters, and illiterate or heretofore excluded populations may now have easier access to knowledge. In addition, since the correlation between education, training and development is clearly established, development strategies are placing ever higher stakes on widespread access to education, and continuing education in particular, now considered to be a strategic growth factor.

In the health field, new technologies such as video-conferencing and medical encyclopedias on CD-ROM allow a multitude of health facilities around the world to have universal and instant access to any sort of medical information. Many hospitals, laboratories and universities are already equipped with networks and are able to tele-observe medical diagnosis, analysis and evaluation transmitted from one corner of the globe to another. In developing countries, these applications can create new possibilities in the area of education and expertise.

Access to networks and their content

The emergence of a society founded on knowledge can be envisaged only after the creation of conditions allowing for universal access to products and services of a cultural or commercial nature, distributed over networks. At the outset, we saw that disseminating information and its value-added contribution formed the heart of economic and cultural activities in the new knowledge-based society. Thanks to the acceleration of technological innovation, the industrial stakes involved and competition, the new network technology and infrastructure are going to become

much less costly than the price of their content and more accessible to the greatest number. By contrast, access to the information disseminated over these infrastructures will be a much more complicated matter, indeed a problematic one. The cost of services could constitute a significant constraint, resulting in a gap between those possessing the means of financing access to the content in question and those unable to accede to information and disseminate it.

At this point there arise questions as to the use of the new information and communications technologies and access to their content. How is it possible to promote broad access by individuals, businesses and countries lacking the necessary financial resources, and thereby share the advantages of the knowledge-based society? What role can be played by the owners of the infrastructures, the producers of the programmes, the authors, publishers, governments and international organizations, in broadly disseminating information to segments of the population, or to entire countries lacking the resources for access? How shall we find the right balance between low-cost information widely disseminated and financed by advertising, governments or international organizations and value-added information that permits genuine access to knowledge and decision-making? The debate that has arisen on these topics underscores just how precious and costly a resource knowledge has become. It also shows how important it is for public authorities to implement a regulatory framework designed, on the one hand, to guarantee free access to the great diversity of information, and, on the other, to promote free competition and pluralism in a balanced economic environment.

The challenge of globalization

The problem of access to content has a corollary that is characteristic of the closing years of the twentieth century, namely, the globalization of communications. The world is facing a new process, begun a few years ago, that features a spectacular development of information technologies and the creation of planetary networks; it symbolizes the worldwide triumph of market economies and the liberalization of international trade. At a more basic level, governments in general are faced with the challenge of globalization and international opportunities opened up by widespread use of satellites and other global networks. This process coincides with the disappearance of national territories, space having lost its articulations and boundaries, its grey zones. Traversing these immense, now-accessible spaces, human thought pays no heed to boundaries and pushes monopolies aside. This unprecedented development is quickening the pace of elimination of political borders and favouring the steady emergence of new rights resulting from the use of information technologies, and recognized by governments.

The opening-up of society to the world at large is also quickening the pace of industrialization of cultures, partly owing to the formation of conglomerates on a global scale in the fields of information, telecommunications, the audiovisual field and leisure. The globalization of markets forces these businesses to meet fierce competition head on, in a context in which only the most powerful survive, thereby becoming real power structures – to the extent of raising the issue of the 'governability of the earth'. This process of concentration, which increasingly impedes the entry of new players, or excludes the weakest of them, is a matter of particular concern. It has the potential to put an end to freedom of information and pluralism. What is more, the international character and hegemony of the big global oligopolies constitute a threat to the cultural products of small markets and increase the risk of standardization or impoverishment of local cultures.

Faced with this process of globalization, most governments appear to lack the tools required for facing up to the pressure from important media changes. The new global order is viewed as a daunting challenge, and it most often results in reactions of introversion, withdrawal and narrow assertions of national identity. At the same time, many developing countries seize the opportunity represented by globalization to assert themselves as serious players in the global communications market. Some have committed themselves to an impressive shift towards innovative policy in audiovisual communications, while others have invested in the highly strategic software industry, thereby acceding to value-added services. In all these countries, the new information and communications technologies seem to be a priority in plans for economic development. It is a matter of political and strategic choice in the restructuring of global communications. In order to penetrate international markets, these countries have had to rely on their ability to innovate and create in the communications field.

History shows that the countries which fail to take advantage of the opportunities offered by these new technologies in the fields of information, electronic data processing and telecommunications will inevitably suffer slower development and decreased power of 'negotiation' in the new global communications landscape. History also teaches that countries which merely surrender to the mechanisms of the global market may lose their sense of identity and their culture. Clearly, the challenge is fundamental. It is a matter of combining the fruitful tensions between the specific identities and cultural expressions of each country, the centrifugal forces of globalized markets, and common membership of the human species in all its diversity. This is a tremendous challenge, calling for new action and dialogue, for negotiated, balanced collective responses.

The main features of the Report

Questions such as the foregoing are at the heart of the debate on the major changes in world communications. They are made even more urgent by other, less well understood issues arising from the impact of new information and communications technologies on cultural life and the functioning of society, as well as from the actual character of the information society and the promises it holds out.

We believe it is too early to draw the proper conclusions about the use of these new technologies and their impact. This Report attempts, rather, to describe technological progress at the present time and in the foreseeable future, and – without jumping to hasty conclusions – to point out the most clearly discernible changes in terms of development and cultural, social and political expectations. By proceeding in this way, we avoid viewing the information society and its new technologies as the automatic result of some sort of determinism. The emphasis is placed, rather, on the dynamic, multifarious and heterogeneous character of these phenomena: the new information and communications technologies do not spread at the same rate as they are created, but depend on critical mass, which alone determines, in most instances, whether they are disseminated selectively or universally to the various societies.

There are three major sections to this Report. Together they paint a global picture of the technological changes in the field of communications, analyse the transformations in the media landscape and explore problems involving public authorities, information and democracy. The Report thus attempts to mirror the major changes in communication and likewise their effects on the media, individuals and societies.

Part 1 describes technological progress in information and communications, and shows how the surge in the digital revolution and the convergence of technologies constitute a major innovation likely to contribute to the development of the information society. The expression 'new information and communications technologies' is used in the Report to designate the new communications techniques developed in recent decades. These techniques are at once material objects, or tools and procedures, and also non-material entities such as the knowledge, con-

tent and symbols required for creating, renewing or transmitting information. The innovative aspect of these tools, then, refers not just to the material support media of the technologies, but also to their content, and their manner of being disseminated or appropriated in general. In our analysis, the techniques in question cover the three major branches of communications: telecommunications (telephone, cable and satellite transmission), electronic data processing (in the broad sense, including personal computers and game consoles), and audiovisual products with their large family of traditional activities such as radio broadcasting, the electronics industry and the cinema.

At the present time, these three distinct technologies are tending to coalesce, becoming everyday tools for leisure and work. Accordingly, Chapter 1 presents the major technological changes, based on three transformations: the digitization of images, sound and data, digital compression, and the growing power of electronic components. Progress in these areas is part of a technological upsurge that is set to overturn completely the existing conditions under which information and knowledge are produced and disseminated. This will enable us to store and transmit information of any type – voice, image, text – free from any constraints of space, time or quantity.

Such a method of processing information electronically leads inevitably to the merging of activities which, from a historical point of view, existed and developed independently. Therefore the same chapter takes up the topic of convergence, a recurrent theme in the study and analysis of the new information and communications technologies. This new paradigm refers to the gradual merging of the three sectors of communications, and allows us to imagine innovations unthinkable just a few years ago. At present, the major information technology (IT) and mass-consumption electronics firms are in a race to innovate. The result will be hybrid instruments sharing features of IT, telecommunications and mass-consumption electronics.

The computer is one of the principal sources of the changes occurring at the end of this century. Its ever-shorter life-span forces IT systems builders to innovate incessantly and renew their products, while adapting to the requirements of a demanding market in constant flux. The spectacular development of networks, and especially the improved performance of electronic components, linked to the steady lowering of prices, leads us to envisage several competitive strategies. The first favours multimedia; the second promotes the merger of IT and television; the third furthers the notion of computer networks. The various trends are presented in Chapter 2 of the Report.

Irrespective of the trend in the design of computers, their performance and expansion are dependent on their being interconnected. This underscores the essential role that must be attributed to the network of land connections (telephone and cables) and wireless connections (microwave and satellite). This concept is the focal point of Chapter 3, which attempts to show how the digital revolution creates a condition of abundance which brings fundamental changes to the rules of the network game. A new technological era is dawning, and it favours both network connections and the establishment of a veritable spider's web covering the entire planet: the coming information society will rely on that network.

The other topic treated in this chapter is the Internet and its stunning growth, even in developing countries. Besides presenting its success and its global reach, we shall focus on its potential in the fields of university research and education. Currently, most universities and research centres in the world are connected to the Internet, which has become, for an ever-greater number of users, researchers and scholars, a vast, living encyclopedia. Nevertheless, although the Internet can be credited with having revealed the huge need for services of this new type, it does have some limitations: at the moment, its use tends to exclude languages other than English, and raises the issue of security and surveillance, among possible abuses such as non-transparent money-laundering, undesirable content of a bigoted, racist or pornographic nature, and computer piracy. Yet another problem is that of data-overload and traffic jams, which appear to have worsened with the introduction of images that consume large volumes of computer memory. Lastly, we cannot leave unmentioned the fact that the Internet is on the way to becoming a powerful commercial medium, whereas originally it was designed for the free and friendly exchange of information.

The predictable saturation of the network and the introduction of multimedia made it inevitable that a broad-band digital network combining the various services would be created – information highways. One of the main characteristics of these highways is their ability to transmit an infinite variety of information simultaneously and interactively. At the present time, such highways are the subject of envy and of grandiose ambitions. In the most industrialized countries, a stream of reports considers information highways a priority for a society's entry into the new type of economy, increasing the productivity of existing activities, and creating new ones. Some go so far as to compare the effects of the future information society, with its highways, to those of the railways and electrification in an earlier time. This highway-building project, elevated to the status of the founding myth of the information society, is being met with scepticism and concern in many developing countries, however. The great fear is that the majority of countries on the planet will become marginalized or excluded from the possibilities afforded by information highways, particularly in the area of development. Perhaps in response to these concerns, the Midrand Conference (South Africa, 1996) proposed a global scheme for information highways, to be shared by both industrialized and developing countries.

Chapter 4 is devoted to major economic changes, and attempts to show, on the one hand, what the course of technological convergence has done to transforming the information economy based on knowledge and growth and, on the other, how it has drastically altered the structure of work. This chapter's first point is an illustration of how the new information and communications technologies dematerialize the economy: its wealth no longer comes from the manufacture of material goods but from activities and services. It also shows how, in the IT domain, the value of software and services now far surpasses that of machines. One point of interest in this analysis is the revelation of the exponential development of software, which has become one of the strategic raw materials of the information society. The other important aspect of this chapter concerns the noteworthy major economic changes in the key sectors of communications. The chapter shows how, in most countries, the demand for information of all kinds appears to be undergoing rapid expansion. Moreover, it is the information market – including software, computers and other communications products – that is showing the most rapid worldwide growth.

The second point of the chapter concerns the major changes in the world of work. The arrival of entirely virtual businesses is still on the distant horizon, but an ever-growing number of 'telecommuters' is becoming a reality in some developed countries. Thanks to the computer, the fax machine and other communications tools, home workers eliminate hours of commuting and are able to enjoy greater flexibility in scheduling their work. Businesses can profit handsomely in terms of smaller office-space needs and reduced social welfare contributions. The chapter takes up the example of India, which has become one of the principal software service centres, with growth that could reach more than 60 per cent by 1998. Low labour costs and a skilled labour force are attracting the biggest Western companies to India's data-systems management services. The final topic of the chapter is the globalization of the information economy. The key concepts in this process are: concentration, globalization and deregulation.

The communications war entails mobilizing larger and larger amounts of capital, to finance innovation and to acquire dissemination rights. In this context, the major international industrial conglomerates are developing strategies and alliances aimed at ensuring their future dominance in developing communications markets. Information in the broad sense of the term has become a rare, precious and costly commodity. The globalization of the information economy is in fact rooted in the dominant position acquired by market economies in the gradual liberalization of world trade, first under the GATT, then the new World Trade Organization (WTO), and lastly by virtue of the ubiquitous planetary networks which quicken the pace of circulation of merchandise, capital and information.

Chapter 5 first takes up the internationalization of media, then governmental regulation and security policies in the wake of the development of global transmission networks. The first item shows that societies are more and more interconnected, thanks to networks and network products which operate globally. This phenomenon is illustrated by a portrait of the large transnational television channels, operating regionally or globally. These are considered to be the most powerful, influential or symbolic actors. The analysis shows, however, that the internationalization of their programmes is more and more likely either to lag behind the expectations of their local or regional audiences, or to be out of touch with them. Access to globalization requires organization of a number of regional or national audiovisual forums. The search for common linguistic references, or a stock of images common to national or regional cultures, as practised by networks such as Star TV, CNN or MTV, is a new process, and often contradicts the single, standardized vision of the internationalization of cultures. The analysis also shows a new pattern of communication flows: although the large Western networks remain solidly established, a growing number of Latin American, Arab and Asian broadcasters are launching their own channels via satellite, and often compete with the major channels in reaching their own communities. The second goal of the chapter is to give some idea of changes in government reactions to the globalization of media. We discover that various countries have adopted different measures as regards regulation of the programmes of private or public television operators, the implementation of anti-monopoly mechanisms, or rules for broadcasting quotas.

Chapter 6 takes up the important issues raised by the new information and communications technologies. These are mainly regulatory, cultural and political. The first issue is copyright and intellectual property. The combination of technological progress and the dematerialization of the products of communication brings both opportunities and risks, which have not yet been dealt with by legal systems; these include invasion of privacy and protection of privacy, protection of personal data, intellectual property, network security and confidentiality – a host of issues that also give rise to the problem of legal access to the content of these technologies. In this regard, there is a lively debate between those who view free access to the networks as a fundamental right, like other basic rights, and those who believe that access should be geared to particular circumstances and the nature of the information (public, corporate or private). A third group views network access as merely another commercial service.

The second major issue is the serious problem of inequalities that mark off rich and poor countries, and privileged and excluded groups within the same society. Most developing countries are facing the challenge of new technologies which originate in and are disseminated from places outside their own borders. In most instances, these countries feel excluded from this progress and continue to deplore the obvious worsening of imbalances in the flow of information exchanges between North and South. The gap between high-income countries and the majority of Southern countries is growing ever wider, and

suggests that the much heralded global village could be essentially the lot of the richest countries, where databases, software and programs are concentrated and stored. On the whole, the gap appears to be widening while, at the same time, assistance to development in the communications field – on the wane for several years now – continues to shrink.

The third major issue is the standardization of programme content, along with the inevitable reaction of turning inward, self-isolation and rejection of things foreign. This situation poses new ethical, political and legal questions that the traditional media have not had to face before. In developing countries, there is concern about the standardization of local cultures under the influence of impoverishing, reductive content which trivializes everything. The risks are great and consequential: probable disappearance of vulnerable, community cultures, weakening of cultural foundations, the temptation to react by withdrawing to extreme positions of assertion of identity, and threats of violent confrontations between ethnic groups. Developing countries as well as a number of European states are jealous of their cultural and linguistic identities, considered by many to be a basic component of their national sovereignty. The new transnational media are perceived as a threat to local identities.

Differences are emerging between countries which produce, disseminate and own programmes, and those which import them. The former encourage the thorough internationalization of markets and the globalization of trade. The latter view the audiovisual field as a service and an industry whose cultural objectives assume the existence of a special framework arrangement to be negotiated within the appropriate intergovernmental entities such as GATT or WTO. What is certain is that the globalization of content also raises the issue of the place, role and future of public services in a drastically altered audiovisual landscape. Can they survive in the face of increasingly intense competition? Do they in fact still have a future? Has it been radically called into question? Faced with these questions, public television services are having to deal with the issues and challenges of renewal, adaptation and survival.

Lastly, Chapter 7 is devoted to the new opportunities offered by the new information and communications technologies and other activities devoted to development. For the majority of researchers and communications specialists, the paradigm of technological transfer is a thing of the past. The new information and communications technologies offer developing countries the opportunity to make 'technological leaps' which should allow them more rapidly to achieve the requisite levels of equipment and connection to information networks. More and more governments share that view, and are choosing the most advanced technologies in order to establish, renew or support their communications infrastructures. For example, in the space of less than ten years, India has become the world's second biggest producer of software; the Republic of Korea is maintaining its position as world leader in the production of chips; in 1997, China's national telecommunications operator became the world's largest provider of mobile phone services. The great majority of developing countries, however, are not experiencing similar growth, and seem to be up against constraints and obstacles that must be either overcome or kept under control, if they intend one day to build bridges to the networks and services of the coming information society.

In Part 2 we reach the heart of the Report, where we set forth the full range of transformations of world media landscapes as a result of the digital revolution and the new information and communications technologies. The focus is on the most obvious developments in the various sectors of the written press and audiovisual media. The digital revolution and technological progress are seen to entail a multiplication of information media, favouring a continually growing supply of programmes, together with

fragmented behaviour of listening and reading. These changes bring with them very broad social modifications in the use of the press, radio and television, as well as the way their audiences receive them.

Part 2 is made up of four chapters, dealing, in order, with the major changes in the world of the press, news services, radio and television. Chapters 8 and 9 are devoted to the press and news agencies, without which written and electronic journalism would be unable to offer a comprehensive view of national and international news. In the first section we analyse the manifold world of the press, characterized by a multiplicity of models according to the political, cultural and economic environment of each nation. This world is facing a twofold crisis: the first is the result of the economic crisis affecting certain regions of the world, and the other is a consequence of the important technological changes that have occurred in the press sector.

We also present the effects of the breathtaking progress in journalistic trades and the work habits of journalists and other staff in that profession. Lastly, two examples taken from the world press illustrate the major changes that have occurred since the 1990s. We first look at the independent press of Africa, which, despite lingering illiteracy, has grown alongside the democratic process and in some cases has even curbed efforts by the official press to find new grounds for its legitimacy. The second example is the Russian press, which played a decisive role in weakening the previous regime. This press is facing growing difficulties, reflected in dwindling circulation and a spectacular increase in the price of paper, printing and distribution.

How does it stand with the news agencies? Three of them, active on a global scale (Associated Press/USA, Reuters/United Kingdom and Agence France Presse AFP/France), are the source of about 80 per cent of the public's information worldwide. For some, these figures are evidence of their hegemony in the circulation of information. Others take the view that they illustrate the problems such worldwide organizations have in surviving. Furthermore, the need to make major investments, especially in leading-edge technology, forces these services to expand into financial markets that are deemed most profitable, or to enter televised news, which has prospered with the development of new channels transmitted via satellite.

Chapter 10 explores the new landscapes of radio, marked by various radical changes in the areas of politics and technology. Our first point is that, of all the media, radio remains the cheapest means of transmission and the only medium able to reach the most remote rural areas. For many countries, the radio is still the primary source of information. Furthermore, the war of the radio waves has shown over and over again that radio is a major issue, whose social role is not limited to mere entertainment, but is capable of serving diplomacy, politics, and even propaganda and hate. In this regard, we look at the development of various radio experiments in the world, noting the emergence of local and community radio in developing countries, under the influence of the democratic process and international broadcasting. An example cited is the British national radio service, the British Broadcasting Corporation (BBC), which serves as a world standard for the quality of its programmes and its journalistic accuracy.

We next describe the new technological innovations in radio broadcasting, in particular the new system of digital transmission called Digital Audio Broadcasting (DAB), which is destined radically to change the listening habits and ergonomics of radio by opening up new prospects and applications. Lastly, we present a site inventory of community radio, widely considered to be a local, democratic substitute for official and commercial broadcasting. We note that, in the various experiments described and in different political, technological and cultural contexts, we find the same determination to open up new paths to participation by local populations in the operation and management of community radio.

In Chapter 11 we analyse major transformations in the world of television, the result of digital innovations and compression techniques. We examine the effects of these changes, which are beginning to open up new television frontiers: improved technical quality, more programmes on offer, significantly lower broadcasting costs, pay TV, new interactive services. Regarding the last point, we show that with interactive television the viewer is no longer a passive consumer of programmes, but an actor enjoying free and individual use of the medium. Pay TV and pay-per-view were followed by near video on demand (NVOD), offering a programme that starts anew every fifteen minutes, and finally video on demand (VOD), which allows the consumer to choose any programme at any time. We take our illustrations of these new systems from Videoway, of Quebec, a foreshadowing of information highways.

These technological revolutions are bringing profound change to the audiovisual landscape and giving rise to spectacular industrial battles. The economic war will involve about ten conglomerates which make and break alliances designed to acquire the basic elements of pay TV: control of the subscriber and access to programmes. The problem will clearly be one of providing programming for all the new broadcasting alternatives. A corollary is that the new media war will involve broadcasting rights to sporting events and highly successful films, creating concern that this feature will involve gargantuan financial bidding, thereby excluding the small countries of both the industrial and the developing world.

The final portion of this chapter is devoted to the study of the audiovisual landscapes throughout the world. The majority are experiencing enormous changes resulting from the technological transformations already alluded to, from the process of democratization and the globalization of media and their content. Accordingly, many governments are attempting to adapt to the situation and speed up the reorganization of their media. Others are caught up in problems related to the transition, and are trying to effect change within highly conservative traditions. Others again are choosing to turn inward, attempting to defend increasingly porous borders.

On the basis of these trends, we present a regional panorama of global television that is sensitive to the characteristic features of the various countries, but also underscores common elements. The strategic role of television, which has become the primary cultural activity in many countries, is conceived of by some as essentially a commercial operation, based on free enterprise and competition. Other countries look at television as a mixed private/public system in which strictly economic facts coexist with socio-cultural and political concerns. Lastly, others again consider television to be a public monopoly, with exclusively public funding.

Commercial television predominates in the United States and in the majority of countries of Latin America. In these countries, the state has withdrawn from television either partially or totally, while retaining control over its operations – for instance, through regulatory agencies. Some countries, like Brazil and Mexico, have become heavyweights in the world audiovisual market, and have even managed to create transcultural products while expanding energetically in the rest of the world. In most European countries and in Canada, television has developed as an extension of the former public-service monopolies which dominated the audiovisual scene. Since the 1980s, European television has evolved into a mixed system consisting of well-established commercial broadcasters and a public television that has often run out of steam. The two systems are different in kind and in their objectives. Private television is driven by commercial imperatives, whereas public service television is perceived as an instrument of cultural and social development. In many countries of the region, this difference is encouraged and preserved, since it reflects two complementary images of the role of television in society.

In the countries of the former socialist bloc, state

monopolies are giving way to pluralistic broadcasting systems. Although the media landscape is undergoing significant alteration in the wake of political changes, it continues to reflect disparities at the level of infrastructures and media practices. Overall, a genuine audiovisual market is in the process of emerging, in which the creation and even the disappearance of channels obey the laws of supply and demand. The emergence of the ideas of competition and wooing audiences is quickening the pace of transition, and is also the subject of debate within public and private professional media circles. Some are keen to underscore the progress made in deregulation as part of the movement toward European integration, whereas others emphasize the dangers of accelerated liberalization, and the threat of mortgaging the independence of the media, and thereby the process of transition to democratic rule. Lastly, the transition of state-run channels to a public-service mission often meets with resistance, notably the weight of conservative traditions embedded in the previous system.

In developing countries in transition to democracy, television is state property, but commercial or community channels are emerging. According to the degree of liberalization of the media, some public services are being given their independence and are gradually becoming accessible to the full range of interest groups, including minorities. Although goodwill is often not lacking, it is still the case that certain ideals of public service (such as editorial independence regarding political and economic interests, direct financing, quality production, etc.) are meeting with difficulties as regards training, management and technical ability.

In other developing regions, most television systems are state monopolies devoted to fostering the civic solidarity required by the drive to develop. In such cases, 'public service' is out of the question, and they are often considered to be instruments of political control in their editorial policies.

In addition to the major trends in the evolution

of television worldwide, we decided to include examples of some ten countries whose systems are participating in the dynamics of development and growth as reflected in their programme output and their ability to stand up to international competition. In the majority of developing countries, however, these examples include disparities in the financial resources available for production as well as the technical resources needed for creating programmes. Regional tables are provided for the purpose of comparing the audiovisual situation in these various countries.

Part 3 of the Report attempts to explore and update the relationship between information, law and public authorities. It is more analytical than descriptive, and consists of five chapters designed to analyse the legal basis of information dissemination and the threats it is encountering in the world at large.

Chapter 12 presents the concept of the right to information as founded in law and practised in various parts of the world. In the first section, the development of the legal framework for freedom of information is presented. Among human rights, the right to information occupies a primordial position, alongside the right to freedom of opinion and expression, which it entails. Article 19 of the Universal Declaration of Human Rights proclaims that right. The implementation of the declaration in various national contexts, however, illustrates the degree to which political systems influence the nature and progress of media as regards their content, organization and markets. Freedom of information in many countries – in democratic ones, in particular – is often in fact at odds with the principles of international agreements. In other countries, freedom of information has been the result of long and painful struggles, marked by episodes of reversal and progress. In yet other countries, where credible, independent information is lacking, freedom of information remains an ongoing struggle, a conquest yet to be consolidated. Lastly, in regions of conflict, information becomes either disinformation designed to inflame the public and

deceive the enemy, or an instrument of hatred and violence.

In the second section we present the various activities of UNESCO in the field of communication. We also try to show how, following the Second World War, the concept of free circulation of information became an issue in the Cold War. While the countries of the West were defending the principle of free and unrestrained circulation of information as laid down in Article 19, Communist countries upheld the notion of controlled information based on bilateral agreements. The developing world, meanwhile, condemned the inequalities in information and communications, and criticized the media of Northern countries for disseminating images of their own lives considered prejudicial or inaccurate. These divergent views marked the debates on the concept of a New World Information and Communication Order (NWICO) within international organizations throughout the 1970s and 1980s, notably those of UNESCO.

Meanwhile, political transformations in Central and Western Europe since 1989 were making it possible for UNESCO to reassert its constitutional foundations. At its General Conference of 1989, it adopted a new communications strategy based on the democratic principles of its constitution, regarding first of all the 'free flow of ideas by word and image'. The fact remains that the debates concerning NWICO have enabled the international community to become more fully aware of the disparities in information and communication both between nations and within them, and of the urgent need to expand communications resources in developing countries. On the basis of this consensus, UNESCO will develop its new action programme incorporating three main objectives: 'encouraging the free flow of information, at international as well as national level; promoting the wider and better balanced dissemination of information, without any obstacle to freedom of expression; developing all the appropriate means of strengthening communication capacities in the developing countries in order to increase their participation in the communication process'. The main vehicle of this action is the International Programme for the Development of Communications (IPDC).

The third section of this chapter shows how technological and economic revolutions have contributed to the rapid expansion of freedom of information. In the former socialist bloc as well as in certain developing countries, the media have had, and continue to have, a not insignificant impact on political developments, as catalysts and instruments of more rapid democratization.

Chapter 13 takes up threats to and violations of freedom of expression in the world. Although freedom of the press is making headway, it is far from being the general rule. Many governments still try to control the media. This is illustrated by an analysis of the Internet, which has become an unavoidable player in the media landscape, able widely to disseminate all manner of services, well beyond national borders. The Internet's explosive growth has fuelled a broad debate, attributable to the growing divergence between user communities, which are deeply suspicious of any government intervention, and the tendency of public authorities to want to monitor, control and even censor the network.

Chapter 14 examines current dangers to democracy. Although not threatened by a reborn totalitarianism, it is in fact called into question by economic developments, in which profits and success loom increasingly larger as the criteria affecting the achievement of freedom of expression. The creation of giant national and transnational communications conglomerates reinforces the industrial character of the media. Multimedia corporations control either directly or indirectly not only newspapers, but radio stations, television channels and on-line networks, often overlapping national boundaries. Thus the media have become new powers able to change the rules of democratic evolution. What is at issue is not merely the media's role as monitor of the public authorities

(what the Anglo-Saxon countries call the 'watchdog role' of the media) and contributor to enlightened civic choice, but the fact of the media's actually becoming a substitute for the public authorities through systematic influence over public opinion, involving use of the most sophisticated techniques of persuasion. In this changing environment, the growing power of new technologies raises concerns. One example is the use of virtual images and news summaries consisting of spliced images: used with poor judgement, such presentations can deceive and create risks not envisaged by current regulations. Now that the media are able to generate images that are more real than reality, it has become harder to distinguish truth from falsehood. Press and television images are manipulable by technological miracles far more difficult to detect than the crude fabrications of the 'Timisoara mass grave' (Romania). If we fail to remain vigilant, technological magic can now make virtual reality into an actual merger of the real and the unreal, a drift that threatens to undermine the foundations of democracy.

These dangers are all the greater at the present time as television news comes more and more under the constraints of real time and its instantaneous character. For some, this technological magic provides arguments for initiating 'cyber-democracy' projects, enabling citizens to participate directly in the taking of political decisions. This idea has given rise to an intense debate in academic and political circles, where critical and sceptical attitudes predominate. With this new form of direct democracy, the entire range of issues is now raised: the future of our institutions, our cultures, our beliefs and the democratic debate itself.

Chapter 15 takes up the increase in violence in television programmes, video games and other media. Currently, the influence of this factor on children is the subject of much controversy, as shown by the contradictory results of a number of inquiries. Absence of agreement, however, fails to address the concern of parents, educators and political figures faced with a trend that is expanding globally.

In conclusion, the Report presents a few alternatives to the new situation in global media. It shows how users, cultural communities and non-governmental organizations are taking advantage of the opportunities afforded by technological progress to argue for broader participation in the flow of information on the networks. They intend to offset not only the excesses of governments and other abuses of power, but also those of the global market and its ambition of planetary expansion. The success or failure of this third way depends on the ability of societies to act with awareness of these new, emerging communitarian forms attempting to anchor themselves in the values of sharing, solidarity and peace.

Methodology

In the light of the breadth and sheer quantity of questions raised by this report, it has become more necessary than ever to have a framework for understanding the issues, especially as communications are infinitely complex, all-encompassing and difficult to decode. Communications are not only conceptually difficult to grasp, but they have the added complication of drawing on several human and social sciences, thus raising simultaneous questions across disciplines. For instance, issues such as the content of new information and communications technologies, access to them, the industrialization of programs and the question of public service are all entangled with present-day issues such as globalization, development and democracy.

With a view to preserving these issues in all their complexity and interconnectedness, we have avoided the kind of analysis that compartmentalizes matters, most often on the basis of outdated or even invalid conventional doctrine. To such an analysis we prefer a more general angle, one that attempts to describe and explain. We seek to remain resolutely multidisciplinary in our approach, the better to grasp the hidden, complex and diverse phenomena of world communications. To that end, we base our approach on a number of examples which amount to demonstrations of decoding of what is actually going on in the field. In addition, as regards the meaning of the key concepts in communications, we have added a full Glossary at the end of the Report, which frees us from making such definitions within the text. Also, a bibliography points out those recent publications where the writer has found information and analyses that seemed germane.

Problems

- The Report does not set out to embrace the entire universe of global media in detail, or to review the entirety of national television broadcasting. The objectives of this study preclude entering into an analysis of a multitude of difficult issues of a practical and theoretical nature. Nevertheless, for the purpose of shedding light on the major world regions and highlighting crucial aspects of their situation, the constraints they face and the strategies used by the leading actors in terms of innovation and development, we have used a number of case-studies, selected on the basis of typical approaches to development, and with a view to preserving balance between geographical regions and nations.

- In the majority of instances, documentary evidence and statistics become rapidly obsolete, because of the ephemeral nature of communications tools, and because of political and economic fluctuations. That problem is exacerbated by the divergent – not to say contradictory – character of some quantified data. With this in mind, we have taken particular care, with the assistance of My von Euler, to update and check the accuracy of the statistics gathered from various national and international sources. Thus the presentation of tables, charts and other quantified illustrations goes beyond mere quantitative issues, to become an aid to a more qualitative understanding of the contents of the Report.

Technical evolution of the information society, 1820–1990

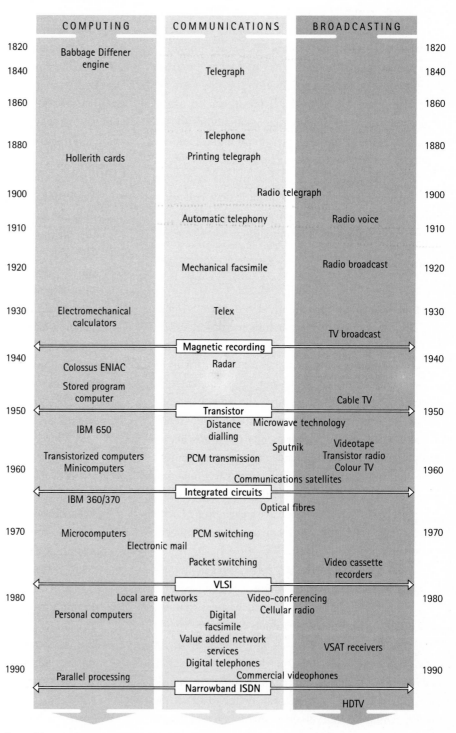

Source: *Telecommunications and Broadcasting: Convergence or Collision?*, Paris, OECD, 1992.

The goals of the Report

Our primary objective is to transcend the framework of specialized study and reach out to a wider readership, hoping to provide people with food for thought, as well as an indication of the paths to be followed and the essential topics for discussion, so that readers can understand and go more deeply into the basic aspects of communications on the eve of the twenty-first century. Secondly, we are committed to reflect the variety of tendencies and opinions, regional interests and judgements that are by nature subjective, all the while maintaining a philosophical approach that is faithful to the values of democracy and the fundamental documents on the right to freedom of expression. We believe this is the only path to knowledge consonant with the nature of communication.

Part 1

New information
and communication
technologies:
change and
challenge

'Optic fibres',
by P. Dumas/Eurelios

The end of the twentieth century is marked by change of revolutionary scope and scale, characterized by a series of transformations such as technological convergence and world-wide media coverage, not to mention the globalization of their content. These in turn are leading the way to a true revolution, one based on information and knowledge, referred to by Alvin Toffler as the 'third wave'. The issues at stake are of immense significance, for they imply a break with the past, heralding a new era of economic, social and cultural development fundamentally different from anything that has gone before.

The origin of these far-reaching changes is to be found in the advances in new information and communication technology, progress speeded up by the digital revolution and the convergence of the computer, telecommunications and audiovisual industries. In the space of only a few years, the unprecedented growth in the research dedicated to these sectors has resulted in a wide range of innovations leading to the convergence of various techniques, convergence that in turn has become tangible reality. Communication systems have unified, to such an extent that telephone transfers and television pictures no longer circulate on separate channels. Computers and television sets are one and the same thing, telephones are linked to the Internet and mobile phones are connected to laptop computers. These changes also have far-reaching sociological implications, not only in terms of the ways we use the new technologies but also in the ways we have recourse to their services, and for what purpose.

At the same time, the fact that computers can now be interconnected has marked a new step in innovation with the emergence of worldwide communication networks. At the forefront of these is the Internet, a living encyclopedia which makes no distinction between telephone, satellite or television to route the information it contains. Optimum performance of the network will not be achieved, however, until very high performance circuits have become commonplace.

That movement is now under way, through the growing integration and interconnection of new information technology with telecommunications resources. It can be seen in information highways, the synthesis of technological convergence resulting in widespread interactive multimedia offers. This break with the past, one of the major undertakings for the next century, symbolizes a society in which network-distributed information and intelligence will be the major forms of wealth. Most governments are persuaded that such is the case, and are already preparing vast schemes with information highways as their priority to enable their societies to take part in a new economy, to enhance the productivity of already existing industries and to create new ones.

With this in mind, economic actors in all sectors of the information and leisure industries – including suppliers of telecommunications hardware and infrastructures – are already taking up their positions. Groups are being set up for this purpose, launching intersectoral alliances which have generally led to high market concentration and internationalization.

These upheavals, both technological and economic, are radically modifying the ways in which we use communication, both at work and in the home. New possibilities for training, education, employment and leisure activities hitherto reserved for an élite can now be afforded by all. People communicating now have powers of transmitting and receiving information undreamed of even ten years ago. That fundamental breakthrough, which backs up the concept dear to Bill Gates of 'information at your fingertips', both enhances individual action and at the same time questions the very nature of the state, national frontiers and cultural roots. Combined with geopolitical change, it raises a number of questions about legislation, the gaps existing between nations and within them, the risk of rendering local cultures uniform, and the role of public services when forced to compete with domestic and supranational private programmes.

Chapter 1
Technological change

The accelerating progress in new information and communication technology is essentially based on three fundamental changes: the digitization of images, sounds and data; digital data compression; and the growing power of electronic components. These innovations have made possible the gradual replacement of analog equipment by digital systems that are clearing the way for greater interactivity between end-users and terminals.

The digital revolution

Digital technology marks a true revolution which goes far beyond purely technical upheavals. On the one hand, it will lead to the integration of information transmission networks and reception hardware, and, on the other, it will simultaneously enhance a new relationship with the media and the way in which we consume the information they convey. Basically, this revolution stems from the spectacular progress made in micro-electronics, leading to the digitization of images, sound and data. In conventional so-called analog systems, sounds and images were converted into electrical signals so that they could be transmitted on physical support systems such as wires and optic fibres, or in electromagnetic wave form via terrestrial broadcasting networks or by satellite. With digitization, the same signals are coded into strings of numbers represented in binary form as packets of 0s and 1s, which then constitute a data processing file. The problem with these basic files, however, is that they are extremely demanding in terms of transmission capacity. Digital compression has solved the difficulty, by reducing the flow of information to decrease the time and therefore the cost of transmission, without modifying the quality and content of the information itself. In radio broadcasting, digital techniques and particularly that of data compression will make it possible to transport, on a single transmission channel (be it via cable, terrestrial broadcasting or satellite), several services (television, radio, data transmission, telecommunication), or several

Convergence, a new paradigm

The general process of digitization has resulted in the emergence of a new feature: the convergence of telecommunications, computer and audiovisual technologies, which were previously separated by techniques, legislation and modes of distribution. The new concept has given rise to different definitions and interpretations according to each operator, institution or researcher concerned. Harmonized, common development of convergence is difficult to find, because each state is strongly influenced by its own history and the different levels of development of its telecommunications and audiovisual sectors. However, the structural transformation of the public sector and new legislation look forward to the development of such convergence. Several angles of approach are possible. Some authors see convergence as comprising three different features or levels: the technical convergence mentioned above, economic convergence (the concentration of firms and the integration of services) and convergence in legislation. Others add the convergence of social customs and expectations. The Organisation for Economic Co-operation and Development (OECD) distinguishes three other types of convergence: technical, functional and corporate.

Technical convergence refers to the use by the communication industry of signal digitization. It is evaluated according to the progress in the digitization process in the three communication sectors. Computer technology is by definition completely digitized. Digitization in telecommunications is an ongoing process which is already highly advanced in terms of both transmission and packet-switching. Finally, the audiovisual industry is making giant leaps in the digital world. Technical convergence, then, refers to the adoption of the general process of digitization.

Functional convergence refers to the diversification and increasingly hybrid nature of the services offered by communication media which hitherto have been distinct. This means radio broadcasting services will be able to transmit signals other than information or entertainment programmes; in addition to the conventional services of dialogue and data transmission, the telephone industry will also be able to transmit entertainment; cable-based distributors on their side will be able to provide telephone services. Functional convergence may thus be summed up as free competition between the radio broadcasting, telecommunications and computer technology sectors, and the disappearance of the traditional boundaries between these three industries.

Corporate convergence refers to the new capacities of the communication companies to diversify their sources of finance. In this way, companies telecasting audiovisual programmes will be able to make viewers pay for them direct, and will no longer have to limit themselves to indirect revenue such as advertising or state subsidies. The same principle applies to telecommunications companies, which will now be able to seek other sources of finance than direct fee-paying alone.

The distinction in technical terms, therefore, between the various sectors of the communication industry is less self-evident, owing to the fact that information is processed in digital form and that the transmission infrastructure itself (cable, satellite, terrestrial broadcasting) is multi-purpose. Functional convergence and that of the companies involved is thus melting the barriers between the different sectors of activity.

While opinions are unanimous with respect to the reality of convergence, particularly in terms of its technological nature, debate is still heated about the lead times that will be needed to provide each home with programmes that are interactive, easy and fast to use. Some believe it will happen tomorrow, others talk of its realization ten or twenty years hence.

Convergence is, in fact, an ongoing process. The speed of technical breakthroughs, and the political and economic uncertainty and even resistance they encounter and create, make any definitive analysis of the concept impossible. Convergence is basically a social construct, based on technological as well as economic, legal and political logic. In consequence, neither the information society nor the communication tools it requires (information highways, multimedia, interactivity) will come into being, even if the technological conditions for their realization exist, unless there is political, economic and legal endorsement, and unless, above all, there is support for the project from a majority of users.

Convergence

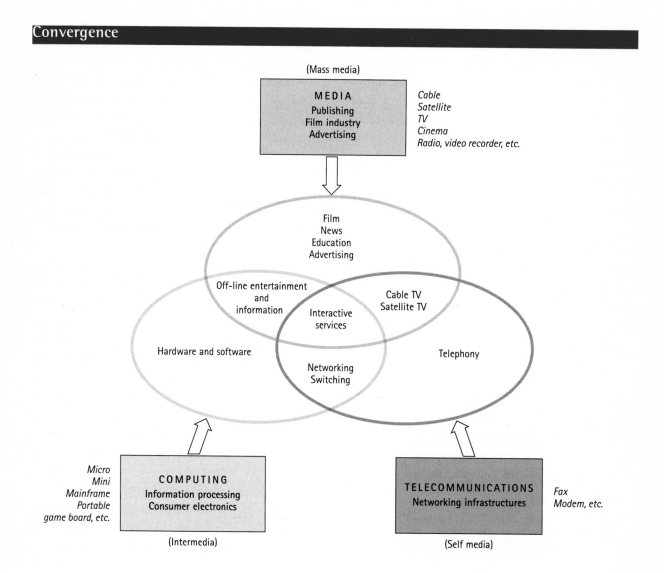

Chapter 2
New terminals:
from multimedia
to network
computer

As a result of technological convergence and progress in digitization, the laboratories of computer technology and consumer electronics firms are competing in the race for innovation and sophistication. All of them are looking for multi-purpose, comprehensive solutions which correspond to recent trends and practices in communication: integration, high definition, miniaturization, ergo-nomics and mobility. New products called 'information appliances' are emerging, combining computer, telecommunications and consumer electronics technology. Some are designed as specialized appliances such as wireless telephones with read-out, keyboard and Internet connection, others, called 'wearables' resemble portable computers and are as powerful as a mid-range microcomputer, are voice-controlled and weigh little more than a personal stereo. Others again are multi-purpose, enabling users to telephone (and display their correspondent), to consult databases, to access the Internet and to watch television channels. One single piece of equipment will combine all these functions, providing general, instantaneous access from the home to every service. The battle for this future medium is already raging. The consumer electronics industry is competing with the information processing industry to define the new terminal, but for the time being no one knows which will have the upper hand: an interactive, multimedia type of television, or microcomputers that have also become smart receivers. The debate seems even more complex with the rising power of the Internet and of digital television. The microcomputer, already endangered by the Internet, is now threatened by the decision taken by the Federal Communication Commission (FCC) in April 1997 to impose on the approximately 1,500 United States television stations a brief timetable for the change-over to digital. The battle for the small screen of the future has accordingly begun. The principal consumer electronics and microcomputing companies are now jockeying for position to control the huge American small-screen market, estimated to

Informatics manufacturers are now merging the operations of computers and television. A multimedia computer will provide TV programmes, access to the Internet and all its interactive services simultaneously.
Photo: M. Ginies/Sipa Image

be worth some $150 billion. To tackle this mass market, several strategies are in competition. The first of these focuses on an increasingly integrated, upmarket, multimedia type of computer; a second favours an amalgamation with television, while yet a third targets network computers.

Multimedia

Almost every single manufacturer today offers so-called multimedia configurations providing the end-user with a combination of power and audio-video functions, not to mention the CD-ROM (Compact Disc Read-Only Memory) reader. This new type of configuration handles not only texts and graphics but also still pictures, video and sound. Multimedia applications were first developed locally via an optical disc known as a CD-ROM, containing interactive programs with games, and educational or reference works. The multimedia computer, which has already invaded the worlds of publishing, the graphic arts and architecture, is now penetrating the music market with the automatic production of scores, the photography market with digital picture processing, the film industry for post-production work, special effects and image processing. It is in training, games or research work, however, that multimedia applications have seen the highest speed of growth.

With the development of the Internet and the

techniques of sound and image compression, multimedia-dedicated programs can also be consulted or downloaded. Using a microcomputer equipped with a modem together with a subscription to an access service or network computer (a computer connected direct to the network), end-users can access thousands of multimedia services and consult CD-ROMs remote, and will shortly be able to watch television or a film on their microcomputer.

Estimated number of PCs sold per day worldwide, 1995–2000 (in thousands of units)

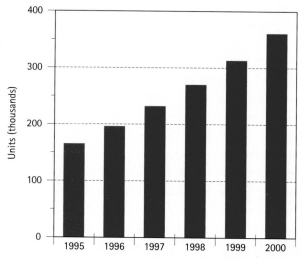

Source: Dataquest, from *Le Monde informatique* (Paris), 31 May 1996.

Television trends

Faced with the massive attack from computer manufacturers, consumer electronics firms are also benefiting from all-digital technology and its convergence to position themselves in this new market by imposing television as the dominant support medium to consume multifunctional services. This competition has been stepped up by the FCC announcement of a timetable for the change-over to digital television. Since then the major American and Japanese manufacturers of information systems have been working on the amalgamation of PC and television. The preliminary target is the family and the living-room. The screen being offered to viewers consists of a multimedia chain for everyone, parents and children alike. It combines television programmes with access to the Internet and the entire range of interactive services. This means that the viewer, in the course of a tennis-match, can review the players' achievements or placing. He or she may also send electronic messages, telephone, listen to the radio or surf on the Web.

Network trends

After multimedia machines and multi-purpose terminals, computers at the end of the 1990s have become communicative. Large software firms and manufacturers of professional information systems are launching a new generation of machines called 'Network Computers' (NC). Their bare-boned architecture (since they use networking power they have no need of operating systems or software), low price (between $500 and $1,000 for a professional version), manufacturer-independent technology, and simplicity of use and maintenance make them a highly competitive candidate to replace PCs, considered too sophisticated and over-expensive. With the Java language, a sort of universal software translator developed by Sun, the NC will be able to run any application, no matter what its source operating system. In response to the threat of the NC, Microsoft is preparing to launch at the start of 1998 a competitor called Windows Terminal (WT), a new type of network computer that is even more straightforward than the NC.

Digital Versatile Disc (DVD)

With digitization and the progress made in storage technology, the future of the traditional CD-ROM seems uncertain. The experts forecast that by the year 2001 the DVD with its capacity of 4.7 Gb will have turned the CD-ROM with its 680 megabytes into a museum piece, and will form the multimedia support *par excellence*. This is another technological revolution which came about as a result of the decision in December 1996 by several consumer electronics companies, which were arguing about the characteristics of the future digital video disc, to agree on a single format and its name: Digital Versatile Disc or the Digital Video Disc (DVD). A single DVD will contain anything from 4.7 Gb to 11 Gb, i.e. from seven to a little less than thirty CD-ROMs. It will be able to host films as well as data-processing applications or video games. Ultimately it will replace all the formats stemming from the current CD range, including audio CDs, CD-ROMs, CD-Is and video CDs.

With these new functionalities, the industry has succeeded in developing a product capable of interesting both the leisure industry and the professional world. The DVD can contain films, music, encyclopedias and training programs. For the consumer, it is capable of hosting 133 minutes of film on a single side with digital high-definition quality. For the computer world, it provides large storage capacity and fast data access. The fact remains that the DVD market, which is expected to be worth $4 billion in the year 2000,[1] represents major potential for the global consumer electronics industry. The experts forecast that 340 titles will be available in 1997, which will expand to more than 700 titles by 1998.

The DVD opens up other perspectives, whether in terms of back-up space (DVD–RAM) or for archival storage (DVD–R). The large industrial groups, however, have yet to agree about the common standard for a recordable DVD. While the product has been technically finalized, its commercialization raises certain doubts. A launch without prior notice to the market would raise the problem of protecting works and their encryption in order to prevent piracy. For this reason, the Hollywood majors have already imposed regional codes to prevent their worldwide distribution strategy from being compromised by the circulation of films in the DVD format.

1.   According to Dataquest Consultants and IDC-DVD, reported successor of the CD-ROM (*Le Monde informatique* (Paris), 11 October 1997, p. 28).

Chapter 3
Networks: the foundation for the information society

The combination of breakthroughs in the digitization, storage and processing of information on the one hand, and the convergence of technologies on the other, has strengthened the existing networks (satellite, cable, Multipoint Multichannel Distribution Service/MMDS), and accelerated the setting up of new high-speed networks, enabling new information technology and the telecommunications industry to combine in complementary fashion.

Satellite broadcasting networks

Most of the satellites in service before 1989 were low- or mid-power systems outputting signals whose reception required an expensive, large-scale dish antenna. They covered territories such as Australia, the United States or the (then) Soviet Union and provided telecommunications and radio broadcasting services for local relay stations. The same process is still employed by a large number of cable TV systems in North America, Latin America and Europe, and has been put into use in recent years in Asia. Concomitant with the upgrade to mid-power and recently to high-power satellites such as the direct broadcasting satellite, there has been a reduction in the size of dish antennae. With the emergence of the digital age, the new generation of satellites is likely radically to increase the supply of interactive services accessible to the general public.

The digital satellite market is booming. Market share is probably greatest in the countries of southern Europe and in developing countries where the penetration rate for cable TV is low, even non-existent. From South-East Asia to Latin America, most countries are once again targeting this market at a time when a new system of world coverage is being set up in parallel using constellations of satellites basically dedicated to the mobile telephone sector.

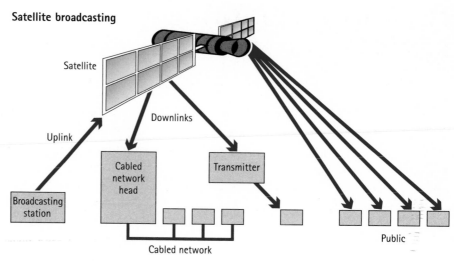

Source: *Dossiers de l'audiovisuel* (Paris, INA), No. 52, 1996.

Cable networks

Cable TV uses a wireframe support (coaxial cable or optic fibre) in order to transmit several programmes simultaneously from the operator of a specialized TV station to subscriber households. With a few exceptions, the geographical coverage of cable TV channels in practical terms is confined to urban areas, owing to constraints in the field and criteria of economic efficiency. Cable TV operators today are fully aware of the new capabilities of satellite retransmission which, through data compression, have boosted the range of programmes on offer and brought new interactive services into being. To meet the competition from satellites, cable TV operators use various transmission resources and data compression to enhance their capacity on coaxial cable networks. They also rely on new optic fibre architectures and on progress in Asymmetrical Digital Subscriber Loop technology (ADSL). This is a digital transmission technique provided by telecommunications operators to broadcast pay-per-view video over their copper wire telephone network, hence the name Video Dial-Tone (VDT). The process makes it possible to transmit up to four television signals at the same time as telephone conversation. In other words, the subscriber can talk on the telephone and watch a video programme transmitted at the same time over the same telephone line. The advantage of this type of technology is the ability to offer pay-per-view video type services over the telephone network without any major investment, as long as the home of the subscriber and the telephone switchboard are both equipped with transceivers.

The change which has had the greatest impact on the current radio broadcasting environment is without doubt the emergence of optic fibre (light modulation) cable as a potential means of transmitting communication signals. Thanks to optic fibre, telephone companies and cable TV operators can provide broadband video services which would be impossible with conventional metal wiring networks, or, at any rate, only at greater cost and with less efficiency.

Digital terrestrial networks

Terrestrial broadcasting is still the main means of telecasting, enabling more than a billion television viewers worldwide to receive their programmes, despite the developments in other telecasting means such as cable or satellite, which offer greater capacity in terms of the number of channels available. Conventional technology has made a comeback through the new possibilities provided by a technology for digital data compression known as MMDS. This process leads to improved picture and sound and above all makes it possible to broadcast four times the number of programmes received through the conventional analog technique, as well as enhancing spectrum management. In concrete terms, television programmes are picked up via a dish antenna which receives a multitude of programmes. A specific MMDS technology transmitter with a range of 5 to 10 kilometres broadcasts the pictures. In surrounding villages or rural areas, a small receiver antenna can distribute the signals to between ten and fifteen households.

Broadcasting each digital microwave stream, however, will require the installation of a special network of transmitters and relay links. The investment may be competitive compared with the cost of a satellite repeater, which is generally rented at around $600,000 per year. The technique is currently developing at high speed in regions such as Africa, the Middle East and the Russian Federation, as well as Central and Eastern Europe, where homes are too widely scattered for the installation of cable networks to be economically viable. There are a number of digital terrestrial broadcasting projects currently under way. The British Government was the first to propose the introduction of digital terrestrial broadcasting in the United Kingdom as early as 1998.[1] Some thirty digital terrestrial channels will be launched prior to this date. Without having either their sets or their aerials altered, more than 70 per cent of British homes will receive these programmes with the aid of a special decoder. The United States of America, however, was the first to develop a concept of a digital terrestrial broadcasting system, initially designed for high-definition television (HDTV). The Federal Communication Commission (FCC) sees the advent of digital terrestrial broadcasting as a means of enhancing the efficiency of spectrum management. To foster development of the system, the Commission recently decided to issue 10,000 licences. Finally, in Japan, terrestrial broadcasting of digital television will become possible between the years 2000 and 2005.

Mobile networks

Mobile communications are booming today, thanks to their ability to 'free' the end-user completely of wire

connection constraints. Mobile systems form the terminal link in a communication network, and provide the multi-purpose and integrational functionalities required by the recent trends in technological convergence. A mobile telephone equipped with a modem and connected to a portable computer can thus be converted into a genuine mobile office, since it can receive and send faxes and files, and access e-mail services from anywhere around the world. It is in the cellular telephone market, however, that growth in mobile communications has been greatest. In the developed countries, which are well equipped with stationary communication systems, the cellular telephone matches the diversity of professional and personal uses and requirements. In the developing countries, it represents an advantageous solution, capable of making up for the shortcomings of the conventional telecommunications infrastructure, particularly in underprivileged areas or those with a low population density. In general, the mobile communications market has one of the highest expansion ratios in the telecommunications sector, with an annual growth rate close to 20 per cent. In all, the number of subscribers worldwide should rise from 40 million in 1995 to 100 million by 1998. Mobile phones are thus switching from being upmarket to mass market. That development is likely to be to the detriment of wireframe networks, which may be abandoned by a vast group of end-users in favour of a telephone number that will follow them wherever they go.

Mobile communication: a segment of globalization

In terms of distribution and penetration, the developed countries are not those with the highest growth rate. While the United States still leads Europe, Asia for its

1. The proposals are set forth in 'Digital Terrestrial Broadcasting – The Government's Proposals', *Sequentia*, Vol. III, No. 8, July/August/September 1996.

Number of cellular mobile telephone subscribers per thousand inhabitants, 1995

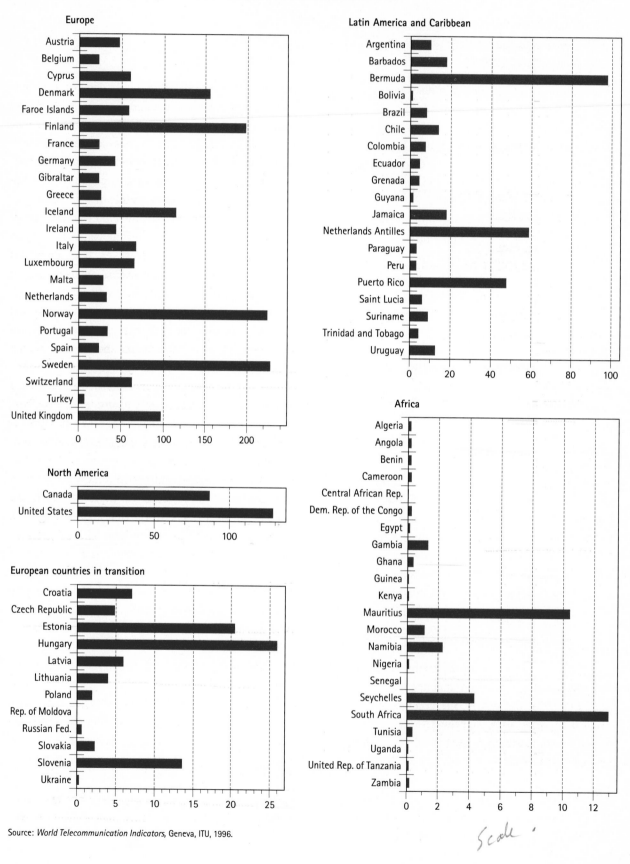

Source: *World Telecommunication Indicators*, Geneva, ITU, 1996.

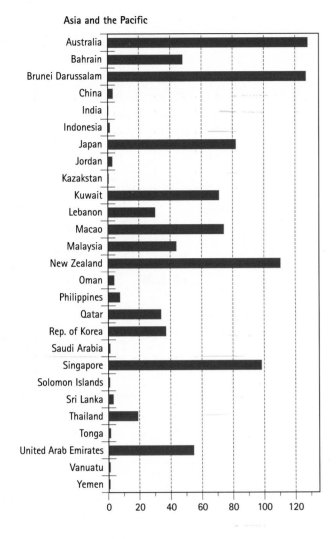

Asia and the Pacific

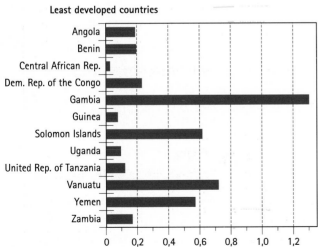

Least developed countries

part has the greatest growth worldwide. In 1996, the installed base of cellular phone subscribers in the Asia-Pacific region (not including Japan) stood at 12.6 million, 7 million of whom were in China alone, where the network has expanded in spectacular fashion. The figure for the region should reach some 53 million by the end of the decade.

In Africa and the Middle East, the advent of cellular services has opened the door to the private sector, both foreign and local. The wave of liberalization since 1990 has resulted in the granting of licences to private operators. Since that date the number of subscribers to cellular services has grown by an average of 78 per cent per annum. From 2.3 million in 1995, the number should have soared to nearly 13.7 million by the year 2000.[2] In Eastern Europe and the newly independent states of the former Soviet Union, the number of cellular phone subscribers could reach 5.5 million by the year 2000. The growth announced will be driven by heightened competition and further deregulation.[3]

All the above countries would therefore seem to have opted for the fastest and cheapest solution. The cellular phone is rapidly becoming something of a panacea, above all as a result of the progress in worldwide telecommunications projects.

Major satellite mobile telephone projects

1997 has seen the emergence of a new type of radio-telephone service with the launch of the first generation of low-orbit satellites, which will ultimately render terrestrial relay links completely obsolete. These new satellite systems are fully-fledged telephone exchanges in orbit, designed to transmit communi-

2. Pyramid Research Inc., 'Cellular and PCS Markets in Africa and the Middle East', Cambridge, Mass., 1996.
3. Pyramid Research Inc., 'Cellular and PCS Markets in Eastern Europe and the Newly Independent States', Cambridge, Mass., 1996.

The principal satellite radiotelephone projects

Project name	Main investors	Industrial partners	Operators	Cost of project (in US$)	Number of satellites	Date of service start-up	Type of service	Cost of communication
East	Matra Marconi Space			1 billion	1		Telecommunications and multimedia	
Globalstar	Loral Space and Communications and Qualcomm	Aérospatiale, Alcatel, Daimler Benz, Finmeccanica and Hyundai, Telital and Ericsson	France Télécom, Vodafone, Air Touch Communications, Dacom.	2.5 billion	48 (low orbit)	1998	Telecommunications	$0.50 to 0.65 per minute
Iridium	Motorola	Lockheed, Raytheon, DEVCOM, Siemens	O.tel.o, STET, Sprint, Korea Mobile Telecom Corp.	3.8 billion	66 (low orbit)	1998	Telecommunications	$2 to 3 per minute
Odyssey	TRW and Teleglobe	Mitsubishi, Magellan, Panasonic, Northern Telecom		3 billion	12 (medium orbit)	2000	Telecommunications	$1 per minute
Teledesic	Microsoft and McCaw cellular communication	AT&T		9 billion	840	2001	Information highways, video conferences, multimedia	
Ico	Inmarsat	Hughes Electronics, NEC, Ericsson, Samsung, Panasonic, Mitsubishi and Wavecom	Over forty, including DeTeMobil	3 billion	10 (medium orbit)	2000	Telecommunications	

Sources: 'Upwardly Mobile', *Network Review: Communications Week International* (London), 3 June 1996, pp. 32–66; 'Le projet satellitaire Iridium poursuit son développement' [The Iridium Satellite Project Continues to Develop], *La Tribune Desfossés* (Paris), 27 March 1996, p. 14; 'Gros satellites solitaires et petits en essaims se disputent le marché des télécommunications', *Le Monde* (Paris), 13 June 1996, p. 21; 'Téléphone: les concurrents sur orbite', *L'Usine nouvelle* (Paris), 30 April 1997.

cations by means of 'satellite-hopping' until they reach their destination. They ensure nothing short of complete and permanent coverage of the planet and a level of performance unequalled by any of the existing terrestrial infrastructures. By the year 2000, the satellite-based radiotelephone industry may well include five rival networks. The first Iridium network, which was piloted by the American company Motorola, was launched on 5 May 1997. It is planned to have all sixty-six satellites that make up the system in place by September 1998. From that date the first subscribers will use a complex portable to receive and

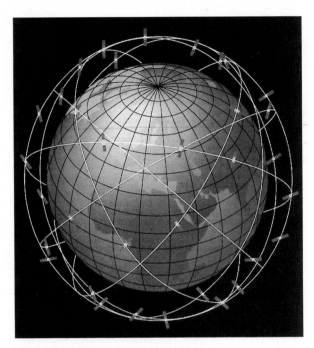

Globalstar satellites placed in low orbit from 1998. More than 850 satellites will compose a first constellation in the next few years, to provide mobile telephone services at planetary levels, automatic search, electronic mail and multimedia services.
Photo: APT Journal/Globalstar

transmit by voice, fax or computer data, but at a price of around $2,000 in addition to the cost of the communications, i.e. $2 or 3 per minute. The cost will no doubt start to fall as other networks come onstream, for instance Globalstar, a competitor that is already in position to give infrastructure back-up for national operations. Competition will become even fiercer with the launching of the other constellations such as Bill Gates's network, Teledesic, which was given the go-ahead by the FCC in March 1997, and many others such as ICO, Odyssey, Skybridge or Orbcomm.

The Internet – network of networks

The Internet is a sort of worldwide co-operative society composed of a multitude of dispersed networks, in which individuals and social groups develop independently of any specific place, culture or country. The Internet has no owner. It is managed by a community of users, and finances its operating costs via its members, who pay connection fees to *hubs* (or

The standards battle

The mobile communications market represents enormous potential growth. The economic issues at stake are such that the battle has already started between two rival digital transmission standards. On the one side there is the American technology known as Multiple Access by Code Distribution (AMRC or CDMA), and on the other the European standard called the Global Standard for Mobile Communications (GSM). Technically, the differences between the two are minute, but they are mutually incompatible.

Mobile communications seem destined to a fate similar to that of video cassettes for VCRs: in the coming years, one of the competitors will have to go. That is why each type of technology, supported by its countries and companies, is redoubling its efforts to prove its superiority. The battle is being fought not only in the European and North American theatres, but elsewhere around the world where the markets have yet to be exploited. The winner will gain equipment supply contracts worth several billion dollars, and thus reign single-handed over the mobile telephone market.

It is also worth noting that discussions are open in international forums about Global Mobile Personal Communication by Satellite (GMPCS) systems to ensure the free circulation of terminals. The issue calls for worldwide co-ordination so that all telecommunications operators and public administrations can, among other things, ensure access to and free circulation of the GMPCS, define a utilization standard, and find a solution to distribution taxes.

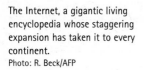

The Internet, a gigantic living encyclopedia whose staggering expansion has taken it to every continent.
Photo: R. Beck/AFP

network nodes) entrusted with routing the data exchange, or to local providers who connect up to the hubs. It is a tangible illustration of the way in which the general communication system has changed, and embodies current convergence by offering an ever-increasing number of services, with audio and video functions integrated with most applications. As a result, the Internet has become a tool for use by the general public and by private users, whereas it was initially designed to provide a communication medium for military and, subsequently, academic use.

The Internet:
a vector for internationalization

Almost 200 countries were connected to the Internet in 1997. North America has taken a considerable lead in the use of the network, since it utilizes virtually three-quarters of all network access sites. The phenomenon is gradually gaining ground on the other continents, particularly in the developing countries. Despite the many difficulties due to the limited number of telephone lines, access by developing countries to the World Wide Web is growing fast. The growth is particularly noticeable in Latin American countries, where almost every single university is connected to the Internet. In Africa, most countries

are also connected to the Internet. In South Africa, the number of host computers per 1,000 inhabitants grew by 147 per cent in the period 1994–95 alone, while the traffic in Burkina Faso is increasing at the same speed as in the industrialized countries (about 100 per cent per year). The presence, albeit symbolic, of places such as Eritrea, the Faeroes, Fiji and Lesotho gives some indication of the globalization of the network. Furthermore, while the presence of a number of countries such as China, India and Indonesia is as yet quite modest, the size of their populations is bound to propel them into the front ranks fairly soon. In general, current growth in network use is exponential in the full sense of the term. A few figures give some idea of its scale: between 2 and 3 billion messages are exchanged every month around the world. Approximately 75 million people are equipped with an electronic mail-box, which they may or may not use, and almost 100,000 commercial service sites are currently listed. At the end of September 1996, at least 500,000 servers were in operation around the world, a figure which is estimated to double every three to four months. The result of this boom is that nearly 30 million pages of information are currently available. According to Internet experts, if the trend continues, every facet of human knowledge will be on the network in less than ten years from now. In 1996, the Internet had some 40 million internauts (users). With a current growth rate of 12 per cent per month, it is estimated that by the year 2000 the figure will rise to 100 million people. With its worldwide expansion and the increase in throughput rates, the Internet is currently opening to other sectors such as the worlds of industry, electronic shopping, the various media, and scientific and academic information.

Number of Internet hosts worldwide, 1991–97

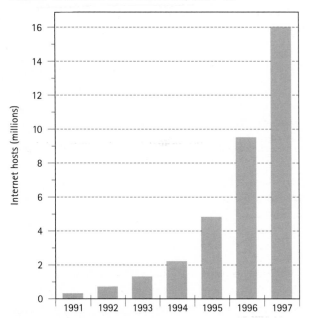

Source: Network Wizards (http://www.nw.com).

The Internet:
new arena for the global economy

According to the various published estimates, data exchange on the Internet is distributed as follows: 60 per cent for trade, 27 per cent for research, 9 per cent for administration and less than 5 per cent for education. These percentages are likely to change in favour of the corporate sector, which is making

increasing use of the Internet to penetrate markets around the world and for interchange with customers. Certain estimates indicate that trade activities could generate revenue of between $7 billion and $40 billion in the year 2000. More optimistic analysts mention figures of up to $150 billion. In 1996, however, network trading only generated sales worth between $600 million and $1.2 billion.[4] A whole new industry is humming in, on and around the Internet: new software systems such as Java and Navigator have been developed to facilitate access to and navigation through the network, and new generations of machines such as *network computers* connected directly to the Web have been launched on to the market.

Companies enter the network and attempt to take advantage of it to engender savings in terms of management costs and/or to stimulate new markets. Banks and funding agencies are providing on-line services specializing in settlements, share trading and the transfer of financial securities. Finally, electronic trading is becoming increasingly widespread, with more and more intermediaries making purchases on the network.

According to some observers, the danger is that the massive influx of the industrial, financial and advertising worlds may make its use by scientists marginal and may even signal the end of the Internet as we know it today. Others estimate that the number of Web pages in circulation, unlike other media, is limitless and that the network can therefore absorb any such initiative. The risk is not so much the arrival in strength of the financial and advertising sectors, but the apathy that may spread through the Internet community when faced with the sheer wealth and quality of commercial service sites.

4.   'A Planetary Supermarket on the Internet', *A World Overview. The Economy and Society in 1996*, 1996 edition, pp. 22–3, Paris, *Le Monde*.

Internet host distribution by geographical area and type of domain		
Domains[1]	Number of hosts	Relative distribution (%)
Territorial domains		
Africa	103 304	0.6
Asia and the Pacific	1 631 176	10.1
Europe	3 510 881	21.7
North America	1 190 518	7.4
Latin America and the Caribbean	165 674	1.0
Total	6 601 553	40.9
Non-territorial domains		
Commercial	3 965 417	24.6
Educational	2 654 129	16.4
Networks	1 548 575	9.6
US military	655 128	4.1
Government	387 280	2.4
Organizations	313 204	1.9
International organizations	1 980	0.0
Undefined domain	19 094	0.1
Total	9 544 807	59.1
World total	16 146 360	100.0

1. A domain is the first level of composition of an electronic address (the second being a sub-domain and the third being computers). There are territorial (national) domains and seven non-territorial ones. The latter comprise machines connected to international networks (.com; .int; .net; .org) or networks which are part of the United States administration (.edu; .gov; .mil).

Source: Network Wizards (http://www.nw.com), 1997.

The Internet: a new media competitor

In the media sector, the Internet also seems to be making inroads as a new information carrier, capable of transmitting news in real time equally as well as the written press, radio or television programmes. Today, each of the major media is setting up sites on the Web in an attempt to compete with the other conventional media in the fields of news, entertainment and leisure activities. Written press and television sites generally offer articles and photographs, and even audio or video recordings, while in recent months radio stations have started using the Web to broadcast programmes around the world, either live or recorded. Finally, the Internet is a serious threat for fax machines and even telephones. The use of e-mail is expanding at an infinitely faster rate than fax machines in their day. The various telephone services available via the Internet at cut-price rates are worrying the conventional telephone companies, which have attempted in vain to parry the attack on legal grounds. According to the IDC consultancy firm, the number of telephone users on the Internet is set to rise from 500,000 in 1995 to 10 million in 1998 and 16 million in 1999. This market, which was worth only $3.5 million in 1995, is expected to reach $560 million by the end of 1999. It should expand rapidly through the activities of the American software firms Microsoft and Netscape, which are integrating the telephone function into their navigation program on the Internet.[5] In the United States, however, the Federal Communication Commission (FCC) has dashed their hopes by declaring telephony on the Internet legal.

The Internet: a chance for education

The Internet offers infinite potential for training and education. It already forms one of the greatest sources of information and documentation accessible anywhere around the planet. Several thousand scientific and technical publications can be consulted, generally free of charge or for a modest sum. Finally, it is one of the world's most extensive e-mail systems, with integrated newsgroup and discussion services (UseNet news) for joint projects linking universities. In the United States, an FCC objective since May 1997 has been to ensure 'universal' access to the Internet in the nation's schools and libraries. As of 1998, more than 100,000 schools will enjoy such access at a special low rate of between 20 and 90 per cent of the ordinary cost to the user. The Internet enables university staff and researchers in developing countries lacking libraries or documentation centres to overcome their scientific and cultural isolation and remain in close contact with the international scientific community. It will completely transform their conditions of work by enabling them to access the vast resources of the leading research centres and universities in the industrialized countries. With this aim in mind, several experiments have been set up in partnership with UNESCO or with scientific establishments such as ORSTOM (France) and non-governmental organizations such as Greennet (United Kingdom). The Internet can also be a valuable means of enhancing the image of national cultures. For the first time in Africa, Niger has set up a site to visit its archaeological riches, while Benin has launched a service dedicated to voodoo.

Internet hosts in Africa, 1997	
Country	Number of hosts
Algeria	28
Angola	2
Benin	9
Botswana	24
Burkina Faso	1
Burundi	1
Central African Republic	6
Congo	1
Cote d'Ivoire	202
Democratic Republic of the Congo	1
Egypt	1 615
Eritrea	1
Ghana	203
Kenya	273
Lesotho	1
Madagascar	27
Mali	15
Mauritius	122
Morocco	477
Mozambique	31
Namibia	262
Niger	5
Nigeria	4
Rwanda	1
Senegal	69
South Africa	99 284
Swaziland	226
Togo	5
Tunisia	39
Uganda	17
United Republic of Tanzania	3
Zambia	173
Zimbabwe	176

Source: Network Wizards (http://www.nw.com), 1997.

5.　　Reported in 'Internet: la bataille du téléphone bon marché' [Internet: Battle for the Low-price Telephone], *Le Figaro* (Paris), 4 March 1997, p. 8.

The chronological history of the Internet

	Up until 1969	1970–75	1975–80	1981–85
Internet	1968, UK: First packet-switching network 1969, UCLA: Launch of Arpanet	1970: Use on Arpanet of Network Control Protocol (NCP)		1982: DoD imposes TCP/IP support 1983: NCP is abandoned in favour of TCP on Arpanet. 1983: Arpanet is divided into Arpanet and Milnet
Other networks			1976–77: UUCP is developed and integrated with Unix 1977: Theorynet 1979: UseNet 1979: CompuServe	1981: BITNET 1981: CSNET 1981, France: Teletel (minitel) 1982: EUnet 1983: EARN 1983: Fidonet
Politics Organization	1957: USSR launches Sputnik. In response, USA creates ARPA in the DoD 1962: Report by Paul Baran from the RAND Corp., on distributed communication networks	1972: Set-up of internetworking workgroup (INWG)	1979: ARPA sets up ICCB, Internet Configuration Control Board	1983: Internet Architecture Board replaces ICCB
Transmission speeds Nb of nodes	1964: 4 nodes	1971: 23 nodes	1977: 111 nodes	1981: 213 nodes 1983: 562 nodes 1984: 1 024 nodes 1985: 1 961 nodes
Protocols Application	1969: First RFC Host Software Steve Crocker	1972: Telnet (RFC-318) 1973: File transfer (FTP) (RFC-454) 1974: V Cerf (et al.) lays down the bases for the future TCP protocol (RFC-675)	1977: Specification of electronic message format (RFC-733)	1982: TCP and IP are finalized 1982: EGP Exterior Gateway Protocol 1982: Mail Format (RFC-822) 1982: SMTP 1983: Domain Name Servers

Source: Arnaud Dufour, *Internet*, Paris, PUF, 1996 (Que sais-je? series).

1986–90	1991–92	1993–94	1995	1996 onwards
1986: Creation of NSFNet 1987: Creation of SWITCH 1988: Internet Worm (virus) 1989: RIPE 1990: Arpanet ceases to exist	1991: Creation of NREN by the High Performance Computing Act 1991: Creation of Renater 1991: Creation of Ebone	1993: Creation of Dante 1994: 25th anniversary of the Internet 1993–94: Explosion of WWW 1994: First Virtual is the first cyberbank 1994: Merger of RARE and EARN into TERENA	1995: NSFNET ceases to exist (replaced by interconnected networks)	Challenges: Management of growth of next-generation IP Commercialization and privatization Protection Ethics
1987: UUNET 1989: Merger of BITNET and CSNET into CREN 1989: Creation of RIPE		1994: Théry Report (France)	1995: Launch of Microsoft Network (MSN)	Competition Interconnection
1988: Creation of CERT 1989: Creation of IEFT and IRFT under IAB	1992: Birth of the Internet Society ISOC 1992: IAB becomes the Internet Architecture Board and is integrated into ISOC	1994: Development of trading activities on the Internet		Funding of ISOC ?: ILFT
02/1986: 2 308 nodes 11/1986: 5 089 nodes 12/1987: 28 174 nodes 1986: NSFNet 56 kbit/s 1988: NSFNet 1.5 Mbit/s	01/1991: 376 000 nodes 01/1992: 727 000 nodes 10/1992: 1 136 000 nodes 1991: NSFNET backbone at 44.7 Mbit/s	01/1993: 1 313 000 nodes 07/1993: 2 056 000 nodes 01/1994: 2 217 000 nodes 07/1994: 3 212 000 nodes	01/1995: 4 852 000 nodes 07/1995: 6 642 000 nodes	
1986: NNTP 1987–89: PEM 1989: SUN RPC 1988–89: SNMP 1988–91: POP 1989–94: PPP	1991: Gopher 1992: World Wide Web 1992–93: MIME	1993: Mosaic 1994: Netscape	1995: Internet Phone	?: IPng ?: VRML ?: Java, revival of World Wide Web

The Internet, however, will prove its true value in the field of education only when the network can offer interactive functions with a much higher degree of efficiency, particularly in terms of sound and video images. Current research led by American academics sponsored by private partners is aiming to launch Internet 2 by 1998. The new network should be faster and more powerful, and can be used for interactive training and distance learning, with real video-conferences between teachers and students, for instance. For their part, satellite operators such as Astra and Eutelsat are striving to develop a powerful broadband technology to download in particular games or entertainments of an educational nature which the public is using more and more. This is sure to provide the worlds of recreation and education with a real teaching aid, promoting and illustrating knowledge and know-how.

The Internet movement has therefore been launched. Various sectors within it are already taking shape (based on individual, collective, cultural, educational and commercial initiatives), implying a change in the ways in which we produce, exchange and learn everything. The Internet will only reach maturity, however, by ensuring a harmonious balance between the various facilities and multiple interests present on the Web, and it is only by strengthening the networks reserved for education, training and culture, on the one hand, and, on the other, by reinforcing basic liberties and moral principles, that the Internet will form part of an ethical cyberspace.

Information highways

Information highways can be defined as a high-speed global network capable of routing to subscribers at high speed a series of new interactive services, such as distance learning, data bank querying, teleshopping, telemedicine, pay-per-view television, picture phoning, etc. These would seem to be the basis for a true technological, economic and cultural revolution, destined to eliminate all geographical, temporal and cultural frontiers. In industrial circles they are compared to the grand civil engineering projects of the nineteenth century, such as the construction of cross-continental railways, or the first motorways. They will enable users to upload or download information to and from any point on the network, and to obtain information tailored to their requirements. At the same time, information users can become information suppliers. Information highways are not a single physical network but a series of local, regional, national and international infrastructures linked to form a worldwide information highway.

Like any other grand technological project, they have aroused heated debate which boils down to a confrontation between those who are for and those who are against their development. Some merely see them as yet another technique which will render the reality of social relationships even more 'virtual', accentuating individualism within society and further widening the gaps in development not only between nations but also within them. Others, on the contrary, consider that if the information highways do indeed come about, they will lead to far-reaching changes, particularly in the sectors of creative art, education, adult training, health and culture – changes, they add, which are likely to create new demands for other services. Most states support the latter point of view, and have built the concept into their strategies to combat the increasing challenges created by international competition. As a result, information highways have become a focal point for political, industrial and cultural issues.

Major projects

The United States was the first to announce the launch of an information superhighway (Information Super Highway). The project, since then baptized the National Information Infrastructure (NII), is led by an interministerial committee (the National Information Super Highway Task Force) in charge of the operation in its experimental design stage. The project, which

The information highways are a major challenge for governments: giving access to the greatest number, promoting cultural plurality and regional and linguistic differences, and assuring diversity of opinions and ideas.
Photo: Lebon/Sipa

has been allocated a budget of $1.5 billion, is the spearhead of the economic revival of the United States and will hopefully generate hundreds of thousands of jobs, either directly or indirectly. A number of pilot experiments are already under way which are precursors to information highways. The most ambitious of these include the Full Service Network set up by Time Warner in Orlando, Florida, which serves 4,000 homes and provides a complete Video on Demand (VOD) service, and the project launched by Bell Atlantic in northern Virginia which provides approximately the same services and aims to be in 8 million homes by the year 2000. The purpose

of these experiments is to test the market and determine the consumer demand for such new services.

The European information highway project was set forth in 1993 in the White Paper entitled *Growth, Competitiveness, Employment.* It was a reaction and a response to the American challenge, and focused more on the concept of the information highway itself than on its infrastructures. During a meeting in Corfu (24–25 June 1994), the Council of Europe discussed the community policy on the information society on the basis of the Bangemann Report (whose official title was *Europe and the Global Information Society. Recommendation to the Council of Europe*). The recommendations, which gave special emphasis to telecommunications, favoured a liberal approach to the sector as well as harmonization of national legislation with respect to media ownership, the protection of private life and intellectual property rights. Three weeks after the meeting, the Brussels Commission adopted an action plan on the ways and means of setting up a 'global information society'.

With respect to applications, the United Kingdom launched the first experimental information highway, the British Telecom Interactive Television (BTITV). Italy has already initiated its first interactive television experiment in Rome and Milan, in partnership with the American company Bell-Atlantic.

Japan reacted in 1994 to the American information highway project mainly through two public institutions: the Ministry of International Trade and Industry (MITI) and the Ministry of Post and Telecommunications (MPT). The stated aim was to set up by the year 2010 a broad interactive communication network providing a range of high-definition multimedia services. The MPT started by setting up a pilot experiment in the region of Kansai. The innovative feature of the Japanese approach to entering the information society is the fact that it is focusing its efforts on the requirements of that society and on intellectual creativity.

The Dialogue Conference

At the opening ceremony of Telecom 95 (October 1995) in Geneva, President Nelson Mandela of South Africa challenged the world community to eliminate the distinction between information-rich and information-poor countries as a critical way of eliminating economic and other inequalities between North and South. Mr Mandela declared: 'As we head towards the twenty-first century, the development of a global information society based on justice, freedom and democracy must be one of our highest priorities.' The meeting in Midrand (South Africa) was the first step in that direction. It was a major event for the developing world, which for the first time was able to discuss the potential offered by the information society to satisfy needs in the cultural, educational and economic sectors of the developing world.

● DIALOGUE AND MUTUAL VISION

The information society must be built on a set of common standards, based on tolerance and the respect for difference, on co-operation and the concentration of efforts, and on the convergence of national visions to a single worldwide vision shared by all. The main proposals for dialogue concerned the following subjects:

- Instituting measures of information technology facilities, processes and applications in both developed and developing countries, to ensure that the gap between the information 'haves' and 'have-nots' can be assessed and bridged.
- Setting up permanent observatories throughout the world, with very high leadership and participation of civil society, to monitor developments in the information society and proactively help the people understand what is happening and what their opportunities are.
- Calling on governments to promote the information society in developing countries.

● COMMON PRINCIPLES AND COLLABORATIVE ACTIONS

Through close co-operation between the developed and the developing worlds at the highest level, it will be possible to set up and develop efficiently a truly global information society, and to prevent certain countries from becoming marginal in relation to others. The fundamental questions raised by the participants concern a number of principles such as universal service, a precise regulatory framework, long-term socio-economic development, co-operation and competition at worldwide levels, the diversity of languages and cultures, co-operation in technological fields, private investment and competition, the protection of intellectual property rights, etc.

● FACILITIES FOR DISCUSSION

Two opening forums, one focusing on business issues and the other on civil society, brought together captains of industry, academics and labour and community leaders from the delegations. They underlined the need for co-operation and partnership between the public and private sectors to reach the common goals of the information society. In the forum on civil society, discussions concerned a wide variety of issues linked to the impact of the information society on people and societies. The forum presented recommendations designed to overcome the threat of a two-tier society, to evaluate the gap between the 'haves' and the 'have-nots', and to include the developing countries in the G7 pilot projects on the information society.

● PILOT PROJECTS

The eleven G7 pilot projects need to be extended in order to become plans for a truly global information society. The other subjects identified are to be linked with the numerous initiatives existing at regional, national and international levels, such as the African Information Society Initiative (AISI) of the Council of Ministers of the UN Economic Commission for Africa (ECA).

The Information Society and Development (ISAD) conference was a watershed in the development of the relationships between the developed and developing worlds. It embodies a real awareness of the importance of the information highways as a challenge for development, and of the fact that a truly global information society can be built only with the participation of the vast majority of the countries on this planet.

Sources: *ITU News*, Nos. 8/96 and 9/96; Midrand press pack, ISAD.

Since the advent of these projects, governments have become aware of these new challenges and have fostered debate or reports on the information society. In France in 1994, Gérard Théry, the promoter of the French Minitel videotex system, returned a report on information highways to the government and suggested that by 2015 every home and every company in the country should be connected to the new network. In Canada in 1994, the Ministry of Telecommunications published a report on the 'Canadian Information Highway'. And in its report published in September 1995, the Information Highway Advisory Council presented the Canadian answers to the challenges of the highways.

In China, three projects baptized the 'Golden Bridge' (a high-speed digital network linking thirty capitals and 12,000 companies), the 'Golden Gate' (connecting corporate computer systems) and the 'Golden Card' (a network of electronic banking systems) aim at massive development of the communications and telecommunications sectors. To reach that target, China has budgeted expenditure of $61.7 billion between now and the year 2000. Two-thirds of that amount are dedicated to the construction of the 300,000 kilometres of optic fibre designed for the high-speed network. Other countries, such as Australia, the Republic of Korea and Singapore, have also scheduled the development of high-speed networks and of the new technology they require to connect up homes, schools and companies to the information highways.

South Africa, Indonesia and the governments of a number of developing countries have decided not to be left behind and are putting forward reports defining their strategies to be part of the information society. At the same time, and with the same aim in mind, regional and international organizations are developing initiatives around the information society. In 1994, the International Telecommunications Union organized the first World Telecommunication Development Conference. On that occasion, the Vice-President of the United States, Al Gore, launched the concept of a worldwide information infrastructure – 'GII, the global information infrastructure' – which he defined as a 'planetary information network that transmits messages and images at the speed of light from the largest city to the smallest village on every continent'.

One year later, at the invitation of the European Union, the group of the world's most industrialized countries (G7) held a Ministerial Conference on the Global Information Society. It outlined eleven pilot projects to guide the development of the information society, and undertook to associate the developing countries in discussions of wider scope. In pursuit of a common vision, in May 1996 at Midrand (South Africa), together with the European Community and South Africa, the G7 organized the Information Society and Development Conference (ISAD), with representatives from developing countries, the countries of the G7, those of the European Union, and United Nations agencies.

The issues

The giant task of constructing the information highways and the estimated cost of setting them up are a golden opportunity for computer manufacturers, software publishers, consumer electronics manufacturers, telecommunications network operators and other groups of information holders. The industrial task is that of making information highways and their applications available to a public about whose future behaviour nothing is known. No one can say with any certainty whether the public are going to want new interactive services. But for the manufacturers, the potential market is enormous, and justifies taking the risk. With this outlook in mind, numerous alliances between firms are being set up to control the global information industry (see the chapter on technological change).

Over and above the commercial and industrial mechanisms which for the time being seem to be the driving force behind the construction of the information highways, the cultural and scientific issues must not be neglected.

The new infrastructures are not just technological vectors, mere solutions put forward by market forces. They also represent, according to certain official policy speeches, a new facility to which users around the world may have at least minimum access, on equal terms and enjoying equal quality, no matter what their geographical location. There is a major risk, however, that access may become the privilege of high-yield markets, particularly where new value-added services are concerned, which therefore raises the problem of the predominance of private interests in the development and organization of the information highways. The issue, therefore, resides as much in the technological capacity to create an information society as in the ability to promote the conditions for harmonious social, economic and cultural development on an international scale and thereby ensure access for the greatest possible number.

Access to the networks presupposes a reliable universal service at an affordable price, meeting the fundamental needs of individuals for education, science and culture. This implies that users, whatever their origin, must be able to acquire the basic 'digital skills' and have sufficiently user-friendly interfaces to benefit from them.

It is equally essential that the pluralism of opinions and ideas be guaranteed, and that software which is not necessarily of commercial value be developed. It is also necessary that the plurality of cultural goods on offer and participation by all linguistic and regional viewpoints be fostered, in order to avoid uniformity and standardization of network content.

Finally, in a digital universe which is already deploying its networks and drawing its new frontiers, there is a strong risk that the differences in the levels of development not only between nations but within them may simply widen. This risk is particularly significant in developing countries, which will have to implement clear-cut, audacious strategies to enable users to take advantage of the information highways. The temptation to seek to control access to them, on the grounds that some programmes do not correspond to either religious or political national standards or values, could result in highly prejudicial delays in developing the new communications infrastructures. The free flow of information is an essential prerequisite, not only for the exercise of democratic rights but also for social and economic progress. That being said, to reduce the current debate to questions of market forces or purely technological issues would be to miss the point. The major challenge facing the countries promoting the information highways is a multiple one. On the one hand, the difficulty lies in ensuring that the greatest number of people have access to the highways, and for the same reason, in removing every obstacle or barrier of any kind that might impede or hinder the advance of the highways within nations and between them; the challenge, on the other hand, lies in promoting the diversity of programmes both in their content and in their origin, such that each and every community or sector of society is able to express itself and thereby ensure the survival of its culture, language and traditions, without being systematically tied down by economic considerations linked to market laws. In this connection, the concept of public service urgently needs to be redefined to adapt it to the realities of the information highways. In other words, thought should be given to the measures that must be taken at government level in order to ensure that access to the information highways is open to all, that the most elementary needs, notably in terms of culture and education, are guaranteed over and above purely economic considerations, and that the services meeting these elementary requirements are financially accessible to the greatest possible number.

Excerpts from speeches and schemes on the information highways

. . . a planetary information network that transmits messages and images at the speed of light from the largest city to the smallest village on every continent. . . . This GII will circle the globe with superhighways on which all people can travel. . . . These highways – or, more accurately, networks of distributed intelligence – will allow us to share information, to connect, and to communicate as a global community. From these connections we will derive robust and sustainable economic progress, strong democracies, better solutions to global and local environmental challenges, improved health care, and – ultimately – a greater sense of shared stewardship of our small planet. . . . [This national infrastructure] will consist of hundreds of different networks, run by different companies and using different technologies, all connected together in a giant 'network of networks', providing telephone and interactive digital video to almost every American.

Excerpt from the speech given by the Vice-President of the United States, Al Gore, to the ITU World Telecommunication Development Conference, Buenos Aires, 21 March 1994.

The cost of information today consists not so much of the creation of content, which should be the real value, but of the storage and efficient delivery of information, that is in essence the cost of paper, printing, transporting, warehousing and other physical distribution means, plus the cost of the personnel manpower needed to run these 'extra' services. . . . Realizing an autonomous distributed networked society, which is the real essence of the Internet, will be the most critical issue for the success of the information and communication revolution of the coming century or millennium.

Excerpt from Izumi Aizi, 'Building Japan's Information Infrastructure', *Nihon keizai shimbun*, 16 April 1993.

The broadband network must be fully bi-directional. . . . It must be easy for any person to provide services. . . .

Universal service rules must be adopted, designed to provide a basic service to all Australians for low cost. Cross-subsidization may be necessary. . . .
We believe that the Government should publish as much information as possible over the public data network as a public service.

Excerpt from *Electronic Frontiers,* Australia's submission to the Broadband Services Exports Group.

Throughout the world, information and telecommunications technologies are generating a new industrial revolution already as significant and far-reaching as those of the past. It is a revolution based on information. . . . Information has a multiplier effect that will energize every economic sector. With market-driven tariffs, there will be a vast array of novel information services and applications. . . . Since information activities are borderless in an open market environment, the information society has an essentially global dimension.

Excerpt from the Bangemann Report *(Europe and the Global Information Society)* to the Council of Europe, Brussels, May 1994.

In its simplest form we can see the Information Highway in objects as near to hand as the telephone, television and personal computer . . . Canada has already got a part of the electronic infrastructure needed to provide Canadians with applications and convergent services linked to wireless, telephone, data transmission and other communication services . . . Many Canadians have access to the Information Highway via banking services, TV service on demand or commercial uses such as videoconferencing.

Excerpt from the Final Report of the Information Highway Advisory Council, *Connection, Community, Content: The Challenge of the Information Highway,* Industry Canada, September 1995.

Source: *World Telecommunication Development Report,* Geneva, ITU, 1995.

Chapter 4
Economic change

The differences in production between the broadcasting and telecommunications industries are rapidly dwindling as a result of the progress in new information and communication technology combined with the convergence of computer science. The disappearance of these barriers has resulted in the development of existing industries (consumer electronics, computer technology, video games, etc.) and the spawning of new services (electronic commerce and publishing, mobile communication, teleshopping, etc.). These changes have required major investment, underlining the industrial and commercial character of the media and the scale of financing they need. At the same time, the high cost of research and development has led companies to sign alliances setting up multimedia groups on a world scale, their aim being to obtain greater outlets on the international market. Worried by the potential loss of a substantial part of their own media capacity, states have set up authorities to supervise and regulate the market-place at national or regional levels. The present chapter discusses the salient trends of the communication market.

A knowledge-based economy

The move towards the information society is characterized by the general dematerialization of the market-place, a feature which has affected every economic sector and has resulted in new modes of economic exchange and corporate organization. It has freed the economy of the conventional constraints of distance and the scarcity of resources. Digital technology and data compression have produced means of creating information that can be multiplied to infinity, making the information economy one of abundance and profusion. Essential wealth no longer resides in the physical substrate on and with which information is conveyed, but in the growing production of paperless goods and in the development of know-how, which has itself become a strategic resource.

The triumph of software over hardware

On the global information technology market, the value of software and services caught up with that of hardware as early as 1991 and exceeded it in 1992, with sales of almost $200 billion out of a total market worth $380 billion. By the year 2000 it is estimated that services will be worth more than $660 billion out of a total of $1,000 billion.[1] This new development has enabled the program and software industry to overtake manufacturers of hardware. The real added value is no longer held by computer constructors such as IBM or Compaq, but by the manufacturers of microprocessors and operating systems. Up to the present date, the computer industry has always been dominated by Intel, which supplies 80 per cent of all the microprocessors used around the world, and by Microsoft, which holds an identical market share in terms of operating systems (Windows 95, Windows NT, MS-DOS), hence the nickname of 'Wintel' often given to personal computers (PCs) today. The operating systems of the one and the microprocessors of the other form the core of more than 80 per cent of the PCs sold around the world, and the two companies lie at the heart of the computer revolution.

Microsoft, the creator of the MS-DOS operating system, is worth more on the stock market today than the American giant IBM. It is astonishingly powerful and financially profitable, with sales of approximately $4.6 billion and a net profit margin in the order of 25 per cent. It also has a major advantage: its domination of the program market for microcomputers – tools which are still an essential prerequisite for access to the Web. Since its launch in August 1995, the firm's latest generation of operating systems for general public microcomputers, Windows 95, has sold 25 million copies. Windows NT, the professional version of the system, has just become the world leader. Finally, Microsoft is the fourth-ranking publisher of CD-ROMs worldwide and is now launching projects for broadband operating systems, as well as the development of a programme navigation and guide system for interactive television. Intel, for its part, has become the driving force for growth and profit in the world of information technology. The enterprise, with net sales for 1995 skimming $20 billion, in 1996 announced a leap of 41 per cent in profits. Its turnover has increased every year by more than 30 per cent to reach $20.8 billion in 1996, with a net profit margin of 20 per cent. Financial analysts estimate that Intel will be soon the most profitable company on the planet, ahead of traditional industries, for example Shell or General Motors.

1.   'Information Technology Market Slides towards Services', *01 Informatique* (Paris), 21 February 1992, quoted by C. Goldfinger, *L'utile et le futile* [The useful and the useless], p. 72, Odile Jacob Publications, 1994.

The qualitative level of the human resources in a country and the capacity of its citizens to use new technology and thus make optimum use of their know-how have become vital factors in competitiveness. The correlation between know-how and economic growth is henceforth an established fact. Development strategies around the world now invest in knowledge, education and training, as the new keys to success for modern economies.

At the heart of this movement lies the exponential development of software systems and services. Real added value is no longer contained in technology or production, but in the ways we use them both. This tendency is particularly noticeable when the situation of businesses in the communication sector, whose activities are exclusively paperless, is compared with that of companies producing hardware. Globally, software and services have superseded the

Information industry and GDP growth worldwide, 1990–94 (percentages)

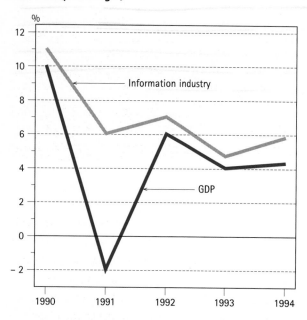

Source: ITU and OMSYC data quoted in *Television and the Future*, produced by RAI for the UN Television Forum, New York, 1996.

new as well as conventional media: radio broadcasting, information technology, satellites, cable TV, cinema and many other related activities. In this chapter, we focus on the major economic changes in key communication sectors: audiovisual products and services, information technology and telecommunications.

Estimated relation between the information service and equipment market, 1990–2000

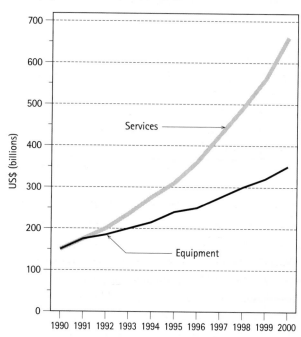

Source: C. Micas, 'Industries et marchés de l'informatique dans le monde', *Communications et stratégies* (Montpellier), No. 4, 1991, p. 130.

manufacturers of computers and other technology in generating revenue, profits and capital gains.

A growth-based economy

In every country around the world, the demand for information in every form seems to be steadily increasing. The three sectors of the communications industry (telecommunications, information technology and audiovisual products and services) in 1994 totalled sales of $1,430 billion, or 5.9 per cent of the world's gross product. In other terms, for every $1,000 that the planet earns and spends, $59 are generated by the sectors of the communications industry.[1] Its high-speed growth is notably the result of constant demand from the Asia-Pacific region and Latin America.

The communication market can cover a relatively wide range of business activities, including

The audiovisual field

In the new audiovisual environment, the most immediate problem perhaps is competition from new forms of image distribution, linked to the development

1.   *World Telecommunication Development Report*, Geneva, International Telecommunication Union, 1995.

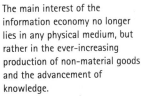

The main interest of the information economy no longer lies in any physical medium, but rather in the ever-increasing production of non-material goods and the advancement of knowledge.
Photo: Munoz-Yague/Eurelios

of digital television. The latter has introduced direct pay-per-view systems, thus creating an upheaval in the freedom of television enjoyed up to the present time by commercial advertising.

In Europe, the audiovisual market is expanding at a sustained rate, on the order of 10 per cent per year. Growth of this nature, 1 per cent higher than the world market rate, has every chance of being maintained with the start-up of ninety-eight new television channels in 1995. This increase in supply is the result of the development in European satellite capacity, with the launch in 1995 of the first services making use of digital technology, but also of the continuation of deregulation, notably in Central and Eastern Europe and in the Scandinavian countries. The growth is due to three factors: the expansion in cable TV infrastructures (with an increase of 11.6 per cent in the number of cabled homes in 1994 in the thirty-three European countries); the growing number of cable subscribers (with an increase of 11.5 per cent in the fifteen member states of the European Union); the upswing in investment in television commercials (with an average increase of 14.7 per cent in 1994 throughout the fifteen member states); and finally the development of pay-per-view channels and the growth in their subscribers (+25 per cent).

On the North American continent, pay services are also the driving force behind growth. According to the Institut de l'Audiovisuel et des Télécommunications en Europe (IDATE), 51 per cent of the turnover in the American audiovisual sector comes from pay television, whereas public TV no longer represents more than 40 per cent of the market. The same trend can be seen in Asia and in Latin America, where the trend in the audiovisual sector is continuing towards direct financing by the consumer, thereby widening the gap with the logic of indirect financing generated by TV commercials or licence fees.

One might question whether this new tendency is likely to marginalize general-interest television, but the facts indicate that mass-media broadcasting is far from being a thing of the past. Even if the TV market share has decreased sharply, the size of its audience is still enormous and its power of attraction still strong. The television market worldwide seems to be based on hybrid forms of coexistence and financing combining the various forms of commercial advertising and direct payment systems. Another feature is the ongoing reconciliation between the cinema and television industries as well as the increasingly international nature of programmes. As a rule, the arrival of private general-interest or pay TV channels is accompanied by an increase in the television commercial market. This current expansion is taking place to the detriment of the advertising revenue for public television channels.

The information technology sector

The computer industry features a number of prominent trends. The first concerns the market for electronic components, the key to all technological innovation. Component performance characteristics (miniaturization and computing power) and the ongoing decline in their prices have boosted the market for electronic hardware. The market for these components is also growing steadily wider with the digitization of every possible electronic product, with outlets in buoyant sectors such as telecommunications, computer technology and multimedia. American and Japanese companies are the leading manufacturers worldwide of electronic components. Since 1984, they have also dominated the professional and general consumer computer markets.

The second change concerns the spectacular growth of the multimedia industry. The health of the market is due to the expansion of the general consumer sector for hardware and products. In 1993, in the United States, the number of CD-ROM readers in homes outstripped the number of CD-ROMs in the workplace. Out of an estimated total installed base at that time of 7 million readers, 4.5 million were in homes and 2.5 million were in companies. From 1993 to 1994, product sales in the publishing sector no less than tripled, generating a growth rate in publishing turnover of 85 per cent, which rocketed to 186 per cent in the first quarter of 1995.[2] Since then, the computer manufacturers have started to reposition themselves on the general consumer segment, an upheaval caused by the potential market of hundreds of millions of homes to be equipped in the coming years. The installed base worldwide of personal microcomputers (PCs) has, so to speak, exploded. According to the consultancy firm IDC, the European market grew by 7.1 per cent in 1996, thus placing it far behind the Middle East and Africa (20 per cent), the Russian Federation (17 per cent), the United States (21 per cent), China (25 per cent) and Japan (33 per cent).[3]

Professional estimates indicate that the world will have 250 million microcomputers at the turn of the twenty-first century, with sales of 132 million microcomputers in the year 2000 alone, without counting portables or mainframes. The market potential represents an annual sales figure of $264 billion in the year 2000 as against $148 billion in 1996 and $125 billion in 1995.

This being said, the aforementioned developments in microcomputer technology are taking place in a high-risk market against a backdrop of intense competition. Microcomputer technology has become a market in which volumes and economy of scale have become essential in order to compensate for decreasing prices and narrowing profit margins. To be profitable today in the microcomputer sector, a company has to sell at least 1 million machines[4] per year. On top of this, ongoing technological changes, never-ending price wars to sell machines that become obsolete increasingly rapidly, and decreasing profit margins have made the microcomputer market vulnerable, and a reshuffle of the players and their cards[5]

---

2.   According to the American Software Publishers Association (SPA), quoted in 'En attendant' [In the Meantime], in *Média pouvoirs, 50 ans de médias* (Paris), Nos. 39/40, 3rd and 4th quarters 1995.

3.   'L'ère de la communication sans l'Europe?' [The Communication Era without Europe?], *Le Monde Économique* (Paris), 25 March 1997, p. 1.

4.   According to Erich Ochs, vice-president of the survey consultants International Data Corp. (IDC), 'the PC market is increasingly becoming a volume market, and the break-even point of volumes to produce in order to be profitable is rising', quoted in 'Microcomputing has Become a High-risk Market', *Le Monde* (Paris), 6 July 1996, p. 12.

5.   In 1996, the leading world microcomputer manufacturer, the American firm Compaq, announced price cuts of up to 21 per cent on its range of professional PCs equipped with the Intel Pentium microprocessor. Those rates have been decided in reaction to sales figures lower than their scheduled targets. Other manufacturers, such as Hewlett-Packard and Digital Equipment (DEC), have fallen into line

is likely. The weakest manufacturers are already winding up their ventures in computer technology.[6] At the same time, other manufacturers are positioning themselves and taking the initiative in innovation, by creating new architectures capable of breathing new life into the multi-purpose microcomputer of the future, combining computer and television technologies. The issue has more to do with preparing the machine of tomorrow, a user-friendly hybrid resulting from the convergence between television sets, computers and games consoles. All the major manufacturers have realized the scale of this development and are preparing for a radical change in their end market. In this respect, the Japanese firms are proving to be unusually aggressive. The NEC group, which has a 20 per cent stake in the capital of Packard Bell, claims, with its new partner, second rank worldwide, with 4.2 million machines sold and net sales of $8 billion. The same offensive is being launched by the other Japanese constructors Fujitsu, Hitachi and Sony.

Control of the Internet: the computer industry's Battle of the Bulge

The Internet is a new distribution platform not only for value-added services but also for programs and multimedia works. It is a highly prosperous, new market with some 40 million users to date. In the United States, 11 per cent of American families are already subscribers to on-line services and 19 per cent have regularly used the Web over the course of the last twelve months.[7] In Europe, according to the strategic survey published by the directorate in charge of electronic media for the European Commission (DG 13), service demand seems to make greater use of distribution over an Internet type of network than that via CD-ROM.[8]

In fact, these new market opportunities anticipate a major upheaval in the computer industry and foreshadow the impact that the Internet will have on the use of computers. They are all part of a technological, commercial and legal battle for the

control of the Web, between computer technology and software majors such as Microsoft, IBM and Compaq and small innovative firms like Netscape for navigation software, or Sun Microsystem for Internet application development tools. The latter's success can be explained more by their aggressive strategy in relation to the dominant position of Microsoft[9] and by their diversification policy, notably with respect to multimedia and Internet applications, than by their technological skills alone.

Faced with these new pretenders, the majors are changing strategy to adapt to the new shape of the computer market. Microsoft is henceforth preoccupied

and applied immediate price reductions of up to 26 per cent. 'Compaq Restarts Personal Computer Price War', *Le Monde* (Paris), 6 March 1996, p. 15.

6. The French computer company Bull, from which the French Government is gradually withdrawing its stake, suffered a downswing in losses in its personal computer business in 1996, as did the ICL and Escom groups. The French company has had to sell off its microcomputer business to the American manufacturer Packard Bell. The same fate befell the Italian firm Olivetti, which was unable to reach the requisite critical mass: it sold 800,000 PCs in 1996, while the minimum break-even point stands at around 1 million units. The PCs that represented 22 per cent of group turnover are largely responsible for the group's losses, which were estimated at 1.3 billion French Francs for the first semester of 1996, with a debt load of nearly 8 billion French Francs.

7. According to an inquiry by *Business Week* published in the summer of 1996, quoted by *Multi-media Made in USA,* p. 73, Paris, Institut Multi-Médias, 1996.

8. Quoted in 'L'édition électronique face à ses incertitudes' [Electronic Publishing Faced with Uncertainty], *Le Monde* (Paris), October 1996, p. 25.

9. The purpose of this vast multimedia offensive is to reconquer a program market, 80 per cent of which is controlled by Microsoft. For Larry Ellison, CEO of Oracle, 'the priority of Oracle is clearly that of multimedia: by the year 2000, a quarter of our sales will be realized by the multimedia division', quoted in *Multi-media Made in USA,* p. 88, Paris, Institut Multi-Médias, 1997.

with network navigation-aid software, given the success of firms such as Netscape Communications and Sun Microsystem. The first of these two companies has become sector leader with a market share of almost 74 per cent gained with its program Navigator,[10] a software system that has introduced new interfaces such as guidance and navigation instruments for users to find their way through the jungle of addresses on the Internet. To counter the aims of Microsoft, the firm is striving to maintain its position and title by launching a new version of its Navigator program, that provides users with much wider possibilities for sound and video applications. The firm has also set up a subsidiary whose objective is to develop another version of Navigator to equip televisions as well as cellular telephones or games consoles. In 1997 Netscape also intends to launch a new browser called Communicator, with a small modular knowbot (or knowledge-seeking robot) called Constellation. In addition to management of all the standard Net functions (Web, e-mail, newsgroups), the virtual, information-seeking robot will enable internauts to receive personalized information automatically, without having to make regular use of the module themselves. In the near future this type of knowbot should be able to help people in all sorts of ways, whether to book a plane ticket at the best price, or to sort information in order to have a personalized daily review of the press.

Microsoft, which only has a 4 per cent market share in this sector, is trying to make up for lost time by launching three versions of its Explorer software, a program equally capable of navigating through the information found on the hard disk of a computer and that found on the Web. The programs are integrated directly with software systems such as Windows or Microsoft Office and supplied free of charge to end-users. The strategy, aimed at increasing the sales of Windows-based software and operating systems, has not been welcomed by Netscape, and the company has filed a complaint with the American Department

Market distribution of Web navigators

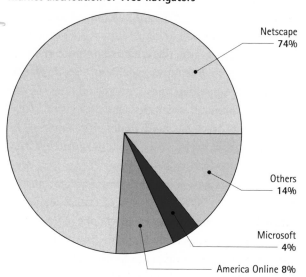

Source: Forrester Research, from *Le Figaro* (Paris), August 1996.

of Justice on the grounds of anti-trust practices.[11] Informed sources report that Microsoft held a 28 per cent share of the global 'navigator' market in January 1996 as against only 4 per cent three months later.

The real potential, however, lies in conquering the promising Intranet market, i.e. the application of Internet tools to corporate in-house networks. In this area, Netscape seems to be a few lengths ahead of its competitors. Its software system Navigator 3.0 is apparently compatible with sixteen different types of operating systems, which is a powerful sales argument for companies that generally have a heterogeneous installed base of computers. In comparison, Microsoft's Explorer software can be used only with its own operating systems Windows 95 and Windows NT.

10.	According to the American consultancy firm Forrester Research, quoted in 'Netscape-Microsoft: A Duel to the End', *Le Figaro* (Paris), 28 October 1996, p. 31.

11.	'Browser Battle Goes On: Netscape Writes to DOJ', *Broadcasting & Cable* (New York), 26 August 1996, p. 54.

The second of the firms mentioned, Sun Micro-systems, has been the first to launch into the supply of computers tailored to operating centre servers on the Internet. The company is undeniably the current leader on the Internet, with a 56 per cent market share. It is developing new software systems of the Java-OS type, which enable applications to be distributed via the Internet and which work on any type of personal computer or operating system.

Even the players in the computer industry agree about the central role of the Internet and are framing strategies to make the most of this new revolution in the field. As early as June 1996, the IBM group focused its strategy on networking and the development of electronic commerce solutions. Today, all the PCs of the firm are equipped with the latest version of the navigation software system Netscape. The firm also provides on-line aid and direct links with a quantity of Web pages designed to attract a family audience. The IBM Web site usually offers free software which can easily be downloaded with a simple click of the mouse. Hewlett Packard has similar aims, and has enabled its servers to carry out transactions as well as perform video retransmission. To do so, in May 1996 the firm signed an alliance with Netscape in order to sell the Web server and Netscape navigator in the software package supplied with each HP machine. Apple, which is currently in economic difficulties, is fighting the same battle: the company is focusing its new strategy on the Internet by proposing an access that aims to be simple, efficient and inexpensive. The constructor is betting heavily on this card by launching the Pippin, a combined CD-ROM reader console and Internet terminal. Apple has also undertaken to integrate Internet functions on all of its machines.[12] The firm's new strategy breaks with the in-house policy of norms and standards. It is also militating for a policy of all-out reconciliation and partnerships, even with Microsoft, with which the constructor has signed an agreement whereby European users of the PowerMac, the top-of-the-range

What the majors are worth

- **INTEL**
Sales: $16.2 billion in 1995.
Net income: $3.6 billion.

- **MICROSOFT**
Sales: $5.9 billion for the 1994–95 fiscal year; $6.42 billion at the end of the third quarter of the 1995–96 fiscal year.
Net income: $1.4 billion in 1994–95; $1.6 billion at the end of the third quarter 1995–96.

- **SUN**
Sales: $5.9 billion in 1995.
Net result: $355.8 million.

- **ORACLE**
Sales: $2.96 billion in 1995.
Net profit: $441.5 million.

- **NETSCAPE**
Sales: $80.7 million in 1995.
Net loss: $3.4 million.

Source: *Le Monde* (Paris), 2 November 1996, p. 15.

computer from Apple, will have access to Microsoft Office office-automation applications.

Telecommunications

The telecommunications industry entails both the production of hardware and infrastructures (satellites, telephones, wireframe networks, corporate networks and personal radio communications) and the supply of services. It forms the basic infrastructure for any

12. 'Apple', *Multi-media Made in USA*, p. 4, Paris, Institut Multi-Médias, 1996.

modern economy, as well as being an important link in all international exchange of goods and services. Over the course of the last decade, the telecommunications sector has been shaken by lightning technological changes and competition from powerful networks as a result of the convergence of computer technology, software publishing and the media.

These developments have meant that the telecommunications industry has moved away from its conventional role of a public service providing telephone facilities alone, to become a branch of business generating new services and products considered to be key factors in international competitiveness and productivity. The world telecommunications market boasts a very rapid growth rate projected to continue well beyond the year 2000. Estimated at $800 billion in 1996, it is expected to reach $1,200 billion by the year 2000. The sales figure for telephone lines approached $600 million in 1993 as against $575 million in 1992. On top of this should be added the figure of almost 34 million mobile telephone subscribers in 1994.[13]

The region of South-East Asia is seen as one of the strategic zones for telecommunications, a sector considered to be a priority in any development policy. Japan has the largest telecommunications market in Asia. The penetration rate for telephones has increased by more than 30 per cent since 1984, with 61.7 million subscriber lines and a teledensity (the number of telephone lines per 100 inhabitants) of 49 per cent in 1995.[14] Meanwhile, the digitization of the network is continuing and should be completed by year-end 1997. The Japanese market also serves as a benchmark for other countries in the region. The prospects in China are impressive, with a sector that is genuinely booming. Other development programmes of unprecedented scale have also been set up in Indonesia, the Philippines and Thailand, transforming the region into a battleground between the world's major manufacturers and the main exporters of telecommunications technology.

The Chinese Leap

A powerful phase of growth in Chinese telecommunication infrastructures began in 1990. Since then, the number of telephone subscriber lines has multiplied by ten (to reach 68.7 million lines). The Chinese Government intends to develop its system at a rate of 10 million lines per year, or approximately 15 per cent of world production, with a target that fluctuates between 70 and 100 million lines by the year 2000. To obtain this rate of expansion, in its ninth governmental plan (1996–2000) the Chinese Government forecasts it will have to invest more than $60 billion. The rate of development is even faster in the sector of the mobile telephone, which has a growth potential that is virtually unique in the world, even though regulation continues to be restrictive. This evolution is particularly noteworthy with regard to fixed telephones for which the Chinese Government in May 1997 authorized China Unicom, a national operator competing with the state monopoly China Telecom, to run its own independent local telephone networks in three regions of the country. In taking this step, the authorities have permitted foreign firms working in partnership with China Unicom to enter the Chinese telephone market with its enormous potential. Forecasts anticipate 10.5 telephone lines for 100 inhabitants by the year 2000 as opposed to only 4.6 lines at present. It is expected that the Broad Band Integrated Digital Network, which is the Chinese version of the information highways, will be installed by the year 2010.

Sources: 'China Assigns Priority to Telecommunications Development', *Financial Times*, 9 April 1996; *Annual Report* of the Observatoire des Systèmes de Communication [Communication Networks Observatory] (OMSYC), France, February 1997.

13.   *Conjoncture 96* (special issue of *Les Échos*, pp. 151–2), Paris, Editions Breal, 1996.
14.   'Japon: l'empire des mobiles' [The Mobile Empire], *Réseaux et Télécoms* (Paris), June 1996, p. 18.

privatization

National legislation to protect telecommunications monopolies is gradually being modified in every country. The movement and the philosophy behind it began in the middle of the 1970s in the United States. The trend then spread to Japan, the United Kingdom and the rest of Europe. In 1997, the movement became global with the agreement signed in Geneva (on 15 February 1997) within the framework of the World Trade Organization (WTO). The agreement marks the gradual end of the monopoly in telecommunication services (telephone, service transmission, etc.). The signatories of the agreement together represent 90 per cent of a world market evaluated at $800 billion in 1996, with an annual growth rate of more than 10 per cent.[15] According to WTO experts, the complete opening of the market to competition should result in price cuts, benefiting consumers first and foremost, thereby spurring an upswing in growth in every country.

In the industrialized countries, the trend has already had a positive effect on the growth of the sector and should make a significant contribution to improving the situation of employment.[16] Africa, on the other hand, shows some sluggishness of growth in the telecommunications sector, no doubt due to the general slowdown of economic activity in the region. The results recorded by Africa for the period between 1990 and 1995 were lower than those of the other developing regions.

The main obstacles to the development of the telecommunications sector are connected with the cost of infrastructures, to their financing, to regulatory problems and to price policies. According to the International Telecommunication Union (ITU), investments of some $7 billion will be needed between now and the end of the century for sub-Saharan Africa to have one telephone line per 100 inhabitants.[17] Many African analysts fear that the domestic monopolies which are currently disappearing will have been replaced by international cartels in a few years.

15. 'La fin des monopoles' [An End of Monopolies], *Le Monde* (Paris), 18 February 1997, p. 15.
16. According to a survey carried out by Bipe Conseil for the European Commission, the opening of the telecommunications sector to competition should result in the creation of 1.3 million jobs between the present date and the year 2005. The jobs will not be directly created in the telecommunications sector, but the latter will provide a cumulative effect for the other sectors of the European economy. 'La libéralisation des télécoms va créer des emplois en Europe' [Liberalization of Telecommunications to Create Jobs in Europe], *Les Echos* (Paris), 27 January 1996, p. 12.
17. P. Tarjianne, 'Développement des systèmes d'information et de communication pour l'Afrique' [The Development of Information and Communication Systems for Africa: Problems and Prospects], Rencontre sur l'Afrique et les Nouvelles Technologies de l'Information [Meeting on Africa and New Information Technology], Geneva, 17–18 October 1996.

World telecom service turnover (in billions of US$)

Region	Fixed telephone		Mobile telephone		Data transmission		Other		Total	
	1995	2000	1995	2000	1995	2000	1995	2000	1995	2000
North America	146.7	162.0	24.3	47.2	24.5	31.5	9.5	10.0	205.0	250.7
Western Europe	136.3	153.2	20.0	40.7	16.0	20.7	19.7	23.7	192.0	238.3
Asia/Pacific	99.0	120.1	19.0	44.9	11.2	16.9	7.6	9.9	136.8	191.8
Other	43.8	69.1	8.3	36.3	4.9	9.7	2.8	5.9	59.8	121.6
Total	425.8	505.0	71.6	169.1	56.6	78.8	39.6	49.5	593.5	802.4

Consequences for employment

In the developed countries, jobs and professions are undergoing deep changes affecting every single area of the workplace. The information sector, considered to be one of high growth, has a high demand for personnel, although the impact on employment depends on the technology in question and the structure of the market. As a rule, employment is increasingly concentrated in the production of paperless goods and the supply of services. Between 1990 and 1995, the film industry generated 127,000 jobs in the United States – more than the car, pharmaceutical and hotel industries combined. Hollywood nowadays is a bigger employer than all the manufacturers in the aerospace industry put together. Another noticeable trend is the creation of new jobs in services using new information technology, such as telecommuting and teleshopping. The potential for creating jobs in the information and communication technology sector lies in the use of the technology and not in its production, and in services rather than in industry; this explains the negative trend in employment in the industries that produce new technology, and the relative stagnation in employment among the industries that use new technology and the services that produce it, but the positive employment curve in the services that use the technology. The environmental sector and non-trading services, particularly education, are also prime areas for creative applications of information and communication technology.[18] The arrival of the networks and the explosion of the Internet, however, have seriously disrupted the organization of work and production. New services such as teleshopping could reduce employment in the conventional industries such as retailing, or result in transfers. The time and money saved could be devoted to the purchase of products and services which in turn create jobs. When CDs and videos are accessible via on-line servers, all that users will have to do is select the digital file corresponding to the music or film that they wish to hear or watch. The CD or video production line will disappear to the benefit of other surrogate areas. The Internet, for instance, could disrupt the conventional software distribution circuits (software shops) by making it possible to distribute software as an on-line service.

Remote companies are also being set up, structured as networks and focusing their capital outlay on information systems that form the basic tool of their business activities. Their operations are gradually being enhanced via a maze of collaborators interconnected by interactive networks that are modifying the ways in which people work everywhere. (See 'Indian Innovations' on page 70).

Telecommuting

At the dawn of the twenty-first century, telecommuting is developing in giant leaps. According to the International Labour Organisation (ILO), 7 million people telework full-time or part-time in the United States, with more than 1 million in the United Kingdom, 250,000 in Germany and 200,000 in France. At the heart of this trend lies a series of factors linked to the boom in paperless business, the development of global networking and the decrease in telecommunication costs. Technology no longer poses a problem: it is available, simple to use and relatively inexpensive. In theory there is nothing to stop properly equipped employees from putting their skills to good use hundreds of kilometres away from their company.

Like all new technology, however, telecommuting is the subject of heated debate. Its proponents put forward a whole series of items in its favour: savings in travel costs and time, the tailoring of work to personal rhythms, reconciliation between business and the rural environment. Its critics, on the other

18.   C. Freeman and L. Soete, *Technology and Employment*, Maastricht, Maastricht University Press, 1993.

hand, feel that it does not guarantee employees' social benefits, that it entails a risk of confusion between one's job and one's private life, and that employees have to make themselves more readily available, without any real recompense. They also feel that telecommuting eliminates not only manual work, but even certain professional jobs, those that can be replaced by expert systems or intelligent machines. Others claim that telecommuting does not contribute to the continuing high rate of unemployment, but on the contrary provides an opportunity for new growth of the job market. Others again maintain that a tele-commuting economy actually exists, encompassing not only the major corporations which are currently off-shoring, but also the clusters of professional micro-companies that analysts call the 'Soho' (Small Office Home Office) market, one with significant potential, since it comprises a large number of companies, usually with fewer than ten employees.

The various forms of telecommuting

- Telematic work at home or home automation.
- Work in a satellite centre, a delocalized micro-branch of a firm linked to it by telematics.
- Work in telepremises for different companies by independent telecommuters or by employees of the administrative body for the telepremises.
- Nomadic, mobile, itinerant telecommuting, such as sales representatives or technical sales executives in frequent telematic contact with their permanent base.
- Part-time telecommuting.
- Telecommuting based on teleservices from the home or telepremises (taking appointments for a doctor's surgery, telephone calls for prospecting services, company after-sales services, etc.).

Source: P. Morin, *La grande mutation du travail et de l'emploi* [Major Changes in Work and Employment], Paris, Les Éditions d'Organisation, 1995.

Key figures

- 47 million: the current number of American telecommuters (occasionally working from home), according to the Link consultancy firm. If telecommuting is taken to mean a job in which the home is the main workplace, this figure is much smaller.
- 70 per cent of American companies have already set up some form of telecommuting (Source: *Fortune Magazine*).
- No more than 55 per cent of the active population in the United Kingdom work full-time inside a company.
- 10 million Europeans will be telecommuting between now and the year 2000 (DG XIII Objectives).
- 35 per cent of the French population say they are ready to try working at home, according to a poll carried out by *Télétravail Magazine* on a sample of 1,000 persons. The outlook is particularly attractive for those under 40 years of age. The main advantage anticipated is better management of working hours (44.5 per cent of sample).
- 7.5 million: the number of working hours lost by people in the Paris area every day in transport (Teleurba survey, January 1996).

Source: *Le Monde Informatique* (Paris), 12 July 1996.

Globalization of economic activities

The globalization of economic activities has resulted in enhanced concentration in the communication sector, strong growth in the world market for new information technology and an acceleration in the development of electronic commerce.

High media concentration

Concentration is one of the major trends featuring the communication business in the 1990s. The term refers to the consolidation of corporate positions through takeovers, mergers or alliances, or simply by absorp-

Indian innovations

As early as 1986, the Indian Government launched a development programme to set up a high-quality software industry targeting the world market. Today, the three leading Indian data-processing firms (CMC, Tata Consulting Services (TCS) and Tata Unisys Ltd) specialize in the production of software systems. Their rate of development is increasing virtually parallel to that of their installed base, and high-power growth is anticipated in the software market for the coming years. Exports rose from $114 million in 1990 to $351 million in 1994.

With a population of more than 900 million inhabitants, India has labour available which is specialized, highly skilled and low-cost. These people are trained in the leading universities and polytechnic schools, from which 250,000 engineers and scientists graduate every year. To boot, some 5,000 Indian engineers today are members of the research teams of Silicon Valley (California) and serve, on their return home, as intermediaries for setting up Indo-American joint ventures. This means that, given the quality of its computer engineers and the low cost of domestic production, India has become a 'target' for the major foreign groups of computer manufacturers and software publishers. It has also become a key site for service activities (data capture, data processing and accounts management systems).

The scope of action in this sector in India is widening all the time, and the country has become easily the number one supplier of teleservices, with 400 companies and 20,000 programmers and computer engineers. Consortiums such as TCS (4,000 operators) have extremely serious references in computer project management (such as an electronic management system for a British bank, a management system for the administration of the port of

Kuwait, etc.). Some of the most important companies in Switzerland, such as the Swissair airline company, financial institutions, and even the Swiss National Bank, have chosen to develop software in partnership with TCS. The company is currently engaged in nearly 500 projects in some forty different countries. Since 1987, its sales figure has more than tripled to more than 1 billion rupees, 80 per cent of which are generated by software exports.

Parallel to teleservices, another system has seen particularly high growth: 'body shopping', or the hire on-site of teams of computer engineers working several weeks abroad as part of a specific contract and at wages significantly lower than those paid to local staff. According to a report by the World Bank, the average monthly salary of a programmer in India is $225, compared with $600 in Singapore and $2,500 in the United States. The starting salaries paid to Indian computer engineers are approximately 10 to 15 per cent of their American counterparts.

In order to develop its software industry and attract customer companies, the Indian Government has set up technopoles such as 'Silicon Platform' in Bangalore, with proper infrastructures and international telecommunication links by satellite. Companies that have set up in-country, including Texas Instruments, Motorola, IBM, etc., benefit from tax breaks and customs duty exemptions on imports. The Indian Institute of Science, reputed to be the best science university in the whole country, as well as various other institutes, trains specialists on-site in areas ranging from software systems to aeronautics. In all, the Bangalore technopole comprises 70,000 employees, 7,000 of whom are engineers working in high-technology sectors.

tion. It is inseparable from product diversification, of which it is also the financial result. Concentration is increasingly part of the overall process of globalization, involving cross-border investments aimed at acquiring shareholdings in companies in foreign countries. Globalization thus ensures return on initial capital outlay and increases market share.

Like the other sectors of the economy, that of the communication industry also bears the stamp of high corporate concentration, achieved by acquisitions, alliances or the start up of new companies to widen the scope of market penetration and business activities. In the audiovisual field, as well as the press, publishing and leisure sectors, international conglomerates are emerging with the purpose of controlling not only the transmission system (manufacturing network, cable, satellite, etc.) but also the programmes they convey. The latter have become the key issue in the digital war. The boom in digital programme streams and the advent of information highways has led to the setting up of vast banks of programmes, precisely because these are the raw material which will supply the networks and generate most income on the audiovisual market. The players in the communication industry have already made their calculations. Ted Turner, owner of CNN, has been buying out production studios, while Microsoft has been buying up the reproduction rights for museum pieces the world over for years. The fact is that film studios and museums are a valuable source of programmes for cultural and leisure applications. Other players are taking part in a frantic race of mergers and acquisitions of firms specializing in the media and in entertainment (Time Warner with Turner Broadcasting System (TBS), Disney with ABC Capital Cities, Westinghouse with CBS and Viacom with Paramount and Blockbuster). These alliances have resulted in the appearance of conglomerates such as News Corporation, Sony, Time Warner Inc., Finivest, Bertelsmann and Havas, which have reached scales previously unheard of in the media and leisure industries. The features they have

in common are globalization, integration and 'critical mass'. The largest group is the giant Time Warner-TBS (Turner Broadcasting System) which, ahead of Disney/ABC-Capital cities and with sales of $20 billion in 1995, combines assets as varied as *Time*, *Fortune* and *Sports Illustrated* magazines, the cable-TV news channel CNN and Warner Bros film studios, not forgetting its music outlets and the Atlanta basketball team. Each of these divisions in itself also comprises a complete range of other companies, publications and professions. The worldwide, diversified scale of the firm enables it today to generate approximately 25 per cent of its income outside the United States. By the year 2000, that percentage will have risen to 40 per cent.[19] Following its merger with ABC Capital Cities, Disney now tops the world list in the field of leisure. The American giant is active in three branches. The first of these combines cinema (Walt Disney, Touchstone, Hollywood and other studios) and audiovisual (ABC television network bought up in 1996). It represents almost half of the turnover. The second branch consists of the theme park industry and represents one-third of all the activities. Finally, the third branch comprises consumer products and by-products (about 20 per cent of the turnover) commercialized in some 600 Disney outlets around the world. The media market is dominated by between five and eight major firms known as the 'World Companies', with other groups of regional or secondary status trailing far behind.

The creation of groups on scales such as these, with such high-power diversification, is an eloquent illustration of the major trends that characterize the media industry at the end of the twentieth century. In this sector, at least four groups in 1994 saw their sales climb over the $10 billion mark. Most of the top

19. R. McChesney, 'The Global Struggle for Democratic Communication', introduction to *Monthly Review*, summer issue, May 1996.

Share of advertising expenditure by three media (press, TV and radio) in millions of US$, 1996

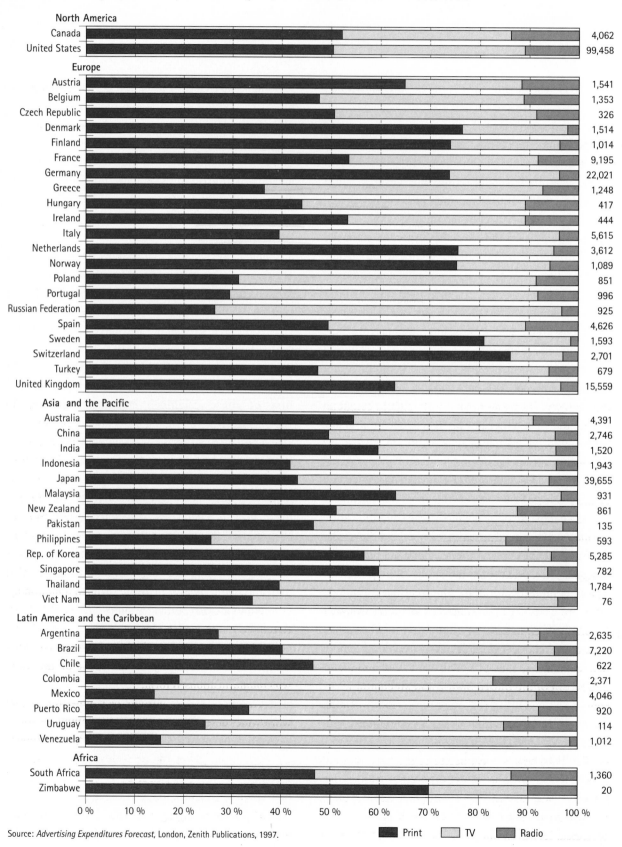

North America

Country	Value
Canada	4,062
United States	99,458

Europe

Country	Value
Austria	1,541
Belgium	1,353
Czech Republic	326
Denmark	1,514
Finland	1,014
France	9,195
Germany	22,021
Greece	1,248
Hungary	417
Ireland	444
Italy	5,615
Netherlands	3,612
Norway	1,089
Poland	851
Portugal	996
Russian Federation	925
Spain	4,626
Sweden	1,593
Switzerland	2,701
Turkey	679
United Kingdom	15,559

Asia and the Pacific

Country	Value
Australia	4,391
China	2,746
India	1,520
Indonesia	1,943
Japan	39,655
Malaysia	931
New Zealand	861
Pakistan	135
Philippines	593
Rep. of Korea	5,285
Singapore	782
Thailand	1,784
Viet Nam	76

Latin America and the Caribbean

Country	Value
Argentina	2,635
Brazil	7,220
Chile	622
Colombia	2,371
Mexico	4,046
Puerto Rico	920
Uruguay	114
Venezuela	1,012

Africa

Country	Value
South Africa	1,360
Zimbabwe	20

0 % 10 % 20 % 30 % 40 % 50 % 60 % 70 % 80 % 90 % 100 %

Source: *Advertising Expenditures Forecast*, London, Zenith Publications, 1997.

■ Print □ TV ▨ Radio

The top ten world audiovisual companies: audiovisual turnover in billions of US dollars, 1994

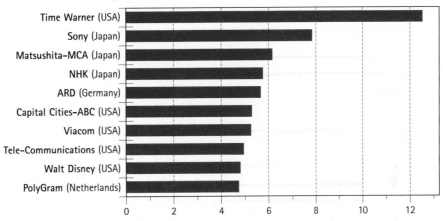

Source: *Idatenews* (Montpellier), IDATE, 1996.

ten groups in the world today are diversified conglomerates. Of the top ten groups in the sector in 1994, five were American, three were Japanese, one was Dutch and one was German. Many of the major groups also obtain a large part of their earnings outside their country of origin.

In the field of telecommunications, the list of examples of concentration, particularly in the United States, has grown much longer since the law on the deregulation of telecommunications was passed by Congress in February 1996. The first deregulation in 1984 put an end to the monopoly of AT&T (founded by Graham Bell in the nineteenth century) by splitting it up into eight divisions, seven of which were 'Baby Bell' companies, each of which inherited a monopoly in a region of the United States, and an eighth, which kept the name of AT&T and its long-distance communication networks. With the adoption of the most recent law in 1996, legislators brought monopolies to an end in every sector of the telecommunications industry with an eye to greater competition between long-distance operators and regional firms in their respective markets which had hitherto been protected. However, one year after the adoption of the

law, competition is finding it hard to take hold. On the contrary, there is a trend towards concentration that appears to favour the monopoly of regional firms: SBC Communications, the biggest of the local telephone companies, grew out of the purchase of Pacific Telesis by Southwestern Bell. Two other Baby Bells – Nynex and Bell Atlantic – are preparing a merger. In the view of some analysts these alliances foreshadow a return to the single-operator system as was the case with AT&T before the 'big bang'. Others hold that legislators will oppose any return to such a monopoly. Moreover, the attempted merger in June 1997 between AT&T, leader in national and international communications, and SBC was pronounced anti-competitive and contrary to the spirit of the 1996 telecommunications reform.

An even more important fact, however, is that worldwide deregulation of the telecommunications market has, for the first time, favoured the emergence of cartels with global status. The recent takeover of the American company MCI by BT (British Telecom) has rocked the telecommunication services industry by completely changing its scale. For the first time, a telephone operator will be able to exert strong pressure in the leading business areas around the world. BT, which will have control of the new group, baptized Concert, will be able not only to consolidate its position on a deregulated American market but also to strengthen its penetration of the Asian market-place, considered to be the most buoyant sector for the future. In the takeover, in addition to its commercial aggressiveness, MCI will contribute its Internet know-how and a customer base of some 3,000 international firms, as well as its shareholding in the News Corporation multimedia group owned by Rupert Murdoch. The new group now ranks fourth in the telecommunications sector, behind the Japanese company NTT, the American firm AT&T and the German firm Deutsch Telekom. With an annual sales figure of £25 billion and 43 million customers (professional and private) in seventy countries, the group forms a large-scale network more global in scope than any of its competitors.

Globalization of the new information and communication technology market

The information technology market, including software, hardware and other communication products, currently has the fastest growth rate in the world. In 1996 it represented $650 billion, equivalent to one-tenth of the gross domestic product of the United States. According to the statistics of the World Trade Organization (WTO), the market has expanded each year since 1990 by approximately 15 per cent, when the average growth rate for world trade in the same period was 8 per cent. The rate of expansion is even more impressive given that prices are rapidly falling, particularly in the program sector and that of all the software tools serving the exponential growth of the Web. The heavyweights in the sector are American, with IBM, Motorola, Intel and Microsoft, or Asian, with NEC, Toshiba, Samsung and Acer, while the Europeans also have several majors, notably Philips, Siemens, Thomson and Alcatel.

In terms of exports, Japan and the United States dominate international trade. In 1995, Japan exported some $106 billion-worth of goods, while the United States came close to $100 billion. The European Union arrived in third position with $57 billion, but this figure does not include trade inside the European Union.

Many Asian countries figure among the top ten exporters in the whole field of international trade, notably Singapore (fourth position), the Republic of Korea (fifth position), Malaysia and China. The ten leading exporters represent sales of $435 billion out of a total of $595 billion-worth of exports worldwide. A large number of developing countries, however, have trade deficits both in equipment and in services, and are hesitant about encouraging over-rapid deregulation of their foreign trade.

The information technology market saw the signing on 12 December 1996 of a free-trade agreement between the United States and the European Union, to come into effect between now and the year 2000. The purpose of the agreement, drafted as part of the first WTO ministerial conference, is to eliminate trade barriers on imports of computers, semiconductors, telecommunication equipment and integrated circuits.

Development of electronic trading

The emergence of world networks has provided a genuine infrastructure for international trade. This has oriented the development of the industrialized countries towards a global information economy, based on the delocalization of companies and free trade. The very nature of the Web and its capacity for digital data transmission make the Internet a prime channel for trade in any paperless product or service. The launch, for instance, of virtual telebanks without any branch office could well become the norm in the coming century. As a rule, any product that can be printed in an electronic medium (book, newspaper, picture, video, etc.) can be sold and delivered instantaneously via the Internet. In 1995, electronic trading on the Web represented sales worth $0.5 billion, and close to $0.25 billion in the first quarter of 1996 alone. By the year 2000, the experts estimate the world market for electronic trade will be worth more than

$7 billion. The difficulties connected with the novelty of the market and with its international character should not be underestimated, however. A number of quandaries still remain, notably with respect to the fiscal and legal status of these transactions.

Major importers and exporters of selected goods, in billions of US dollars, 1995

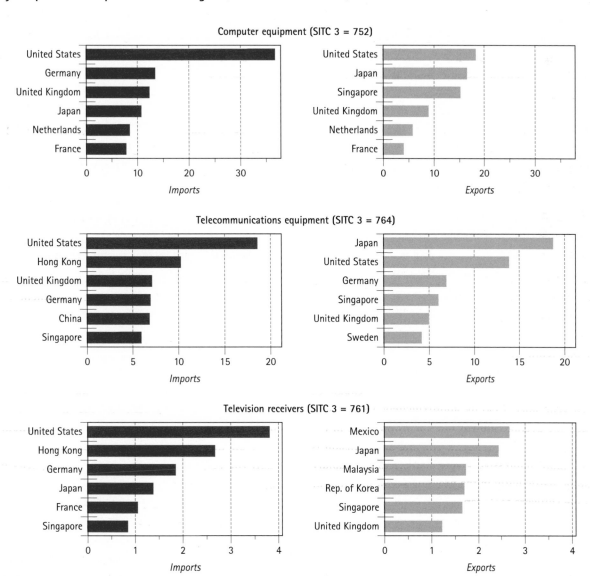

Source: UNICC (http://www.unicc.org), 1997.

The Intranet

The global explosion of the Internet has had repercussions in the corporate sector, and fostered the setting up of a new private network, baptized the 'Intranet'. It is based on the use of the architecture and protocols of the Internet within a company. The result is a significant reduction in operating and telecommunication costs as well as an improvement in the flow of information.

The network knows no frontiers and enables the telecommunications costs of a company to be reduced by a factor of up to ten. Data transmission costs the price of a local call, no matter what volume of data is transmitted or the distance over which it is sent. When the transmission rates on the network have sufficiently increased, companies will be able to communicate in real time very cheaply by video conference. Companies connected to the Intranet have a fantastic tool for trade, technology and competitor monitoring. A vast database can be efficiently used to monitor competitors and contact potential partners. Finally, the Intranet is an extremely powerful marketing tool, whereby not only can millions of potential consumers be contacted, but above all personalized dialogue can be set up with each of them, precisely targeting their requirements at extremely competitive cost.

With all these potential advantages, projects are multiplying in every company, no matter what their size, sector of activity or objectives. In 1996, more than 30,000 companies around the world were present on the Internet. Infatuation with the Web has led to a boom in the market for Intranet services and systems. According to the Californian consultancy firm Zona Research, Intranet programs are currently outstripping the software systems developed for the Internet; in 1996 they represented a market worldwide of $2 billion, which should reach $8 billion by 1998. Finally, the Input company estimates that 75 per cent of the sales realized in 1996, either direct or indirect via the Internet, in fact concern the Intranet. This is no doubt what has motivated companies to find rapid solutions to the data security issues posed by the Internet in order to finalize the adaptation of the network to their in-house needs.

If the Intranet confirms its promise, it will have a revolutionary impact on the ways in which we work, on the one hand by considerably increasing the speed and efficiency of exchange between company employees, and on the other by enhancing the performance of their everyday activities.

Chapter 5
Media globalization
and regulation

Globalization of communication

Parallel to the globalization of the major communication corporations there has been a two-way split, featuring a strong trend towards concentration in one direction, and the geographic dispersal of business activities all around the world in the other. At the same time, the spectacular progress in new information technology, particularly in satellite broadcasting systems, as well as the explosion in the numbers of subscribers to the Internet and the boom in its applications, have increasingly encouraged the media to become international and to develop global broadcasting networks. Globalization is the new concept, a term indicating the ways in which our modern societies are increasingly connected by these networks and their products that operate on a world scale. The present chapter describes some of the cross-border TV channels, illustrating one form of communication globalization.

Image globalization

The development in cross-border TV stations accelerated powerfully at the end of the 1980s. Some are privately owned general-interest channels (Super Channel, Star TV) or public service systems (TV5, BBC World Service), while others are specialized in newscasting (CNN, Euronews, etc.), sport (Eurosport, Screensport, etc.), leisure (Disney Channel) or music programmes (MTV, MCM). They reach millions of homes around the world via cable networks or via collective or individual reception of satellite signals. In order to overcome language obstacles and increase their audience, cross-border stations are investing increasingly in national-language programmes (CNN, NBC, Star TV) or multiplex sound channels enabling televiewers to choose among several languages (Eurosport, Euronews). As a rule, TV stations are basically financed by revenue from commercials on the domestic market but are increasingly likely to target the international scene. In addition to commercials,

Globalization of communication, a major challenge calling for
a community-based, supportive and equitable response.
Photo: Malanca/Sipa Press

some channels (CNN, Star TV) obtain a growing share of their revenue from pay-per-view systems via cable TV networks, as well as from hotel and individual subscribers. The success of cross-border television is due to a series of factors that are basically technological in nature: the boom in satellites, the proliferation of installed bases of dish antennae over vast regions of the world, progress in the miniaturization of TV control rooms, cameras and small-scale transmission stations which together have done away with distance and time.

Cable News Network (CNN)

CNN is the channel which best embodies the instant, global, worldwide status of television. The channel today can reach every region around the world via a network of satellites covering the whole planet. In 1995, the channel was distributed in more than 120 countries, beaming its programmes into more than a thousand hotels around the world and reaching more than 70 million homes. But it was the coverage of major events such as the abortive coup d'état in the former Soviet Union or the Gulf War that pushed the channel to the forefront of the planetary news system. The aim to serve an international audience means that it repeats part of its newscasts every twenty-four hours

to provide televiewers worldwide with a panorama of the main news at any time, hence the importance of CNN International, the version of the channel's news bulletin tailored for international audiences. It combines the international programme of CNN and televised newscasts from Headline News, the other non-stop news channel of the Turner empire that telecasts a summary of the day's events every half-hour. CNN and Headline News are the most profitable products of the Turner Broadcasting System (TBS), the mother company that also comprises Turner Network Television (TNT) and TBS Superstation. In recent years, the group has been putting into practice a diversification strategy by exporting its various models worldwide. In June 1997, CNN regionalized its news programmes aimed at North and South America, Asia and Europe. The revised formula consists of adapting the editorial content to the targeted regions. Broadcasting is in Spanish for the South American market and English for the rest of the world. The channel operators have announced plans for alternative cultural and language versions, aimed in particular at the Arab, Indian, Japanese and Russian markets. This new policy does not rule out the extension of the TBS network round the world. In Europe, it has become the majority shareholder in the German non-stop news

Coverage of CNN by name of satellite

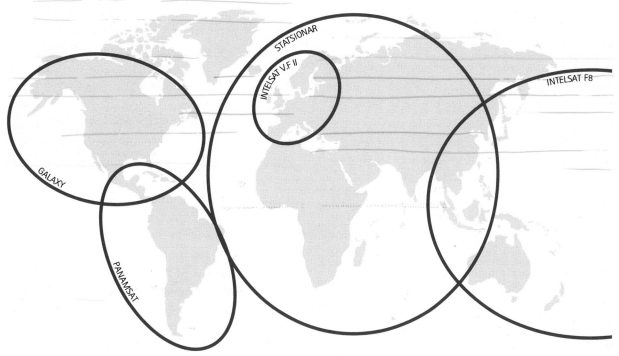

Source: F. Balle, *Médias et sociétés*, op. cit., p. 519.

channel NTV and in the Russian station TV6 Moscow. Targeting the European, Caribbean and Central American regions, it has also recently launched two channels which are already highly prosperous in the United States, one specializing in animated cartoons, The Cartoon Network, and the other in films, Turner Network Television (TNT). The TBS group, with earnings in 1995 of $3,437 billion, has just merged with the Time Warner company to give birth to the largest global communication group in the world, ahead of Walt Disney-ABC. Observers expect the synergy generated by the two groups to buttress CNN's news potential, particularly in view of the journalistic input from the Time Warner group (*Time Weekly, People, Fortune, Sports Illustrated, Entertainment Weekly*, and so forth). Notwithstanding this important influx, however, CNN has to contend with other competitors surfing in on the wave of satellites,

players who have also become aware of the strategic power and potential of information.

BBC World Service

The BBC World Service ranks as a serious alternative to CNN. A subsidiary of the BBC, it covers practically all five continents. It broadcasts a non-stop news programme twenty-four hours a day. To cover its operating costs it receives neither licence fees nor state subsidies and strives to balance its accounts through sales. In addition to its newscasts every hour, the BBC World Service adds news magazines and the best documentaries produced by the BBC. In recent years, it has improved its coverage through partnership agreements with regional or local channels such as the South African pay-TV network M-Net, and American and Japanese channels. While the BBC World Service seems to be the main rival for CNN, other news channels with specific linguistic or regional viewpoints are joining the throng.

Euronews

Euronews is the leading satellite-based multilingual European news channel, jointly set up by eleven European public service channels. Via the Eutelsat II-F1 satellite, it covers all of Europe, including the central and eastern regions, as far as the Near and Middle East. Televiewers have access to programmes broadcast non-stop twenty-four hours a day on a separate frequency for each of the six languages available: Arabic, English, French, German, Italian and Spanish. The originality of the channel is that the news bulletins are image-only telecasts, with voice-over journalists simply commentating on the pictures, reports and magazines provided by members of the European Radio-Television Union (UER). According to its proponents, by presenting a coverage of regional and world current events from a European point of view and in six different languages, Euronews can claim to be the European equivalent of the American channel CNN.

Other worldwide networks

Other networks have spread over all five continents. The largest of these today is that of the Rupert Murdoch News Corp. group. It is the fourth largest communication empire in the world, with a 1995 sales figure of $9 billion (profits of $626 million from the press and $400 million from television). The Murdoch Group has a worldwide television network connected by satellite, notably comprising the fourth-ranking national American network FOX TV, the British encrypted BSkyB and the Star TV channel. After starting out as a small programming stream in Hong Kong, Star TV has grown to seven channels and is now the largest network in the Asia-Pacific region. It covers practically all of Asia, with a perimeter that includes Australia, China, Japan, Pakistan and even the Near and Middle East. The network includes news,

sport and music channels, and has seen spectacular growth, particularly in South-East Asia and in India. Finally, Rupert Murdoch has announced his arrival in the near future in Japan with JSkyB, the United States with AS-KyB, and the United Kingdom with the launching in 1998 of a digital stream of 200 theme channels and services.

The American operator Direct TV also has the same target, and is developing joint ventures with partners from different regions around the world. In Latin America, the company intends to launch a stream of 142 channels, telecast in Spanish and Portuguese. After consolidating its presence in Asia, the operator intends to target the Japanese market in 1997 by going on-air with Superbird C, a stream of a hundred specialized theme channels. The company also intends to penetrate the African and Indian markets with the forthcoming launches of Direct TV India and Direct TV Africa.

The French-language channel TV5 is also battling to gain planetary coverage by using four satellites: Eutelsat II-FI to cover the whole of the region from Helsinki to Casablanca, Statsionar 12 for the whole of the African continent, Anik E1 for North America and finally PanAmSat1 to reach Latin America and the Caribbean. Since its start-up in January 1984, TV5 has operated continually in an associative French-language framework including the French-language Belgian Radio and Television Authority (RTBF), the Swiss Radio Broadcasting authority (SSR), France 2, France 3, the French National Audio-Visual Institute (INA), the Financial Broadcasting Authority (SOFIRAD) and the Canada Quebec Television Consortium (CTQC) comprising the main broadcasters and producers in Quebec and Canada. The programmes on the channel basically comprise televised newscasts and magazines presented as the counterpoint to CNN, together with fiction, entertainment and theatrical and musical productions by the various French-language television channels.

Another network with planetary status is the

MTV music channel, which was launched in 1981 in the United States and has not ceased to expand since then. It has consolidated its position in every region of the world with MTV Europe, MTV Asia, MTV Brazil, Mandarin MTV and MTV India. This regional fragmentation is part of the new strategy of the channel, which consists in adapting to the cultural conditions of each region. Also worth noting is the arrival of new channels specializing in financial news such as CNBC, Dow Jones, Bloomberg and Reuters, which are vying for position on the world money market.

Newcomers

Although the international circulation of televised programmes has always been dominated by the developed countries, notably in North America and in Europe, major changes are taking shape. The trend is towards enhanced co-operation and a somewhat timid balancing of the flow of communication. The international circulation of programmes is becoming less of a mismatch as a growing number of Latin American, Arab and Asian broadcasters launch their own satellite TV channels. In this field, the conventional North–South cleavage appears somewhat narrower in relation to the other gaps between regions or major language communities. Asia, Latin America and the Middle East are asserting their presence and expressing a greater demand for news with a regional focus, while channels with international or regional status are developing and often competing with those of the Northern hemisphere. In Latin America, the Mexican broadcaster Televisa has invested more than $250 million in the Panamsat company to set up its own satellite TV channels. The Mexican operator provides a pay-per-view service in the United States and in Spain. In Argentina, the Canal Sur channel telecasts a selection of news and entertainment programmes representative of South America over both American continents. For the Arab world, the Middle East Broadcasting Centre (MBC) channel telecasts from London via Arabsat to the whole of the region. Funded

essentially by Saudi Arabian capital, it is picked up every day from Morocco to Iran with a programme featuring news, entertainment, cinema and religious broadcasts. News nevertheless remains the priority focus of the channel, with the recent acquisition of the UPI news agency networks and the modernization of the studios and the editorial department. MBC today is fully equipped for digital broadcasting, but that eventuality will be possible only with the launch of Arabsat 2.

Now that it has gone global, television displays whatever is happening around the planet, from the fall of the Berlin Wall to the massacre of Srebrenica or the genocide in Rwanda. It has become a bona fide worldwide counterculture that undermines totalitarian regimes and renders state control of content ever more difficult and illusory. However, even if international television has enabled peoples that were previously deprived of images to open their windows onto the world, many feel concern about the power, the spirit of conquest and the scale of the networks, which have become nothing short of empires.

Regulation around the world

Regulation is a means of reconciling the economic interventionism of public authorities and the market forces in the audiovisual field. Domestic regulatory systems for the audiovisual sector feature a number of factors linked to the political, economic and cultural specifics of each country but also to economic and technological change around the world.

The radical technological upheavals of the 1980s, combined with the expansion in television stations broadcasting by satellite and their increasingly international nature and structure, have caused major changes in the audiovisual field in every country. First of all they attacked the monopolies held by national broadcasting authorities which traditionally have always controlled the various functions of programme production, programming and broadcasting. Marketing and globalization have also brought the development of new markets with the emergence of private operators and the growth in their numbers, thereby undermining the conventional balance that existed between public and private sectors. These changes have been further amplified by the new possibilities of transmission opened up by digital broadcasting, as well as by the emergence of multimedia groups against a backdrop of internationalized markets, and finally by the growing importance of private interests in the audiovisual field.

Faced with these new upheavals – which are likely to amplify during the course of the next few years – certain states have drafted a number of laws or taken decisions of a statutory nature. National contexts call for different strategies according to political traditions or patterns of media ownership.

In countries where radio and television are a state monopoly, their management is generally controlled by the executive body, which governs the administration and guides decisions concerning the production and broadcasting of programmes. This structural concept tends to disappear as the democratic process evolves. A public broadcasting authority is distinct from a state-controlled television service in that it enjoys editorial independence guaranteed by law and operates in a highly competitive environment. The state manages frequencies in order to prevent them from being used in an uncoordinated manner, and often supervises the financial management of the enterprise. On the other hand, regulation, wherever it exists, is controlled by independent authorities entrusted, according to the country in question, with regulating or supervising the programming activities of the private and public television operators. The authorities are generally placed outside the administrative hierarchy and are theoretically free from any judicial or political influence. Some are endowed with decision-making powers enabling them to organize the domestic audiovisual market-place and to control the legality of the conditions in which programmes are broadcast by private and public operators, and

are even authorized to sanction occasional breaches of the law.

It would be difficult in a single chapter to quote all the texts issued by regulatory authorities or legislative bodies. It is possible, however, to highlight a number of systems and illustrate concerns common to them all.

Highly varied systems

Generally speaking, different countries have different approaches to the authority in charge of regulating the audiovisual and telecommunications industry. In some countries, there is a single statutory body. This is the case in the United States, where the 1934 Communication Act entrusted the regulation of the vast area of the telecommunications and audiovisual sectors to a single agency, the Federal Communication Commission (FCC). The FCC is responsible for frequency management, supervision of the telecommunication networks operators (prices, service quality, network interconnection, etc.) and regulation of international communications on behalf of the United States. The organization of statutory authorities in Canada is quite similar to that in the United States. The regulatory body is the Canadian Radio-Television and Telecommunications Commission (CRTC), set up in 1961; its main assignment is to allocate radio and television frequencies and to define the operating conditions of each licence-holder, particularly with regard to the quotas of Canadian works broadcast and to the enhancement of domestic production. Since 1976, the CRTC has also monitored the telecommunications market, in which it strives to maintain a balance among the different operators. In Japan, the Ministry of Post and Telecommunications (MPT) is responsible for communications in the broad sense of the term, including postal services, telecommunications and broadcasting. In Italy, the Bill presented by the Italian Government in July 1996 provided for the creation of a higher authority to supervise the audiovisual and telecommunications sectors. In other countries, the two branches of communication are governed separately, for example by the Office of Telecommunications (Oftel) and the Independent Television Commission (ITC) in the United Kingdom, or the Autorité de Régulation des Télécommunications (ART) and the Conseil Supérieur de l'Audiovisuel (CSA) in France. In practice, no country has a completely unified statutory structure, and it is only as a result of convergence pressures that attention is being brought to bear on the information and communication industry.

Effects of convergence

With the digital revolution and the convergence between the older industries such as the telephone and cable sectors, many conventional communication services, such as audiovisual services, can be routed through telecommunication networks. In some countries, cable operators can provide audiovisual and telephone services via the same physical medium. With the liberalization of telecommunications, new markets are developing and new operators are claiming the right to use competitor services on the same transmission system. The United States was the first country to take this change into account with the new telecommunications act adopted in February 1996, which completely opened up the communication industry to competition. The act enables the three major operators – long-distance telephone companies, local telephone companies (the seven Baby Bells) and cable operators – to compete in a general free market system.

Anti-trust laws

Anti-trust laws have been introduced into national legislation. They usually place ceilings on shareholding in the capital of television channels. If a closer look is taken, however, and the legislation mentioned above is kept in mind, regulation in this area – particularly in the United States and in Europe – is more akin to deregulation than regulation of the

audiovisual sector, a finding in keeping with the principle of liberalization which is characteristic of most countries nowadays.

In the United States, the provisions of the 1984 Act on the concentration of operators on the American market have been slackened. The Act stipulated that no audiovisual consortium was allowed to reach more than 25 per cent of the American population, and it was out of the question to leave two stations on the same local market in the hands of a single owner. In the latest version of the law, the admissible percentage of the nationwide audience for all the stations controlled by a single owner was raised to 35 per cent (it is currently 25 per cent). The networks today are also authorized to have their own cable companies.

In the United Kingdom, the Bill to amend the 1990 law which was submitted to Parliament in July 1996 came into force on 1 November the same year. The new terms of the broadcasting Act relate to plurimedia ownership. They are intended to boost synergy between progress groups and local radio and television operations. Planned acquisitions have to be submitted for approval to the Radio Authority and the Independent Television Commission, whose task it is to see that the public interest rule is applied on the basis of diversity of opinions and programme content.

Broadcasting quotas

Many countries around the world have adopted rules that are both economic and cultural in their objective, forcing broadcasters to comply with quotas for programming and production of national works. By legislating on the quota question, states have sought to react to the consequences of the process of internationalization of the media on national television and film production and on the circulation of goods and services.

In Canada, the regulations stipulate that 60 per cent of all programmes broadcast annually must be Canadian in origin, and 50 per cent of those broadcasts must be during prime time. On Radio-

Canada stations, a 60 per cent minimum of Canadian programmes must also be broadcast during prime time. Canadian pay-TV stations have to allocate at least 20 per cent of their revenue to the production of Canadian programmes. In Lebanon, the audiovisual law adopted by the Lebanese Parliament in November 1994 stipulates that 40 per cent of all the programmes broadcast on national channels must be Lebanese in origin. In France, statutory requirements include quotas for broadcasting films and audiovisual productions (40 per cent French and 60 per cent European), conditions for telecasting films, advertising rules and regulations, the protection of children and adolescents, and due regard for the French language.

The effectiveness of these measures seems somewhat debatable, given the fact that viewers are free to watch other international channels if the domestic programmes do not suit their tastes, with the result that the ultimate effect of the measures may be diametrically opposed to their initial purpose. On the other hand, a calculated policy forcing broadcasters to allocate part of their resources to production may be a viable alternative to broadcasting quotas.

Europe and audiovisual regulations

European regulations for the audiovisual field are based on the celebrated 'Television without Frontiers' directive of 1989. The purpose of the document was to co-ordinate certain provisions laid down by law, regulation or administrative action in member states of the Union concerning the pursuit of television broadcasting activities.

The most controversial aspect of the directive was the obligation for all European television channels to devote a majority of certain time-slots to broadcasting programmes of European origin. The requirement resulted in considerable disagreement during the drafting of the directive and in the somewhat thorny dealings with the United States during the trade talks of the Uruguay cycle at year-end 1993. Compliance by TV channels with the above-mentioned obligation has yet to become the subject of any systematic monitoring, and this feature of the directive remains one of the main concerns for industry professionals and legislators alike.

The revision of the directive and its effects on the improvement of the circulation of European audiovisual works within member states of the European Union will be items on the agenda for the European Commission and Parliament in 1997. While the 'Television without Frontiers' directive remains the key document in the audiovisual policy of the European Union, another White Paper on *Strategic Options to Strengthen the European Broadcasting Industry* was published in April 1994 and constitutes the basis for the current agenda, which aims to outline a community policy on these questions for the future.

This initiative is equally intended to be the first step in a further procedure to adapt European rules and regulations to forthcoming technological change, featuring the convergence of television, telecommunications and information technology.

Chapter 6
The major implications of new information and communication technology

The digital revolution combined with the setting up of open, interconnected, interactive networks has fostered a number of radical changes, the most important of which have resulted in the dematerialization of products, growing concentration in cultural sectors and the globalization of communication networks. The overall trend, associated with the free circulation of products around the world, raises a number of questions of a statutory, cultural and political nature. Over and above the issues raised by the progress in technological convergence and industrial conflicts, there remain a number of problems: those concerning the place of copyright and neighbouring rights in the future information society, those with respect to national cultures and their diversity in the general trend towards globalization, and finally those of the new information and communication technology in economic, social and cultural development.

All these areas are both significant and strategic in the quest for enhanced democracy in the information society – the only factor that might induce the participation of all political, cultural and linguistic viewpoints around the world.

Copyright and intellectual property

The scale of the technological upheavals that go hand in hand with the dematerialization of products has confused the judicial concepts on which intellectual property rights were based, and has sparked wide-ranging debate about the ways in which copyright should be applied and complied with in a digital environment.

Major principles and their development
Copyright and neighbouring rights form one of the very first areas of international co-operation. International structures for the protection of copyright were set up from the end of the nineteenth century onwards. The 1886 Berne Convention was the first multilateral

agreement instituting the international protection of literary and artistic works. Since then, the convention has been revised several times, most recently in 1971. It guarantees creators a high level of protection of their rights (moral rights, economic rights relating to the reproduction, representation or public performance, broadcasting, adaptation and translation of their work). The Universal Copyright Convention, adopted under the aegis of UNESCO in 1952 in Geneva and revised in Paris in 1971, obliges signatory states to ensure effective and adequate protection of copyright, leaving them free to adapt that protection to the requirements of their socio-economic reality. It was this convention that introduced the © symbol followed by the name of the copyright holder and the year of first publication, to replace the registration formalities required by certain legislations. Finally, the Rome Convention, signed in 1961, provided a flexible, international legal framework for the protection of performers, producers of phonograms and broadcasting organizations.

All these texts were drafted well before the digital revolution, and cannot directly take into account the developments that have occurred in this area since 1961. Chapter 1 discussed the enormous advantages of digital technology compared with analog systems. Digital technology also provides a major opportunity for intellectual and creative works in that they can be disseminated an infinite number of times. That self-same power of dissemination, however, can also lead to the violation of copyright, notably through piracy and other forms of computer crime. Around the world can be seen an increasing number of flourishing unauthorized businesses manufacturing and marketing illegal 'smart card' decoders for the reception of telecasts without the payment of any licence fee. Piracy and the other forms of counterfeiting are a major problem whose economic consequences cost tens of billions of dollars every year. All these risks are a cause for concern among creators and have led states to examine the usefulness

of creating a special legal system for the new digital environment.

At the international level and as part of the work carried out by the World Intellectual Property Organization (WIPO), most participants consider it unnecessary to draft new special legislation. Two basic viewpoints have emerged on the subject, however. The first consists in applying distribution rights together with reproduction rights to works transmitted via digital means. This is, for the most part, the position defended by the United States, which proposes to consider transmission as a form of distribution, whether it involves 'on-line' transmission or the dissemination of the reproduction of a work recorded on a material medium. The American position requires that international transmission be considered as a form of import.

The second viewpoint regards the act of digital transmission as an act of public communication. This is the position of Argentina, Australia, Canada, Japan, the member states of the European Union, and Uruguay, a point of view backed by several non-governmental organizations. Public communication rights would be combined with reproduction rights when the end-user makes a copy of the work transmitted. The WIPO treaties on copyright and neighbouring rights adopted on 20 December 1996 in Geneva contain no provision with respect to reproduction rights in the digital environment for lack of agreement on this sensitive point. On the other hand, Article 8 of the Copyright Treaty implies that the digital transmission of works via networks is an act of public communication governed by the exclusive rights of right-holders.

The adoption of this article, however, was linked to an interpretative statement to the effect that 'it is understood that the mere provision of physical facilities for enabling or making a communication does not in itself amount to communication within the meaning of this Treaty or the Berne Convention'. The declaration further indicates that the provisions of the treaty with regard to limitations and exceptions (Article 10) do not prevent a signatory from applying Article 11(2) of the Berne Convention. The statement seems to suggest that the provision of the physical facilities for enabling or making a digital communication is not a sufficient stage in the digital communication of works to warrant protection under copyright laws. It leaves a number of questions unanswered with respect to the liability of providers of wide-area networking servers in the process of digital transmission.

Balancing interests and agreement

At regional and national levels, the issue has become particularly acute with the publication of the US White Paper of September 1995. Drafted by the Working Group on Intellectual Property Rights of the White House Information Infrastructure Task Force set up by President Clinton in 1993, the document contains detailed proposals for adaptation of the US Copyright Act to cyberspace. Their concern has also been echoed in Canada with the report of the Information Highway Advisory Council, which was published the same year.

The importance of protecting intellectual property also led the European Community in 1988 to present a Green Paper containing an economic and judicial analysis of the various problems raised by the new information technology in legal terms. Multilateral discussions held during the drafting of the paper resulted in the adoption in 1995 of the Green Paper on Copyright and Related Rights in the Information Society. It lists a catalogue of fifty-five problems concerning future copyright. The paper followed the Bangemann Report of June 1994, which considered the protection of intellectual property to be a crucial element in the development of a European multimedia market. The European Commission has announced another Green Paper specially devoted to the legal protection of encrypted signals, and has raised the possibility of intervention by the Union to make technical protection systems mandatory when the former have been sufficiently

developed and accepted by industry. Finally, also worthy of note is the CITED project (Copyright in Transmitted Electronic Documents) developed under the ESPRIT programme.

UNESCO's contribution

For its part, UNESCO, which initiated the Universal Copyright Convention (1952), was an active participant in the Diplomatic Conference organized by WIPO in December 1996 with a view to adopting a new protocol to be appended to the Berne Convention. The presence of UNESCO at the conference, as well as at those organized by the European Commission on Copyright and Related Rights on the Threshold of the Twenty-first Century (June 1995) and at the Intellectual Property Conference of the Americas (July 1996), was intended primarily as a means of achieving a consensus on an arrangement reconciling the respective rights of authors, producers, copyright holders and the general public, as well as those of exporters and importers of protected works.

UNESCO also launched a wide-ranging consultation with specialists in the field of communication, publishing and development. In that connection, worthy of note was the organization in co-operation with the Spanish Government of an International UNESCO Symposium on Copyright and Communication in the Information Society (Madrid, March 1996).

Discussions at the symposium focused on three major subjects:
- The outlines of a national policy to set up the basic infrastructures for the digital transmission and broadcasting of information (the role of the state and of private operators), and the norms that should govern the operation of those infrastructures, as well as the principles for regional and international co-operation in the area.
- The guidelines to follow in order to adapt national legislations so as to ensure that they protect the legitimate rights of authors and other

right-holders in the digital and multimedia environment and enhance harmonization of those rights at the international and regional levels.

• Strategies for national policies aimed at fostering the creation and development of cultural economic sectors, the digital broadcasting of works and performances, and distance learning, with a view to international and regional co-operation in this area.

The discussions also enabled Member States of the Organization, especially those from developing countries, to acquire up-to-the-minute legal and technological data in the field of intellectual property rights.

The symposium was followed by a series of regional meetings of Committees of Experts on copyright in the information society (basic infrastructures, the protection of rights and their social and cultural impact). The first of these, for Latin America, the Caribbean and Canada, was held in Bogotá in September 1996. The second, for Asia, the Pacific and the Arab States, was organized in New Delhi in November 1996. The Committee of Experts of Europe is scheduled to meet in Monaco in March 1997 and that of Africa in 1998.

On the whole, the various meetings have agreed on the need to simplify legal rules at the international level, in order to maintain a three-way balance of (a) the rights of authors in relation to those of the traditional cultural economic sectors and of information highway service providers, (b) the rights of right-holders in relation to the public interest (both of which are contained in the Declaration of Human Rights), and (c) the interests of countries exporting 'copyright' in relation to those of importer countries, notably the developing nations.

The above balance is closely connected to the issue of the access to information and to new communication technology and contrasts the views of three groups of thinkers: those that relate network access to a fundamental right on the same grounds as other rights; those that consider access must be modulated in relation to the varying contexts and types of information in question (information which is access-free, in the public domain or restricted); and finally, those that would make all network access part of a commercial service.

The problem is complex and multidimensional. The absence of legal protection is not supportive of creativity worldwide, and it is equally obvious that over-protection is not conducive to access to the networks by research workers and academics of developing countries. The correct balance therefore remains to be found between the right of creators to benefit from the use of their work and the needs of users to access those works and use them freely.

One further suggestion, developed by a number of non-governmental organizations in particular, militates in favour of a political alternative, based on non-market mechanisms ensuring right-free access for underprivileged countries to digital productions connected with social and economic development. Other ideas, based for example on consumer initiative or on codes of ethics developed ad hoc by information professionals, may suit the complexity of the problem and ultimately be more effective. This only underlines, however, the vital role of dialogue and co-operation among the various parties concerned, which, alone, may enable the right balance to be found between the interests of some, the duties of others and the solidarity of all.

Major imbalances

Economic obstacles

The development of the information society raises the issue of the inequalities which are a feature of both the industrialized and the developing countries, and which at the same time come between the rich and poor within the same society.

The developing nations are confronted with the challenges of the new technology, the production and

How to approach copyright and intellectual property rights: the Canadian example

The Final Report of the Information Highway Advisory Council, published in September 1995, examines copyright legislation and practices in the context of a digital environment. Salient excerpts are presented below.

● PRINCIPLES

In the context of accelerated digitization of information, the federal government should adopt principles for copyright based on the following:

● maintaining a balance between the rights of creators to benefit from the use of their works and the needs of users (including the education and learning community) to access and use those works on reasonable terms;

● encouraging industry, creators and user communities to develop and implement an administrative and regulatory framework that is easily understood and implemented by all interested parties and not seen as a barrier to access or use of the content on the information highway;

● recognizing creativity as required for the information-based economy and the multiple roles of individuals of the information highway (creators, disseminators and users of information);

● encouraging the creation of works that are critical to a national and cultural identity and economic development.

● BROWSING

The new technologies present unprecedented challenges for the protection of works. If the information highways are to be viable and sustainable, creators must be guaranteed continued protection of their works. At the same time, users must be assured of fair and reasonable access to those works. In its final report, the Copyright Subcommittee concluded that 'the act of browsing a work could mean either accessing a work, even if it is temporary or ephemeral in nature, or the making of a copy'.

● FAIR DEALING

In the context of copyright, accessing and reproducing works in a digital environment is increasingly complex. It is important that users comprehend better the extent and nature of copyright liability.

● MORAL RIGHTS

Moral rights include, among other things, the right to paternity and the right of integrity of the work. The right of integrity is attached to the honour and reputation of authors who, in order to seek remedy, must show that their reputation has suffered from the modification of their work. The alteration or mutilation of originals of certain artistic works also infringes the author's right of integrity.

● CROWN COPYRIGHT

In the council's view, ensuring universal and easy access to public information on the information highways does not require the abolition of Crown copyright, but instead a more liberal approach to making works of the Crown available to the public should be adopted.

● DISTRIBUTION RIGHT/OWNERSHIP

The right to communicate to the public by telecommunications currently contained in the Copyright Act clearly applies to the electronic transmission of works to the public. There is therefore no need to introduce any new rights, such as an electronic distribution right.

● ADMINISTRATION

Upon review of the range of mechanisms that could be developed to track and enforce copyright on the information highways, the council concluded that the above combination of technological, policy and legislative solutions was appropriate. The industry itself, with the assistance of the federal government, is best suited to developing the technological solutions.

● PUBLIC EDUCATION

Both users and creators and the industry in general need to better inform themselves about the rights of creators and the responsibilities of users on the information highway. The federal government can lead by example by exercising copyright in a responsible manner, by participating in copyright enforcement programmes and by ensuring that government works are broadly and routinely distributed.[1]

1. *The Challenge of the Information Highway* (Final Report of the Information Highway Advisory Council), September 1995.

Inequality still separates the industrialized from the developing countries, just as it does the affluent from the socially disadvantaged members in a given society.
Photo: P. Wender/Sipa Press

Newsprint consumption, 1970–94

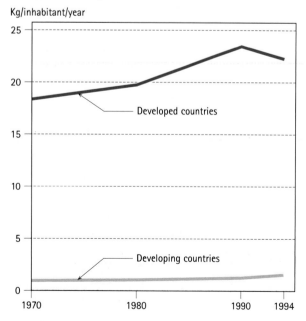

Kg/inhabitant/year

Source: *UNESCO Statistical Yearbook 1996*, Paris, UNESCO, 1997.

distribution of which take place outside their frontiers. A large majority of these countries feel excluded from that progress and some continue to denounce the aggravation of the obvious imbalances in the flow of information exchange between the North and the South. The debate began as long ago as the 1980s within UNESCO and in other international circles, about the idea of the New World Information and Communication Order (NWICO) (See Part 3, Chapter 2).

The talks have at least brought to the attention of international opinion the extent of the disparities and distortions that exist in the area of communication and new technology, imbalances suggesting that the vision of a global village which so many have held for so long will basically be attained by the richest or most recently industrialized countries in which the data banks, software systems and programs are gathered and stored. The gap is particularly wide in Africa, which has only 1 per cent of the telephone

**Estimated number of television receivers
per 1,000 inhabitants, 1970–94**

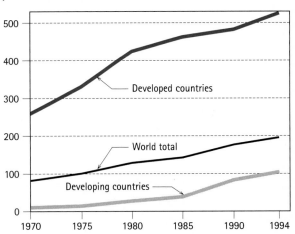

Source: *UNESCO Statistical Yearbook 1994, UNESCO Statistical Yearbook 1996,*
Paris, UNESCO, 1995, 1997.

**Estimated circulation of daily newspapers (number
of copies per 100 inhabitants) by estimated illiteracy rate
(in %), 1994**

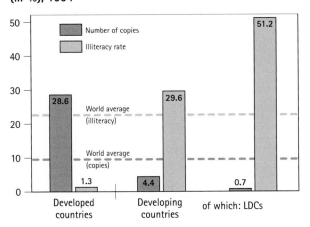

Source: *UNESCO Statistical Yearbook 1996,* Paris, UNESCO, 1997.

lines available in the world, but 12 per cent of its population. In 1994, there were more telephone lines in the city of Tokyo alone than in the whole of Africa, when the population of the continent is thirty times greater than that of the Japanese capital. Inside Africa there are also remarkable differences in development. Over the last decade, the number of telephone lines per 100 inhabitants – known as teledensity – has doubled in the Maghreb. In South Africa, the number has increased by more than 200 per cent and is now close to 10. Teledensity in sub-Saharan Africa has stagnated, emphasizing the disparity between the affluent and the underprivileged countries. The same observation holds true of information and communication. The inequalities are just as pronounced in terms of audiovisual equipment as for the production and content of their programmes. The same applies to the consumption of the written press, of radio and

**Average connection fee and monthly subscription fee for residential telephone service
by region, 1995 (in US dollars)**

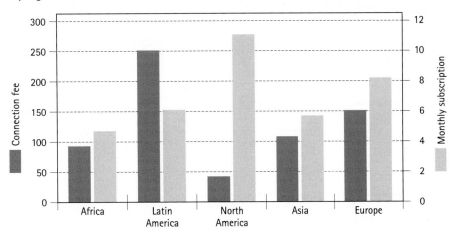

Source: *ITU Statistical Yearbook,* Geneva, ITU, 1996.

Penetration of satellite/cable TV in households (percentages)[1]

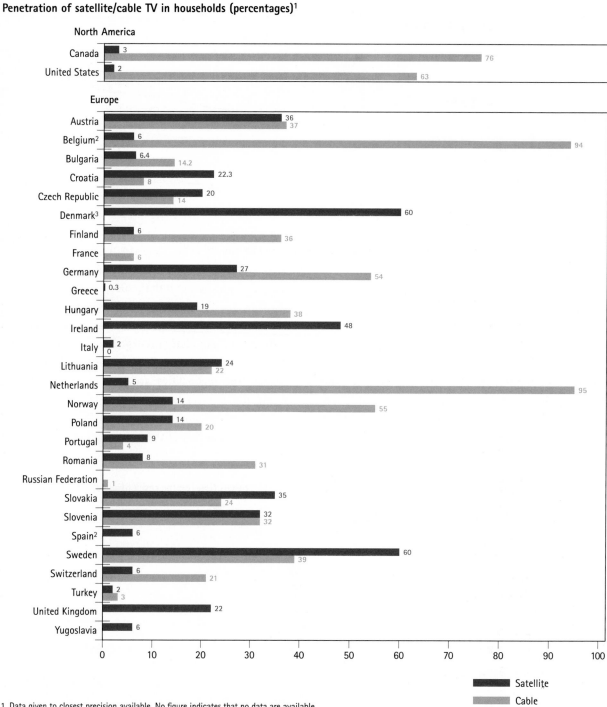

1. Data given to closest precision available. No figure indicates that no data are available.
2. Includes SMATV.
3. Includes SMATV and cable.

Source: *Market and Media Facts*, 1996–97, London, Zenith Publications.

Asia and the Pacific

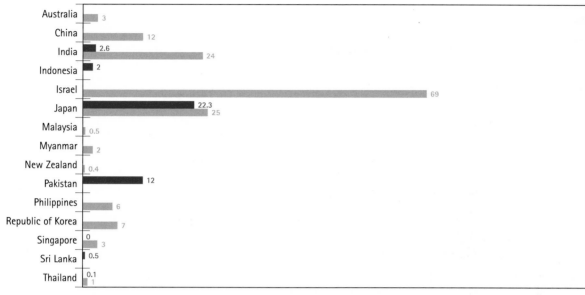

Latin America and the Caribbean

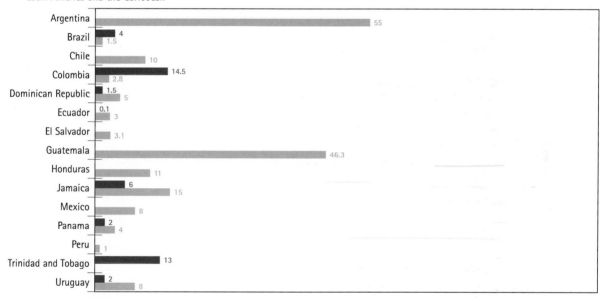

Africa

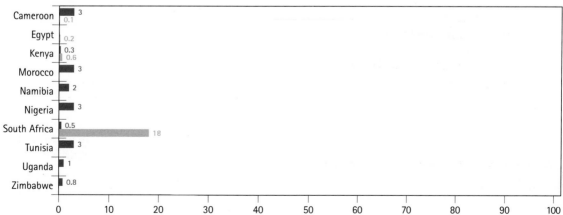

Countries reporting a percentage of the population having no access to postal services[1]

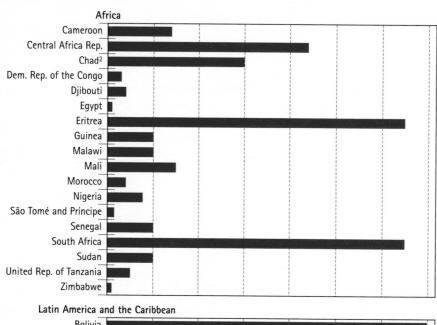

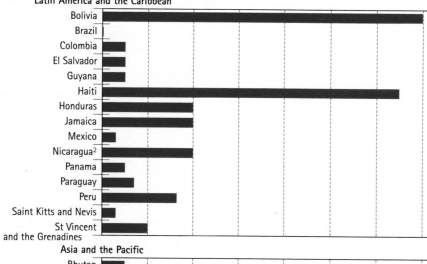

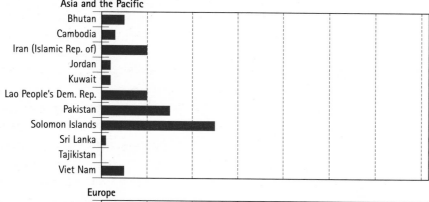

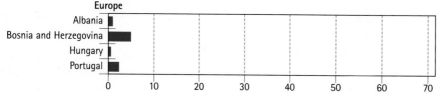

1. No residential postal delivery or possibility to collect post at a post office.
2. Data refer to 1994.

Source: Postal statistics, Berne, UPU, 1995.

television programmes, and to the flow of programmes from producer to consumer countries. This imbalance has been still further highlighted with the emergence of digital technology and the broadcasting of programming streams. Market globalization favours communications between developed or newly industrialized countries or within such countries, or links between major cities and rural zones. In the economic sphere, the imbalances reflect both the highly unequal economic development of nations, the diversity of their political systems and the specific character of each society. They can be explained as much by the past as by certain current effects of globalization.

These somewhat pessimistic observations must, however, be tempered by the emergence of a number of Asian and Latin American countries that have worked wonders where telecommunications and audiovisual technology are concerned. Some even form the driving force behind economic growth rates that contradict the climate of recession in the rest of the world. Others have begun policies for technology transfer and adaptation by offering attractive subcontracting capabilities and thereby offshoring communication multinationals. The example of India given in Chapter 3 is highly significant in this respect.

Cultural and linguistic obstacles

The imbalances between nations and within them, together with the acceleration in the globalization of the contents of programmes, also arouse concern about the dangers of cultural and linguistic standardization. Developing countries are at risk from standardization of local cultures through a form of planetary brainwashing caused by the white noise of poor programme content. These dangers may have grave consequences, such as the marginalization and possible disappearance of fragile community cultures, the weakening of cultural foundations, the temptation to withdraw into an identity coinciding with religious beliefs, and the threat of violent inter-ethnic conflict. While the existence of these dangers raises questions

of ethics and political sovereignty, they have also been used by some states and their single parties as a convenient alibi to justify their stranglehold on the media and the use of the media.

The member states of the European Community also appear to be jealous of their cultural identity and make it a fundamental factor in their national sovereignty. They are striving to protect their audiovisual production by a policy of broadcasting quotas adopted within the framework of the directives of the 'Television without Frontiers' programme. The economic issues implicit in quotas became a subject of confrontation with the United States during the GATT trade talks in 1993 (now the World Trade Organization). There are two contradictory viewpoints on the subject. The United States is pushing for the free circulation of programmes, while Europe and Canada intend to protect their cultures and their film industries by arranging programming rules. The Americans wish to encourage a form of total market internationalization and the globalization of trade, whereas Europe and Canada consider the audiovisual field to be a service whose cultural purpose justifies its treatment as a special case in relation to the overall GATT agreements. Hence the importance for the European Union to have an audiovisual and cinema policy designed to preserve cultural identities, to strengthen economic development and to create jobs in the audiovisual sector. However, according to the European specialists, the results of the GATT trade talks (in December 1993) hardly changed anything, either in terms of the current market situation, which favours American programmes, or with respect to the risks of furthering their market domination with the arrival of digital clusters of TV programming streams.[1]

1. P. Rogard, 'Pour une politique européenne de développement à la création cinématographique et audiovisuelle' [For a European Policy to Develop Cinema and Audiovisual Creation], in *Les cahiers de l'audiovisuel* (Paris), No. 5, September 1995, p. 9.

As digital technology rapidly develops, however, the scope of deregulation is widening in Europe to include the private telecommunications sector. The latter is to become a competitive market from 1998 onwards, and should facilitate the circulation of images. In addition, the future prospects outlined in the European Commission's Green Paper on the audio-visual policy of the European Union are already those of a demand focus on 'profitability in an open, dynamic global market' based on a largely free trade attitude. On top of this, the renegotiations of the 'Television without Frontiers' directive reached a compromise with some difficulty as a result of strong reluctance on the part of countries such as Germany, the United Kingdom and Italy, all of which demanded the straightforward abolition of the quota policy.[2] Together, these new trends have led the European Union to think about implementing a different policy basically aimed at strengthening the broadcasting industry.

The other major issue is the risk of linguistic standardization. An example frequently quoted is the fact that the vast majority of programmes circulating on the Internet are in English and that the main navigation software systems are not capable of reading characters other than those of the Latin alphabet. These fears apparently are being allayed by the market trend towards linguistic diversification throughout the system. With the stupendous growth of the Internet, English-speaking countries owned only 70 per cent of sites in January 1997 as against 90 per cent a few months before. Today three language groups are extending their reach throughout the network: Germanic (German, Dutch and the Scandinavian languages) with 11 per cent; Romance (French, Italian, Portuguese and Spanish) with 9 per cent, and Japanese with 5 per cent. The world's other languages are used on only 5 per cent of the sites. This is a poor showing if the Internet is to be multilingual and sensitive to the whole family of cultures. Yet the latest technological progress in automatic translation makes data pro-

cessing possible in a number of languages. Moreover, for exponential growth of network navigating and surfing tools, the setting of common standards adapted to the various non-roman scripts, and public and private investments in on-line services, could transform the network fundamentally in the medium term by giving every user access to a huge amount of data in foreign languages using non-roman scripts.

The future of the public service

Media globalization together with the arrival of competition from international and national private television channels raises the issue of the status, role and future of the public service in the new audiovisual fields around the world.

For many years, public television channels enjoyed a period of stability based on a monopoly. There are three main reasons for their domination. The first of these is technical, and concerns the use and distribution of frequency spectra considered to be a collectively owned, rare resource. In this area, the state played the role of a microwave 'regulator', to prevent frequencies from being used in a disorganized and anarchic manner. This function is generally performed today by an authority independent of the government, its role being to enforce conditions of fair competition. The second reason concerns the public service role which is conferred on all the broadcasting services. The power of radio and of television seems truly vast from the political, social or cultural viewpoints, since it provides the general public with access to cultural information programmes that they would not be able to receive elsewhere or otherwise. The third and final reason is linked to the traditional distrust of public authorities with respect to the market's capacity to

2.   The European Union Ministers of Culture, on 20 November 1995 in Brussels, agreed to maintain the status quo in the audiovisual quota issue. On the other hand, the fifteen member states have undertaken to hold a new debate within the next five years on the 1989 European Directive on 'Television without Frontiers'.

perform the public service assignments imposed on the broadcasting industry.

The crisis in public service broadcasting

The arrival in the 1980s of private operators and distributors on the market had as its consequence the end of the supremacy of public television channels, a setback which then depleted their audience ratings and advertising market share. Technological innovations in the satellite area also led to the development of new markets, accompanied by an increase in private capital and publicity investments in television. Since then, the growth in private channels has taken place to the detriment of advertising revenue for public television, undermining the traditional balance between the public and private sectors. These various reversals have occurred in an environment of increasing internationalization and worldwide televisual exchange.

All around the world, clusters of private, general-interest or specialized digital television channels are springing up in audiovisual market-places which are becoming increasingly turbulent. Against this backdrop, the public channels have had to face stagnating or diminishing public subsidies, forcing them to reduce their expenses or seek other sources of revenue such as the introduction of TV commercials. Reduced government involvement in public service channels in several countries, notably those in Europe, has accelerated the rate of change in the audiovisual market-place and thrown the public television sector into disarray.

The public service challenge

The future of public service broadcasting depends on a clearer distinction between public service and public sector, which are two very different concepts altogether. Privately owned television operators exist that provide educational or cultural programmes, traditionally classified as being the role of the public service. In the United States, for example, the major networks such as CBS, ABC or NBC also provide pro-

grammes of an educational and cultural nature, as does the federal CBC-Radio Canada network. These programmes are all part of a complementary, diversified offer. The assignments and obligations of the public service are not necessarily incompatible with the ownership of corporate capital, and the difference between private and public as diametrically opposed sectors is no longer pertinent.

The concept of public service seems nevertheless to be gaining ground in Europe, and is even moving towards that of universal service, notably where the texts of the European Union are concerned. Universal service is relatively far removed from the Canadian or French concept of public service, and lies somewhere between the Latin and Anglo-Saxon definitions. Generally speaking, a universal service is seen as a compensatory factor within a market-controlled regulation system.

The future of the public service also depends on a clearer distinction between public service and commercial television, which obeys market laws first and foremost. The public service should be free of economic and financial considerations dictated by audience ratings and market share, to carry out its role as a social link. In a world open to the internationalization of data flow and image exchange, a public service should provide basic landmarks of a historical, cultural and political nature for a nation. It should embody, among other things, the relationship that a people has with both its image and its imagination – hence the importance of the provision by public television of true diversity and pluralism to its viewers. These are the two concepts which are the key both to the identity of the public service and indeed to that of democracy. It is no doubt through a form of television in keeping with the tradition of the BBC, far removed from political or economic power, that the public service will really accomplish its mission of informing the general public, a role more vital than ever for the democratic working of contemporary society.

Chapter 7
Opportunities
and prospects

Progress in new technology and its speedy development has resulted in many new applications such as multimedia products and services, and 'intelligent' interfaces. These new possibilities, which began in industrialized countries, have gradually spread around the world and offer new opportunities for distance learning, health and many other activities designed for development. Access to knowledge and information via new networks can be a positive contribution to the sustainable development of different sectors of society. The question, however, is how to apply the new information and communication technologies effectively to development and how to use them in order to bridge the gap between the rich and the excluded, between nations and within those self-same nations.

The question stems from the heated debate between researchers and communication professionals about the conditions for transferring new information and communication technology to developing countries. A certain number, the advocates of the 'modernization paradigm', consider that the transfer of new information and communication technology is a major stimulant for the development process that, in the long run, will enable the developing countries to catch up with the industrialized countries. For others, the opponents of 'cultural dependence', any such transfer would merely be a step further not only towards inequality, but even towards the destruction of the cultural identity of societies in the Southern hemisphere. Finally, for others again, both the paradigms of transfer and dependence are outdated. New information and communication technology and its applications provide developing countries with the ability to perform a kind of 'technological leap-frogging' that could enable them to reach the connection capacity required for the information networks far more rapidly. Similar forms of leapfrogging might also enable economies with a high level of skilled labour to switch to 'value-added' economies.

An increasing number of states share the latter

point of view and have opted for the most advanced forms of technology to implement or renew their communication infrastructures. To reach their objectives, on the one hand they have adopted policies of adaptation and technological transfer by offering attractive subcontracting capabilities, thereby relocating communication multinationals; on the other hand, they are investing in communication programmes or setting up new communication infrastructures (software, audiovisual production, etc.).

Other countries, particularly in South-East Asia, have achieved something of a feat in telecommunications and the audiovisual field. Some of these nations even form the driving force for economic expansion that counterbalances the climate of recession elsewhere in the world. South-East Asia currently enjoys the highest rate of economic growth worldwide and operates as an accelerator for the whole continent: 11 per cent per year since 1983 compared with a global growth rate of 6 per cent. Its telecommunication equipment population is now close to that of the industrialized countries and in some areas is even a length ahead of European states. Thailand, for instance, which started from nothing in 1986, today has the world's highest penetration rate in radio communications. China, India and several countries in South-East Asia have launched their own satellites. Nevertheless, it would probably be a mistake to think that all developing countries could automatically attain this level of development.

The countries in this region of the world find themselves in widely differing economic situations as a result of a series of factors, the most important of which are the ability to attract investment, the educational level of the population, the economic policies adopted by their leaders and, finally, their co-operation with the industrialized countries and the impact of all these factors on new information and communication technology and its applications. In fact, most of the developing countries are confronted with economic and political alternatives of a strategic

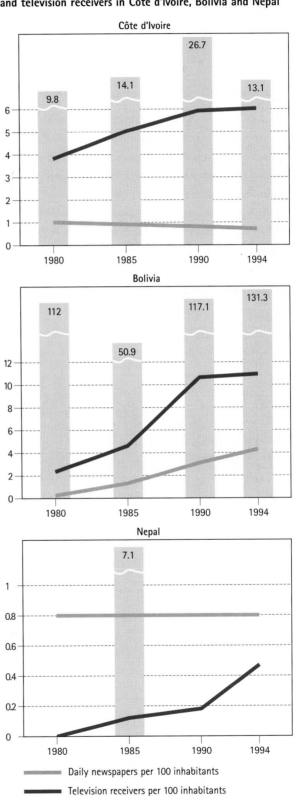

Comparative data on newsprint consumption, newspapers and television receivers in Côte d'Ivoire, Bolivia and Nepal

Côte d'Ivoire

Bolivia

Nepal

▬▬ Daily newspapers per 100 inhabitants

▬▬ Television receivers per 100 inhabitants

▨ Annual newsprint consumption (kg) per 100 inhabitants

Source: *UNESCO Statistical Yearbook 1996,* Paris, UNESCO, 1997.

The Arab World and the information society

Although it began in the industrialized countries, the development of the new information and communication technology is gradually spreading to the whole world, offering tremendous opportunities for every society to access knowledge and know-how. This trend can be seen in the Arab countries, with the installation of communication infrastructures capable of providing new opportunities for distance learning, health and many other development-

oriented activities. With 250 million inhabitants, a gross domestic product of $12 billion, an installed telephone base of 450 billion lines (or more than 5 subscriber lines per 100 inhabitants), the 'Arabsat' regional satellite system, an installed television base ratio higher than 10 per 100 inhabitants, and an installed radio base ratio higher than 25 per 100 inhabitants, the Arab world is well placed to tackle the global information society. Gulf states, i.e.

Telephone lines per 100 inhabitants

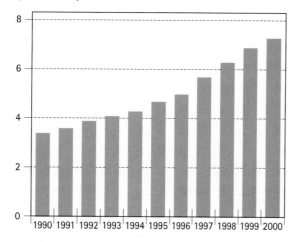

Internet hosts (thousands)

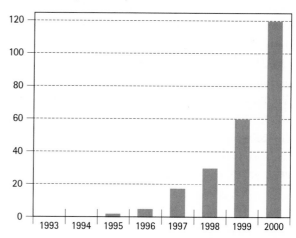

Cellular telephone subscribers (thousands)

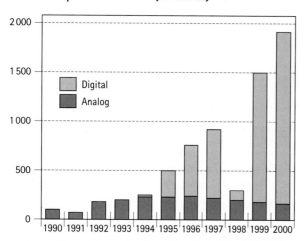

Outgoing international telephone calls (billions of minutes)

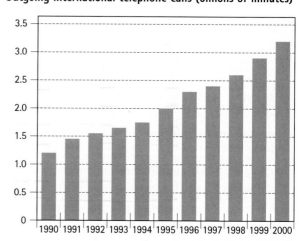

Source: *Indicateurs des télécommunications des États arabes 1996,* Geneva, ITU, 1996.

Bahrain, Kuwait, Qatar and the United Arab Emirates, have practically reached the objective of a universal service. They have almost all fully digitized their networks and offer state-of-the-art services characteristic of developed countries (ISDN, the Internet, GSM standard cellular mobile telephones, digital television, etc.).

Less advanced Arab states (Comoros, Djibouti, Mauritania, Somalia, Sudan and Yemen) have inadequate access to the Web. The issue for these countries is how to improve access to telecommunications against a backdrop of low-level economic development. In the third group of Arab states, the level of development in telecommunications is situated between that of the wealthy countries of the Gulf and that of the less advanced countries in the region. This group includes the Maghreb countries (Algeria, the Libyan Arab Jamahiriya, Morocco and Tunisia) and the Levantine countries (Egypt, Jordan, Lebanon and Syria), together with Oman and Saudi Arabia.

Some countries in this group since 1990 have obtained the best results in terms of telecommunications

among the Arab states: Morocco, for instance, has almost tripled its network of subscriber lines since 1990; in 1995, Syria increased its telephone line system by 42 per cent, and Tunisia now ranks third in the region for its rate of growth in subscriber lines.

During the coming years, most Arab states will be faced with the task of accelerating progress in their telecommunications sector in order to bring them up to the level that some developing regions have reached (Asia and Latin America) and to expand their service offers, both of which are indispensable prerequisites for active participation in the new global information economy.

Arab states have an advantage, compared with other developing regions, in that they can count on diversified sources of potential financing. Private capital in the region also plays a far from negligible role: according to World Bank estimates, Arab holdings overseas total some $350 billion. In addition, telecommunication companies in the Gulf are not only an example of successful development, but can also provide technical and financial support to operators in the other Arab countries.

Full development of the information society in the Arab states will be possible, provided that governments use the new information technology efficiently, notably to reduce the gap in development between nations and within them. With this outlook in mind, satellite operators, and the users and creators of content as well as specialists in information and computer technology, have vast possibilities for initiating innovative approaches in the field of communication, taking into account the potential for development and market opportunities. Within this framework, the ITU and UNESCO are working together to promote the use of telematics for social, economic and cultural development in the region. An important step in this process was the creation in March 1996, endorsed by both organizations, of an association for co-operation in the area entitled the Regional Arab Information Technology Network (RAITNET).

Radio and television receivers per 100 inhabitants

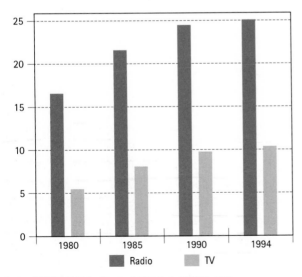

Source: *UNESCO Statistical Yearbook 1996,* Paris, UNESCO, 1997.

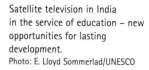

Satellite television in India
in the service of education – new
opportunities for lasting
development.
Photo: E. Lloyd Sommerlad/UNESCO

nature, but also with constraints and obstacles that they will have to overcome or manage if in the future they wish to set up gateways with the networks and services promised by the information society. These obstacles are financial, technical and political in nature.

First and foremost, the introduction of new information and communication technology requires extremely heavy investment, estimated at several hundred billion dollars, a sum that most developing countries can neither raise nor commit. In addition, most of these states are currently confronted with obstacles to development and are subject to structural

adjustment plans that force them to limit their expenditure. Second, the hypothetical presence of these countries on the future electronic networks presupposes the installation of terrestrial or satellite telecommunication networks, the management and control of which seem incompatible with the obsolete and under-equipped level of local telecommunication services. Third, the future information society presupposes fair, universal access to the Web for the whole population of a country. The geographical dissimilarities within these countries, however, are alarming. They stem from the political options that have been adopted by governments which are generally centralizing in outlook, resulting in fairly top-heavy media concentration, with telecommunication services located in the capitals and major provincial capitals.[1]

Together, those problems and obstacles clearly illustrate the challenges that the developing countries must face: implementing a new information and communication policy in order to modernize, democratize and diversify the services on offer.

The first of these challenges entails favouring a worldwide strategy for the reform of communication services. The need to modernize communication equipment presupposes the transfer of the new technology and intensive use of the services it provides. The funds required, however, are such that modernization inevitably entails monopoly deregulation, a fact which has now become the reference framework for any upgrade or modernization of communication policy. Most developing countries are fully aware of this need, and have already opted for deregulation or privatization by having their companies join the trend of internationalization and partnerships with the major operators in the industrialized countries.

Without subscribing to some form of liberal economic determinism, privatization can probably solve a number of requirements, including that of providing the specific value-added services necessary for any connection with telecommunications networks. On the other hand, privatization can be seen as a legitimate means of socio-economic change only if every class of society gains some benefit from it. This is precisely the reason why privatization must be accompanied by a statutory framework guaranteeing that all sectors of the population, in particular those people living farthest from the major cities, have access to the basic information and communication services, just as, through partnerships or alliances, it should facilitate access to every form of information and communication flow, whether by telephone, audiovisual programmes, the written press, etc. Finally, the success of privatization presupposes the existence of an open market, strong local enterprise, and fair market rules and regulations to counterbalance the risk, inherent to privatization, of the emergence of new monopolies.

The second of the challenges mentioned above is linked to the conditions in which access is gained to technology and to its content. Most developing countries have modest, even outdated telephone services and audiovisual equipment, which cannot easily be adapted to the digital transmission used by electronic networks. The experts take the view that this deficiency can be made up by satellite technology which will complement the existing terrestrial cellular telephony systems and transport large amounts of data at low cost. The system of transmission by satellite seems to offer several advantages, notably that of covering vast areas and reaching populations in regions with difficult terrain and hostile climates that cannot be covered by Hertzian means. Satellites make it possible to broadcast educational and cultural programmes and distance learning courses throughout a country, and finally to connect up to electronic networks.

This last point seems worthy of note, since the technical capabilities and possibilities of planetary networks, the most well-known of which is the Internet, seem closest to the idea of open, limitless communication. It is also a practical, economical solution for developing countries if they wish to have access to a universal system of communication that

---

1. Three examples illustrate the disparity between countries: in 1992, 71 per cent of the installed base of telephones were located in Abidjan (Côte d'Ivoire). The subscriber line average for the whole country was 0.7 per 100 inhabitants compared with 4 per cent in Abidjan. In Benin, of the 25,500 lines available, 60 per cent were installed in Cotonou, which has only 10 per cent of the population. Finally, of the 41,000 direct lines in Ghana, the main line rate was 0.5 per 100 inhabitants, but was 2 per cent in Accra and 0.1 per cent in rural areas.

can make good a number of deficiencies, notably in terms of point-to-point communication (telephone, telex, fax, etc.).

The third challenge mentioned above concerns the capability of developing countries to adopt an overall strategy that links the transfer of information and communication technology to a training and research policy. Access to know-how and training in every country is a major priority. The acquisition of know-how and knowledge, which today fill the role played first by land-ownership and later by capital in transforming modern society, has become a priority in national development strategies. New information and communication technology is seen as an important means of completing and consolidating the traditional techniques of teaching and learning. Virtually everywhere around the world, development programmes are making increasing use of satellite

television, telematics, and even video-conferences in education, health, family planning and community development. The technology permits transmission throughout the national territory of adult training programmes and distance learning courses tailored to suit all kinds of publics (leading to greater flexibility, faster learning and a wider audience). The technology offers immense possibilities for reaching vast numbers of people, with more efficient and attractive teaching methods than those used in traditional education.

In addition to these advantages, if the various costs of training, such as travel in developing countries between badly-serviced rural areas are taken into account, distance learning based on new technology seems particularly cost-effective, and will become even more so as its use develops. In the medical field, new technology such as picture phoning, video-conferences and medical encyclopedias on

Improving access to telematics for development

An international survey entitled 'The Right to Communicate: At What Price? Economic Constraints to the Effective Use of Telecommunications in Education, Science and Culture and in the Circulation of Information', was jointly undertaken in 1992–93 by UNESCO and ITU. The survey details the needs of the education, science, culture, communication and information sectors in terms of telematic services and data transmission. It provides examples of more appropriate pricing systems and other special arrangements successfully used to benefit these sectors, together with an analysis of the factors that affect prices and the international market trends that result from them. The survey examines some of the options available to the authorities to solve problems of inadequate use of telematic services by sectors of public interest and discusses the balance to be struck between the concept of a public service and the principle of non-discrimination. The survey shows that the Internet – and in more general terms, all

forms of co-operative networks oriented towards specific applications – is an important model for improving access to telematics, with advantages for user groups, telecommunications operators and public authorities alike.

Overall, the strategies and recommendations in the survey point to a promising approach to quality telematic access, at reasonable cost, for users in sectors of public interest linked to development.

The approach implies:
- co-operation among users to identify, consolidate and promote the demand for telematic services;
- the development and expansion of such services on the basis of market principles and possibilities;
- enlightened public policy, the purpose of which should be to promote the setting up of telematic infrastructures and their use by sectors linked to development, including measures for price reforms based on the cost of access.

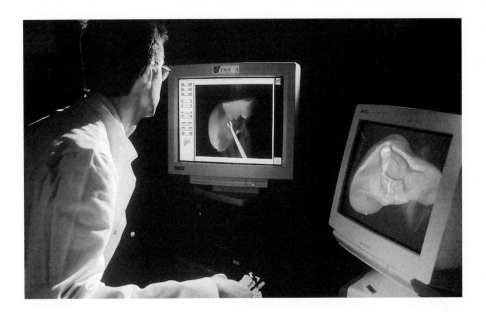

Many developing countries are availing themselves of the new information and communication technologies for purposes of distance education, health services and other developmental activities.
Photo: P. Pailly/Eurelios

CD-ROM are responding increasingly to a demand which already exists at the experimental level. In a few years, doctors, hospitals, laboratories and universities will be networked and capable of telemonitoring diagnoses, analyses and examinations transmitted from one end of the world to the other in record time, via computer and video systems. Examples of experimental applications are already on the increase, notably between hospitals in developed countries.

It is not enough to buy technology to gain access to the information society, however, nor should a straightforward purchase be seen as a miraculous solution. Access entails a considerable degree of effort, information, learning and popularization that developing countries will have to uphold if they wish to benefit from technological change and have the tools necessary for their autonomy, namely new information and communication technology. Nor should the latter be seen as some sort of magic wand far removed from the socio-economic facts of life of the countries into which they are introduced. The technology concerns every kind of user: researchers, academics, students, company executives, etc., who have to adapt to their new environment and learn to use their navigation system properly in order to optimize its potential.

In addition and in parallel to this, technology transfer has to be supported by a research drive. This consists, first of all, in analysing the breakthroughs made in information technology, the conditions permitting its transfer, and its interaction with the local socio-economic environment, and discovering the ways in which all these factors occur and interrelate. The result will be a clearer understanding not only of the use of technology, its effects, and the economic and technical constraints, but also of its advantages and the room for manoeuvre in its application. Within this global framework, research can provide a genuine form of 'strategic surveillance' used to guide policy-making by developing countries with respect to technological options.

Research is also a prerequisite for development which is often put to one side by countries that are consumers of new technology. Many developing countries since their independence have built highly diversified industrial tools in the field of communication systems, while remaining technologically dependent on supplier countries. They often find themselves confronted with R&D issues designed, driven and developed in industrialized countries. The latter have taken the high ground in the field of new technology – or are seeking to do so – by developing scientific research, taking the view that the capability to appropriate and assimilate technology depends on the degree of mastery and development attained in the strategic sector of research and development, a

Interactive television in support of distance education

A pilot distance education programme introduced by UNESCO and the International Telecommunication Union (ITU) has been launched in Morocco in collaboration with the Ministry of Education there. The aim is to achieve a link-up between the audiovisual and telecommunication sectors and to explore ways in which it can be applied to the country's education system. The project will seek to solve the problem of budgetary constraints and meet the most pressing pedagogical needs. These concerns were voiced at the Jomtien World Conference on Education for All (March 1990). A plan of action was subsequently prepared by UNESCO and ITU in May 1995 to estimate the potential of interactive television in regard to schooling and teacher training.

The principle of interactivity is vital to learning in that it fosters constant improvement in the training process, as students and teachers learn to adapt. It also triggers interstudent dialogue, thereby creating interest and curiosity. The communication of knowledge accordingly is no longer unidirectional, leading as it does to spontaneous reaction and lively comment on the part of students.

The purpose of the Moroccan project is to furnish an umbrella blueprint for improved teaching by updating telecommunication infrastructures and upgrading teacher training. The introductory phase of the project will concentrate on elaborating and finalizing the different stages of educational studies and teaching methodology with the assistance of a representative sample of teachers. It will then be extended to the country as a whole and in particular to southern Morocco with its largely illiterate rural population.

This second phase involves a training programme for some 2,000 teachers, 500 school directors, administrators and technical staff. It also provides for five training centres in each of the main provinces of Morocco. Each centre will be equipped with the latest in technological and information system resources for fifty pupils, and be placed under the supervision of the School of Radio and Television in Rabat, which will circulate and disseminate information. The teaching documentation centres will be linked to a data transmission network for ease of communication with students, principally through e-mail and a CD–ROM system available in a virtual library which teachers may use. The project is to be managed by technicians, engineers and administrators under the supervision of a project chief.

This project will be of three years' duration. The first year will be devoted to preparatory work, including staff training and the purchase and installation of interactive equipment. The distance education system will take off in the second year. And finally, by the end of the third year, the teaching methods should be tried and tested and the technological aspects well under control. The system will be extended to all twenty-two provinces of the country by the year 2008. The overall cost is estimated at $6 million. Half of this sum will be provided by the Moroccan Government, with the other half being paid by international institutions and agencies. Feasibility studies are now under way to assess the possibility of extending the project to other developing countries such as Bangladesh and Cape Verde.

branch of activity in which the most advanced countries have dominant positions.

The last point in this chapter concerns the issue of international co-operation in the field of communication. The balance sheet, after several decades of international co-operation for development purposes, is disappointing. On the one hand, it shows that very few countries have entered the newly industrialized country category, and that the use of traditional methods of development aid to enhance economic growth must be re-examined. The efforts made by the international community must be upheld and widened to include other underprivileged regions around the world, through a different approach to co-operation. In concerted fashion, this must include international organizations in order to facilitate partnership agreements with the private sector, include professional skills and ensure marketing and management know-how, and enhance understanding and knowledge with respect to the new legislation on the independent written press and the audiovisual field – in short, a different conception of co-operation altogether, leading to an authentic transfer of knowledge, in a spirit of balanced interests, solidarity and sharing.

Co-operation and UNESCO

● IPDC 97:
   $2 MILLION FOR NEW PROJECTS

At the closure of its meeting (17 to 21 March 1997), the Council of the International Programme for the Development of Communication (IPDC) agreed to fund thirty-six new projets for a total of $2 million. The projects are intended to provide the developing countries, and Central Asian countries having a transitional economy, with media training and infrastructures in order to close the communication and information gap between the industrialized and developing nations. They are also part of UNESCO's new communication strategy, which aims, on the one hand, to show how information and the media help to promote democracy and development and, on the other, to assist developing countries to step into the information society which is now emerging. The approved projects relate in particular to the least developed countries of Africa, Asia and the Caribbean.

In Africa, IPDC is to provide support to two regional or interregional and nine national projects. The former involve updating the use of the Internet tool for the Pan African News Agency, and media support for democratization and long-term development in West and Central Africa.

National projects which involve infrastructures and training in Africa include in particular: support for the Eritrean press agency ERITNA (computer equipment supply), aid in setting up a community radio for the women of Nankumba Peninsula in Malawi, and boosting the output of independent newspapers in Rwanda, where 95 per cent of the press corps have either been killed or gone into exile since the 1991 massacres.

Among the nine national projects for the Asian Continent, IPDC is contributing to the Silk Roads Radio News, an independent network for the exchange of information by radio in the former Soviet republics of Central Asia, support in the form of equipment and technological training for newspapers in the most remote regions of China, and collaboration on computerizing the national information network in Papua New Guinea.

In regard to the Caribbean, IPDC has selected three projects involving funding and in-service training. These should result in a series of three fifteen-minute documentaries on the African heritage of the descendants of runaway slaves in Guyana, Jamaica and Suriname, in addition to two training programmes covering everything from radio broadcasting and newspaper reporting to the media in general, distribution and marketing.

● TELEMATICS IN THE SERVICE
OF DEVELOPMENT

An African Regional Symposium on Telematics for
Development was organized in Addis-Ababa in April 1995
by the International Telecommunication Union (ITU), the
United Nations Economic Commission for Africa (ECA),
UNESCO and the International Development Research Centre
(Canada). The symposium brought together more than a
hundred specialists representing real or potential telematics
user associations, service partnerships, telecommunications
operators and the appropriate government organizations, as
well as representatives from some twenty regional,
international and bilateral co-operation organizations
working in this field in Africa. The conference proposed a
certain number of regional and national strategies that were
approved in May 1995 by the Conference of Ministers
responsible for Economic and Social Development and
Planning.

After the ministerial conference, the ECA, in
collaboration with the other organizers of the conference
and with their approval, set up a High-level Working Group
on Information and Communication Technologies in Africa,
which then developed a regional action plan entitled the
'African Information Society Initiative' (AISI). This was
approved by the conference of African ministers in 1996. At
the international level, planning work and fund-raising has
already begun, the aim being to establish a programme with
a budget of $11.5 million. The programme is entitled
'Harnessing Information Technology for Development' and is
headed by ECA, the World Bank, UNESCO, ITU and UNCTAD,
and should help to launch AISI as part of the United
Nations system-wide Special Initiative on Africa.

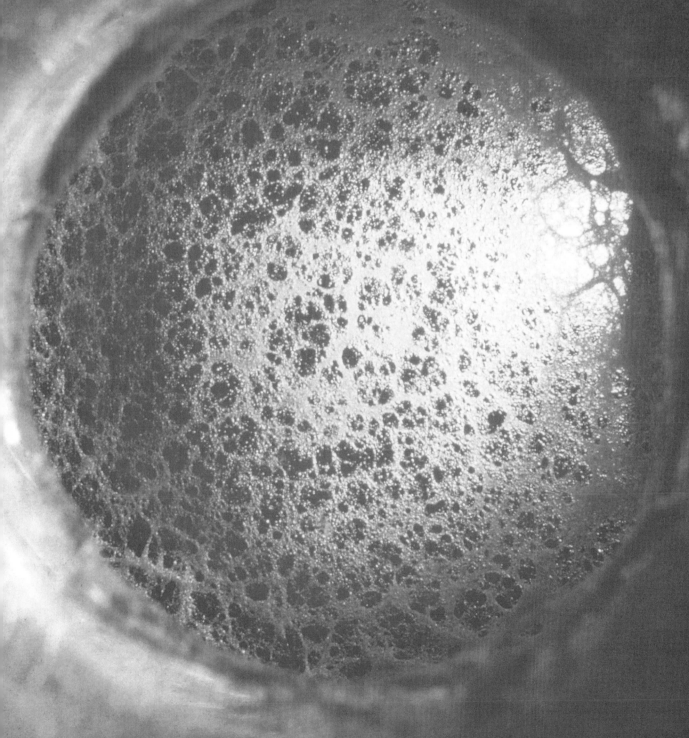

Part 2

Changes in media environments

'A flask with pure evaporated DNA'
by Erich Hartmann/Magnum Photos, Inc.

Although the digital revolution and the economic and technological changes that it has fostered have affected every sector of the communication and information industries, the greatest impact has been in the written press and the audiovisual media. In the new technical resources, publishers and broadcasters have found vastly enhanced means of reaching their target audiences. But the breakthroughs are the forerunners of far-reaching sociological upheavals, not only with regard to the ways in which we use the press, radio and television, but also in the ways they affect us.

In the written press sector, the new technology has had widespread repercussions in newspapers and magazines. The computerization of editorial work has had a revolutionary impact on the techniques of journalism, creating new jobs and changing old ones. It has provided publishers with an opportunity to take part in the digital revolution which is now under way, notably by enabling them to provide on-line newspapers on the Internet.

In the radio market, broadcasters have taken advantage of the new transmission systems to diversify the programme offer and improve listening comfort, the trend now being to provide high-fidelity digital satellite programmes, or even to create a site on the Internet.

In the television sector, data digitization and image compression techniques have led to a vast increase in the programme feed with a qualitative improvement both in pictures and sound. The same technology also provides new possibilities for interactivity that may, on the one hand, revolutionize the way we watch television and, on the other, enable viewers actually to affect what happens in the programmes.

New modes of information consumption

The increasing number of information media has encouraged non-stop growth in the range of programmes on offer, with theme channels, specialized magazines, and local radios of an associative or community type in particular, but has also resulted in fragmented listening and reading behaviour patterns. The consequence of this enlarged, personalized form of consumption is likely to favour the transfer of the programming function from broadcaster to viewer. 'Zapping' and repeat broadcasts via digital programme streams or VCRs mean that users can consume video and audio services on demand, whenever and however they wish.

Digital television will enable users to access a wide range of new services, such as pay-per-view TV, the downloading of video games or software, or channels specializing in sports or teleshopping. Based on the North American model, these services are currently developing with increasing speed by making viewers pay for programmes as they consume them, in the same way that they pay for their electricity or telephone services. The requisite decoders are already on the market around the world and are the cause of industrial battles about rival standards. Their regulation is a vital issue in the audiovisual management of digital television, because they are the key to consumer households, the means of monitoring viewers' choices, and that of ultimate control over contact with the customer.

The profusion of networks and audiovisual channels raises the question of what programmes are to be fed to them, since new support media will not sell if attractive, quality programmes are not developed to be shown on them. Content has become a precious, rare and costly commodity, resulting in bitter struggles for exclusive coverage rights and hence control over distribution.

New media environments

The technological advances used by the media, their internationalization, progress in democracy, and freedom of enterprise and expression have led to upheavals in the media landscape everywhere around the world. Clear-cut traditional geographical divisions have given way to a wider range of market diversity and subtler shades of distinction. The conventional divides between a virtually uniform, poor Southern hemisphere and a wealthy, homogeneous Northern hemisphere have narrowed. New trends are emerging, with certain countries such as Egypt, India and Turkey making inroads in the press sector, while others such as Brazil and Mexico are making their mark in the audiovisual field, having learnt how to compete on equal terms with the major industrialized countries. Yet it is still the case that the majority of the developing nations and small industrialized countries have neither the same financial resources nor the critical mass to feed their television channels with programmes. The danger therefore exists that some nations may dominate the programme market, with the concomitant risk of a certain form of cultural standardization. And while the profusion of information systems provides users with greater freedom of choice, it also creates greater inequality – even within the same country – between those who can afford to pay for programmes and those who cannot.

Chapter 8
The press

Newspapers are the oldest media. Their heyday ended with the Second World War, and their decline has been frequently prophesied ever since, to the extent that today they are no more than a minor factor in the media market. In spite of these difficulties one should not underestimate the dynamism of newspapers in certain developing countries, however, or the scale of the technological changes they have undergone, or their high degree of diversity around the world. Indeed, the situation of the press is highly dissimilar from country to country, operating on the basis of a number of models that vary in relation to the different political, cultural and economic contexts inherent in every nation. There are a number of similarities, however: everywhere in the world the press is confronted with a twin dilemma, one produced by technological change, the other the result of the economic recession that has hit some regions of the world.

Main changes in technology

In reaction to technological breakthroughs and competition from pictures, newspapers are seeking to maintain their market share by increased diversification, with a considerable degree of determination. They are players of increasing importance in the other communication sectors, including the audiovisual field, radio, telematics, publishing, bill-posting and direct marketing, and are gradually spreading their activities to include the multimedia market by offering their services on the Internet.

Production: digitization and remote printing

Technological developments and digitization have impacted a number of links in presswork, making newspapers more accessible and more convenient for readers who have now also become television viewers, as well as providing newspapers with new means of adapting more easily to competition from pictures. The same technical advances have also enabled the press

Changes in presswork

The computerization of editorial staff has caused a real upheaval in working habits but has also marked a genuine development in presswork. Computers fascinate some people and frighten others, and have fostered bitter resistance from print union representatives. The possibility for journalists everywhere to type their own articles, type copy and enter it directly into a computer system has completely transformed the profession. Keyboard operators previously responsible for inputting copy, and who themselves had replaced traditional typesetters, have already gone in some countries and will disappear in the medium-term elsewhere. Similarly, the manual mounting of pages previously prepared by the editing supervisor and carried out by typesetters and copy preparers is beginning to disappear in some publications, to give way to computer-assisted page make-up. On top of this, as a result of the automation of the printing sequence, the numbers of staff in newspaper printing shops, from reel hands to controller hands to typographers, graphic artists and photo-engravers, have been considerably reduced.

The advantage in microcomputing for journalists is that they do not have to be permanently present at the head office of the newspaper. For several years now, reporters with the major publications around the world have been using laptop computers to type their text (and their illustrations) on site at their assignment and front-end them into the production process via any telecommunications network.

The widespread adoption of these techniques and their influence on the gathering, transmission and use of information have had an impact on journalism in general, which no longer entails working for only one of the media, as is still the case in some countries. Journalists now need to be versatile in order to be capable of switching from one branch to another.

These new processes, enhanced by digital transmission, have penetrated the market because of the need common to every newspaper to go to press as late as possible in order to print the most up-to-date news and keep manufacturing costs down. Production has become more streamlined, but an entire breed of print workers is on the verge of extinction as a result.

---

to give greater emphasis to photographs in relation to text, to graphics over the written word, to colour over black and white. The prototype for this model is the American daily *USA Today,* which marked a milestone in the history of the press by opting for a new concept in the use of colour, in particular as a means of enhancing information and guiding the reader. These options have not been copied everywhere in the world press, however.

Fax transmission

As a result of progress in telecommunications and satellites, texts, photographs and graphics can now be transmitted by facsimile from one continent to another. Since the first transmission by the *Asahi shimbun* from Tokyo to Sapporo in 1959, which took half an hour per page, the process has considerably improved. From New York, the *Wall Street Journal* dispatches its pages to Hong Kong in less than three minutes. Today, facsimile is used at both ends of its capabilities. On the one hand it is used for short-haul transmission: in Algeria, for example, the daily newspaper *Le Soir d'Algérie* transmits its pages from its head office in Algiers, where they are made up, to regional printing shops in Oran and Constantine. In Switzerland, the pages of *24 Heures* and the Geneva *Tribune* are transmitted to a common printing centre in Lausanne. At the other end of the spectrum, facsimile is used for long-distance international

Number of daily newspapers: highest and lowest values of number of titles per country within the region, 1994

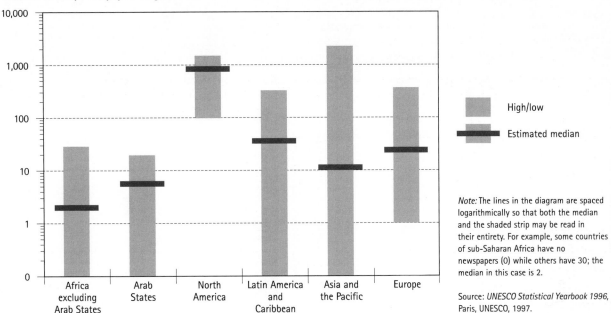

Note: The lines in the diagram are spaced logarithmically so that both the median and the shaded strip may be read in their entirety. For example, some countries of sub-Saharan Africa have no newspapers (0) while others have 30; the median in this case is 2.

Source: *UNESCO Statistical Yearbook 1996*, Paris, UNESCO, 1997.

transmission. Dailies such as the *International Herald Tribune*, the *Financial Times* and the *Guardian*, and likewise the Egyptian paper *El Ahram*, the Japanese newspaper *Mainichi shimbun*, the Greek paper *Avriani* and the Italian *Gazetta dello sport*, are simultaneously printed in several sites around the world.

Photojournalism

This form of presswork has been impacted by major breakthroughs, notably in terms of digital storage and image transmission capacity. The current trend is towards complete digitization of the whole of the photographic image chain, from film-free cameras to the scanning and production of printing plates, via image processing on workstations where photographs can be displayed on-screen, to be cropped and retouched before being inserted into the final page make-up. Layout artists can thus make up the whole newspaper direct from computer to printing plate, without having to edit hard copy and film in order to copy the plate itself. Most of the leading news agencies such as Associated Press, Reuters and Agence France Presse provide their subscribers with equipment permitting the reception of digital photographs, and most dailies are equipped with a digital processing sequence to receive photographs transmitted either by their regional editorial staff or directly by news agencies.

Printing and distribution

Newspaper production is now fully controlled by computer. From web tension to ink feed, from the registration of four-colour prints to the inserting of quires, down to the counting of copies at the delivery unit – all these steps are programmed and executed by computer. Computer technology is equally present throughout the newspaper distribution system. Every day, computers calculate the number of copies to be deposited at each point of sale, suggest optimized routes for carriers, control the printing of addresses and trigger requests for subscription renewals.

Whereas almost all the editorial staff in industrialized countries have become 'computer literate', and many newspapers in Latin America and Asia have followed their example, newspapers in the Arab World and Africa have taken the leap to computerization only recently. Elsewhere, the move is taking place in small steps.

Electronic publishing

The written press in the world faces new challenges from networks.
This could be an opportunity to strengthen the printed media and
cultivate readership loyalty. But this assumes an ability to present the
public with more attractive and relevant materials.

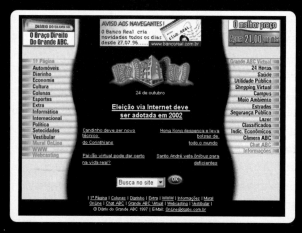

LA CRÓNICA DE HOY

DIRECTOR GENERAL: PABLO HIRIART / AÑO UNO

Nacional
Internacional
Negocios
Deportes

Academia
Cultura
Medio Ambiente
Espectáculos

Gente de Harvard y Yale quiere enterrar la revolución, dice LEA

DOBLE
NO CIRCULA
Jueves
1 y 2
EXCEPTO LOS AUTOMOVILES CON CALCOMANIA CERO
5 y 6
EXCEPTO LOS AUTOMOVILES CALCOMANIA UNO Y CERO

LA CRÓNICA DE HOY
México, D.F.
JUEVES 23 DE OCTUBRE DE 1997

Luis Echeverría llevó una ofrenda a la tumba del general Lázaro Cárdenas. Ahí habló de la actitud poco revolucionaria de los presidentes que estudiaron en el extranjero. Como buen maestro de los mensajes cifrados, mandó uno de sus fobias y otro de sus filias. El que no coordinaba ni a sus nietos, je, je...

Editorial
Artículos y Columnas
Suplemento Dominical
Foro de discusión

Contingencia en el DF: el ozono llegó a 250 imecas

Welcome to ALAYAM Home Page
ALAYAM الأيام

| ALAYAM | Local News | Arabic News | News In English | Columns | Sports | Daily | Bookshop | Cartoons |

الأعداد السابقة
Previous Issues

السبت الاحد الاثنين الثلاثاء الاربعاء الخميس الجمعة
Sat - Sun - Mon - Tue - Wed - Thu - Fri

ملتقى القراء   BAHRAIN TRIBUNE   News In English

Bahrain Online   Search   Interesting Links

سوق العملات
Money Exchange

Today's Weather

'97 WORLD SERIES
Marlins Win
Game 5, 8-7

The New York Times
ON THE WEB

AUTOS
A New Look

"All the News That's Fit to Print"   **Friday, October 24, 1997**   ● Weather

Sections
● Front Page
● Politics
● Sports
● Op-Ed
● Travel
● Real Estate
● Job Market
● Cartoons

● Week in Review
● CyberTimes
● Business
● Editorials
● Arts & Leisure
● Books
● Automobiles
● Diversions
● Web Specials

News by Category | Forums
A.P. Breaking News | A.P. Radio
Classifieds | Services | Search

FROM TODAY'S TIMES
Hong Kong Stocks Plunge, Tremors Felt in Global Markets

IN CYBERTIMES
Cracked Computer Code Underscores Limits of Security

Seeking the Missing in Algeria

Tour the Site | Help Center | Low Graphics | Table of Contents | Privacy Information
First Time Users: Register Here
New York Times Home Delivery

digital
Granma
INTERNACIONAL

Edición disponible en los idiomas

Español ● English ● Français ● Português ● Deutsch

Che   PREMIOS Granma Internacional

® Copyright. Granma Internacional/Edición Digital. 1997. Todos los derechos reservados
Se autoriza la reproducción total o parcial de estas páginas WEB, siempre que se indique los titulares del Copyright.
Cualquier información adicional por favor comuníquese con
redac@granmai.get.cma.net

Granma Internacional es una publicación editada en La Habana, Cuba. Avenida General Suárez y Territorial.
Plaza de la Revolución José Martí. Apartado Postal 6260 C.P. 100699 Telex: 00511-355-0511-221
Fax: (53-7) 33-5176 y 33-5826 Teléfono: 81-6265 y 81-7449. Fiz: 91 3333 ext 19 y 23

Bienvenue sur les pages de la
TRIBUNE DE GENÈVE
Le leader des quotidiens genevois

EDICOM

Édition du jeudi 23 octobre

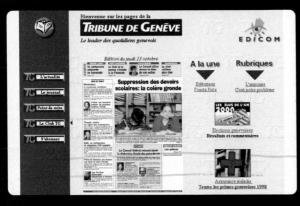

TG L'actualité
TG Le journal
TG Point de mire
TG Le Club TG
TG S'abonner

Suppression des devoirs scolaires: la colère gronde

A la une
Éditorial
Points forts

Rubriques
L'annuaire
C'est notre problème

LES PLUS DE L'AN
2000

Élections genevoises
Résultats et commentaires

Assurance maladie
Toutes les primes genevoises 1998

KUENSEL
BHUTAN'S NATIONAL NEWSPAPER
The Only Authentic Site From Bhutan

SATURDAY, October 18, 1997

Dashain festival celebrated

- Red Cross visits Bhutan
- Chillies can be saved
- Bad timing - Kuensel Editorial

- Apple tree fungus can be controlled
- Police complete human rights course

Last Week's Issue

الأنوار
Al Anwar, The Internet Edition

BEIRUT   THURSDAY, OCTOBER 23, 1997   Nº 13 111

رئيس الحكومة يكشف جولاته الخارجية
تهربا من معالجة الاوضاع الاقتصادية الداخلية
محاولة الهراوي فتح معركة الرئاسة باكرا باءت بالفشل
والخلافات المعلنة بينه وبين الحريري لصالح التمديد

الشيخ ياسين يدعو للجهاد ضد اسرائيل
السلطة الفلسطينية تحذر من انفجار الاوضاع

مبارك: نتنياهو غير جدير بالثقة ولا يحترم اتفاقات السلام الموقعة

القاهرة: تنفيذ حكم الاعدام في ٤ اصوليين

تعزيزات للجيش الجزائري حول العاصمة

Development of the written press in developing countries

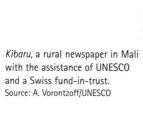

Kibaru, a rural newspaper in Mali with the assistance of UNESCO and a Swiss fund-in-trust.
Source: A. Vorontzoff/UNESCO

Egyptian newspapers have the fastest growth in the Arab World.
Source: A. Nabeel/AFP

Diversity of types and models

The press gains new freedom

In democratic countries, the press is often considered as the 'fourth estate', responsible for keeping watch over the social pact between government and governed, thereby enabling citizens to make enlightened choices and to express their opinions. Its independence is given body and form in particular under Article 19 of the Universal Declaration of Human Rights, which, referring to the free flow of information, calls for the elimination of all barriers to seeking, receiving and spreading information and ideas, both within states and beyond their frontiers.

In countries in democratic transition, the press is seen less and less as an instrument in the service

The independent press flourishes in
Manila (Philippines) – newspapers,
tabloids and comics.
Source: C. A. Arnaldo/UNESCO

In China, the end of the state
monopoly in newspaper distribution
has resulted in new networks using
the postal services, home delivery
and vending.
Source: M. Geneta/AFP

of governments. Freedom of enterprise and of speech together have disrupted the old monopolies and led to radical changes in the media environment, with competition between newspapers now even becoming heated. Readers today have a choice of several publications which are often critical of those in power, with the result that current threats are more economic in nature, such as limited or controlled advertising markets, prohibitive tax liabilities, hyperinflation, and so forth.

In a minority of other countries today, the press is still a monopoly in the hands of the state and is used to serve political, economic or social aims defined by government authorities or the party in power. Elsewhere, in areas of unrest or war zones, certain sections of the press, controlled by either one of the parties in the conflict, are used to disseminate their propaganda and spread their ideologies. Newspapers in these cases provide disinformation to manipulate the population, and in extreme cases may be transformed into hate-mongers, inciting to violence and crime. The examples of Rwanda and the former Yugoslavia are still fresh in our minds.

Daily press, wide diversity

The daily press has developed to highly varying degrees, according to country, region and historical background. It is on the decline in the majority of the most developed countries and on the upswing in various developing countries. As far as dailies are concerned, in 1995 the highest circulation was the privilege of Japan, with the plethoric *Yomiuri shimbun*, which has a print run of approximately 10 million copies per day. One overriding feature of the high-run newspaper market is intense concentration, with a sector dominated by a limited number of large national private press groups, including Asahi in Japan, Bertelsmann in Germany and Indian Express in India, international corporations such as Pearson and the News Corporation in English-speaking countries, or publicly owned groups such as Dar Al Ahram in Egypt.

Apart from *The Wall Street Journal* and *USA Today*, which are international in scope, neither Germany nor the United States has a press 'capital', the major dailies with nationwide circulation being located in several large cities such as Hamburg, Frankfurt, Munich, New York, Los Angeles or Chicago. The United States remains the country where the local press is most highly developed, as was testified by the 1,532 titles in circulation in 1994.

Market penetration by newspapers varies according to the size of the country, its journalistic history, its rate of literacy or even its technological development. A few facts and figures give an idea of their impact in various countries. The 1995 figures for industrialized countries where readership is on the

downturn indicate that Norway was in the lead with 610 newspapers sold per 1,000 inhabitants (the 1994 rate was also 610), followed by Japan with 576 (down from 580 in 1991), Sweden and Finland with 464 (472 in 1994) and Switzerland with 365 (372 in 1994). Still on the basis of 1995 circulation figures, readership has increased in other countries, such as Egypt with 67 newspapers per 1,000 inhabitants, India with 26 (up from 21 in 1991), Malaysia with 123 (up from 117 in 1994) and Sri Lanka with 29 (28 in 1994).[1]

These figures illustrate the wide differences between countries and regions. In most African, Arab or Caribbean countries, there is a degree of convergence. Circulation and penetration are still weak even if certain titles that have emerged with democratization – such as the *Vientiane Times* with a print run of 350,000 copies in Laos,[2] *Liberté* with 352,000 copies in Algeria, *Evenimental Zilei* with 120,000 copies in Romania,[3] *Motomoto* with 40,000 copies in the United Republic of Tanzania – have revitalized the sector, generally as market leaders.[4]

Form and content

Quality newspapers stand out for the wealth of their news and the depth of their investigation. Worth citing among many others in this respect are the *Washington Post* in the United States, the *Independent* and the *Guardian* in the United Kingdom, *Frankfurter Allgemeine Zeitung* in Germany, *Le Monde* in France, *El País* in Spain, *El Mercurio* in Chile, the *Straits Times*

1. World Association of Newspapers, *World Press Trends*, London, FIEJ/Zenith Media, 1997.
2. 'Laos: vers une libéralisation des médias', *Medias-pouvoirs* (Paris), No. 38, 1995, p. 7.
3. 'La presse roumaine vit mal sa nouvelle liberté' [The Romanian Press Misses out on New-found Freedom], *Le Monde* (Paris), 12 March 1996, p. 28.
4. A. J. Tudesq, *Feuilles d'Afrique, étude de la presse de l'Afrique sub-saharienne* [African Notes: Study of the Press in sub-Saharan Africa], Éditions de la Maison des Sciences de l'Homme Aquitaine, 1995.

The top thirty daily newspapers in the world in 1996: Asia leads the world press[1]

	Thousands of copies distributed
1. *Yomiuri shimbun* (Japan)	14 485
2. *Asahi shimbun* (Japan)	12 660
3. *Mainichi shimbun* (Japan)	5 867
4. *MZ guangbo dianshi* (China)	5 348
5. *Xinmin wanboa* (China)	5 227
6. *Bild Zeitung* (Germany)	4 644
7. *Nihon keizai shimbun* (Japan)	4 550
8. *Chunichi shimbun* (Japan)	4 394
9. *The Sun* (United Kingdom)	4 007
10. *BJ guangdo dianshi* (China)	3 372
11. *Daily Mirror* (United Kingdom)	3 168
12. *Beijing wanbao* (China)	3 073
13. *Sankei shimbun* (Japan)	2 876
14. *Jiefang riboa* (China)	2 272
15. *Daily Mail* (United Kingdom)	2 077
16. *Baokan wenzhai* (China)	2 053
17. *Hokkaido shimbun* (Japan)	1 991
18. *Yangcheng wanbao* (China)	1 913
19. *Zhongguo dainshi ba* (China)	1 813
20. *Wall Street Journal* (United States)	1 784
21. *Beijing ribao* (China)	1 784
22. *Wen hui bao* (China)	1 721
23. *Komsomolskaia Pravda* (Russian Federation)	1 582
24. *Joong-ang Daily News* (Republic of Korea)	1 500
25. *Trud* (Russian Federation)	1 442
26. *Shizuoka shimbun* (Japan)	1 426
27. *Zeitunggruppe WAZ* (Germany)	1 140
28. *Neue Kronen Zeitung* (Austria)	1 075
29. *Nishi-Nippon shimbun* (Japan)	1 022
30. *The Times of India* (India)	978

1. Ten Chinese, nine Japanese, one from the Republic of Korea and one Indian are among the thirty peak sales figures in the world.

Source: *World Press Trends*, London, FIEJ/Zenith Media, 1997.

in Singapore and *El Watan* in Algeria. Quality newspapers address a wide-ranging readership elite, generally decision-makers, with the result that their influence is considerable, even if their circulation figures remain generally low (with print runs of a few hundred thousand). A number of these titles, such as the *International Herald Tribune*, the *Wall Street Journal* and the *Financial Times*, are considered to be international publications, even though their circulation is still far below that of some national titles such as the Japanese newspaper *Yomiuri shimbun* cited above.

The popular press and papers specializing in analysis and commentary are powerful purveyors of news around the world. The best known of these papers are *Bild Zeitung* in Germany (with a circulation of 5 million), the *Sun* in the United Kingdom (4 million), *Sabab* in Turkey and the *New York Post* in the United States. They are recognizable by their screaming headlines, short articles and eye-catching photographs. The success of the so-called 'sensational' newspapers is due not only to the type of news they provide but also to the style of language they use, bordering on the colloquial, and to their graphic layout based on illustrations, scare headlines and tabloid format. In some countries such as the United Kingdom, these dailies have become a real power base, in which the spotlight is on sensationalism to the detriment of any explanatory or factual reporting. Unlike the countries in the Northern hemisphere, South-East Asia or Latin America, the countries south of the Mediterranean and in the Arab and African world do not have popular newspapers with high circulation figures. On the other hand, the sports newspapers are widely read, such as the *Gazetta dello Sport* in Italy, *Graphic Sports* in Kenya and *El Hadef* in Morocco.

Generally speaking, in terms of the number of dailies published around the world, the developed or newly industrialized countries have an obvious lead in comparison with Africa or the Arab World. The

The press in the Russian Federation

Newspapers in the Russian Federation from 1990 onwards were confronted with a radically new socio-economic situation, the repercussions of which were far-reaching. In 1992, more than 80 per cent of the newspapers published within Russian territory still belonged to the Communist Party. The decree by President Boris Yeltsin putting an end to the activities of the Party also deprived every title of most of its financial resources. Since that date, competition has hit the press sector, bringing in its wake the difficult process of reconversion to a market economy.

● ROCKED BY THE CRISIS

Since 1990, the situation of the Russian press has worsened as a result of economic difficulties linked to new market demands. Between 1991 and 1993, *Pravda* sales fell by 500,000 copies, while those of *Izvestia* plummeted from 4.7 to 1.1 million and those of *Trud* from 18 to 1.5 million.[1] In the small towns and rural communes the state of the press is even more critical, caused by the absence of advertisers, the low-level income of the population and the growing cost of distribution. In reaction to these setbacks, a law to support the local press was adopted by the *Duma* in 1995. It provides for the purchase of new printing equipment as well as coverage of the costs related to the production and purchasing of paper, while the public postal service is to defray the costs of distributing newspapers. This assistance for the local press does not include newspapers belonging to political parties or specialized titles. Despite these obstacles, in 1996, 59 per cent of the Russian population read a newspaper every day, 61 per cent listened to the radio and 86 per cent watched television. Very few of the newspapers or magazines they read, however, have acquired any real financial independence, whether from the state, political parties, industrial groups or banking syndicates.

● MARKET MOVES

With the liberalization of the economy, the Russian press environment has totally changed. Some newspapers have simply been renamed: the Leningrad *Pravda* has become the *Saint Petersburg News*, although the old editorial staff is still the same, and the *Kommunist* review is now known as *Free Thought*. Although other newspapers, former mouthpieces for the Communist Party in particular, have changed owners, the majority of them are now controlled by a few large corporations in the banking and power production sectors. The leading Russian oil group Loukoil, for instance, has a 20 per cent stake in the well-known daily *Izvestia* and its print run of 550,000. Another, the giant Russian gas company, Gazprom, has acquired a 20 per cent stake in *Komsomolskaya Pravda*, which has one of the highest circulation figures in the whole of the Russian Federation. Russian banks also have interests in the press. The Menatep bank, at the head of a veritable industrial empire, has a share in the Independent Media Group, which publishes an English-language daily and the Russian editions of *Cosmopolitan* and *Playboy*. Imperial, another bank connected to the Gazprom group, controls the economic daily *Kommersant*. Finally, the Most bank has created a modern-day empire with the daily newspaper *Sevodnia*, the radio station Echoes of Moscow, the television channel NTV and the news magazine *Itogui*.

Concentration on this scale has aroused considerable debate in the Russian Federation. For some, the fact that large companies should have shareholdings in the media is a normal economic process common to every democracy. For others, the process is fraught with danger for pluralism and for democracy, all the more so in that the main groups that control the media are also close to the political power base.

1. Figures taken from P. Alessandri, 'Les médias en Russie' [The Media in Russia], *Médiaspouvoirs* (Paris), Autumn 1993.

Sources: 'La liberté des médias en Russie a fait "un pas en arrière", selon un rapport européen' [Media Freedom in Russia Steps Backwards, Says a European Report], *Le Monde* (Paris), 7–8 July 1996, p. 3; 'Fédération de Russie: nouvelles lois de soutien à la presse écrite' [Russian Federation: New Laws in Favour of the Written Press], *Iris* (Strasbourg), March 1996, Vol. 2, No. 3, p. 13; 'Les médias russes sous l'emprise croissante des grands groupes proches du Kremlin' [Russian Media Increasingly in Hands of Power Groups Close to Kremlin], *Le Journal de Genève* (Geneva), 10 December 1996.

circulation for dailies in absolute figures is a clear illustration of this adverse balance: 319 copies per 1,000 inhabitants in developed countries, and a little under 33 per 1,000 inhabitants for the rest of the world.[5]

The periodical press in various parts of the world has seen radical change and marked growth. One such market move is the specialization of the titles in this sector in order to address a specific readership 'target', addressing a common centre of interest for both men and women. Highlights in this sector include association magazines, such as the *ADAC-Motorwelt* review for motorists' associations in Germany, with a circulation of 9.2 million, and *Modern Maturity* for pensioners in the United States, with a circulation of 27 million. Other examples include specialized technical journals in the economic or professional sectors; general public magazines such as television reviews (*TV Guide* in the United States, which sells 16 million copies, *Sorrisi e Canzoni TV* in Italy with a readership of 2.3 million); women's magazines such as *Elle* in France, *Harper's Bazaar* in the United States and *Grand Hotel* in Italy; news magazines, almost all of which are imitations of *Time*, which was launched in the United States in 1923, such as *Der Spiegel* in Germany, *Espresso* in Italy, *Cambio* in Spain or *L'Express* in France; intellectual, academic, quality reviews with low sales but high impact, such as *Les Temps modernes* in France or the *New York Review of Books* in the United States; the religious press, such as *Le Pèlerin* in France or *La Croix du Bénin* in Benin; and finally the entertainment press for youngsters such as *Mickey Mouse Magazine*. Just as for dailies, the situation of periodicals around the world shows tremendous inequality. Most of the magazines are published in America, Asia and Europe.

All the above publications differ in terms of the ways in which they are owned and distributed. Some of them are held by families, as is the tradition in Germany, Japan and provincial France. Others belong to large industrial companies, as in India (Tata) or Italy (Fiat), as well as to public authorities, as is the case in China, Cuba, Egypt and Tunisia. In most cases, however, they belong to press groups, this being often the case in Europe, Latin America or North America. The development of these groups has resulted in widespread internationalization, notably in the periodical sector with the launch of magazines of international scope and status such as *Fortune, Playboy, Elle,* etc. Other differences in the press concern their methods of distribution: depending on the historical traditions of the country in question, newspapers are sold from kiosks or by newsagents, delivered to the doorstep or bought from vending machines.[6]

Decline and downturn in circulation

In most countries, newspapers have gone through a serious recession characterized by a general downturn in sales, a loss of advertising market share, dwindling readership among the younger generations and a general decline in the influence of the press compared to radio, television and now to computers. On top of this should be noted the increase of distribution and production costs and the rocketing rise in the price of paper between 1994 and 1995. The steep increase has come close to 40 per cent since 1995 and has weighed heavily on the financial position of newspapers. The rise is also held to be responsible for the difficulties that newspapers around the world are currently facing and even for the winding up of some papers.[7] These restrictions illustrate the extent to which

5.   For more on this subject see J. Barrat, *Géographie économique des médias*, Paris, Éditions Litec, 1992.

6.   The statistics and information in this chapter are taken from: C. B. Johnston, *Winning the Global TV News Game*, Focal Press, 1995; *World Press Trends*, FIEJ, Paris, 1996; C. J. Bertrand, *Média: Introduction à la presse, la radio et la télévision*, Paris, Ellipses, 1995.

7.   This sudden surge in the price of paper has led the International Federation of Newspaper Publishers (FIEJ) to vote a resolution denouncing 'the dramatic effect of price

newspaper production is a capital-intensive industry, and the consequences of the crash it is currently facing for the other sectors of the press. In terms of circulation, in 1995 alone dailies in Europe were down 0.69 per cent and in the United States they lost 1.32 per cent. Newspaper circulation figures in these two regions of the world have declined by 7 per cent over the last ten years, while periodicals have lost some 8 million readers. In Central and Eastern Europe there has been a major downturn in circulation, with a fall of 70.25 per cent in the Russian Federation and 20.07 per cent in Estonia. Only in Bulgaria, with a rise in readership of 74.19 per cent, and in Latvia with growth of 25.79 per cent, have the trends been upwards between 1993 and 1994. On the other hand, newspaper circulation has increased in Asia and in Latin America, with growth in countries such as Brazil (22.68 per cent), Colombia (5.81 per cent), Malaysia (4.68 per cent), Singapore (5.87 per cent), Turkey (63.91 per cent) and India (28.51 per cent). In terms of sales, Japan tops the list with 72.7 million copies a day in 1996, i.e. an increase of 0.9 per cent over 1995. The United States comes in second place at almost 57 million copies per day. China is in third place with its 2,200 newspapers, of which the top ten total sales of 28.5 million copies each day.[8]

In terms of advertising revenue, the press is continuing to lose market share to television and radio. In many countries, notably in the European Community, there was a general recession in this area for the print media between 1991 and 1994. Since 1994, however, the situation has improved, and revenue from advertising is beginning to rally, indicating for a number of countries that the end of the slump is in sight. In the United States, revenue from advertising grew 5 per cent in 1995, with sales of $36 billion compared with $34 billion in 1994.[9] The greatest rates of growth since 1991, however, have occurred in countries such as Malaysia (with a rise of more than 120 per cent), Brazil (131 per cent), India (97 per cent) and South Africa (97 per cent). In China, the advertising market is positively booming, with revenues of $140 million in 1996, compared to a mere $12 million

increases on the economic health of the press industry'. 'These increases will inevitably end in a reduction of the number of newspapers, and publications with low circulation figures are in danger of disappearing altogether,' went on the FIEJ, which pointed out to paper manufacturers that 'these high price rises are going to undermine the foundation of their own trade', because they lead to increased 'diversification of newspapers in electronic forms of news circulation'. – 'La presse investit le multimédia' [The Press Lays Siege to the Multimedia], *Le Monde* (Paris), 3 June 1995, p. 28.
8.   According to T. Balding, director of the International Federation of Newspaper Publishers (FIEJ), at a speech given during the Ninety-fourth Publishers' Congress, Washington D.C., 20 May 1996.
9.   'Les éditeurs de journaux s'inquiètent du déclin de la diffusion dans les pays industrialisés', *Le Monde* (Paris), 22 May 1996, p. 28.

The independent press in Africa

The democratization process that began in the early 1990s in Africa has resulted in the emergence of a privately owned, independent press in several countries. Although these newspapers are often produced on a small scale and have only limited readerships, they are all vying for position in the democratic debate. Many titles, such as *La Gazette du* *Golfe* in Benin, *Sud Hebdo* in Senegal or *Le Messager* in Cameroon, have met and continue to meet with widescale popular success. The role and the development of the private press have varied according to the traditions, region and type of political regime in each country.

In 1997, there were approximately a hundred private

newspapers published fairly regularly over the whole continent. Most of these are dailies, although some appear fortnightly or monthly, but almost all their business is concentrated in the cities.

The independent press is confronted with a number of obstacles that are cultural, economic and political in nature, including illiteracy, low purchasing power, the narrowness of national markets, etc. Mali, for instance, has four national dailies for its 10 million inhabitants, poor readership purchasing power, a high rate of illiteracy, distribution limited to large provincial towns and meagre advertising resources, not to mention the prohibitive cost of paper. In addition, the role played by a number of titles in forming public opinion for some governments is a source of concern, and for others a source of inspiration in their attempts to silence the press, including making publication subject to prior authorization, the withholding of information, customs duties, exorbitant tax liabilities, intimidation and lawsuits brought against newspapers and their editors.

Other, more direct obstacles stem from monopolies imposed by public authorities on raw materials and equipment, a form of control which is difficult to circumvent and which some simply see as another form of censorship in disguise. On top of these problems lie other constraints linked to the general economic backdrop and to the devaluation of the CFA franc, which have led to increases in manufacturing and transport costs, rising numbers of bad debts and a fragile advertising market. In 1996, the latter represented little more than 20 per cent of newspaper revenue. The companies that dominate the market are mainly foreign, and prefer radio and television or space advertising in the international magazines that have wide circulation in the region.

Parallel to these constraints, the independent press in Africa has also made a number of slip-ups. The lack of qualified journalists due to the insufficient number of training programmes has led some newspapers to spotlight current events and seek the sensational stories, or to support partisan points of view and settle scores, and in many cases the development of ideas connected with

political parties makes it difficult to distinguish between informative reporting and the press that specializes in commentary.

Several initiatives have been taken to overcome the mishaps that are inherent in any young press sector. A number of newspaper editors have created the Newspaper Publishers' Society (SEP), a pool of regional scope based in Benin that aims to unite local independent newspapers. Other publishers, such as the Sud Communication Group in Senegal, have organized press groups around several activities, including newspapers, radio, publishing and printing, and have set up their own training programmes. Finally, others again have tackled the issue of professional ethics with the creation in 1995 in Yamoussoukro (Côte d'Ivoire) of an observatory on press freedom, ethics and a professional code of conduct (OLPED).

In spite of these efforts, the independent press has yet to find its feet in the African media environment. It is still weakened by a restricted readership of literate people confined to cities and suburbs. In order for it really to take part in the democratic debate and win the fight for pluralism, it has to face a number of challenges, the most important of which are:

- Modernizing equipment (fax machines, word processors, desktop publishing).
- Maintaining and preferably increasing the frequency of publication.
- Finally, enhancing training facilities to improve professional skills and develop the spirit of enterprise.

Within this framework, from 1993 onwards UNESCO began setting up a project for the 'Development of an Independent and Pluralistic Press in Africa' in sub-Saharan Africa. The project includes the organization of in-service training activities, the supply of equipment, the installation of effective distribution networks and other operations connected with the exercise of the profession. In 1996 the project provided further training for 108 journalists, thirty-three of whom were women, in some twenty countries of Central and West Africa, as well as the creation of a pilot publishing centre in Cameroon.

Daily newspapers in Africa: number of titles per 1,000 inhabitants, 1994

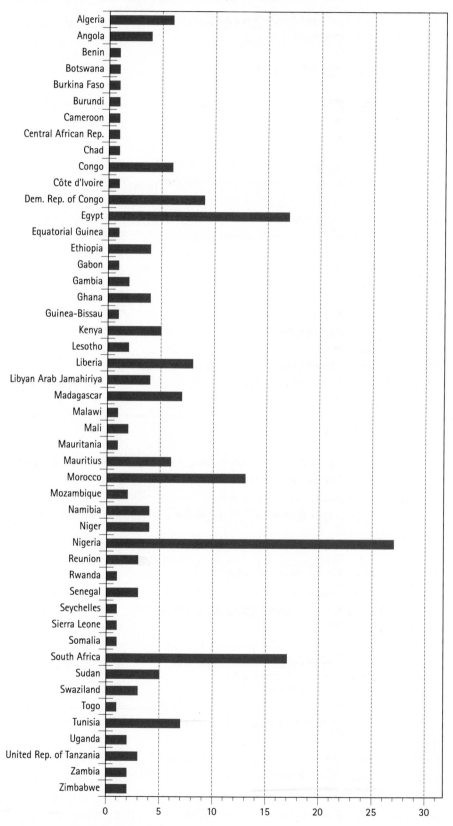

Source: *UNESCO Statistical Yearbook 1996,* Paris, UNESCO, 1997.

Daily newspapers in Africa: circulation per 1,000 inhabitants, 1994

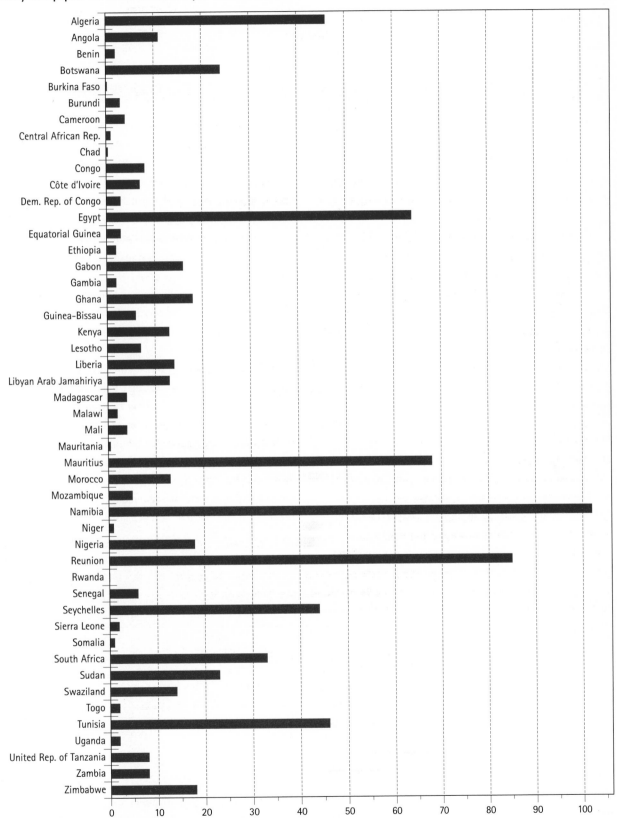

Source: *UNESCO Statistical Yearbook 1996,* Paris, UNESCO, 1997.

The Internet reinvents the press

More and more newspapers around the world are opening servers on the Internet in order to provide their readers with an electronic version of their content. In August 1996, there were more than 1,500 newspapers and international magazines available on-line, 1,400 of which were on the World Wide Web alone.

The first attempt at electronic publishing dates from 1992 by the daily newspaper the *San José Mercury News,* which enabled computerized readers to access the electronic edition of their newspaper. By 1997, testing had widened to include the leading titles in the international press (the *International Herald Tribune, Le Monde, Al Hayat,* etc.), all of which are henceforth accessible on the Net.

The United States has the lion's share with 765 publications (almost 400 of which are periodicals), to which should be added some 123 Canadian titles. With approximately 300 titles on-line, Europe is also present on the market, as are Africa, Asia and the Arab World, although to a lesser degree.

Generally speaking, all the on-line newspapers provide a wealth of often personalized news items and at particularly high speeds. Some, such as the *New York Times,* complete their texts and photographs with spoken commentaries, while others have set up newsgroup debates with their readers. These technological innovations have enhanced the written press, enabling it to face up to competition from radio and television on better terms. In addition, via the network, local and national newspapers can address a diversified public, spread around the entire planet. All these experiments are being closely monitored by the publishing world, which has been able to identify other potential audiences such as research assistants, students, journalists, financial analysts and teachers, forming a vast market that may in the medium–term provide sufficient return on development costs, estimated at several million dollars per year.

Although they are fully aware that electronic publishing is not a miracle solution for the economic straits in which the profession currently finds itself, many experts feel that the written press may be able to overtake television again, thanks to the Internet. For the time being, few of the sites providing electronic publishing services are profitable. Participation in the new electronic media is none the less considered by publishers to be a long–term investment that may guarantee the survival of newspapers as a medium in itself. Whatever the case, it is a means of increasing the conventional range of news packages and services, and may even attract a younger readership, not in the habit of even looking at newspapers.

Sources: '1 500 journaux en-ligne' [1,500 On-line Newspapers], *Le Monde* (Paris), 8–9 September 1996, p. 29; 'Gutenberg survivra-t-il à l'édition électronique?', *I&T Magazine* (Strasbourg), p. 14; 'L'édition électronique: des profits à l'horizon?' [Electronic Publishing: Promise of Profits?], *FIEJ Newsletter,* No. 4, March 1997, p. 1.

---

in 1991. Home China watchers say that this market is set to grow at an annual rate of 20 per cent in the years to come. The reasons are twofold: on the one hand, there is the launching of new press groups, particularly private ones, the first of which has set up shop in the Guangzhou region; on the other hand, the state monopoly on distribution has come to an end. Already by 1997, 775 titles had their own distribution network using the postal system as well as door-to-door delivery.[10]

10.   'Dix fois plus de journaux en Chine' [Ten Times More Newspapers in China], FIEJ Newsletter, No. 4, March 1997, p. 4.

Chapter 9
News agencies

Newspapers everywhere are dependent upon the wire services that in addition to countless dispatches provide them with current event overviews or reports from correspondents in the field. Even in the satellite age, the written press and televised news bulletins cannot by themselves provide their public with a complete account of the national and international news every day without the help of news agencies which disseminate thousands of wires twenty-four hours a day, often in several languages. The wire services that have the greatest coverage worldwide are the Associated Press (United States), Reuters (United Kingdom) and the Agence France Presse (AFP) (France).

The Associated Press agency is a pool of close to 1,500 American newspapers as well as thousands of radio and television stations. The Agence France Presse, on the other hand, is the oldest of the worldwide news agencies. It has a much narrower domestic market than the American agencies and has to contend with serious financial problems: more than three-quarters of the agency's sales are generated in France, in particular through subscriptions from ministries and government offices that represent 50 per cent of its revenue. While this form of economic dependence might raise a few queries about the editorial freedom of the agency, many press observers recognize the agency's reputation for quality and professional reliability.

Reuters is the world leader in news, with 260 bureaux through the world, capable of real-time transmission of texts, data, video and computer graphics. It comprises 1,600 journalists, photographers and camera-operators who can be mobilized at any given time. It was the first wire service to recognize the necessity of diversification in order to avoid its disappearance from the press scene. Reuters has succeeded in its strategy, since more than 90 per cent of its revenue is generated by diversification products, ranging from the foreign exchange market to that of shipping via the stock market. In all, the group

Agence France Presse (AFP) is the oldest of all major world news agencies, and one of the largest, together with the Associated Press (United States) and Reuters (United Kingdom).
Source: Attias/Sipa

employs a staff of 10,000, and in 1995 had a sales figure of £2,309 million. Listed since 1984 on the London and New York stock exchanges, Reuters Holding PLC is controlled by a pool of British and other press groups guaranteeing its editorial and financial independence. The pool has a right of veto against any decision endangering 'the gathering and dissemination of news and information, the principles of independence, freedom and integrity'.[1]

The three major agencies have a singular role in the international circulation of news. On their own, they process and disseminate more than 80 per cent of the international information that is broadcast every day around the world. Their services are vital for the major as well as the small-scale dailies, from the powerful television networks down to local radio stations.

Obviously there are other agencies in the world. Some can claim the rank of international agencies,

such as the Russian agency Itar-Tass, the Japanese agency Kyodo, the Chinese agency Xinhua, the German agency DPA or the Spanish agency EFE; others have purely regional scope and status, such as PANA, the Pan-African News Agency, or the Caribbean News Agency, CANA. Finally, most of the other agencies are limited to national scope and pick up the wires from the major agencies for their coverage of international affairs.

News agencies find it increasingly difficult to cover the costs of journalist networks installed all around the world with the revenue from subscriptions paid by the media. As a result, the agencies must continually innovate to reduce their costs and diversify their products and customer base.

1. 'Reuters: la Rolls de l'info' [Reuters: The Rolls Royce of the News World], *Le Nouvel Observateur* (Paris), 3–9 August 1995, pp. 4a ff.

Financial news agencies

In recent years, the major traditional agencies, together with a few newcomers, have specialized in the money markets, which are considered to be more lucrative. From the 1960s onwards, Reuters was the first to have the idea of diversifying its products by launching a financial and business news 'wire' service. It was an astute move, since by 1995 sales of news to the media represented no more than 5.5 per cent of the agency's turnover. The highest revenue comes from the 600,000 computer terminals installed in 149 countries which subscribe to the highest-density financial wire service in the world. Since the 1980s, however, Reuters no longer holds the monopoly of the financial news market. Newcomer, specialized agencies such as Bloomberg TV, the American television network CNBC and the Dow Jones group (with the Wall Street Journal and the AP-DOW Jones agency) together with European Business News (EBN), have also launched services targeting the financial news market. In 1995, Agence France Press set up the French version of Bloomberg Television (Bloomberg TV). In 1996, the global market for financial news stood at some $5 billion, a huge market which has prompted some agencies to extend this lucrative sector to include the televised news market.

Televised news agencies

In addition to the supply of texts, photographs, data and graphics, some agencies have also launched into the gathering, processing and dissemination of current events pictures, mainly destined for television. With the development of the new channels transmitted by satellite, broadcasters no longer able to cover growing reporting costs have turned to the services provided by the major agencies. Even the leading television channels such as the American networks or the BBC, who take pride in their traditional rigour in news reporting, call on agencies for video coverage of international current events.

Bureaux/correspondents for selected news agencies
Location of AP-TV, Reuters and WTN local bureaux/correspondents by region

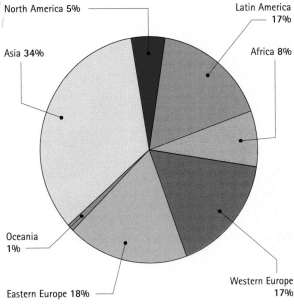

North America 5%
Latin America 17%
Africa 8%
Asia 34%
Western Europe 17%
Oceania 1%
Eastern Europe 18%

Source: *Global News: A Two-way Street?*, New York, RAI/KPMG, 1996.

EFE

23 bureaux in Spain
137 cities covered in 102 countries

Source: http://www.efe.sp

AFP

165 correspondents in foreign countries
4 regional centres:
Paris, Washington, Hong Kong, Nicosia

Source: http://www.afp.com

ITAR-TASS

74 bureaux stations
in Russian Federation and CIS
62 bureaux in 59 countries

Source: http://www.itar-tass.com

XINHUA

30 bureaux in China
7,000 journalists in Chinese provinces
100 bureaux worldwide
4 regional offices
500 correspondents in other countries

Source: *Le Trimestre du Monde* (Paris), 2nd quarter, 1992.

The Caribbean News Agency (CANA) was set up with the assistance of UNESCO and Germany.
Source: UNESCO

Cabo-Press, the national news agency of Cape Verde, created with the assistance of UNESCO and the International Programme for the Development of Communication.
Source: D. Roger/UNESCO

For several decades, the sector has been dominated by Visnews and UPITN, later to become respectively Reuters Television (RTV) and Worldwide Television News (WTN), with as their majority shareholder the American network ABC. The development of new technology in video transmission and the growth in market demand for news have led some of the major television channels to set up their own news agency. The American network CNN has launched CNNI, which broadcasts news programmes and at the same time offers its services to other broadcasters around the world.

Televised news agencies over the last five years have had a real growth rate estimated at around 50 per cent, generating income of some $250 million.[2] With the advent of digital technology, the market should expand by a further 50 per cent over the next ten years. Henceforth, the major agencies are capable of transmitting video and audio information everywhere around the world and in real time, a technological revolution which will no doubt entail an increase in the worldwide picture flood.

2.   'The Changing Role of News Agencies', *Diffusion UER*, Autumn 1995.

United News of Bangladesh, the Bangladeshi independent news agency

As soon as it was established in January 1988, the independent agency United News of Bangladesh (UNB) launched a major programme to develop its national and international news-reporting network. The objective was to cover all Bangladesh's rural areas, to supply news to the principal regional newspapers and to expand coverage of international events. Today, the agency plays a key role on Bangladesh's pluralist press scene. Its central news service alone has a staff of thirty-seven, comprising nineteen editors and eighteen journalists, with a daily output of between sixty and sixty-five national news items. For international coverage, the United News of Bangladesh has its own correspondents based in London and New York, who produce on average between 150 and 170 news items a day. The regular work schedule is divided into three distinct six-hour shifts, starting at 8 a.m. and finishing at 2 a.m. the next morning.

Moreover, UNB is the only Bangladeshi news agency which boasts a fully computerized news service and which uses the latest transmission technologies. The computerized service has many advantages, not least the speed with which information can be received and dispatched. The network's aim is to process the information received from the main office and transmit it to the other regional offices.

UNB's other technological innovation has been to introduce and develop a news service in Bengali. Thanks to UNESCO support, this service will enable its subscribers to access publications issued in Dhaka in the vernacular. An Internet server in Bengali will also be developed in order to supply news to the media in the United Kingdom, the United States and other regions of the world.

The agency has introduced an up-to-date colour photo service which receives photographs via satellite from foreign news agencies such as Reuters and Agence France Presse. UNB's own photographic material is also published in the major Dhaka dailies.

In addition to these technological innovations, UNB has developed a network of partnerships with various news agencies such as Associated Press of America, American News Agency and other international agencies engaging in information exchange. The agency is a member of the Organization of Asia Pacific News Agencies (OANA), the Commonwealth Press Union (CPU), the Asian Mass Communication Research and Information Centre (AMIC) (Singapore) and AsiaNet (Sydney).

The United News of Bangladesh (UNB) is the first independent agency to develop, with UNESCO and IPDC help, a computerized service in the Bengali language.
Source: UNB

Chapter 10
Radio

The radio is the most widespread branch of the media on every continent: it is the cheapest and the easiest to access, permitting real-time communication with audiences wherever they may be. It is the branch whose use has become most commonplace, in particular in developing countries, on the one hand because of the relative marginality of television, which is still an urban feature, and on the other because of the difficulty for most of the population in gaining access to the written press. In addition, group listening provides radio with a wider audience and thus enhances the introduction of new social practices. Finally, the production of radio programmes does not require vast technical, financial or human resources.

The history of radio illustrates the wide variety of its uses for propaganda, political or utilitarian purposes. Its power is awesome when employed by dictatorships as a weapon of propaganda and hate-mongering. The example of the Mille Collines 'free' radio station in Rwanda is still fresh in all our minds. When radio is used as an instrument of government authority, its power is political. When used as a catalyst for development and preventive purposes, it can be utilitarian. Over and above these various uses, radio has always been a window onto the outside world, thereby playing a decisive role in the democratic process, a fact which many countries have recently recognized.

In the last few years, radio has considerably evolved around the world. In addition to public service radio and commercial stations, particularly in Latin America, there has been the development of a whole series of so-called community radio stations, enabling social groups to make their voices heard, including religious communities, universities, ethnic minorities, etc. They generally have a modest budget, and often manage to survive thanks to the unpaid work of their personnel and to voluntary contributions from their sponsors and listeners, as well as occasional revenue from advertising.

New radio environments

In Africa, radio is much more widespread than television or the written press, both of which continue to
be urban-concentrated media. The democratization
process that is taking place in a number of African
states has led to significant changes in the audiovisual
landscape throughout the continent. In countries such
as Benin, Burkina Faso, Guinea, Mali and Senegal, the
end of the monopoly of public radio-broadcasting has
resulted in the setting up of regulatory and legislative
bodies favourable to pluralism; despite a stated desire
for openness, however, there is strong resistance to
change, further exacerbated by administrative en-
tanglement. The rare attempts at setting up private or
commercial radio stations have found it difficult to
penetrate a radio market traditionally dominated by
the public sector. As a general rule, public authorities
control the whole process of frequency allocation and
give precedence to stations in the public sector, a
status quo which explains the infatuation of African
audiences with international radio stations. As a result,
the absence of pluralism on a local and national scale
in the long run can pose a threat to the cultural
identity of a country.

West Africa is the region which has the greatest
number of commercial radio stations, both specialized
and general-interest, such as Africa No. 1 in Gabon,
Horizon FM in Burkina Faso, Radio Multi Media and
Radio TSF in Cape Verde, Radio Jeune Afrique
Musique and Radio Nostalgie in the Côte d'Ivoire, and
Sud FM in Senegal. In English-speaking and Portuguese-speaking countries, except for Guinea-Bissau,
Namibia, Nigeria, South Africa, Uganda and Zambia,
broadcasting legislation does not provide for the
creation of private radio stations. In South Africa, the
radio environment adjusted to post-apartheid society
with the launching in 1997 of seven such stations run
by new operators from the native African business
community. Most African national or private stations
produce a large part of their programmes in English,
French or Portuguese. The trend was enhanced with
the appearance in 1992 of FM stations broadcasting
in the music and news format. Countries do exist,
however, such as Angola, Madagascar and the United
Republic of Tanzania, in which radio stations broadcast all their programmes in local languages. While
radio remains the only true form of mass media, FM
broadcasting reaches only certain capitals or large
cities. Just like cable television or digital radio, direct
satellite broadcasting for the moment lies beyond the
means of African countries, owing to the cost of the
requisite technical facilities.

In the United States, four companies dominate
the radio scene: CBS (Columbia Broadcasting System), NBC (National Broadcasting Company), ABC
(American Broadcasting Company), which are all part
of the same channel network system, and MBS
(Mutual Broadcasting System), which was set up by
a group of advertising agencies. The Networks form
a galaxy teeming with clusters of local television
channels and radio stations, most of which are geared
to regional and local audiences and generally
specialize in news and classical music programmes,
etc. Others broadcast for ethnic, linguistic or religious
minorities. There were 6,230 commercial stations in
1970, 8,099 in 1983 and more than 9,400 by 1990.
Most are affiliated to the Networks. Parallel to these,
educational radio stations originally set up on university campuses have given birth to a public service
radio network with a commercial-free status and
cultural scope, National Public Radio, which in 1996
included some 1,400 affiliated radio stations. The FCC
(Federal Communication Commission) is the American
broadcasting authority which controls and regulates
the market, as well as allocating frequencies and
issuing broadcasting licences in accordance with the
recommendations of the Communication Act of 1934.
In contrast with a downturn in revenue in 1995, the
radio industry saw a slight upswing of 6 per cent in
1996, in particular as a result of the buoyancy of radio
stations in the South and West of the United States.

Radio receivers per 1,000 inhabitants, 1994

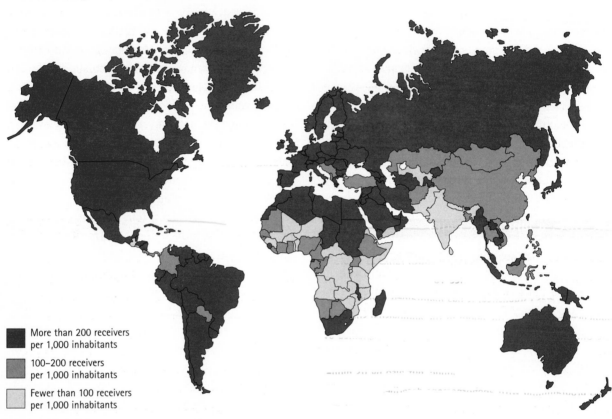

More than 200 receivers
per 1,000 inhabitants

100–200 receivers
per 1,000 inhabitants

Fewer than 100 receivers
per 1,000 inhabitants

Source: *UNESCO Statistical Yearkook 1996,* Paris, UNESCO, 1997.

In Europe, competition from television has been a contributing factor to the decline in radio audiences. In general, public service radios have resisted the downswing and maintained their ratings. In France, radio has a range of commercial and public service stations that completely cover the territory. Choice includes a panoply of news, practical advice, music and shows. Listener ratings are constantly rising for music and public service radio stations and grew from 20 per cent in 1992 to 23 per cent in 1996. In the same year, 95 per cent of the French population had at least one radio receiver.[1]

In Central and Eastern European countries, the upheavals resulting from the collapse of the Communist system have radically changed the radio landscape of the region. Since 1989 several commercial or international foreign radios have taken advantage of the twin process of democratization and liberalization to create their own station or to sign alliances with local radio stations broadcasting in the FM bandwidth. In general, these new stations supply the same type of programme: essentially popular music, financed by advertising, with short news-flashes. Their penetration strategy is also virtually identical: they seek out local partners in countries with the most open markets, supply the equipment, reinject part of the programmes broadcast by the parent

1.   'La radio atteint l'âge de la maturité' [Radio Comes of Age], *Le Monde* (Paris), 8 November 1996, p. 32.

station and train a local production crew. In terms of audience, radio stations with international scope and status do not have the same appeal that they had during the Cold War. They now lag behind commercial radio stations, which are seen to symbolize more accurately the Western way of life and the leisure culture. According to the specialists, these radio stations help introduce a market economy through their commercials.

In Poland, when the legislation on broadcasting came into effect in December 1992, more than a hundred radio stations were already broadcasting illegally. On the other hand, several private stations and some forty radio stations belonging to the Catholic Church were broadcasting general-interest and religious programmes on a temporary authorization basis. In 1993, the National Broadcasting Council, the regulatory authority in charge of broadcasting, granted licences to three national radios: Radio Zet (Warsaw), Radio RFM FM (Krakow) and Radio

The BBC, a landmark radio

The British Broadcasting Corporation (BBC) ranks as a role model in the world of radio. Since 1927, when the corporation was established, it has maintained a high audience level despite the boom in the audiovisual supply in the United Kingdom. Its listener loyalty may be explained by the quality of the services it provides, addressing every single sector of a wide-ranging public, but also by its high-class programming with anchorpersons described as a 'unique breed who combine popularity with excellence'.[1] The reputation of the BBC is also based on a news service which abides by the rules of accuracy and impartiality, and has become an international byword.

In this area, the five national stations that comprise the BBC use their own network of correspondents in the United Kingdom and overseas, and on occasion that of the BBC World Service (the international service of the BBC). Funding for the radio is exclusively generated by the licence fee levied each year on owners of radio receivers. This allowance prohibits the BBC from resorting to any other form of financing. According to Sir Christopher Bland, Chairman of the BBC's Board of Governors in 1996, it ensures 'the quality, range and diversity of BBC programmes . . . and enables us to serve our licence-payers and enables us, sometimes, to step aside from the race for massive audiences'.[2]

The five stations mentioned above cover the whole of the national territory, including Northern Ireland, and comprise thirty-eight regional and local stations. Each is specialized, based on a segmentation of the population according to the main age-groups. Radio 1 addresses a young audience and mainly broadcasts modern music intersected with newsflashes. Radio 2 targets the 30-plus public with more varied musical programming and a strong news input. Radio 3 is a cultural radio station which focuses on classical music and drama. Its audience is smaller, estimated at less than 2 per cent of the market, but extremely loyal. Radio 4 is a station dedicated to political and cultural debate, most often broadcast live. Radio 5 Live is the BBC's latest national radio channel, having replaced Radio 5 in 1994. It broadcasts sporting news and information twenty-four hours a day on medium wave. In 1997 it reached an audience of 5.53 million listeners. This noteworthy improvement is largely due to the station's menu of non-stop news and sport (soccer and rugby). The BBC entered the digital age in 1995, when it set up a series of ambitious Digital Audio Broadcasting (DAB) projects for every programme on all five national stations.

1.   'Preparing for Tomorrow', *EBU Diffusion*, Autumn 1996, p. 45.
2.   Sir Christopher Bland, President of the BBC, 'Meeting the Challenges', *EBU Diffusion*, Autumn 1996, p. 6.

Religieuse Maryja. Radio Zet is a success story. It broadcasts its programmes via satellite throughout the whole of the territory and is relayed by twenty-five local affiliates. It also broadcasts to the Ukraine, Bulgaria and Belarus.[2]

In Hungary, until the legislation on broadcasting was adopted, frequency allocation was decided on the basis of a moratorium promulgated in July 1989 by the last Communist government, which was upheld by the new government and endorsed by the Hungarian Parliament. A number of radio stations such as the Anglo-Hungarian station Calypso, the American-Hungarian station Bridge, and the commercial Radio Danubius were set up as early as 1989. The pirate radio Tilos, launched in Budapest in 1991, still continues to broadcast under the name of Piros Radio. Legislation on frequency allocation was not adopted by the Hungarian Parliament until 1993, thereafter providing the legal basis for the allocation of frequencies to private broadcasters.

Technological change and audience fragmentation

Radio broadcasting is not immune to technological upheaval, and the current situation is teeming with developments. In terms of the progress that has been made, worth mentioning are multiplexing, the miniaturization of receivers, the diversification of power supplies, frequency modulation and the considerable improvement in quality of reception. All these advances have made radio more mobile, more convivial and less expensive. Thanks to the transistor, it has become a part of society and has spread everywhere, even into cars, with radio systems that today include their competitive counterparts: audio cassette or compact disc (CD) players. Adaptation to digital technology by professional audio broadcasting studios and systems such as the digital stereophonic sound system NICAM, and above all the digital Radio Data System (RDS), have transformed radio listening. The RDS service, developed during the 1980s, is now operational in several countries. It enables auxiliary signals to be simulcast in stereo with the main programme, before being decoded by integrated circuits in a standard receiver. The latter decodes the identification signal of the transmitter and of the programme as well as traffic news for motorists. It can also display the name of a station in unencrypted form and steadily track the optimum transmitter, which means drivers can stay tuned to a given programme no matter where the vehicle goes. Despite this progress, direct broadcasting of programmes to the public hitherto has been based on the traditional techniques of amplitude modulation, developed at the turn of the century, and of frequency modulation introduced during the 1950s. The new digital system called Digital Audio Broadcasting (DAB) can overcome this handicap by digitizing the audio signal from end to end. This means digital broadcasting is going to do away with the idea of a frequency linked to a station.

These various technological upheavals are going to disrupt radio listening and ergonomics completely by expanding its horizons. Radio will be able to take into account the full range of listeners' tastes and centres of interest. Stations are already specializing, leading to the development of highly distinct broadcasting formats, with audiences segmented in terms of listening formats. Each station opts for a particular style and 'sound', for example by becoming a theme radio exclusively dedicated to the news, such as France Info, which has one of the highest audience growth rates in France, or to classical music, such as the Europe-wide radio station Classic FM. The concept of specialization, which originated in the United States, has gradually been adopted everywhere around the world, since it corresponds to listeners' tastes and expectations in general, particularly those of adolescents.

2. K. Jakubowicz, 'New Media Structures in Poland', *Bulletin of the European Institute of the Media* (Berlin), March 1993, p. 15.

Apart from this new trend, radio is continuing to decentralize with the emergence of local, community and regional radio stations. With low-power transmitters, radio is present in even the remotest of regions with small stations which are both localized and specialized, meaning people everywhere now have a mouthpiece and feel they can play a direct role as citizens. Radio in this sense has replaced the telephone or telegraph. The trend towards free speech has taken on a different dimension in the United States with the 'newstalk' style of broadcasting, based on dialogue with listeners, non-stop twenty-four hours a day, without any music or radio programme as such. Limited until recently to the United States where there are 1,200 phone-in radio stations of this type, the trend is now spreading to Europe, where it has attracted the interest of the major operators.[3]

This diversification of the radio environment will expand even further with the use of satellites as relay stations. Broadcasters are increasingly using satellite transmission for both national and international audiences. Operators use either ancillary frequencies on a transmitter whose main user is a television channel, or digital audio channels available on the satellite. Finally, the 'birds' can also broadcast digital programming streams. Most countries open to cable-TV operators already use these services.

The broadcasts in question are programme packages on various formats transmitted with compact disc quality, with neither commercials nor commentary in between. In Europe, the digital radio of the Astra satellite provides more than twenty-five free-to-air radio programmes, as well as a stream of programmes called Digital Music Express (DMX) which offers subscribers a line-up of more than sixty digital audio theme channels. It is estimated that more than 100,000 listeners in the United Kingdom and Ireland in 1996 replied to the new offer. Listeners can choose the channel of their choice from a stream of programmes. Displayed on their radio or television set they can see the name of the station, the title of the song and the name of the artist that they are listening to. They will also be able to order news broadcasts by teletext on the stock exchange, with sound recorded direct from the stock market itself, which means professionals can stay tuned to the ups and downs of their stocks and shares in real time. Here we step out of the conventional limits of radio broadcasting and into the upmarket realm of the provision of pay services. The frontier becomes blurred, even uncertain, between radio broadcasting in the classic sense of the term and new, specialized, satellite-based pay radio services.[4]

Digital Audio Broadcasting (DAB)

DAB is the acronym for a system of digital audio broadcasting which has the advantage of being particularly convenient for overcoming transmission interference problems. DAB consists in combining a series of services into a frequency band called a base group. Unlike analog radio, in which each programme corresponds to a single frequency, the DAB system combines several programmes or services in one frequency division, or 'carrier'. This enables a multiplex bit stream to be created in which services of all shapes and sizes can be transmitted. A carrier bandwidth of approximately 15 MHz can contain up to five stereophonic programmes simulcast with additional data.

This spectacular improvement in transmission capacity has been made possible as a result of two major innovations: Musicam compression and Coded Orthogonal Frequenced Dated Multiplexing (COFDM). The first reduces by a factor of eight the space

3.   'Cause toujours!' [Jabber away], *Le Monde* (Paris), Multimedia Supplement, 8–14 April 1996, p. 32.
4.   On the subject of satellite broadcasting, see 'Vers la radio numérique par satellite' [Towards Digital Radio by Satellite], *Science et vie high-tech*, No. 17, 1996, p. 32; 'Un nouveau satellite Astra en commande' [A New Astra Satellite on Order], *Le bulletin de l'IEC* (Berlin), March 1995, p. 22; 'Satellite Radio Broadcasting', *Bulletin of the European Institute for the Media*, Vol. 10, No. 2, 1994.

The management of Hertzian frequencies

Hertzian radio broadcasting consists in transmitting information by means of electromagnetic waves. These waves are propagated in the atmosphere, in space and even in solid bodies, without being either seen or heard. Their speed of propagation is the speed of light, that is, 300,000 km/s. However, if the waves did not have different lengths or frequencies they would mingle together and listening to the radio would be impossible. Accordingly, each of the carrier waves of a transmitter is allocated a frequency which serves as a sort of technical identity tag.

Radio broadcasting uses four frequency bands in the electromagnetic wave spectrum, and two transmission modes. The kilometric band (long waves), the hectometric band (medium waves) and the decametric band (short waves) all make use of the amplitude modulation technique (AM). Sound, transformed into an electrical signal, is superimposed onto the carrier wave in the form of a variation in amplitude. The advantage of amplitude modulation is that it allows such waves to be propagated over a very long distance. Travelling over the earth's surface, long waves (150 kHz to 280 kHz) cover over 1,000 kilometres before fading out, medium waves (525 kHz to 1,600 kHz) cover several hundred kilometres, while short waves (6 MHz to 25 MHz) are propagated over very long distances. Limited by the curvature of the terrestrial globe, these waves are reflected on the ionosphere and can thus travel round the world. AM waves, on the other hand, can very easily be disturbed by interference, and cannot as a result be used for stereophonic broadcasting. Hence the recourse to the fourth frequency band, frequency modulation (FM) (metric waves, 87.5 MHz to 108 MHz). In this case, it is the frequency of

the radio signal that is modulated. The amplitude of the carrier wave remains unchanged, the frequency variations serving to carry the signal. The great advantage of frequency modulation is the quality with which sound is reproduced. However, the drawback of FM lies in its limited range, since the waves are propagated in a straight line and collide with the various natural obstacles in their way, reducing their effective radius by the same amount.

The demand for Hertzian space is growing and will continue to grow, keeping pace with the increasing desire of everyone to be kept constantly informed. The frequency spectrum is thus becoming a rare and much sought-after natural resource. The frequency bands available for sound broadcasting are rapidly becoming saturated. However, sound broadcasting today no longer represents the main use to which Hertzian space is put. The emergent technology of digital audio broadcasting (DAB) both permits a saving of the Hertzian resource and makes excellent compact-disc quality reception possible in virtually all situations.

Management of the frequencies allocated to radio broadcasting is undertaken in compliance with the rules established within the framework of the International Telecommunication Union (ITU). It is the International Frequency Registration Board (IFRB) that is responsible for registering and monitoring the application of frequency allocations within the radioelectrical frequency spectrum.

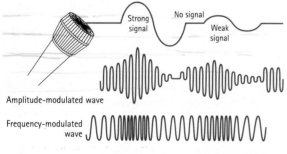

The microphone converts sounds into signals which are in turn modulated either by amplitude (height of wave) or by frequency (number of vibrations per second).
Source: G. Ponthieu, *La Radio*, Paris, CFPJ/Hachette, 1987.

The radio uses four frequency bands and two types of modulation

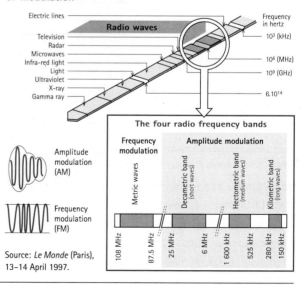

Source: *Le Monde* (Paris), 13–14 April 1997.

Satellite radio for Africa, Asia, the Caribbean and Latin America

A network of satellites scheduled to broadcast digital radio programmes to Africa, Asia, the Caribbean and Latin America is being put into operation by the WorldSpace Inc. company before the end of 1999. The system, which is being constructed by the French firm Alcatel, will reach more than 4 billion persons in developing countries. The operation has been granted licences to use its satellites in the regions concerned. The broadcasting system differs from the Digital Audio Broadcasting (DAB) standard which is regarded as being too costly for populations with fairly poor financial means. The particular technology chosen should place digital radio receivers within the reach of the general public in the fairly short term. Four major groups in the Japanese electronics industry have already been selected to develop and manufacture the new WorldSpace receivers. The company plans to sell about 100 million units in the space of ten to fifteen years. A rate of a million units a year should be achieved within six months of their being put on the market, in theory at the end of 1998. Each WorldSpace network satellite will have three beams with 200 channels each, thereby enabling listeners to receive about a hundred channels. The company has raised $850 million among interested shareholders since it was set up in 1990, has already signed draft contracts with Voice of America and Radio Nederland and is currently negociating with CNN, the BBC and RFI. National radio stations in the target regions too will be associated with this project. Finally, part of the satellites' broadcasting potential will be reserved for educational programmes to be conducted by a foundation being set up by WorldSpace.[1]

1.   'Des radios par satellite pour les pays en voie de développement' [Satellite Radios for Developing Countries], *Ecran total* (Paris), No. 102, 1995; 'WorldSpace va diffuser 100 chaînes de radio numérique sur l'Afrique' [WorldSpace to Transmit 100 Digital Radio Channels to Africa], *Le Monde* (Paris), 29 May 1997, p. 35.

DAB around the world

The first DAB services in the world were launched in September 1995 by the BBC in the United Kingdom and by the Swedish Broadcasting Company in Sweden. Some countries have already tested the system, while an increasing number of others are preparing the same tests in order to promote and develop the system and to transform its technological appeal into viable economic and social use.

The Danish Radio Broadcasting Authorities began trials with digital audio broadcasting from September 1996 onwards.[1] The regulatory authority in France, the Conseil Supérieur de l'Audio-visuel (CSA), in July 1996 launched an invitation for tenders to test digital radio services in Paris and in the Île-de-France region over a period of five years. In Germany the national platform set up in 1991 has scheduled the implementation of pilot schemes in several *Länder*, as well as the testing and launch of regular DAB services before the 1997 IFA (International Funkausstellung) Trade Fair in Berlin, and virtually complete coverage of Germany by the year 2000. In Hungary, the DAB group which started work in 1992 began trial DAB broadcasts in 1995 with a single transmitter in Budapest, and has scheduled the start-up of a DAB service for 1997.[2]

In Canada, the first experiments with the DAB system were carried out in 1990. The purpose of the Digital Radio Research Inc. (DRRI) set up in 1993 was to co-ordinate the tests and promote the system. The new transmitters serving Ottawa and Vancouver which went on the air in 1995 have raised DAB coverage to 35 per cent of the Canadian population. In the United States, a number of mobile demonstrations of digital radio were organized in 1991. Several companies are jostling for position on the DAB market, all of them intending to provide CD-quality radios to the 190 million users of vehicles registered in the United States. According to recent market surveys, Americans spend 97 per cent of their in-car time listening to the radio.[3]

In China, terrestrial broadcasting experiments were undertaken in December 1995 in collaboration with the European Commission and the German DAB platform. In India, the All India Radio (AIR) has pooled the main players involved in DAB and drawn up a timetable for the permanent establishment of the system, scheduled for 2003. Finally, tests were carried out in Mexico City in 1993, and again via the Solidaridad 2 satellite in 1995.

1. 'Satellite Radiobroadcasting', *Bulletin of the European Institute for the Media* (Berlin), Vol. 10, No. 2, 1994.
2. 'Digital Audio Broadcasting Tests in Hungary', *InfoRadio, ITU News* (Geneva) No. 4, 1996, p. 21.
3. 'Radio Networks Moving to Digital', *Broadcasting & Cable*, 5 February 1996, p. 64; 'DAB in the USA: Digital Dream or Dead Air?', *International Broadcasting*, Vol. 18, No. 3, 1995, p. 36.

occupied by a digital sound signal. In audio terms the result obtained is equal to the quality of a compact disc with a throughput of 100 Kbit/s, i.e. the volume of a conventional radio channel. The second innovation, COFDM, is a broadcasting technique which consists in organizing the digital signal into several redundant data packets. The main advantage is excellent resistance to interference, echo and other forms of disturbance. The system was standardized at the European level in 1994 as part of the 'Eureka 147' project, and is now recognized worldwide further to its adoption by the working groups of the ITU-R (formerly the International Radio Consultative Committee/CCIR) as the common global standard for digital radio.[5]

5. The International Telecommunication Union (ITU) is responsible for establishing a single DAB standard worldwide. The union studies technical developments in the field of broadcasting and specifies the technical standards for radio and television broadcasting systems around the world.

DAB has several advantages in relation to analog broadcasting: perfect sound quality free of any interference, capable of serving a mobile audience, and the use of transmitters ten times less powerful than those used by FM equipment, thereby reducing the overcrowding of radio frequency bandwidths by half.

The DAB system is currently being tested almost everywhere in the world, from Denmark to Mexico to China. It is also the focus for industrial wars, since setting it up entails the renewal of the existing installed base of radios. The stakes are therefore very high. The fact is worth underlining, however, that the introduction of digital technology presupposes heavy financial investment, in terms of transmission equipment, the development of new receivers or decoders, and the subsequent launching and production of new programmes. In addition, digital broadcasting technology is not an end in itself. Manufacturers cannot sell large quantities of DAB receivers and other related equipment unless there are interesting, innovative programmes available. Just as other new techniques have had to work their way up on a trial and error basis before being accepted by the general public, DAB will have to undergo the same testing before penetrating the market. Priority, as always, must be given to listeners' needs and the genuine advantages provided by the technology. It is the public which accepts the technology and not vice-versa.[6]

International radio broadcasting

Internationalization is a long-standing facet of sound broadcasting which has most often been associated with the purposes of propaganda.[7] Nazi Germany and Fascist Italy made widespread use of radio to spread their respective ideologies. During the Second World War and the decades of the Cold War that followed, the use of radio for propaganda continued to play an important role, but with the sweeping geopolitical changes that took place at the end of the 1980s, the modes of communication between East and West,

North and South have become less antagonistic. The use of intervention, interference or jamming techniques inherited from the Cold War years have given way to co-operation and international agreements. International broadcasting is now part of the international flow of information and communication, and has become an important vector for the free circulation of information around the world.

At the same time, the democratization of political life in countries in transition has resulted in multiple standpoints on domestic information and news which are more representative of the citizens' manifold expectations, and the development has gradually resulted in a downswing in public interest for foreign broadcasts. The supranational dissemination of information by radio broadcasting seems to have lost its strategic character, in particular in the countries of Central and Eastern Europe.[8] In addition, with economic recessions and budgetary restrictions, there has been a downturn in hourly listening volume. Based on all the radio stations around the world, the airtime for international sound broadcasting dropped from some 16,000 hours per week in 1988 to approximately 12,000 in 1995. On the other hand, the number

6.   P. Dambacher. 'Digital Broadcasting', *IEE Telecommunications*, Series 34, Stevenage (United Kingdom), Institution of Electrical Engineers, 1996; F. Kozamernik, 'Digital Audio Broadcasting – Radio Now and for the Future', *EBU Technical Review* (Geneva), Autumn 1995, p. 2; P. Levrier, 'Le DAB, radio du futur ?' [DAB, Radio for the Future?], *Communication et langage* (Paris), No. 100/101, 1994, p. 48.

7.   J. Wood, *History of International Broadcasting*, London, Deregrinus Ltd, 1992; J. Hale, *Radio Power: Propaganda and International Broadcasting*, London, Paul Elek, 1975.

8.   J. Semlin, 'Déclin et renaissance des radios orientales à l'Est' [Decline and Rebirth of Eastern Radios in the East], *Médiaspouvoirs* (Paris), No. 26, 1992, p. 142; J. Semlin, 'Les radios orientales comme vecteur d'ouverture à l'Est' [Contribution for Eastern Radios to the Opening up of the East], *Réseaux*, No. 53, 1992, p. 9.

of countries with radio stations broadcasting beyond their borders has considerably increased over the course of the last few decades. Similarly, there has been a strong rise in the number of transmitters, from 1,666 in 1986 to 5,000 in 1995.[9] While the leaders in radio broadcasting (the Voice of America, the BBC and Radio France Internationale) regularly reach audiences estimated at between 100 and 130 million listeners, other more modest stations such as Radio Canada, Radio Cairo and Radio Suisse Internationale are picked up by between 5 and 20 million regular listeners.

Major changes and their effects on broadcasting

Big geopolitical upheavals, media internationalization, the increasing emergence of private radio stations and the various democratization processes through which countries in general are going have together produced a number of major changes in the field of international radio broadcasting. The first concerns the form of the media itself. The standard definition limiting supra-national broadcasting to very short wavelengths now seems obsolete. Since the end of the 1980s, several radio stations have started using new technology, in particular that of direct satellite broadcasting, with programme reception by dish antennae or by terrestrial stations with local frequency modulator relays. Many radios such as the BBC, RFI, Radio Pays Bas Internationale, Radio Vatican and Radio Suisse Internationale have obtained authorizations from African, Latin American and Central European countries to broadcast their programmes on domestic airwaves and on the FM band. The BBC was quickest off the mark in obtaining the authorization to rebroadcast its programmes on national or local airwaves in several countries, including Bulgaria, the Czech Republic, Hungary, Poland and the Russian Federation, as well as in a number of African countries. Meanwhile, the Voice of America has succeeded in having part of its broadcasts syndicated in Poland and Bulgaria, and has set up Radio Bridge, a station targeting business people in Hungary. As for RFI, in 1991 it obtained permission to broadcast its Polish programme over the city of Poznań and that of its world service in French on an FM frequency in Sofia. Through broadcasting licences, most of these radios also provide a 'satellite slot service' enabling local stations to pick up and then rebroadcast a part or all of their programmes.

The second change relates to message content. International radio stations are redeploying their strategy, modifying the content of their programmes and changing the tone of their speech. The content, occasionally political, even ideological, of some broadcasts has given way to more general-interest programming, reflecting an aim to be diplomatically and culturally present on the international scene. The new formats contain more programmes focusing on news, magazines and music.[10] In general, the scale and scope of an international radio service are proportional to the political and economic power of its country of origin and to the role that the latter plays in the world. China, France, the Russian Federation, the United Kingdom and the United States have almost continuously been the main broadcasters since the 1960s. In the United States, VOA is the main service operating out of North America. It broadcasts 1,035 hours of programmes all around the globe every week, and in forty-four languages. It is administered by the 'United States Information Agency' and financed by the United States Government. Despite budgetary restrictions imposed by the American administration, VOA is still at the top of international broadcasting, with major resources and infrastructures. During the Cold

9.   According to J. M. Salient, *Passeport pour les médias de demain* [Passport for Tomorrow's Media], Lille, Presses Universitaires de Lille, 1995.

10.   In 1992, 60 per cent of VOA programmes were news, 26 per cent were on-location reports and magazines, 10 per cent were music and 4 per cent miscellaneous. Cited by R. I. Dalage, 'Les radios internationales sont-elles dépassées?' [Has International Radio Outlived its Usefulness?], *Le Trimestre du Monde* (Paris), 2nd Quarter 1992, p. 90.

International radio: estimated total programme hours per week of some external radio broadcasters, 1995

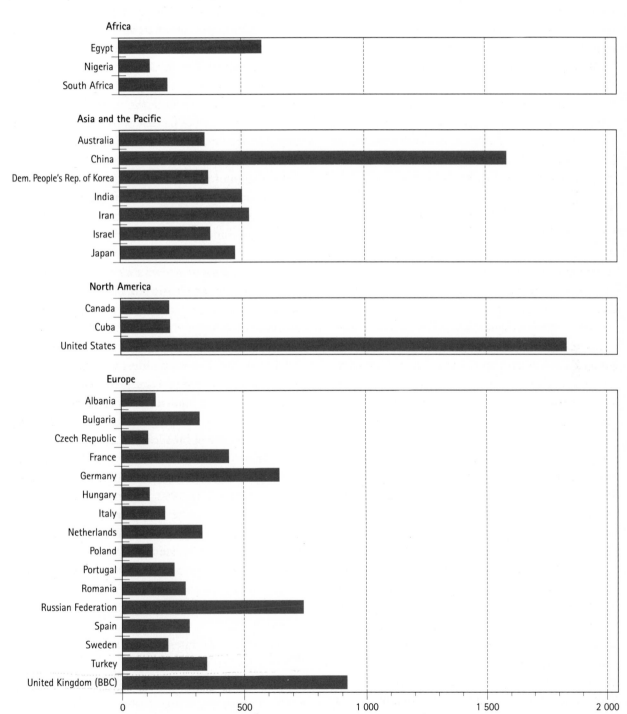

Source: *World Radio and TV Handbook*, Amsterdam, Billboard Books, 1996.

War, VOA focused on developing its broadcasts to the old Communist regimes in the local languages. Nowadays, it is attempting to adapt to the status quo in the international communication market by highlighting its supranational television network Worldnet.[11]

In the United Kingdom, the BBC World Service of the British public broadcasting authority began to transmit on short wave from 1927 onwards for the then British Empire. With an exceptional growth rate, the BBC rapidly gained international status and an image for professionalism and rigour. In 1992, it was broadcasting in thirty-eight languages to one of the largest regular audiences in the world, estimated at more than 130 million listeners. Like VOA, it broadcasts its programmes on the FM band via the 'Intelsat' satellite to a considerable number of countries around the world.

Radio France Internationale first went on the air on 6 January 1975, with as its main objective the broadcasting of daily programmes to French-speaking countries. By 1996, it had gained a new market share and widened its audience, currently estimated at some 30 million listeners. It broadcasts all around the world, with twenty-four-hour non-stop news, music and magazine programmes in French but also in English, Chinese, Portuguese, Vietnamese, etc. Thanks to satellite broadcasting, RFI multiplies its FM radio relays on the medium wavelength and via cable networks to complete its shortwave set-up. In 1997, RFI will be providing its listeners with the first all-digital international radio station, specialized in non-stop news.

In Germany today, Deutsche Welle (DW) is one of the major international broadcasting corporations. In 1990, it ranked fourth worldwide with 568 hours of weekly programmes broadcast in thirty-four languages, to which should be added more than 253 hours of programmes broadcast each week by the DeutschLand Funk (DLF). This new station, which first went on the air in 1962, initially targeted German-speaking people in general, including those in the former RDA as well as in Eastern Europe. Since the reunification of Germany, the programmes of the former RDA radio station, Berlin International, have merged with those of the DW, enabling the German station to strengthen its international broadcasting position and to present a new image of Germany in terms of its cultural, economic and political life. In 1990, the audience of the DW was estimated at more than 100 million regular listeners worldwide.

In the Russian Federation, Radio Moscow, the old radio station of the former USSR, in December 1991 became the international broadcasting authority of the Commonwealth of Independent States (CIS). A former giant on the international broadcasting scene, Radio Moscow International in the 1990s saw its role diminished and its purpose revised owing to the difficulties in restructuring which it has had to face. Its world service in Russian was transferred to the radio of the Russian Federation and renamed the Voice of Russia. Since the break-up of the Soviet Union, the station has lost many of its transmitters which were located in the former Soviet Republics. It has also put an end to a number of international relays and has closed its offices abroad. As a result, weekly airtime dropped from 2,094 hours of broadcasting in 1980 to 1,317 in 1992. There was a similar downturn in the number of languages broadcast, which fell from eighty-eight in 1988 to forty-six in 1992. In terms of content, the trend is towards more infotainment and general-interest programming, with press reviews and news reports, music and promotional programmes on the diplomatic and cultural image of the Russian Federation, in a style more reminiscent of radios in the West than the political hardline of the former Radio Moscow.

In China, the international radio service Radio Beijing was initially developed to target the Asian market, but since the 1980s the station has been

---

11. For more on this subject, see Chapter 11.

broadcasting to countries everywhere. It currently transmits in forty-seven languages. The number of airtime hours per week rose from 1,412 in 1986 to 2,340 in 1995.

In Africa, many radio stations make use of international services. Most of the countries such as Angola, Congo, Côte d'Ivoire, Ghana and South Africa broadcast only a few hours per day or per week, and in a few languages. Nigeria is one of the rare countries on the African continent to have a large-scale international service. Radio Nigeria broadcasts some 322 hours per week in Arabic, English, French, Hausa and Swahili to the whole continent.

In the Arab world, most countries have their own international service broadcasting in foreign languages and Arabic. The leading radio in the region is still the Voice of Arabia, which broadcasts from Cairo. At the end of the 1970s, Saudi Arabia set up its own radio targeting the African and Muslim world. Finally, a large number of stations such as RMC Moyen Orient, Radio Méditerranée Internationale (Midi 1) and Africa No. 1 broadcast internationally without reflecting their governments' viewpoints in any official way. They generally operate on the lines of private radio stations specializing in the 'music and news' format and are financed by advertising.

Democratization in many countries has resulted in the appearance of local radio and television stations, but also in competition from international radio and television networks offering better listening conditions through their satellite coverage. It has led listeners around the world to be more demanding and to choose their stations in relation to quality of programmes and reception. New expectations such as these have encouraged radio broadcasters to innovate in the news sector. In September 1996, in France, Radio France Internationale (RFI) launched a non-stop news programme, broadcast by satellite on shortwave and FM. The BBC World Service has the same designs, and in 1997 intends to launch a current events programme available twenty-four hours a day, in order

UNESCO calling – the science and knowledge radio

UNESCO began to produce radio programmes in the late 1940s. The aim has always been to contribute to the understanding of the ideals that the Organization stands for, through discussion of issues in the fields of education, science, culture and communication. Around fifteen thirty-minute feature programmes are produced each year in English, Spanish or Russian. Their subjects, chosen on the basis of their interest for both UNESCO and the general public, cover a vast field ranging from AIDS to astronomy, from biodiversity to bioethics, from street children to indigenous peoples, from the violence of war to the culture of peace.

The programme catalogue contains hundreds of recordings which are offered on tape or cassette to over 400 national, public, private and community radios in all parts of the world (257 stations broadcasting in English, 60 in French, 60 in Spanish and 42 in Russian) as well as to international short-wave broadcasters. For the last two years, UNESCO Radio has been taking part in the Nexus-International Broadcasting Association Internet experiment of RealAudio on demand. All UNESCO programmes will shortly be available via the Nexus RealAudio server and will eventually be put on UNESCO's Internet site.[1]

---

1.   From 'UNESCO on the Air', *The UNESCO Courier* (Paris), February 1997, p. 39.

to keep abreast of the new habits and concerns of its listeners.

Community radio: novel approach, new audience

Community radio is usually considered complementary to traditional media operations and as a participatory model for media management and production. The term 'community' in this context is used in its geographical and sociological sense, designating the basic unit for horizontal social organization. Community radio stations are designed to encourage participation by a large representative sample of the various socio-economic levels, organizations and minority groups within a given community. The purpose of the stations is to facilitate the free flow of information by encouraging freedom of speech and by enhancing dialogue within the communities concerned in order to promote better participation by their populations. Since 1989, community radios have considerably developed further, thanks to technological innovations and advances in equipment, reductions in the cost of FM transmitters, slacker controls on broadcasting by public monopolies, progress in democracy and the emergence of new private and associative market players.

Community radio is present in every single region around the world. The scale and impact of experiments in this medium vary considerably from region to region. They may last for two months, or extend over one or more generations. Some are totally isolated experiments; others are closely linked to networks at national, regional or international levels, combining conferences, publications or centres of interest or activities. A whole range of experiments in community radio has taken place; some have brought together peoples within the same ethnic group, such as the Hill Tribes Radio in Chiengmai in Thailand, or members of the same industrial group such as the miners in Bolivia, or people from the same village, as in Appam or Dormaa Ahengkro in Ghana,

or the 3,000 inhabitants of a small island like Radio Sunshine in Niue in the Pacific. On other occasions they are backed by denominational organizations such as the World Association for Christian Communication, the World Council of Churches, the Lutheran World Foundation or the International Catholic Association for Radio and Television (UNDA), by NGOs, or by political parties or by development bodies.

Most community radio stations belong principally to the World Association of Community Radio Broadcasting (AMARC) and the International Association of Broadcasting (IAB). The first is a non-profit-making, non-governmental organization, designed to support and serve community radio around the world. It comprises more than 2,000 members on all five continents. As an international solidarity network, AMARC supports the development of community radio by encouraging co-operation and exchange among its members, democratizing radio through national and international action, promoting community radio movements, defending and representing the interests of its members at the international level and providing them with various services. The second was founded in Mexico in 1946 under the name of the Inter-American Association of Broadcasters (IAAB). It received its present title in 1985. The International Association of Broadcasting defends both radio and television broadcasting that conforms to international technological and regulatory standards. In this regard it has been unfailingly critical of illegal community radios and the interference they cause. IAB also militates in favour of broadcasting as a means of freely expressing thought, besides promoting co-operation between broadcasters – public or private, and national and international agencies.

Africa

On the African continent, where more than half the population is illiterate, the educational function of the media is vital. Not only can it contribute to the emergence of a democratic culture, but it can also help prevent the decline in the standard of living and combat poverty with its various consequences such as malnutrition, disease and illiteracy. The end of the state monopoly on broadcasting in a number of African countries has spurred the emergence of community radio. In general, all these stations have started up as a result of drives to decentralize which have benefited regions and rural localities. They also represent a new approach to radio, based on the idea of listener participation in some form or other. Some depend on the broadcasting facilities of public service authorities, with the concomitant risk of undermining their editorial freedom. They are usually operated and directed by one or two salaried staff, in tandem with freelance journalists and voluntary helpers.[12] In order to gain recognition from the public authorities, most local radios have set up regional networks and created associations.

In 1995, in West Africa, there were approximately a hundred local, rural, public service or private radio stations.[13] Most are to be found in rural areas or smaller towns. This is particularly predominant in the countries of Burkina Faso and Mali, which had respectively ten and twenty-one community radios in rural regions (compared with commercial radio stations, which are usually installed in the capitals). In 1991 in Ghana, with the assistance of UNESCO, the Appam community launched a community radio mainly designed to inform the population about health and hygiene issues. A second experiment was launched in 1993 in Dormaa Ahengkro. A similar experiment took place in 1993 in Guinea-Bissau with the start-up of Radio Quele, whose basic purpose was to help combat a cholera epidemic. In Mali, a country well-known for its energetic radio development since the freedom of the press was instituted in 1991, local radios form a part of that development while enhancing participation by communities in the planning and compèring of programmes. Radio Kayes, for instance, broadcasts, in local languages, programmes planned together with independent farmers'

Rural radio in Senegal, a project developed by UNESCO in 1969.
Source: Decker/UNESCO

12.   For further details on this subject, see the contribution of the FAO to the overview of the report *Development of Rural Radio in Africa,* p. 6, International Workshop, Ouagadougou, Burkina Faso, 10–14 June 1996.

13.   'Répertoire des radios privées et locales en Afrique de l'Ouest' [Index of Private and Local Radio Stations in West Africa], Institut Panos, ACCT, August 1995; Institut PANOS/UJAO, 'Presse Francophone d'Afrique Noire vers le pluralisme' [French-language Press in Black Africa Moves towards Pluralism], Paris, L'Harmattan, 1991; Institut PANOS/UJAO, *Le pluralisme radiophonique en Afrique de l'Ouest* [Radio Pluralism in West Africa], Vol. 2, Paris, L'Harmattan, 1993.

associations from the region. Other radio stations such as Bamakan Kayira, Douentza, Bankass, Klédu and Kéné FM all take part in group projects whose aim is the socio-economic transformation of the media landscape and the promotion of education and culture. It is in Mali that the first all-women's radio station was set up. The latter, broadcasting from the suburbs of Bamako (Magnambougou), produces programmes jointly with the listeners' club and women's association.[14]

Similar efforts have been made in Burkina Faso, where the local radio stations together dedicate 40 per cent of their airtime to news, 35 per cent to education and to training and 25 per cent to cultural and recreational programmes. The result is that, in addition to their own programmes, radio stations such as Diapaga, Vive le Paysan, Djibasso or Palabre help to promote health campaigns, women's conferences or training for small-scale farmers. The latest of the community radios, La Voix du Paysan, broadcasting from Ouahigouya in Yatenga Province, went on-air on 19 April 1996. It describes itself as 'a support tool for the construction of democracy and the struggle against desertification and for the eradication of hunger'. The first private radio station in Guinea-Bissau, Galaxia de Pindjiquiti, which went on-air in July 1995, broadcasts programmes focusing on development issues in Creole, Portuguese, Sousso and Wolof. In the same year on the island of Bubaque in the south of the country, a rural radio station run by a non-governmental organization was set up as part of a biosphere reserve project. Finally, in 1992, rural radio stations were set up in the four regions of Guinea (Kankan, Kindia, Labé and N'Zérékoré) with technical backing from Swiss co-operation schemes and enthusiastic support from the local people, who have direct input to programme production.[15]

In South Africa, the political changes which have taken place have given greater scope to independent and community radio, inspired by the National Community Radio Forum of South Africa (NCRF). The

organization recently won an award from the World of Community Radio Broadcasting Association (AMARC), highlighting its major role in the struggle against apartheid and the new battle that it now faces in the construction of a democratic South African society. The NCRF comprises thirty-three groups, all of which are currently setting up radio stations. Its aim is to promote community radio as a serious feature of the South African media environment.

In Kenya, the first Homa Bay community radio was launched in 1982 by UNESCO in partnership with the public radio Voice of Kenya (VOK). For two years, VOK technicians and Homa Bay community members worked together on health, literacy and local enterprise programmes. The radio station was closed down in 1984 for political reasons. In 1996, a new organization overseeing the community radio stations, entitled the Kenya Community Media Network (KCOMNET), was set up.[16] Finally, Radio Sud FM, the first private station in Senegal, went on the air in July 1994. Its aim is to combine commercial and community-style radio in its programmes. The same approach has been adopted in the Gambia with Radio One, an independent commercial station that broadcasts participatory programmes from the town of Banjul, during which listeners can phone in their opinions.

In Mozambique, Radio Pax, a private Catholic radio station that played a major role in the 1960s in the struggle for the country's independence, resumed

---

14. Information taken from 'Waves for Freedom', *AMARC Report on the Sixth World Conference of Community Radio Broadcasters, Dakar, Senegal, 23–29 January 1995*; 'Women's Station Hits the Airwaves', *InterRadio* (Montreal), Vol. 7, No. 2, 1995, p. 4.

15. 'Rural Radio in Africa', *Development of Rural Radio in Africa,* International Workshop, Ouagadougou, Burkina Faso, 10–14 June 1996.

16. 'Kenya: implantation des médias communautaires' [Kenya: Introduction of Community Media], *CLIPS 10* (Montreal), April 1996, p. 5.

broadcasting in 1994 following a break of several years. The station is now located in the region of Inhamizua. In spite of major technical difficulties, it has done a considerable amount of information-gathering on local traditions. It broadcasts programmes specially designed for women and the youth of the region. Other local radio station projects are on line in Chimoio, Maputo, Pemba and Qualimane.[16]

In order to clarify the role, position and social values of community radio in Africa, AMARC organized a pan-African conference on community radio in league with NCRF in May 1997. The meeting showed *inter alia* that there is a unanimous resolve on the part of the African participants to install communication that is non-governemental and non-commercial. Any further discussion will centre on documents and draft charters relating directly to the Declaration of Human Rights, grass-roots communication, and media independence.

Latin America and the Caribbean

In Latin America, the media network, which includes commercial radio and semi-public broadcasting, has favoured the emergence of many local radio stations. The number of community radio stations is particularly large: free radio stations in Brazil, community radio stations in Argentina, participatory radio stations in Nicaragua and popular radio stations in Ecuador and Peru,[17] to which should be added the private educational radios of the Catholic Church. Most of them have commercial licences, but many enjoy privileged status as cultural and educational stations.

The setting up of stations and the production of educational programmes requiring teaching and managerial staff are often financed by sponsorship, with assistance from international organizations, in particular from European foundations of a denominational character. In most cases, community radio stations are the result of the combined efforts of women's associations, farmers' organizations, political parties, unions or youth clubs.

Many small local radio stations have offset printing presses and publish printed documents to support their radio programmes. Some stations distribute audio cassettes and slides. Others work in conjunction with volunteer by-liners called *reporteros populares*,[18] who have grown up in areas which are either underprivileged or ignored by the mainstream media. They are trained in reporting techniques so that they can establish a link between their community and their radio station without any difficulty.

In Bolivia, the 'people's reporters' of local radio stations such as Yungas, Tarija or Don Bosco for the time first in their country's history have started to cover the activities specific to the small, remote villages that lie outside the scope of larger mass media. Focus on local news such as this encourages democratic, lateral communication and develops participation by the local population. Radio Bolivia Gabriel (La Paz), for instance, is visited by 50,000 Aymaras every year. Radio PIO XII involves miners and peasant farmers in the design and production of programmes. They record their musical compositions and take part in the production of radio series.

In the Dominican Republic, Radio Enriquillo is an example of an energetic community radio in the poor southern regions of the country. Since it first went on-air in 1977, it has become a recognized instrument for education and giving the public a voice.

In Peru, the Centro de Communicación Popular de Villa El Salvador near Lima has carried out

16. 'L'Église catholique et les radios locales en Afrique Australe' [The Catholic Church and Local Radios in Southern Africa], *Le Courrier* (Brussels), No. 158, July–August 1996, p. 50.
17. 'What is a Community Radio for a Latin-American?', *UNDA Informations* (Brussels), Vol. 20, No. 1, 1996, p. 4.
18. R. Huesca, 'Participation for Development in Radio: An Ethnography of the Reporteros Populares of Bolivia', *Gazette No. 57*, pp. 29–52, Amsterdam, Kluwer, 1996.

Huanuni, the miners' radio station in Bolivia.
Source: A. Jonquières/UNESCO

experiments, with UNESCO assistance, in the field of communication based on the use of the press, video and cartoons at community level. The cassette-based newsgroup set up in Uruguay and Venezuela by Mario Kaplun is another specifically Latin American form of a community communication system. The newsgroup serves as the link connecting people's organizations and also provides a means of communication with the managers of rural co-operative or farmers' unions. Finally, in March 1996, the AMARC and the Centro de Educación Popular (CEDEP) launched a radio news service entitled Púlsar, which will enable community radio stations in Latin America and the Caribbean to draw greater benefit from the wide-ranging possibilities of the Internet.[19]

Another example is the Latin American Association for Education by Radio (ALER), founded in 1972, which pools some sixty local educational radio stations that are operated in virtually every country in Latin America. Members of the ALER teach more than a million students registered with radio education courses and they reach 15 million others who follow the broadcasts of the 'Airwave University' on agricultural development, health and other subjects.

In the Caribbean, experiments with community radios are less frequent but equally encouraging.

Several are denominational in their outlook. The first community radio went on the air in August 1995, in Saint Vincent and the Grenadines. The project is co-ordinated by the NYC-SVG (for the National Youth Council of Saint Vincent and the Grenadines). The station broadcasts programmes twice a day, focusing on music and interviews with young people and villagers from the communities. In 1995, community radios were also launched in Barbados, Haiti and Jamaica with the assistance of UNESCO.

Asia and the Pacific

In the Philippines, parallel to the conventional radio stations (of which there are more than 500) and television networks (of which there are six nation-wide) covering most of the country, there are some thirty-five local radio stations headed by community groups, denominational associations and educational organizations.

The Network of Tambuli Community Radio, today comprising eight small community stations located in isolated regions, involves the local population in political, economic and cultural life. Set up and managed by local volunteers, the network is

19. 'Púlsar Radio Wire Service is Set to Go!', *AMARC Link* (Montreal), Vol. 1, No. 1, 1996, p. 2.

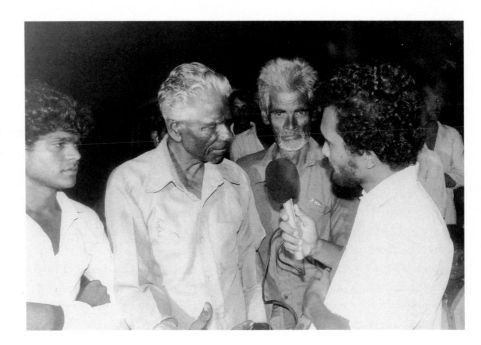

In Sri Lanka, a Mahaweli
community radio producer consults
farmers on problems of education,
irrigation and employment.
Source: C. A. Arnaldo/UNESCO

financed by the Danish International Development
Agency (DANIDA) via the International Programme
for the Development of Communication (IPDC) and
UNESCO. With basic technical training in radio
broadcasting, villagers prepare the news bulletins for
the station as well as programmes focusing on local
subjects highlighting local talent. Open debates on the
airwaves not only maintain a form of constant
pressure on finding solutions to community problems,
but also ensure that they are put into practice once
found. Dialogue with the local authorities is thus more
constructive. The aim of the project is to set up
community radio stations in twelve isolated and
economically deprived regions of the Philippines in
order to improve the free flow of information in the
country, and it was rewarded for its efforts in 1996
when it obtained the IPDC-UNESCO Prize for Rural
Communication.

In Thailand, the radio station in Chiengmai, a
northern region of the country populated by mountain
tribes, has for several years been broadcasting
programmes on substitution crops as part of a government programme aiming to reduce, and ultimately
eliminate, the poppy crop. The Kingdom of Tonga,
anticipating the subsequent production of community
programmes, has already set up the bases for a
network of FM transmitters as well as a short-wave

relay link on the northernmost island in the kingdom.
By using low-cost transmitters specially developed
under the terms of a contract signed with UNESCO,
the Tonga islands now have a complete network
serving all the kingdom's islands and atolls for one-
tenth of the cost of a medium-wave network.

In Sri Lanka, Radio Mahaweli was set up in 1979
on the initiative of UNESCO and DANIDA when the
national authorities launched a construction plan for
a hydroelectric dam. During the six years of the
scheme, the news programmes broadcast by the mobile
radio station enabled the population to be efficiently
moved to new home sites. On the strength of this
success, an FM station has been established in
Guirandurokotte. At present it is community-managed
and is developing medical assistance programmes
through a clinic that it has also set up.

The Mahaweli experiment encouraged UNESCO
and DANIDA to follow up their co-operation in Nepal
and the Philippines. By 1990, thanks to the partnership
of the two institutions, eight of the ten radio stations
that had been planned were already in place in remote
areas of the archipelago.

In Nepal, a project for a community radio, Radio
Sagarmatha, involving a community in the valley of
Kathmandu, commenced transmissions in May 1997
following four years of preparation and negociation

for its broadcasting licences. It has received support from the Nepal Press Institute, the Nepal Forum of Environmental Journalists and *Himal* magazine.

In Australia, the 'Public Radio' community network was given legal status in 1974 and is now officially referred to as the Third Sector, the two others being the Australian Broadcasting Corporation and commercial radio stations. The legislation stipulates that the stations have to be operated by non-profit-making associations and must serve well-defined geographical areas or segments of the population with particular interests. They are self-financed by contributions from the community, and although all commercial forms of advertising are prohibited, they are authorized to broadcast brief messages mentioning the companies that sponsor them.

Community radio has its own national association, the Public Broadcasting Association of Australia, which every year finds itself with ten to twelve new members. It has just set up a national programme service, which regularly broadcasts to more than 130 community radio stations to supplement their own daily programmes. Transmission since 1993 has been performed by satellite, with funding by state subsidy. Of the five channels reserved for radio broadcasting, one is devoted to indigenous broadcasts. Since December 1995, the National Indigenous Radio Service (NIRS) also has been broadcasting by satellite to a hundred stations.

In 1993, two Australian broadcasters, Freda Glynn and Philip Batty, helped set up the Central Australian Aboriginal Media Association (CAAMA), an aboriginal organization that provides a non-stop satellite broadcasting service of aboriginal television and radio programmes over a vast area of Australia. Their pioneering work has resulted in the creation of more than a hundred aborigine associations throughout Australia, each week producing hundreds of hours of radio programmes in nine aboriginal languages, and television programmes likewise. The scheme, which has won the McLuhan Teleglobe Canada Award, demonstrates to what extent aid for underprivileged peoples can help them become responsible for their own lives.

Chapter 11
Television

Major upheavals in the world of television

Like all other media, television has not escaped the upheavals caused by the widespread penetration of new information and communication technology. The major breakthroughs already recorded in the fields of the production, transmission and distribution of pictures have now been further enhanced by the introduction of digital technology and data compression. Digitization has overtaken all the transmission systems (cable, terrestrial and satellite); it has invaded the video chain from end to end (from studio to subscriber), and is increasingly gaining ground in programme production and post-production. In the field of direct broadcasting, digital technology has produced a radical increase in the number of programme streams and services directly accessible to viewers, a technical breakthrough which is going to jolt the programme market, profoundly modify the audiovisual landscape and change the way we watch television, from multiple broadcasts to video on demand, from theme channels to new interactive services such as teleshopping or video games.

These radically new forms of television raise a number of questions which are difficult to answer with any certainty. How are viewers going to react to such a profuse, multifold feed of available programmes? Are they prepared to pay subscriptions or for video on demand? What future do general-interest channels have in relation to the host of theme streams?

All of these issues, which have been the motive for many a spectacular industrial battle, make it impossible today to say what the television of tomorrow will be like. The digital revolution is not purely the mechanical consequence of technological determinism. It is basically a social construct, resulting from a combination of technological, economic, judicial and political developments, and the extent to which it penetrates markets and permeates societies often depends on its combined critical mass alone. This therefore means that the new age of digital television will not be firmly established, even if the technological conditions for it to occur are favourable, without the political, economic and judicial determination also needed for it to occur, and above all without the support of its future users. They are the essential factor, since hands-on use and social appropriation of new technology often work slowly and in occasionally mysterious ways.

The audiovisual markets around the world are going through radical social, economic and cultural upheavals because of these technological breakthroughs, but also because of other satellite processes, such as democratization, economic deregulation and the globalization of the media and of their content. Against this new backdrop, many states are striving hastily to adapt and organize their audiovisual environment. Others, faced with the problems of transition, are trying to bring about change in economies with a long-standing history of conservatism, while others again prefer to retreat inside increasingly leaky frontiers. Yet even transformations of this scope and scale must be seen in relation to the quantitative dissimilarities in reception resources and the qualitative differences in the conditions in which programmes are produced and broadcast.

More programmes, greater segmentation of supply

Commercial broadcasting by satellite made its first appearance in the world in 1962, with the launch of the American satellite Telstar 1, which permitted the exchange for the first time ever of televised pictures between the United States and Europe. Later, the launch into orbit of the geostationary telecommunication satellites Intelsat and Eutelsat, and finally direct broadcasting, were to enhance the coverage of remote transmission and considerably modify audiovisual environments around the world. With technological convergence and the introduction of digital technology in the field of direct broadcasting, the world has entered a new era in television.

TV-viewing hours per person per day in 1996 in selected countries

According to a report entitled *Une télévision dans le monde* [Television around the World] prepared by the Institut Médiamétrie (Paris) in 1996, the development of the cable and digital channels by satellite led to an increase in the number of TV-viewing hours per day around the world in 1995. North Americans maintain their lead with a peak of nearly 4 hours. Southern Europe (Greece, Italy, Spain and Turkey) is in second place with an average of 3.5 hours, ahead of northern Europe (Belgium, Netherlands and Scandinavia) with barely 2.5 hours.

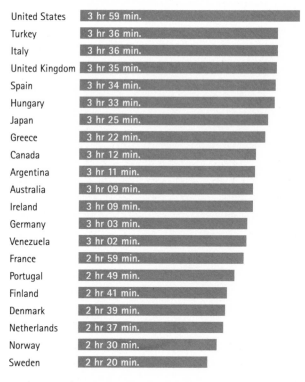

United States	3 hr 59 min.
Turkey	3 hr 36 min.
Italy	3 hr 36 min.
United Kingdom	3 hr 35 min.
Spain	3 hr 34 min.
Hungary	3 hr 33 min.
Japan	3 hr 25 min.
Greece	3 hr 22 min.
Canada	3 hr 12 min.
Argentina	3 hr 11 min.
Australia	3 hr 09 min.
Ireland	3 hr 09 min.
Germany	3 hr 03 min.
Venezuela	3 hr 02 min.
France	2 hr 59 min.
Portugal	2 hr 49 min.
Finland	2 hr 41 min.
Denmark	2 hr 39 min.
Netherlands	2 hr 37 min.
Norway	2 hr 30 min.
Sweden	2 hr 20 min.

Source: Eurodata/TV; Médiamétrie; *Le Monde télévision, radio, multimédia* (Paris), 20–21 April 1997.

The digitization of video signals and the compression of their data will eliminate the main obstacle to, and fundamental feature of, traditional television and its history: the rarity of microwave frequencies and its corollary, the limited number of broadcasting channels. The upshot of these innovations will be a qualitative improvement in television in technical terms, and a quantitative increase in the number of programmes. It is now possible to transmit eight to ten programmes on a single frequency which hitherto carried only a single analog television channel. This has two advantages: broadcasting costs are considerably lower for TV operators, and the supply of programmes for viewers has multiplied. The consequence of this increase in consumption will be enhanced personalization and the transfer of the programming function to the viewer. Given their number, channels have no choice but to specialize. Developing alongside so-called general-interest channels are theme channels (sport, cinema, music, etc.) and channels targeting specific viewers (in terms of age, sex, ethnic groups, religion), as well as new services such as pay-per-view TV, the downloading of video games or teleshopping. As a result, the television sectors of most developed countries now have a twin offer: free-to-air programmes accessible to the general public and pay-TV theme and entertainment programmes designed for those who choose to watch them.

These technological upheavals, combined with the development of pay television, have resulted in fragmented viewership and the introduction of a new type of regulation based on a market closer to telecommunications, a meter market of networks offering services delivered to the doorstep. The television market has moved away from a sector with its own special taxation system to a totally commercial, individualized economy, which increasingly boils down to the organization of the home-based market and a fragmented supply, produced at a distance and in real time. The downturn in viewership has resulted in the ongoing erosion in advertising revenue for traditional general-interest channels. On the other hand, the ratings for pay-TV and theme channels and their revenue from subscriptions and advertising are on the increase.

The real issues in digital broadcasting

The development of television requires a considerable degree of financial investment. In the frenzied climate which currently surrounds digital channels, alliances are struck up – and their allies sometimes struck down – because it is vital to have powerful partnerships for mastery of the basic factors in pay television: control of subscribers and access to programmes.

Decoders

Decoders act as the intermediary between a digital broadcasting network and the device enabling users to access them. Decoders have two main functions: the provision of conditional access to pay-TV channels, and the decoding of digital signals for analog receivers. The aim of broadcasters is to develop a single package, which is small, easy to use, and capable of performing a maximum number of functions. Several operators are currently fighting over that self-same package, each of them seeking to impose their model. The development of digital television depends on there being a clearer situation in terms of standards, and on the cost of decoders.

Alliances

To control these various factors and reign over the world of digital television, the major audiovisual groups, whether as rightholders or as distributors, are tackling the market in a complex dance of alliances, divorces and counter-alliances. Competition takes place against a backdrop of worldwide confrontation when it comes to group takeovers or the introduction of new technology, such as the choice of decoders or the purchase of programme access rights. The digital television market, however, forces operators – who may be friends one day and foes the next – to be highly pragmatic in order to support the development costs inherent to the new audiovisual age. Given the scale of the research budgets that have to be implemented and the consequent need to amortize them on the widest market possible, contractual logic has become the norm, based on sharing markets and know-how in particular. The speed of technological progress, however, as well as hesitancy on the part of decision-makers and operators, and the uncertainties inherent in the digital market itself, make it impossible to project any fixed market overview or analysis, and the alliances are somewhat haphazard.

Sports programmes: big business

The increase in the programme supply raises the problem of finding enough products to feed the new digital programming streams. To gain and maintain subscribers, international and national operators are going to have to fight for programmes, which have become the vital issue in pay television. The battle focuses on the broadcasting rights for athletics events (the Olympic Games, football, boxing, etc.) and for successful feature films. Programmes in the past were amortized by advertising, enabling viewers to watch their favourite programmes free of charge. Today, advertising revenue is no longer enough to offset the cost of purchasing broadcasting rights for 'event' programmes. To access them, the viewer now has to pay. At the forefront of these programmes lies sport. With pay-per-view TV, football fans can watch every national and international match in Europe from the comfort of their homes. Indeed, football is decisive for encrypted channels because it wins them between 30 and 50 per cent of their subscribers. Sport is more of an exclusive sector than feature films, because unlike the cinema industry with, for instance, a dozen major producers in North America, in sport there is only one single rightholder in each country: the national or international sports federation. It is on this form of exclusive market that the major pay-TV channels have built their success.

In Germany, the operator Leo Kirch has succeeded in obtaining the television broadcasting rights from the International Football Federation for the next two football world cups. The exclusive rights have cost the German group and its ally, the Swiss company 'Sports Holding', more than half a million dollars, and now have to be negotiated with the national television channels.[1] In England, BSkyB, the network owned by Rupert Murdoch, really took off in 1992, the year in which Sky Sports began its direct broadcasts of the English first division football championship with Premier League, although the price for obtaining the exclusive rights was staggeringly high: $250 million for the following five years. In 1995, the company had to pay $1 billion to keep the 'football product' on its network from 1996 to 2001. It has also grabbed the American football broadcasting rights from under the noses of the major networks, as well as the broadcasting rights for the Five Nations Rugby tournaments in the United Kingdom for the next five years. In Mexico, the Azteca television channel has bought an 80 per cent stake in the Morelia football team and exclusive broadcasting rights on its matches for 20 million pesos ($2.6 million). The competitor channel Televisa has bought out two other football teams in Mexico and the exclusive broadcasting rights for their matches in the national football championship.

The success of paying event programmes is a precursor to the coming showdown between operators of

[1.] On the subject of the world broadcasting rights for the 2002 and 2006 football world cups acquired by the Kirch group (Germany), the European Commission commented as follows: 'Pay-TV channels are prepared to accept a major increase in their costs to acquire the exclusive rights for sports events. The most astonishing leap (1,000 per cent) occurred in 1996 with the purchase of the syndication rights for the 2002 and 2006 world football championships.' Taken from 'Bruxelles se préoccupe de l'accès aux retransmissions des événements sportifs' [Brussels Concerned About Access to Broadcasting of Sports Events], *Le Monde* (Paris), 15 February 1997, p. 29.

pay television and free-to-air general-interest channels financed by advertising or licence fees. Threatened with being expelled from the football market, the general-interest channels are trying to adapt to the new world by attempting to defend their rights in tennis or cycling, or by contenting themselves with matches of lesser importance.

The stakes are likely to be high, and some football federations are considering developing their own programme stream, as the Netherlands federation is trying to do. Even the major operators want to profit from the market by organizing their own sports events. The leading American cable-TV operator Telecommunication Inc. (with 11 million subscribers) and News Corp., the group owned by Rupert Murdoch, have joined forces to produce and distribute sports programmes destined both for the American market and for the rest of the world.

Governments, regulatory authorities and viewers' associations are beginning to worry about the growing monopoly of pay-TV channels in the broadcasting of sports events. Many observers feel sport has sold its soul and is now held hostage by pay television. Concerned by the trend, in February 1997 the European Parliament put forward an amendment to that effect during the debate on the revision of the 'Television without Frontiers' (TSF) directive.[2] During the same period in Spain, a Bill was tabled before the Cortes, the purpose of which was to prohibit the restriction to subscribers to pay-TV channels of the broadcast of matches in the Spanish football championship.

2.   'EU Aims to Ensure TV Sports Coverage for All', *International Herald Tribune* (Paris), 5 February 1997.

The main interactive television services

Near video on demand

This consists in combining the use of several frequency bands and the periodic start-up of programmes. The latter are broadcast at regular intervals with staggered starting times for the same programme. The disadvantage of this form of near video on demand is that the viewer cannot pause, rewind or fast forward the film. On the other hand, the cost per subscriber of the service is much lower than that of video on demand, which requires considerable technical investment.

Video on demand

This is the most interactive form of digital television. Viewers choose from a catalogue of programmes the one they want to watch, which is then immediately transmitted in real time by a server, permitting viewers to make use of all the functions of a VCR.

Electronic video club

This system is cheaper to operate, using digital compression to broadcast a multitude of programmes on a single frequency. Once they have been stored in the home, the programmes can be viewed at will.

Teleshopping

The aim of this form of interactive television is to provide a service in which customers receive pictures of the products they have selected to purchase. They can access catalogues, place orders in real time and even pay for their purchases direct. Behind teleshopping lies the potential for a complete service industry to be developed.

Video games

The new forms of interactivity are increasingly to be found in video games that take up a large share of youngsters' spare time. The Sega Channel, which was launched in 1994, is a package from the major communication groups Sega, Time Warner and TCI. The channel provides a cable-TV service that enables the games on offer to be downloaded in return for payment of a fee. Competitor services are developing, such as the Game Channel or the Game Show Channel.

Satellite operators around the world

There are about forty television satellites around the world. They may be classified by status (public or private) or by broadcasting reach. Some operators are intercontinental (Intelsat, Hughes Electronics, Intersputnik), while others are regional (Arabsat, Asiasat, Eutelsat, Hispasat) or national (Brazilsat, Palapa, Telecom).

	Organization	Services
Intercontinental operators		
Intelsat	Co-operation of 134 member states: preparing to change status from 'international public service' to commercial (1997). Part of the organization will remain in the public domain to ensure regional balance.	Mainly answering to telecommunication service needs of its member states. Video distribution, Satellite Newsgathering (SNG), DTH and multimedia.
Hughes Electronics	Private. Combines two groups – Galaxy and PanAmSat. Market value of approx. $30 bn and an annual turnover of more than $500 m. Holds some 60 per cent of world market in satellite construction.	Mainly broadcasting and digital network service.
Intersputnik	Founded in 1971 by the nine original members of the Communist bloc. Later joined by Afghanistan, the Lao People's Democratic Republic, Viet Nam and the Democratic People's Republic of Korea. Since 1996 has been an international satellite co-operative comprising twenty-two countries.	International exchange, retransmission of radio and TV, telephone, fax, telex; public and private data exchange, networks for video-conferencing, etc.
Inmarsat	Founded in 1979 by the International Maritime Organization, the specialized agency of the United Nations. Co-operation between 176 member states including Japan, Norway, the United Kingdom and the United States.	Mainly telecommunication service.
Regional operators		
SES	First private operator in Europe, started in 1968.	Transmits approx. sixty TV channels.
Eutelsat	Started in 1985, co-operation of forty-eight European nations.	Mainly telecommunication and telephone services. Provides transmission of: – Central and Eastern European TV channels: TV Shqiptqr (Albania), Duna TV (Hungary), PolSat and TV Polonia (Poland) – Arab States: Space Channel (Dubai), Nile TV and Satellite Channel (Egypt) – Other: Filmnet (NL), TV5Europe (France), RTL2 (Luxembourg), Euronews (multilingual), MBC (Arab), WorldNet (UK).
Hispasat	Spanish telecommunication, programme operated by Hispasat.	Television and telecommunication.
Asiasat	Asia's first regional satellite, totally financed with private funds, launched in 1990. Asiasat is a private company.	Mainly television channels.
Arabsat	International group of Arab countries.	Transmits Arabic public television as well as international television such as CNN and MBC.

Satellites	Reach
Twenty-four satellites currently in orbit, serving approx. 1,700 terrestrial stations (national and international). Fourteen new satellites foreseen before year 2000.	Worldwide.
Galaxy – Ten satellites covering the USA: Galaxy 1 (1983) to Galaxy 9 (1996). PanAmSat – Four satellites covering approx. 100 countries: PAS 1 (1988) to PAS 4 (1995).	Worldwide.
Uses a variety of satellites such as Gorizont, Gorizont 1 (1978), Gorizont 32 (1996), Express 1 (1994), Express 2 (1996), Raduga 1 (1975), Raduga 33 (1996), Gals 1 (1994), Gals 5 (1995) and is now developing its own satellite, Intersputnik 8.	Russian Federation and neighbouring countries.
Has used a variety of its own satellites since 1983: Inmarsat 2F1 (1990), Inmarsat 2F2, Inmarsat 2F3 (1991), Inmarsat 2F4 (1992), Inmarsat 3F1 and Inmarsat 3F3 (1996).	Worldwide.
Astra – Seven satellites: Astra 1A, launched in 1988; Astra 1B, 1991; Astra 1C, 1993; Astra D, 1994; Astra 1E, 1995; Astra 1F and 1G will be launched in 1996 and 1997. It also has 136 relay stations of which some fifty are designed for digital transmission.	21.7 million European homes.
Analog: Eutelsat II F2 (launched in 1991), Eutelsat II F3 (1991), Eutelsat II F4 (1992). Digital: Eutelsat II F1 (1990), Hot Bird 1E (1995). Hot Bird 2, 3, 4 to be launched in 1996 and 1997. Represents altogether 136 relays.	Covers all of Europe and the Mediterranean.
Hispasat 1A (1992), Hispasat 1B (1993), Hispasat 1C.	Spain, Canary Islands and Latin America.
Asiasat 1 (1990), Asiasat 2 (1995), Asiasat 3.	Asia, the Arab States and Eastern Europe.
Arabsat 1A (1985), Arabsat 1B (1985), Arabsat 1C (1992), Arabsat 1D (1993), Arabsat 1E (1995), Arabsat 2A (1996), Arabsat 2B (1996).	Mediterranean countries and North Africa.

	Organization	Services
Selected national operators		
Palapa	PT Telekom and PT Satellite Palapa Indonesia.	Mainly television channels.
France	France Télécom.	Digital and television broadcasting, military use.
Scandinavia	Operated by NSAB (Nordiska Satellitaktiebolaget).	Mainly television channels.
Brazil	Owner/operator: EMBRATEL (National Communications Company).	Data, messages, television and voices.
China	Operators controlled by DFH (Dong Fang Hong).	Communication network.
India	Indian telecommunication and meteorology programme run by ISRO (Indian Space Research Organization).	Telecommunication and meteorological services.
Mexico	Mexican telecommunication programme run by SCT.	National telecommunication programme.

Source: The Satellite Encyclopedia: (HTTP://www.TELE-satellit.com/tse/); *International Satellite Directory*, Geneva, Design Publishers, 1996; F. Baylin, *World Satellite Yearly*, Geneva, 1996–97.

Interactive television

Interactive television is the buzzword in digital television and is expected to result in a clean break with traditional broadcasting. The new digital systems are intended to be capable of reacting to information transmitted by users, in which case viewers will no longer be passive consumers of programmes, but actors able to benefit from completely free, individualized consumption. The issue no longer concerns how viewers will be able to access the greatest selection of programmes, but how they will choose the type of programme that they wish to watch from a stream of offers. In 1997, a set of services in the field of leisure, education and health were tested on certain analog networks or tried out in digital video form.

Videoway, an introduction to interactivity

In Canada, the cable-TV operator Videotron launched the Videoway system in the region of Montreal in February 1990. It is presented as a general public digital telecommunication network produced by integrating a series of services such as cable television, pay television, teletext, video games, e-mail, etc. It offers a mix of infotainment and education programmes, together with a range of services such as telematic games, data banks on various educational subjects or practices and a series of interactive television programmes. A remote control system serves as an electronic guide, enabling users both to control their television and to access all the functions available on the system. The latter is deemed to be interactive, since the viewer can intervene in a programme and react in relation to its content, form or development by choosing from among a number of pre-programmed decisions.

Satellites	Reach
Palapa A1 (1976)–Palapa C2 (1996).	Indonesia, Philippines and neighbouring countries.
TDF1 (1988), TDF2 (1990), Telecom 1C (1988), Telecom 2A (1991), Telecom 2B (1992), Telecom 2C (1995).	Europe and French overseas departments.
Sirius 1 (1994), Thor (1992).	Scandinavia.
Brasilsat-A1 (1985), Brasilsat-A2 (1986), Brasilsat-B1 (1994), Brasilsat-B2 (1995), Brasilsat-B3A (1997).	Whole of Latin America.
China Sat-1 (1988), China Sat-7 (1996), Sino Sat-1, DFH3B to be launched in 1997.	China and neighbouring countries.
Insat 2A (1992), Insat 2B (1993), Insat 2C (1995), IRS 1A (1988), IRS 1B (1991), IRS P2 (1994), IRS 1C (1995), IRS P3 (1996).	India and neighbouring countries.
Morelos 1 (1985), Morelos 11 (1985), Solidaridad 1 (1993), Solidaridad 11 (1994).	Latin America.

In 1996, the Videoway system had more than 300,000 home subscribers, mainly in Quebec. The system has a market penetration rate of 25 per cent, similar to that of the microcomputer, although its uptake is a long-term process, comparable to other mass consumer goods that have succeeded in establishing themselves on the market.

According to the surveys that have been made, the launch of the Videoway system in Canadian homes has resulted in new media habits. In 1994, more than half the subscribers stated that they regularly used the system 53 per cent of the time to watch interactive television, 58 per cent of the time to play video games and 63 per cent of the time to use telematic services. The same surveys show that the Videoway system has generated new listening habits, and that most users prefer the interactive version to the linear version of a given programme. These various new habits suggest the Videoway system is gradually becoming part of the cultural habits of the households that have subscribed to it.

Videoway in fact represents an introductory, familiarization phase to interactive technologies, and a new step in preparing users for the world of UBI (Universality, Bi-directionality, Interactivity). The aim of this new system is gradually to set up a bi-directional digital network in Quebec, offering access to a wide range of products and services direct from the home. UBI is backed by a consortium of partners from the industrial and financial sectors seeking to develop new services (teleshopping, banking transactions, e-mail, access to home automation applications, etc.). The consortium has joined forces with the Université du Québec à Montréal (UQAM) to develop new modes of access to education on UBI.

Sources: A. H. Caron and C. Berre, 'Diffusion de la technologie télévisuelle 'Vidéoway' à l'aube de l'autoroute de l'information' [Launching "Videoway" TV Technology as the Information Highway Takes its First Steps], in *Reinventing Television*, Turin, 1996; J. G. Lacroix, 'Entrez dans l'univers merveilleux de Videoway' [Step into the Wonderful World of Videoway], in: J. G. Lacroix, B. Miège and G. Tremblay (ed.), *De la télématique aux autoroutes électroniques: le grand projet reconduit*, Montmagny (Canada)/Grenoble (France), Presses de l'Université du Québec/Presses Universitaires de Grenoble, 1994; 'Le Projet UBI', *Multimédias, enseignement, formation et téléformation. Les dossiers de l'ingénierie éducative* [Multimedia, teaching, training and teletraining], p. 25, Paris/Montreal, CNDP/Les Publications du Québec, 1995.

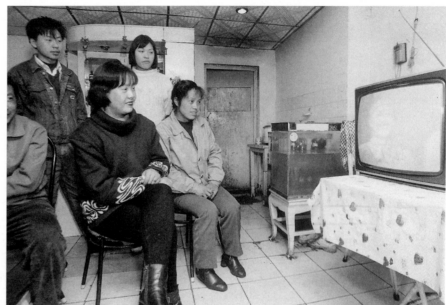

Television in the world – a variety of models, each with its own distinctive features.

Source: P. Kuus/Sipa

Source: Ferrari/SIPA

Television around the world

The media markets around the world occasionally feature contradictory trends between different regions or countries with policy and cultural specifics that are difficult to analyse in a global manner. It is, however, possible to highlight a number of convergent trends. The audiovisual field around the world and the ways in which it is financed are based on a variety of models with different characteristics. In some countries, the strategic role of television is defined according to essentially commercial critera, namely, the market forces of free enterprise and open competition; in others, it is a mixed private–public system, where strictly economic criteria are combined with sociocultural and political concerns; and in others again it is a public monopoly exclusively financed by public funds.

In the latter countries, democracy is in its infancy, or has yet to see the light of day. The state

Source: R. Beck/AFP

Television receivers per 1,000 inhabitants, 1994

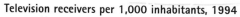

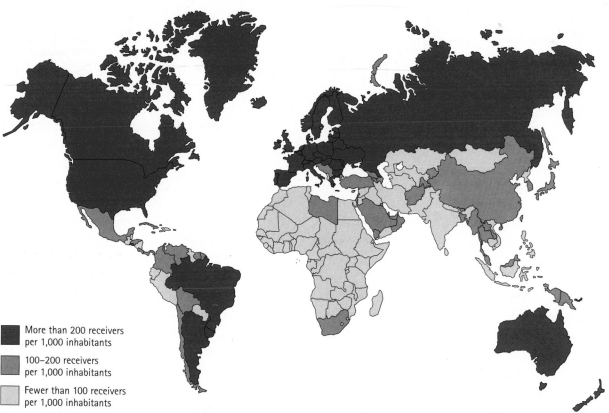

■ More than 200 receivers
per 1,000 inhabitants

100–200 receivers
per 1,000 inhabitants

Fewer than 100 receivers
per 1,000 inhabitants

Source: *UNESCO Statistical Yearbook 1996*, Paris, UNESCO, 1997.

is the main player and directly or indirectly exerts its control over the whole of programme content. This form of television market is currently facing a crisis as a result of the combined effect of several pressures, including that from the upholders of democracy, who criticize the political control of television by governments or the political party in power, on the one hand, and on the other the pressure of competition from cross-border television stations. In the traditional democracies of Western Europe, Asia, the Pacific and Canada, the public–private mix of television systems is the rule. On the other hand, in the United States and in most Latin American countries private television has the high ground. In these countries, the state has almost totally withdrawn from the market, but nevertheless has some control over the operation of television, in particular via its regulatory authorities.

North America

The United States

In the United States there are some 280 million television sets, 72.2 per cent of homes possess at least two, and every adult on average watches more than four hours of televised programmes per day. The audiovisual system is designed and organized on the sole basis of free enterprise and is subject to the principles of competition.

Audiovisual organization in the United States is managed by the governmental agency entrusted with regulating communication, the Federal Communication Commission (FCC). Its work mainly concerns three areas: limiting concentration, laying down the guidelines for programming, and the content of the programmes themselves. The television system comprises four microwave terrestrial broadcasting systems (networks): ABC, NBC, CBS and Fox; more than 2,600 television stations belonging to the Networks called O&O (Owned and Operated) stations or affiliates; an independent station network or one

that is structured as mini-networks; the PBS public service network, which broadcasts to more than 300 relay stations; some sixty cable-TV networks which are subdivided into those supplying basic services, with a line-up of channels such as CNN and ESPN; pay-cable-TV channels specializing in feature films, such as HBO and Showtime; and finally pay-per-view services, invoiced on the basis of real consumption.

The Networks, main components of the audiovisual system in the United States. The Networks comprise stations linked by satellite in order to receive common programmes and advertising messages from a single source. The four Network channels ABC, NBC, Fox Television and CBS cover the whole of the United States, each of them comprising from 176 to 200 stations, 60 per cent of whose programmes are supplied by the Networks. Affiliated stations are contractually linked to the Networks. In return for broadcasting the programmes and advertising provided by the Networks – none of which is allowed to exceed 60 per cent of the station's airtime – the station is paid, receives programmes at competitive prices and is able to broadcast programmes and announcements of its own choice the rest of the time.

In April 1997, Fox Television, most recent of the four principal terrestrial broadcasting networks, and which belongs to the media mogul Rupert Murdoch, moved into second place in the prime-time audience ratings behind NBC. Fox, which has 176 affiliated stations, twenty-two of which it owns outright, owes its profitability to its offbeat programming based on a mix of drama series, sitcoms and sports events that go down well with a young audience.

Parallel to the four Networks are the mini-networks of stations affiliated to the Networks, and mini-networks of independent TV stations. To penetrate an overcrowded market, the latter have to base all the programmes they broadcast on specialization by theme or by type, such as broadcasting feature

influenced by the sheer size of the country, which stretches over four time zones. Television, like radio, was rapidly seen as a tool for communicating and confirming Canadian national identity. In terms of organization, French- and English-language public television channels cohabit with community and private channels broadcast on the terrestrial network, by cable or by satellite.

Canada has eleven television channels on the microwave network, three of which are nationwide and cover the whole of the territory. The national public service broadcasts two distinct programmes, one in English by the Canadian Broadcasting Corporation, and the other in French by the Société Radio Canada. Canada also has a private English-language general-interest channel (CTV), four public education channels (one per province), two private regional channels in English, two private channels in French, and a hundred local stations affiliated to national channels or to provincial networks for their programme feed.

The cable-TV network comprises a range of a dozen theme channels: two public non-stop news channels (Newsword and RDI), two sports channels (TSN and RDS), two video-clip channels (Musique Plus and Much-Music), two channels for youngsters (Family Channel and YTV), two weather report channels (Météo Média and Weather Now), two channels which broadcast the sessions of the Federal Parliament and of the Provincial Assemblies, and a community channel (Télévision Ethnique du Québec), which broadcasts in thirty languages. Viewers can choose to subscribe to a wider range of theme channels, with pay-TV decoders and service on demand. They have several channels at their disposal specializing in feature films (Premier Choix First Choice, Super Ecran, Moviemax, The Classic Channel and Showcase), a country music channel, a scientific report channel (Discovery), and a cultural channel. Finally, for those living close to the United States border or receiving cable TV, viewers have access to the three major American networks CBS, ABC and NBC, to the non-stop news channel CNN, and to the public service television network PBS. American channels have a 22 per cent audience market share in Canada.

In addition to the two general-interest channels, public service television has had two non-stop cable news channels since January 1995. It operates some twenty TV stations and feeds programmes to twenty-eight affiliated local television stations throughout Canada. Public service television does not receive licence fees. The state subsidizes 80 per cent of its budget, the rest of its requirements being generated by advertising revenue.

Analysis of the Canadian audiovisual landscape highlights a number of specific characteristics in its mode of operation and regulation. The Canadian audiovisual system is regulated by an independent authority, the Canada Radio-Television and Tele-communications Commission (CRTC). Like the Federal Communication Commission (FCC) of the United States, the CRTC supervises both radio broadcasting and telecommunications. It grants and renews licences for all radio broadcasters, whether they are pooled as networks or independent, microwave or cable, public or private. Every Canadian channel is placed under its supervision and is subject to specific provisions. Another important feature of the regulation system is the voluntary adoption of rules in conjunction with the players and operators of the audiovisual field to control programmes and advertising messages targeting children. Since 1 January 1994, public and private television channels have been required to abide by a so-called 'self-regulating' code of ethics aimed at banishing scenes of violence from the small screen. In addition, in order to safeguard its independent programme industry, the CRTC requires a certain percentage of Canadian content in the programmes broadcast each day by public or private Canadian television channels.

Western Europe

General trends

Television in Europe has gone through three successive phases in the post-war period: that of a public monopoly, financed virtually exclusively by licence fees, followed by a public monopoly, financed principally by licence fees and revenue from advertising, and recently a system of television paid direct by the customer, either by subscription or on purchase of a service. In the last few years, the audiovisual market has seen sustained growth in the order of 10 per cent per annum, a growth rate which has every chance of being maintained with the launch in 1995 of ninety-eight new television channels, thus expanding the European market to include some 300 broadcasters. The increase in supply is a result of the development in European satellite capacity, with the start-up in 1995 of the first digital satellite services, provided by the Société Européenne de Satellite (SES), which operates the Astra satellites, and by the European consortium behind the Eutelsat satellite.

The most distinctive feature of the 1990s is the rising power of private channels broadcasting in the main by satellite and financed by advertising or as pay-TV programmes. According to the latest television market surveys in Europe,[2] some 383 channels, most of which broadcast commercials, are watched by approximately 761 million people. The same surveys also underline the fragmentation of viewership and a transfer from redundant free-to-air programmes to paying programmes. The market share of pay television has increased twice as fast as unencrypted television, with a growth in turnover of 23 per cent compared with 11 per cent for unencrypted television, against 8 per cent for the video market and 9 per cent for cinemas. According to the IDATE survey, 'this confirms the long-term trend in audiovisual consumption from "free" to "fee"'.

The growth in the choice of television programmes in the course of the same period has been accompanied by a strong rise in demand, as expressed in subscriptions to cable and satellite TV channels, and in the purchase of collective and individual antennae, as well as in advertising revenue. In 1995, the number of homes receiving programmes by satellite and by cable stood at 69.1 million. At the same date, the number of Europeans equipped with dishes or those sharing a collective system for satellite reception was estimated at 19 million, as against 12.6 million in 1993.

According to an inquiry published in 1996 by the operator Astra, direct reception is a marginal market in France, with a bare 1.03 million satellite dishes installed. It is far more substantial in the United Kingdom, with 5 million dish antennae. On the other hand, it is a major market in Germany, where there are 10 million dish homes, to which should be added the 2 million German-speaking households in Austria and Switzerland.[3]

A market shared by three major groups

After a period of mergers, alliances and redress, the pay-TV landscape in Europe seems to have stabilized around three major groups, each of which controls a geographical area: the United Kingdom channel BSkyB, the German channel DF1 and the French channel Canal Plus. In the United Kingdom, Rupert Murdoch, owner of News Corp. and BSkyB, reigns over the British market. More than five-and-a-half million subscribers give the Australian-American group exceptional financial power in Europe. In the first semester of 1996, BSkyB posted profits of $400 million, a rise of 66 per cent compared with the same period in 1995. In addition, the launch at the outset of 1997 of a digital version of the BSkyB

2.   *European Key Facts: Television 96*, published by IP, a subsidiary of the Havas group; *The World Film and Television Market*, IDATE (Montpellier), 1997.

3.   'Les allemands les premiers' [Germans First], *Le Monde* (Paris), 30 August 1996, p. 15.

Audiovisual indicators and GNP for selected European countries, 1994

Country	Households (%)				GNP/inhab. in value at parity of purchasing power
	TV	VCR	Satellite	Cable	
Austria	100	51	36	37	19 560
Belgium	96	46	6[1]	94	20 270
Bulgaria	96	N.a.	6	14	4 380
Croatia	95	42	22	8	N.a.
Czech Republic	98	33	20	14	8 900
Denmark	98	67	60[2]	—	19 880
Estonia	97	19	N.a.	N.a.	4 510
Finland	96	66	6	36	16 150
France	94	68	N.a.	6	19 670
Germany	97	59	27	54	19 480
Greece	96	46	<1	N.a.	10 930
Hungary	96	40	19	38	6 080
Ireland	97	65	48[2]	—	13 550
Italy	99	56	2	0	18 460
Latvia	81	18	24	22	3 220
Lithuania	98	16	16	14	3 290
Netherlands	98	68	5	95	18750
Norway	98	65	14[1]	55	20 210
Poland	98	54	20	14	5 480
Portugal	100	63	9	4	11 970
Romania	89	25	8	31	4 090
Russian Federation	98	20	N.a.	1	4 610
Slovakia	99	27	35	24	6 290[3]
Slovenia	97	47	14	32	6 230
Spain	99	58	3	3[1]	13 740
Sweden	98	74	60	39	17 130
Switzerland	87	62	6	79	25 150
Turkey	93	8	2	3	4 710
United Kingdom	97	79	15	6[1]	17 970

1. Includes SMATV.
2. Includes cable.
3. Data refer to 1992.

Source: *Market and Media Facts,* 1995–96, London, Zenith Publications.

programme stream is seen by Murdoch's potential competitors as the grip of an even stronger 'monopoly' on the pay-TV market.

Germany

In Germany and in German-speaking countries, the DF1 digital programme stream launched by the Kirch group in July 1996 and the analog pay-TV channel Première, owned by Bertelsmann, of the French consortium Canal Plus and Kirch, are in open competition. However, the break-up of the Canal Plus – Bertelsmann alliance, which had intended to produce a joint digital programme stream, has largely contributed to positioning the Kirch group as the sole potential distributor on the digital television market. In 1997 alone, the group intends to invest DM 1.17 billion to feed its DF1 package with programmes. According to the experts, however, the initial results of the stream are disappointing, since four months after its launch only 30,000 German households had subscribed to DF1 as against 200,000 expected by the end of 1996. The same experts estimate that with 15 million households connected to cable TV and 10 million dish homes, the German market is already saturated. Only one digital programme stream may be profitable in the mid-term.

France

In France, the pay-TV market in 1997 was highly favourable to the Canal Plus group, even though it has had to fend off two new digital programme streams since December 1996, Télévision par Satellite (TPS) and AB Sat. The microwave channels forming the TPS-TF1, RTL, M6 and France Télévision package have realized that they could not afford to be left out of pay television without risking a downturn in their audience and, consequently, their income. As a result, the competition between Canal Plus and TPS has heated up, particularly on the theme programme and exclusive coverage rights markets, but the price war is too costly for the narrowness of the French market.

For some experts, the financial viability of three competing digital programme streams seems doubtful, even more so when in Germany, the leading audio-visual market in Europe, the operators agree that there is space enough for only one programme stream. Other analysts estimate that consolidation may take place, the trend being towards the British scenario where the BSB and SkyTV streams have merged after a period of cut-throat competition.

At the international level, the target of Canal Plus was to play the leading role in Europe. Its alliance with the German group Bertelsmann made the French encrypted channel a leading-level potential operator in the European audiovisual market. In only a few months, however, Canal Plus has had to lower its sights further, owing to the withdrawal by the German group, which has found the economic potential of the Compagnie Luxembourgeoise de Télédiffusion (CLT) more appealing. Despite this failure, Canal Plus still holds a powerful position on the world market, with more than 3 million subscribers in 1997, and global growth in its portfolio estimated at 22.8 per cent per year. The group has pay-TV channels in Belgium, Germany, Poland, Spain and Africa, and the international power of the group has expanded even further as a result of its merger with the South African operator NetHold, an alliance which has brought the encrypted channel the markets in Benelux, Italy, Poland and Scandinavia, placing it in the lead of pay television in Europe with 9.5 million subscribers.

Luxembourg

In Luxembourg, the alliance between the Compagnie Luxembourgeoise de Télédiffusion and the AG/UFA Film Union (Bertelsmann Group) has given birth in 1997 to the largest television and radio company in Europe. With approximate sales of $3.7 billion and stakes in nineteen channels and twenty-three radio stations scattered throughout ten European countries, the new group intends 'to fight on equal terms with the American majors'.

Norway

Norway has one public service television channel, the Norsk Rikskringkasting (NRK), which is financed by licence fees, and four private channels, TV3, TV Norge, TV 1000 and TV2. The public channel, a genuine national institution, has the highest viewing in figures, even if the arrival on the market of private satellite channels has shaken the Norwegian audiovisual system. Indeed, the law of 1981 authorizing the setting up of local private radio and television stations financed by advertising has enabled a host of new stations to be set up by organizations, municipalities and associations. With the help of state subsidies and licence fees, the NRK has strengthened its core sectors of news reporting, sports coverage and fiction production. On the other hand, it cannot compete with the private channels in terms of shows and entertainment. Besides NRK, there are four commercial channels. TV3, a cable-TV channel owned by the Swedish group Kinnevilgruppen, initially covered the entire region of Denmark, Norway and Sweden, before focusing on the domestic market with the creation in 1990 of TV3 Norway. Another commercial cable-TV channel is TV Norge, owned by an American group, the Scandinavian Broadcasting System (SBS), the majority shareholder of which is Disney. It broadcasts from 5 p.m. to 2.30 a.m. and frontlines with sport. Since September 1996, when it started to be re-broadcast via a dozen local channels, TV Norge has covered more than 80 per cent of the country. The third private channel, TV 1000, owned by the Swedish group TV 1000 Sverige AB, principally targets a young with programmes focusing on music. The most recent channel, named TV2, was set up in 1992 on the initiative of a pool of private Swedish shareholders, the largest of which is the Schibsted press group.

Central and Eastern Europe

Analysis of the audiovisual fields in the countries of Central and Eastern Europe reveals a number of problems, linked fundamentally to the conditions of transition from a centrally planned economy and the monopolistic management of the audiovisual field to a free market economy and the pluralistic organization of the media. Even though the specific political and cultural characteristics of each country have to be taken into consideration, the period of transition and the problems that go with it may be said to apply to the whole region in that they lie at the heart of policy analysis and decisions with regard to: television and its effects on democracy; the future of the public service, threatened as it is by competition from national private stations and pressure from the authorities; the difficulties of legislating and above all of enforcing that legislation; the concomitant risks of the emergence of other forms of monopolies guided by the logic of viewership 'ratings'; the problem of the specifically European nature of television channels and the quality of their production and programmes; and, finally, respecting cultural pluralism and the interests of the public at large.

Central and Eastern Europe resemble a vast audiovisual worksite for international and local operators, even if the economic conditions in some countries are still somewhat haphazard and advertising is in an embryonic state. The fact none the less remains that the region represents a potential market of more than 420 million viewers, with outlets ranging from equipment (cabling, television sets, satellite receivers, VCRs) to programmes and the production industry.[4] As a result, the major communication groups are taking up positions and developing their penetration strategies for the main countries in the region.

The emergence of channels broadcast by satellite or distributed by cable networks has been the real

4. 'Politiques d'investissement dans l'audiovisuel des pays de l'Europe de l'Est' [Audiovisual Investment Policies in Eastern European Countries], *Communications et stratégies* (Montpellier), No. 1, 1991.

The European Broadcasting Union (EBU)

The European Broadcasting Union (EBU) was set up in 1950 by public radio and television services throughout Europe. It describes itself as an independent international association. It started with twenty-three founder bodies and today has 117 members in seventy-nine countries. Against a backdrop of political upheaval in Eastern Europe, in 1993 the EBU merged with the ORT, the authority in charge of radio and television in the old Eastern bloc of Europe. The purposes of the EBU include negotiating broadcasting rights for major sports events, organizing programme exchange, and promoting co-production. In general, the EBU provides all the operational, technical and legal services necessary for co-operation among member countries. Its lobbying activities in favour of audiovisual audiences, in particular with the European authorities, are gaining ground. In the field of education, at year-end 1996 the EBU set up a European development unit designed, among other things, to produce adult training courses and school syllabuses using new media.

● THE EBU IN FIGURES

- 117 members in 79 countries (66 active members in 49 countries and 51 associate members in 30 countries).
- 1996 sales: 673 million Swiss francs, including 466 million for sport (purchase of broadcasting rights and production costs) and 121 million for the Eurovision transmission network.
- 225 people are employed at the head office (administration and technical centre) in Geneva, which also accommodates 10,000 visitors and delegates of members every year.
- Television: 13 satellite channels and 5,500 km of terrestrial circuits each year route 60,000 hours of broadcasting (25,000 hours of news reports and 5,000 hours of cultural and sports programmes). Eurovision reaches 255 million households, or 640 million potential viewers.
- Radio: two satellite channels provide 1,800 hours of concert and opera broadcasts, and cover 400 hours of sports events and 100 hours of major news events on average per year. Euroradio reaches 400 million potential listeners.

novelty of the 1990s. Before the present decade, satellite television channels were picked up in a marginal, controlled way, carrying programmes produced in the West to a few cable-TV networks or international hotels. With the end of communism, the opening of political and economic doors and pressure from the public eager for new programmes, there have been major upheavals in the audiovisual sector. New channels have been set up in an extended legal vacuum. Satellite reception has developed at high speed, favouring the installation of cable networks and an explosion in the satellite dish market. The figures available indicate that at the end of 1993 more than 3 million households officially received satellite channels, and that this figure had doubled by 1996.

Satellite broadcasting has developed in different ways from country to country. In countries that endeavoured to follow the classic market model, the process was regulated, and the cable-TV operators who were authorized in such countries signed contracts with international broadcasters. On the other hand, TV reception by satellite has developed in an anarchic fashion in other countries, with networks being installed without any licence to operate, more often than not to supply programmes which have been pirated.

At the regional level, several states have organized their own transnational broadcasting strategy, by developing networks broadcasting in the direction of neighbouring countries or by setting up national networks abroad. For its international broadcasting purposes, the Russian Federation uses the old frequency of the first Soviet channel Ostankino, which in 1994 became the ORT. In 1995 the channel was one of the rare links connecting the populations of the former USSR, and between them and certain Central and Eastern European states. The latter have also developed their own satellite broadcasting for the benefit of their communities living abroad. In Poland, the TV Polonia channel broadcasts to the Polish community throughout Europe. In Hungary, the Duna TV station broadcasts a general-interest programme for the 3.5 million Magyar expatriates living in neighbouring countries. Finally, a satellite broadcasting scheme named 'Mosaika', set up as a partnership between Germany and the countries of Central and Eastern Europe, is to broadcast the programmes of each country throughout the region. All the states involved have a vested interest in developing the scheme, given the extent to which nationalities in this region of the world overlap.

While the media landscape is undergoing radical change as a result of major political upheaval, considerable disparities still remain in terms of television infrastructures and the level of their use. On the whole, the reforms that have taken place in the region appear to be irreversible, even if certain measures have yet to produce the anticipated results. While transition seems under control, it is still the subject of debate between political parties and television professionals. Some emphasize with interest the progress made towards eventual integration with the European Community, while others point out the dangers of high-speed liberalization and the risk of media independence being pawned off, with its subsequent effect on the overall process of democratic transition. Finally, others still maintain that the switchover from state-controlled channels to a public form of television service involves obstacles and constraints of a political nature, owing in particular to the sluggishness of current systems and the conservative traditions of the old system.

Poland

Of all the countries in Central and Eastern Europe, Poland is without doubt the most prosperous in audiovisual terms. It has the largest market in the region, since 99 per cent of all households are equipped with television sets and 53 per cent are equipped with VCRs, for a population of 39 million inhabitants. It is also the third largest European market for satellite reception, with 2.5 million dish homes, or some 7 million viewers picking up international channels, to which should be added the 6 million subscribers to cable television. Television attracts the greatest amount of advertising investment, with a 40 per cent market share, as against 30 per cent for the press.[5] In 1994 the market was worth $268 million. Poland therefore represents a promising market for national and foreign operators.[6]

The Polish audiovisual market features a high degree of diversity. It comprises two national terrestrial public service channels, TVP1 and TVP2, which cover practically the whole of the territory; a new public channel, TV Polonia, designed for Poles living abroad; a national private channel, Polsat, which originally broadcast from the Netherlands a programme for Poles everywhere in Europe;[7] a private network of local channels, Polonia 1, broadcast by satellite; twenty television stations that broadcast without any operating licence;[8] and foreign channels such as those of the Italian group Filmnet or the French company Canal Plus, which are accessible on cable in the twenty largest cities of the country. Finally, Poland is taking part in the 'Mosaika' satellite scheme associating Czech, Hungarian, Polish and Slovak television stations.

The highest audience ratings are still held by the two public service channels TVP1 and TVP2, despite

5. 'Central Europe's Cable and Broadcast Market Eager for Foreign Programming', *Broadcasting and Cable International*, February 1996.
6. 'OMRI'S Public and Opinion Research Department', quoted in *Transition* (Washington), 19 April 1996, p. 16.
7. 'Politicians Endanger Independence of Polish Public TV', *Transition* (Washington), 19 April 1996, pp. 28–30.
8. J. M. Smoluch, 'Pologne', in G. Hennebelle (ed.), *Les télévisions du monde: Un panorama dans 160 pays*, pp. 100–2, Paris, CinémAction-Corle, 1995.

powerful gains by the private channel Polsat. The two former channels have cumulated ratings of 78.5 per cent and 44.6 per cent respectively,[9] while Polsat obtains only 28.4 per cent.[10] In 1993, the status of the two public channels switched from a state enterprise to a shareholder company, with the treasury as its only stock-holder.[11]

The law on the audiovisual sector adopted by the Polish Diet in December 1992 came into effect on 1 March 1993. It provided for the creation of a national Polish broadcasting and television council (CNRT), which was inaugurated in April 1993. The law also stipulates the conditions for equity shareholdings by foreign capital when private television stations are set up. The latter are limited to 33 per cent in a broadcasting company and to 49 per cent in a production company.

Russian Federation

Just before the disappearance of the USSR, the Soviet television system comprised four channels, two of which were general-interest, one was educational and a fourth had a regional role, broadcasting a special programme for each of the fifteen former republics. 'Ostankino', the central structure established in Moscow, controlled all radio and television activities. The appointment in 1988 of managers to the board of Gosteleradio[12] who believed in the policy of *glasnost* signalled the start of liberalization at the local studio level. In Leningrad, magazines such as *600 Seconds* or the *Fifth Wheel* opened up a new era in Soviet television which has come closer to viewers' expectations. In June 1990, the then President Mikhail Gorbachev had a law adopted whose aim was to guarantee freedom of speech and pluralism. On 15 July 1990, a presidential decree put an end to the monopoly of Gosteleradio.[13]

New Russian television. With a population close to 150 million inhabitants, 85 television centres, 690 transmitters, 11,000 television relay links,

9,000 receiving stations, 10 non-stop broadcasting satellites, 55 million television sets and a very large-scale television network,[14] the Russian Federation has the largest potential market for television broadcasting in the former socialist bloc.

As in every other country, television in the Russian Federation plays a central role of informing and entertaining. In 1995 more than 93 per cent of the households in the European part of the country had a television set.[15] In 1996, the audiovisual landscape in the Russian Federation was marked by the arrival of private operators and a slump in public service television. Generally speaking, the programmes of public as well as private channels were radically affected by the massive broadcasting of commercials and excessive use of 'heartening' (barter) and sponsoring techniques. In 1996, the Russian television sector comprised five national channels, three of which were privatized, 100 regional public channels, 200 private national channels and more than 200 private regional stations.[16]

9. These are based on the number or percentage of people who have at least had contact with the media under study during the course of a given period (time slot, day, week, etc.), no matter what the duration. Cumulated ratings are related to listening times: cumulated ratings (in percentage).

10. 'Media focus sur Varsovie et étude national sur la Pologne' [Media Focus on Warsaw and National Study of Poland], *Médiamétrie*, March 1996.

11. 'Information and Entertainment in Poland', *Transition* (Washington), 6 October 1995, pp. 13–15.

12. Gosteleradio is the central body with 87,000 employees. It managed radio and television in the former USSR.

13. G. Saffrais, 'La télévision russe, entre democratisation et raison d'État' [Russian Television between Democratization and Real Politics], *Hermès* (Paris), Vol. 19, 1996, pp. 113 ff.

14. A. Garcia, 'Russie', in Hennebelle (ed.), op. cit., pp. 115–16.

15. 'OMRI's Public and Opinion Research Department', quoted in *Transition*, 19 April 1995, p. 16.

16. 'Les médias en Russie', *Problèmes économiques et sociaux*, No. 766, p. 5.

Public service television channels. Alongside a fiercely competitive private sector, public channels have had to contend with serious financial difficulties, due in particular to the lack of subsidies from the state, with a federal budget covering only half the expenditure of its television.

The leading public channel ORT was created by decree on 30 November 1994. It is the result of a semi-privatization system, giving the station the status of a public company in which the state has a 51 per cent stake, the rest of the shares being held by various banks. ORT is the most popular channel in the whole of the Russian Federation. It covers 97 per cent of the territory of the former USSR and has a potential audience of 150 million viewers. It has maintained its general-interest role with a strong cultural and infor-mative bias. In 1994, ORT broadcast a little over five hours per day, when in 1993 it transmitted virtually twenty hours per day. In spite of these restrictions, the channel has maintained most of its audience. It has gone through periods of serious trouble, however, marked by the violent death on 1 March 1995 of its most popular journalist and at the same time its first director-general, Vladislas Listiev.

Rossia (RTR) is the second public channel. It broadcasts over the whole of the territory of the Russian Federation and potentially reaches 87 per cent of the population of the former USSR. After being manipulated by the party in power, the channel has finally acquired a degree of independence and pro-fessionalism which politicians close to those in power often criticize. Its director, V. Popstov, was dismissed on 15 January 1996 for coverage of the Chechen-Ingushetian conflict which was deemed to be 'inappropriate'. The channel is in dire financial straits and in 1994 had to reduce its airtime. The programmes are general-interest in scope and have enabled the channel to maintain its second rank in the ratings.

RMTK is a semi-public channel which broadcasts from 6 p.m. to 11 p.m., to the capital and the sur-rounding region. It is regularly watched by some 20 to 25 million viewers. Its programmes generally comprise on-set variety shows and feature films. Financial difficulties have forced it to share its channel with another private channel, 2X2.

St Petersburg Canal 5 is a channel that covers two-thirds of the Russian Federation. It made a considerable contribution to the debate that shook Russian society during the *perestroika* period. It transmits basically national programmes, and broad-casts feature films and variety shows in the evening. Its in-house production capacity has severely shrunk, making the presence of the channel in the programme market no more than minimal.

Private television channels. The first private television channels were launched from 1991 onwards. The lack of regulation and the input of foreign capital have enabled them to expand particularly quickly, notably in the cable and satellite TV sectors.

NTV is a channel which was created in January 1994 by a pool of Russian shareholders, including the MOST bank. In a single year, it has become one of the greatest success stories in Russian television. It has reached second position behind ORT in terms of audience. Its reception in the Russian Federation is good (approximately 100 million viewers) and it broadcasts every day between 6 p.m. and midnight. In 1995 it almost failed to obtain the renewal of its broadcasting licence because of its independent treatment of news on the Chechen-Ingushetian conflict. In 1995, too, it had a run-in with the law-courts about its programme *Kukli*, whose stars are puppets that comment on the political scene in Russia.

Other private channels such as TV-6 and 2X2 have acquired undeniable popularity. TV6, launched in 1993 by the American Ted Turner with local partners, broadcasts CNN news bulletins, and also children's programmes and feature films, by satellite to cable-TV networks. 2X2 is the oldest of the Russian commercial television channels. It was set up as a partnership with Super Channel. It mainly broadcasts

MTV clips with news bulletins in English supplied by the American channel CBS and Russian-language news bulletins provided by the BBC.

In 1995, the two national public channels, ORT and RTR, and the two private national channels, TV-6 and NTV, on their own accounted for more than 70 per cent of the television audience. The secret of their success is a mix of American and Latin American soap operas, games inspired by channels in the West, talk-shows and occasionally sensational news bulletins.

The Russian Federation is still one of the countries in the region with the lowest rates of cable televisions and satellite dish ownership. Less than 16 per cent of the households in the European part of the country in 1995 had either of these means of reception.[17] Development in cable television is taking place, however, and in some cities represents between 30 and 40 per cent of the total daily audience, equal to the market share of some of the major national channels. In the area of satellite reception, several channels such as the German station ARD, the French stations TF1 and France 2 and the American channel CNN are broadcast non-stop via the Eutelsat, Astra and Intelsat satellites.[18] Finally, the advertising market has seen a remarkable upswing. In 1994, advertisers invested more than a billion dollars in television commercials for the Russian market.

The Russian audiovisual market has entered a new age, one marked by restructuring. Public service television channels are faced with constraints both economic and political in nature: in general, they are still dependent in terms of management and production on foreign capital and programmes, and are also frequently subject to governmental pressure. The absence of any independent regulatory authority makes newsgathering and broadcasting difficult; the dividing line between public and private television as well as access to the media for electoral candidates is still not regulated; and yet the issues at stake in the new television sector in the Russian Federation are considerable, first and foremost with respect to con-

solidating the freedom of the press as a fundamental factor in a democratic state. In this respect, the disappearance in December 1993 of the Ministry of Information and its replacement by the Federal Audiovisual Office (the regulatory authority for public broadcasting) was a sign of the break with the old regime.

Africa

General trends

Just as in other regions, the television landscape in sub-Saharan Africa since 1990 has undergone a deep upheaval. The far-reaching changes have been caused by two major factors: the advent of democracy in several African states and the internationalization of communication. In many African countries, the audio-visual sector, traditionally under political control, has become freer and thus more varied. For some years it has been opening up to international and regional private operators. Possession of satellite reception equipment has been legalized. Pay-TV channels, such as the South African network M-NET or the French station Canal Horizons, have entered the African market and together gained more than a million subscribers.[19] The penetration rate for audiovisual equipment is rising. The number of television sets rose from 600,000 in 1965 to 15 million in 1988, and, even in the absence of reliable figures, it seems that the number of dish antennae and VCRs is continually increasing. In spite of this progress, the African market has yet to be seen as a commercial priority for the

17. 'OMRI's Public and Opinion Research Department', quoted in *Transition*, 19 April 1996, p. 16.
18. 'Sur la nouvelle frontière des réseaux de télévision' [At the New Frontier of TV Networks], *Le Monde diplomatique* (Paris), February 1995.
19. *Africa Film & TV*, Harare, Z Promotions Pvt Ltd, 1996; 'Canal Horizons se développe en Afrique' [Canal Horizons is Progressing in Africa], *Le Monde* (Paris), 15 September 1995.

Audiovisual indicators and GNP for Africa (excluding Arab States), 1994 (figures in parentheses indicate an estimated total number)					
Country	Households (%)				GNP/inhab. in value at parity of purchasing power
	TV	VCR	Satellite	Cable	
Botswana	(15 000)	N.a.	(6 000)	N.a.	5 210
Cameroon	75.9	19.2	3.0	0.1	1 950
Kenya	14	65	0.3	0.6	1 310
Mauritius	(150 000)	60	N.a.	N.a.	12 720
Namibia	9	10	2	N.a.	4 320
Nigeria	53	21	3	N.a.	1 190
South Africa	59	32	0.5	18	5 130
Uganda	(300 000)	70	1	N.a.	1 410
Zimbabwe	(389 000)	6	0.8	N.a.	2 040

Source: *Market and Media Facts,* 1995–96, London, Zenith Publications.

major international broadcasters, even if the middle class, at the pan-African level, increasingly invests in video and satellite reception equipment. As in most countries, the programme supply consists essentially of international productions purchased at low cost, which are usually cheaper than domestic products. None the less, it is worth underlining the large-scale efforts made to promote the exchange of programmes between African national television stations, in particular through the Union of National Radio and Television Organizations of Africa (URTNA), set up in Lagos in 1962, which currently boasts forty-eight member states and also associate members.

The fact remains, however, that Africa is still the region with the fewest telecommunications infrastructures and audiovisual resources in the world. With a few exceptions, the African continent in 1995 had one telephone line per 100 inhabitants and all the lines were concentrated in towns. The inequality is just as pronounced where audiovisual equipment and programmes are concerned. Barely four Africans in every hundred have a television set, or 14.2 per cent of all households, far behind the Asian rate of 55.3 per cent. This means that more than 80 per cent of the population does not have access to television. The most severely penalized of all are the rural populations, who simply do not have the necessary purchasing power.[20] Finally, other gaps are to be found in all African countries, identical to those that characterize many facets of Africa in relation to the rest of the world, between the haves and have-nots within a given country.

New landscapes

An analysis of the African audiovisual environment highlights a certain number of convergent features common to the whole continent. Until the end of the 1980s, particularly in countries with a single political party, television in Africa had always been defined as a political mouthpiece, justifying the action of the authorities. Journalists had the status of civil servants

20. A survey made in the Côte d'Ivoire shows that only 20 per cent of the rural population had access to television, compared with 60 per cent of the urban population. Reported by A. J. Tudesq, *L'Afrique noire et ses télévisions,* Paris, 1992.

and information was generally controlled by the ruling powers. From 1990 onwards, political liberalization and democratization have had as their consequence the emergence of a private press and of a more critical and more credible tone on television. Television still belongs to the state, but does not exclude the emergence of commercial or community channels. Depending on the degree of media liberalization, certain public service televisions have gradually opened up to other points of view. The beginnings of liberalization such as these in many states have enabled changes to be enacted in the legislative framework regulating the media landscape. New regulatory authorities have been instituted, although their structure and purpose vary according to country or region. In Benin, for example, one of the main assignments of the High Authority for Audiovisual and Communication (HAAC) is to guarantee the freedom of the press and the other means of communication and supervise fair access for political parties and associations to the media. This means that the regulatory authorities can both control and corroborate the processes of democratization and political liberalization.

Combined with media internationalization, however, these new features have generated a somewhat paradoxical situation. On the one hand, a number of favourable developments are perceptible: satellite reception, pressure from audiences eager for quality programmes, the launch by some African countries of a second television channel, the emerging audiovisual power of South Africa and Nigeria. On the other hand, because of the worsening in the economic recession, most African countries are forced to adopt structural adjustment plans that require them to limit expenditure and thus deprive domestic television systems of the means they need to develop. Their poverty forces most African television channels to depend technically and financially on partnerships with other countries and on international co-operation. The same dependence affects the broad-casting of programmes, more than 70 per cent of which are of foreign origin. Some countries, such as Cape Verde and Djibouti, import more than 90 per cent of their programmes, a trend reinforced by the use of VCRs. Finally, local production is usually limited to televised news bulletins, news magazines and a few entertainment programmes.

Television in sub-Saharan Africa has always been the subject of debate with respect to its ultimate purpose in African society. As soon as it was introduced, in the 1960s, it was seen as a tool for development and social change. Countries such as Côte d'Ivoire and the Niger developed ambitious educational television programmes, which lost momentum in the 1980s. The serious unrest of the 1980s at least had the merit of waking up international opinion to the serious disparities existing between Africa and the rest of the world in the field of communication. The troubles also highlighted the risk of standardizing local cultures through a form of globalization of transnational programmes, thereby endangering fragile community cultures. With the advent of globalization and geopolitical change, other questions were to be raised, about the role of African television in the democratization process, the purpose and the independence of public service television, and the conditions governing access to new digital and space technology.

These various questions highlight the political, economic and cultural issues that African television has to face: the advent of pluralism supposes a diversified audiovisual sector and independent public television remote from all political or economic pressures. It also supposes the setting up of independent regulatory authorities, with precise purposes and specifications, in a clearly defined ethical, legal and statutory framework. Finally, it presupposes the liberalization of the monopoly on radio and television and a more open approach to private enterprise, particularly at the local level. In addition, the development of television productions that comply with international standards should be an aim for African television channels, which must therefore have the requisite technical resources for co-production and co-operation.

Regional and international players

M-NET is the leading English-language pay-TV network in Africa. Set up in 1986, it has gained more than a million subscribers, 90 per cent of whom are in South Africa. The programmes on the channel are rebroadcast to thirty-five countries across the continent. Broadcasting is by satellite to all the countries except South Africa, which receives broadcasts by terrestrial means. In 1995, the network offered four digital channels: M-NET, Movie Magic, SuperSport and K-TV. In the same year it merged with the Euro-African channel NetHold (2.7 million subscribers) to comprise the MultiChoice digital programme stream, owned by the MultiChoice Future Holding group (MFH). Development of the M-NET network has mainly taken place in the English-speaking regions of Africa. Compared with the major operators world-wide it is classified as a 'junior partner'.

Canal Horizons was set up in 1991 by the French group Canal Plus and the French co-operation company SOFIRAD. The Canal Plus strategy consists in setting up local companies which are partners in the management and broadcasting of Canal Horizons via terrestrial relays. Majority stakes are usually held by local capital with a minority stake taken by Canal Horizons, a partnership arrangement which makes African operators co-owners of the network. Indeed, the overall policy of the French operator is to act as a partner with the African cinema industry. Between 1991 and 1995, some 108 African films were broadcast on Canal Horizons.

In 1995, Canal Horizons had 90,000 subscribers throughout Africa, 18,000 of whom were in Abidjan.[21] Channel executives target to reach 250,000 to 300,000 subscribers in the years to come. Canal Horizons broadcasts its programmes from Paris via the

Eutelsat 'Hot Bird 1' satellite to three major African cities: Abidjan, Dakar and Tunis. An extension programme using MMDS technology to Bamako and Lomé is scheduled. The programme structure resembles that of the encrypted channel Canal Plus. In 1995, 59 per cent of the Canal Horizons programme schedule was based on feature films, 13 per cent on youth programmes and 12 per cent on sport. The erotic shows and televised news bulletins available on Canal Plus are not part of the programmes on Canal Horizons.

TV 5 is a francophone station that began to broadcast its programmes in Africa in 1995 via terrestrial broadcasting networks (MMDS) partially financed by the Canadian Government. The broadcasts with a selection of Belgian, Canadian, French and Swiss programmes can be received in Benin, Burkina Faso, Côte d'Ivoire, Gabon, Mali, the Niger and Senegal. TV 5 Africa is carried by the Russian satellite Statsionar 12 and Intelsat 702. If MMDS systems have spread through Africa, it is because direct reception antennae are expensive for private individuals and MMDS can be installed relatively quickly. One of the most dynamic markets for MMDS systems is Nigeria, where there are approximately fifteen operators and a potential audience of between 100,000 and a million viewers.

Programme importers and co-operation schemes

Importing television programmes takes place under the auspices of various co-operation organizations set up in the different French-speaking countries, in Germany and in the United States. France supplies its programmes via the Canal France International network (CFI), a programme bank that is increasingly beginning to resemble a television channel. CFI also broadcasts news supplied by the AITV International

21. 'Canal Horizons se développe en Afrique' [Canal Horizons is Progressing in Africa], *Le Monde* (Paris), 15 September 1995.

Television Agency. As part of its co-operation programmes, France provides all the equipment necessary for programme reception. The United States provides cultural and scientific programmes via the global Worldnet network and its AfNet scheme. Germany is also present on the market via its Transtel network, and from 1992 onwards with the international television channel Deutsche Welle TV. The United Kingdom, via the BBC World Service Television, still has the largest broadcasting network. The programmes broadcast on these channels are generally amortized through advertising sales, and are provided to African channels in free-to-air or subsidized form.

National TV

African television can generally be classified in three categories, with low-level, average or large-scale infrastructures. The first of these categories usually features a single national channel, with limited airtime, limited audience, and a non-existent advertising market. The profile generally applies to Sahelian and Portuguese-speaking countries. The second category comprises television offering more than one channel, with considerable facilities and airtime use such as in the United Republic of Tanzania (where there are three private channels and one public channel), Zambia and Zimbabwe. Finally, the third category, with large-scale infrastructures, represents a minority of countries such as Nigeria and South Africa: the latter has a state television channel and another thirty or so private and public stations.[22]

South Africa

South Africa is the most dynamic country in Africa in economic terms. In the audiovisual field, it has the largest infrastructures and market in the region. Since the end of apartheid, the audiovisual system has undergone a number of radical changes, in particular with respect to the democratization of the media.

With just over 40 million inhabitants, South Africa has some 12 million viewers, or just under 257 receiving sets per 1,000 people. It was the first country in the continent to have digital broadcasting, with the PAS-4 satellite in 1996. The new supply expanded the South African television market, henceforth shared between a national public broadcaster, the South African Broadcasting Corporation (SABC), and a private operator, M-NET. The two players are striving to diversify their offer in order to occupy the regional and national sectors more effectively, against a backdrop of forecast deregulation and pronounced competition. In August 1996, the South African operator MultiChoice introduced digital television in the form of pay-TV programmes. Three months after its launch, there were some 30,000 subscribers.[23] From Johannesburg, the private channel M-NET also broadcasts its programmes by satellite to thirty-five other African countries.

Faced with competition from private broadcasters, the public television channel SABC has diversified its offer. In addition to three national public channels and two regional stations, SABC has been enhanced with an international service of regional scope and status, as well as a pay-TV satellite programming stream comprising six theme channels specializing in sport, fiction, news and entertainment. To manage these programmes, the public channel has set up a consortium called AstraSat which is open to private shareholdings of up to 60 per cent in its capital.[24] The three national SABC channels in tandem with its two regional stations cover between 60 and 80 per cent of the viewership.

---

22. See L. M. Bourgault, *Mass Media in Sub-Saharan Africa*, pp. 105, 127, Indiana University Press, 1995; A. J. Tudesq, *L'Afrique noire et ses télévisions*, Paris, INA Anthropos, 1992.
23. See 'Africa Turns on to Digital Satellite TV', *Africa Film & TV*, op. cit., p. 41.
24. See 'SABC Whoosh! into Satellite', *COMBROAD* (London), September 1996, p. 5.

The overall strategy of the three major channels, Channels 1, 2 and 3, has been redefined by the Independent Broadcasting Authority, the regulatory authority in South Africa. Henceforth, the assignment of public service television is to enhance the diversity of broadcasting sources, to facilitate access for communities which have hitherto been excluded, and to take into account the political plurality and cultural diversity of the country. The IBA is entrusted with supervising the enforcement of these aims, with regulating the whole of the audiovisual sector and with granting broadcasting licences. Another regulatory authority, the Independent Media Commission (IMC), has also been set up. Its assignment is to supervise fair access to the small screen for social groups and political parties in electoral periods.[25]

Whereas South African television was used during apartheid as a tool for propaganda, its purpose today is to facilitate the integration of the different communities in the country, and to enrich democratic debate within the nation. The main objective of the channel is also to reflect the linguistic and cultural diversity of the country, where there are eleven official languages. The challenge has led the government to remodel the SABC channels on the basis of linguistic, cultural and geographical criteria, while the three new channels – Channels 1, 2 and 3 – symbolize the break with apartheid.

Since this phase of restructuring, South African television has diversified to broadcast some of its programmes in minority languages that were neglected in the past, such as Xitsonga or TshiVenda. Viewers have shown considerable interest in these programmes, with ratings on the rise. The change has also been marked by greater attention to local production, again penalized in the past by a high level of imported programmes.[26]

For international broadcasting purposes, the SABC in 1992 set up Channel Africa, a public channel that broadcasts programmes to English-speaking countries in East Africa. The channel is financed by the South African Ministry of Foreign Affairs. Further to financial problems in 1994, the channel was forced to lower its sights and limit airtime to a few hours per day.[27]

The second player in the South African television landscape is the private pay-TV channel M-NET. It was set up in 1986 by the four main written press groups in South Africa that together have a 90 per cent stake in its capital.[28] Its start-up was seen as a compensatory measure on behalf of the South African written press that has seen its advertising revenue slump as a result of competition from television. The channel broadcasts its programmes via terrestrial means towards the country's hinterland, and via the PAS-4 satellite towards the rest of the African continent. Broadcasting to African countries is based on digital technology in conjunction with the other South African operator MultiChoice. M-NET and MultiChoice are part of the same Euro-African group Nethold. After crossing the break-even point in 1989, by January 1996 M-NET had more than a million subscribers, 90 per cent of whom are situated in South Africa. The station offers a programme stream of four theme-oriented channels, mostly based on American products. Since the station has widened its broadcasting scope to African countries, however, African productions have been integrated into its programme structure. The presence of foreign investors since 1995 has stimulated the South African market. After

25. See J. Cluzel, 'L'audiovisuel en Afrique du Sud – Quelles opportunités pour la France ?' [The Audiovisual Market in South Africa – What's in it for France?], in *Les Cahiers de l'Audiovisuel* (Paris), No. 4, June 1995, p. 87 ff.
26. See 'Controversial Changes Lift Audiences', *COMBROAD* (London), September 1996, p. 5; see also 'Relaunch of SABC TV', *COMBROAD*, March 1996, p. 10.
27. See P. Jallon, 'Afrique du Sud', in Hennebelle (ed.), op. cit., p. 314; 'Channel Africa Saved – for Now', *COMBROAD* (London), September 1996, p. 3.
28. See 'M-NET Breaks the Barrier One Million!', *Africa Film & TV*, p. 38; see also P. Cluzel, op. cit., p. 87.

purchasing the exclusive broadcasting rights for South African rugby matches for the next ten years, the News Corp group owned by Rupert Murdoch finally relinquished them to M-NET in 1996.[29]

South African television therefore appears to be the most dynamic on the continent, with factors such as state-of-the-art technology, and powerful audiovisual groups present on an important potential market to sustain its drive. The government's liberalization policy has brought with it a process of democratization and deregulation which has enriched and enlarged programme choice.

Burkina Faso

Burkina Faso is an African country which is particularly eager to develop the production of African-oriented images. For the last twenty-seven years it has organized the Pan African Cinema Festival (FESPACO), and for several decades has maintained its efforts to set up a local film industry, yet ironically, Burkina Faso is one of the poorest countries in the world. It is situated in the Sahelian zone of Africa and its mainly rural population has little access to even the most basic infrastructures. Against an economic backdrop as dire as this, the role of television is restricted, and essentially confined to urban areas. Television broadcasts first went on-air in Burkina Faso in 1963; indeed, the Upper Volta, as it was then called, with Senegal and the Congo, was one of the very first African countries to have television at all. It remained for many years a totally marginal social feature, its development most often hindered by constraints of an economic and political nature. It was not until 1980 and the emergence of the democratic process that the major upheavals seen elsewhere began to appear in the audiovisual environment of Burkina Faso. New channels have been set up and transmit by digital terrestrial means, cable or satellite. In Ouagadougou, the private channel Multimedia broadcasts the two French-speaking channels, Canal Horizons and TV5, using MMDS digital terrestrial broadcasting tech-

nology, yet in terms of satellite reception – dish antennae are a luxury product for most of the inhabitants of Burkina Faso – there are fewer than 300 dish homes in the whole country. The national television channel TNB is striving to develop its structures, based on a modernization programme begun in 1980. TNB covers less than 15 per cent of the territory and is seen by no more than 20 per cent of the population. In 1978, Burkina Faso had some 6,000 television sets. Further to a financial incentive policy to acquire television receiving sets, today there are more than 80,000, 70 per cent of which are colour sets. There has been a similar rise in airtime. In 1978, TNB broadcast only twelve hours of programmes a week; in 1985, it was broadcasting more than 243 hours a week. That being said, TNB is confronted with serious material and financial constraints. The 500 million CFA francs of licence fees and several hundred million generated by advertising revenue are soaked up by the national electricity company and a government agency, a deflection which weakens the TNB budget and correspondingly restricts its production and programming capacity. The advertising market is highly irregular and represents no more than 0.4 per cent of total revenue for television, which is 60 per cent dependent on imported programmes. The content of these is based mainly on entertainment. Indeed, the increase in airtime has led to a greater dependence on imported programmes, to the detriment of an apparently dynamic local production industry: Burkina Faso in 1989 was the leading supplier of African programmes to the West. In that year alone, the country exported several productions in the form of fiction programmes and magazines as part of the South–North image scheme.

Kenya

Kenya is one of the very few African countries to have an audiovisual system in which a national distributor,

29. 'M-NET Breaks the Barrier One Million!', op. cit., p. 40.

the Kenya Broadcasting Corporation (KBC), and its four channels share the market with a private operator, KTN. The situation is a result of political changes which occurred in 1991 that have led to greater democracy, but is also due to the fact that Nairobi is nothing short of a media pool for East Africa. The capital of Kenya houses the head offices of a number of foreign media organizations, including the PEC (Programme Exchange Centre) and the URTNA (Union of National Radio and Television Organizations of Africa), the organization in charge of the exchange of African programmes.

With an installed base estimated at 2.3 million television sets in 1993 (i.e. eighty-seven sets per 1,000 people), the audiovisual system in Kenya has also gone through a period of major upheaval. Quite apart from the public channels and the private station KTN, another two private channels, Cable Television Network (CTN) and Stellagraphics, in 1995 obtained their permission to broadcast from Nairobi.[30] Pay television is also setting up with the arrival of satellite reception. Its linguistic and geographical proximity (English) make Kenya a potential market for the leading South African operators M-NET and Multi-Choice, which are penetrating the local market by signing up partnerships with Kenyan stations. Kenya also provides them with a possible platform towards the rest of the African continent and the Middle East. The new channel CTN intends to specialize in general-interest programming dominated by entertainment, animated cartoons, music, and news magazines. The channel is owned by Blue Chips Ltd, which is controlled by Australian investors.[31]

The South African operator MultiChoice has penetrated the Kenyan market via a joint venture with the national distributor, KBC, a marriage which gave birth to Channel 2. Since 1995 the station has been offering three pay-TV channels, broadcasting specialized programmes such as Supersport, M-NET's KTV (sport and children's programmes), as well as programmes from M-NET, BBC-WORLD and BOP-TV, a

general-interest channel out of Boputatswana. The channels initially covered only the capital, Nairobi. Today, they have expanded to other cities such as Mombasa, with a subscription rate on the rise. The launch of the Panamsat 4 satellite has multiplied the programmes on offer even further, in particular for viewers who are able to purchase reception equipment.[32]

KBC, the national broadcasting company, is striving to develop and modernize its terrestrial network. It has two stations, one of which has specialized in the production of programmes for nationwide television. KBC broadcasts in English and in Kiswahili on four channels. Imports account for 52 per cent of its programmes, mostly entertainment products. The general move is towards an increase in the broadcasting of imported programmes, from the United States in particular, which provides half of all the programmes shown in Brazil, Egypt, India, the United Kingdom, etc. National production is weak, even though some productions, such as the educational series *Tushauriane,* televised in Swahili, have been resounding successes.[33] KBC has signed agreements permitting the syndication of programmes from several channels or foreign media agencies such as Deutsche Welle, CFI, Reuters Television or the BBC World Television News. KBC in fact is the offshoot of a restructuring of the former public channel Voice of Kenya Television, which was converted into a para-state enterprise open to foreign capital. KBC has not been subject to government control since that phase, although bureau members are chosen by the President

30. C. Scott. 'What Does it Taste Like?', *Media Studies Journal*, Vol. 10, Nos. 2–3, 1996, p. 164.

31. H. P. Bolap, 'Kenya', in Hennebelle (ed.), op. cit., p. 345.

32. 'Satellite Opens Way for Expansion of Pay TV', in *COMBROAD* (London), September 1996, p. 27.

33. A. J. Tudesq, *L'Afrique Noire et ses télévisions*, p. 158, Paris, 1992.

of the Republic.[34] Since 1964, the channel has also housed a journalists' training school, the Kenya Institute of Mass Communication (KIMC).

The private Kenya Television Network (KTN) was set up in 1989, and was one of the first examples of pay television to go on the air in Africa. It was initially owned by the Kenya Times Media Trust group, founded by Robert Maxwell, in association with the party in power, the KANU. It is currently owned by Kenyan businessmen.[35] The channel broadcasts twenty-four hours a day, transmitting CNN International and MTV Europe among others, as well as various local and international channels.

Television in Kenya is part of a general modernization and internationalization process, characterized by the restructuring of public service television, the advent of pay television, the emergence of new private stations and the arrival on the market of foreign operators via joint ventures with local partners. Political liberalization for the time being, however, seems to have led neither to greater diversity in local content nor to the total disappearance of political control. The impact of the new channels should also be put into perspective. They are still limited to the capital, Nairobi, to its 2 million inhabitants, and to the leading hotels in the country. In the end, most of the population of Kenya is rural and remains faithful to the ruling medium: radio.

Asia and the Pacific

General trends

Most markets in the Asia-Pacific region generally have a high rate of growth, with a particularly dynamic audiovisual sector. The region contains more than 60 per cent of the world's population with some 3 billion inhabitants, fast-expanding urban centres and an economic growth rate of 7 per cent per year. The stakes in the region are vast, whether in economic, commercial, technological, political or cultural

terms, having become the world's leading centre for televisual production and consumption.[36]

The region's economic drive extends into the media field, where a genuine revolution has upset every national landscape. Television, without a doubt, has the most powerful growth rate. More than 386 million households in Asia are equipped with television sets, or an average rate of more than 55 per cent.[37] Estimates indicate that by the year 2005 more than 447 million households will be equipped with receiving sets.[38] The arrival of channels from space and their proliferation are another revolution. In 1992 the region averaged 2.4 television channels per country. With digital data compression, there will be thousands of them by the year 2000.[39] On top of this, with the arrival of pay television, revenue from television, estimated at $369 million in 1995, should rise to $2.5 billion by the year 2005. Eighteen per cent of households are connected to cable television today, a rate which should reach 35 per cent by the year 2005.[40] The same ratio applies to the advertising market, which soared from $37 billion to $58 billion between 1985 and 1995. While Japan is still the major beneficiary of this market, with an 84.4 per cent

34. L. M. Bourgault, *Mass Media in Sub-Saharan Africa*, p. 127, Bloomington, Ind., 1995.
35. 'Directory Kenya', in *Africa Film & TV*, op. cit., p. 88.
36. C. B. Johnston, *Winning the Global TV News Game*, Boston/Oxford/Melbourne, 1995.
37. International Telecommunication Union (ITU) (ed.), *World Telecommunication Development Report*, Geneva, 1995.
38. 'The Great Leap Forward', *Broadcasting & Cable International*, April 1995, p. 62.
39. P. Le Corre, 'Télévision: le boom est programmé sur la planète Asie' [Television: the Boom is Planned to Take Place on Planet Asia], *La Tribune Desfossés*, 29 April 1994; cf. N. Vulser, 'Les lendemains qui chantent de l'audiovisuel asiatique', [The Bright Future of Asian Audiovisual Technology], *Les Echos* (Paris), 8 December 1994.
40. 'The Great Leap Forward', *Broadcasting & Cable International*, April 1995, p. 62.

Audiovisual indicators and GNP for Asia and the Pacific, 1994

Country	Households (%)				GNP/inhab. in value at parity of purchasing power
	TV	VCR	Satellite	Cable	
Australia	99	83	N.a.	3	18 120
Bangladesh	10.6	4	N.a.	N.a.	1 330
Cambodia	14	21	5[1]	2[1]	N.a.
China	73	53[2]	N.a.	12	2 510
India	31	6	2.6	24	1 280
Indonesia	40	10	2	N.a.	3 600
Japan	100	85.9	>17	>18	21 140
Lao People's Dem. Rep.	5	1	N.a.	N.a.	157
Malaysia	92	47	N.a.	0.5	8 440
Myanmar	31	42	N.a.	2	115
New Zealand	98	75	N.a.	0.4	15 870
Pakistan	32	25	12	N.a.	2 130
Philippines	57	23	N.a.	6	2 740
Republic of Korea	100	88.6	N.a.	7	10 330
Singapore	99	84	Banned	21	21 900
Sri Lanka	53	6	0.5	N.a.	3 160
Thailand	90	23	0.1	1	6 970

1. Refers only to Phnom Penh.
2. Refers to percentage of adults in Beijing/Shanghai/Guangzhou.

Source: *Market and Media Facts*, 1995–96, London, Zenith Publications.

market share against 15.6 per cent for the rest of the continent, the share of other countries such as China and India is significantly increasing. Generally speaking, the advertising market is buoyant and should see an increase of 75 per cent between 1994 and 2003. According to the *Television in the Asia Pacific to 2000* report, investments worth $39 billion will be made in this sector between now and the year 2000.[41]

New landscapes

Two complementary trends seem to stand out in the audiovisual landscape on the Asian continent: powerful internationalization of the television market, and increasing regionalization. The two trends are reflected equally in terms of ownership and in terms of programme content.

Major international groups such as NBC, MTV, Asian Business News, CNN and StarTV have a large audience in Asia. CNN is watched by 10 million households, ESPN by 6.3 million and BBC World by 7 million households.[42] At the same time, however, local operators are becoming serious contenders at the

41. 'Asian TV Advertising Expenditure 1995–99. Report Round-up', *TV International* (New York), Vol. 3, No. 16, 1995, p. 3.
42. 'The Cable Satellite Landscape: Country by Country', *Broadcasting & Cable International*, April 1995, p. 70.

regional level. In Japan, NHK is part of the wealthiest television network in the world and exports a large percentage of its audiovisual production. Other operators such as the Asia Television Network (ATN) in India, IBC in Thailand and RCTI in Indonesia are positioning themselves on the Asian market. Others again, backed by banks, major industrial groups or political figures, have formed genuine conglomerates such as the Shinawatra Group in Thailand, Biamantra Waxed in Indonesia or Amcorp in Malaysia. Henceforth the audiovisual industry is a fully integrated business sector for Asian groups.

Internationalization and regionalization can also be seen at the programme package level. Asian audiences express a preference for regional programmes in local national languages, a salient feature everywhere around the world. This partially explains the success of the Indian channel Zee TV, 75 per cent of whose programmes are local in origin. The Asia Business News channel is another example of programmes replying to specific regional demands. Other international broadcasters are adapting their programmes to the cultural, political and linguistic diversity of the region.

The Asian audiovisual market is far from being homogeneous, however. Imbalances persist between states and within them. Japan is still the most advanced country in terms of its audiovisual market and the use of new technology. China, India and Indonesia, and also the newly industrialized countries such as Singapore and Thailand, are now buoyant markets, particularly in the audiovisual field. Nevertheless, a number of countries persistently raise questions about the place of 'Asian' or national values in programme content or about the flood of pictures broadcast by satellite.

Regional and international players

The audiovisual communication market in Asia is shared by two main types of operator: local or regional public institutions or major audiovisual groups. The former group is represented by the Asia Broadcasting Union (ABU), located in Kuala Lumpur, which is the Asian counterpart of the EBU. The purpose of this regional organization is to promote intraregional communication and exchange with the other regions of the world. The ABU currently comprises thirty member states and a number of associate members. The organization has woven a network for exchange with similar organizations in Europe (EBU), the Arab States (ASBU), Africa (URTNA), the Caribbean (CBU) and the Pacific (PIBA).[43] The other category of operator comprises the large communication companies of local, regional or international scope and status. Strategies for control of the market are varied, ranging from joint ventures, to total or partial acquisitions of the equity in local stations, or the setting-up of new broadcasting networks.

Satellite Television Asian Region, commonly known under the name of StarTV, is the largest network in the region. It covers some fifty countries, and has a viewing audience which is constantly expanding: 11.3 million households in 1993, 42 million in 1994 and 54 million in 1995. Initially owned by the Hong Kong group of Hutchinson Whampoa and the Li family, 64 per cent of the equity in the station was transferred to the Rupert Murdoch group in 1993 for $525 million. Since then, StarTV has adopted a strategy based on local positioning. The station began by buying the exclusive rights to transmission on the two regional satellites Asiasat 1 and Asiasat 2, with a total capacity of 100 channels and coverage ranging from the Far East to Europe. The network then restructured its mainstream

---

43. The Pacific Islands Broadcasting Association (PIBA) was set up in December 1987 in Tonga to promote measures aiming to develop the audiovisual markets of the region, to train the personnel on the national television stations, and to encourage technical co-operation and audiovisual exchange between the members of the fourteen countries and territories in the region.

programme package by breaking it down into local channels in order to match the linguistic and cultural demands of the region more effectively. Finally, it has multiplied its partnerships with local and national broadcasters in order to give a better position in the various subregions of the continent, in which the Chinese community is highly dispersed. Within this framework, StarTV has set up production sites in Beijing, Bombay, Hong Kong and Taiwan to produce magazines in local languages. The large-scale invest-ments involved have prevented StarTV from making a profit so far, the company having posted losses in 1996 estimated at $100 million.[44]

In India, StarTV has set up its network via a partnership policy with Subhash Chandra, a major operator in the Indian audiovisual field and owner of the private channel Zee TV, in particular. In 1994, the Murdoch group acquired 50 per cent of the capital in Zee Telefilms, a profit-making channel that holds more than 60 per cent of the booming Indian advertising market, which has an annual growth rate of more than 30 per cent. Besides Zee TV, Murdoch also controls four other channels: El TV, Zee Cinema, Star Movies and Channel V. These various acquisitions in India have aroused a considerable degree of criticism, related on the one hand to the potential threat hanging over the cultural identity of the country, and on the other to the risk of seeing Zee TV and the other Murdoch channels take the high ground in the Indian market. In Indonesia, StarTV has adopted the same partnership strategy with the influential operator Indovision, a private broadcaster offering a pro-gramme stream comprising mainly American stations: HBO, ESPN, CNN, TNT and the Cartoon Network. A plan for the joint launch of a new stream of fifteen channels is scheduled for 1997.[45] StarTV also plans to launch new channels in Thailand and in Japan.

Other operators are present on the Asian market. CNN was the first international station to invest massively in Asia, where it has been present since 1982, particularly in Japan. Today it covers more than

twenty countries in Asia and the Pacific, with offices in Bangkok, Manila, New Delhi, Seoul and Tokyo. In addition to its international recipe of non-stop news, CNN every day broadcasts a programme of current events and business magazines for Asia. Time Warner has moved into the Asian market via its base in Singapore, where its subsidiary Home Box Office (HBO) has set up HBO Asia, a pay-TV service special-izing in feature films. The channel is also carried by the Indonesian satellite Palapa, which is received by more than 40 million households. In association with regional television companies in New Zealand and Singapore, the world leader in cable television, the American company Tele-Communications, is pre-paring to launch a pan-Asian channel specializing in business news. This type of programme is already present with the Asia Business News channel, launched by five international and regional press and telecommunications groups including Telecommuni-cation Inc., Dow Jones, Television New Zealand, Siam Ventures (Singapore) and BNN (Hong Kong).

Finally, some local operators such as AsiaNet, Zee TV and Namaste Asian Television are trying to position themselves on the Asian immigration market in Europe and in North America by broadcasting programmes in Hindi and Urdu. Zee TV, for example, has 100,000 subscribers in Europe (1996), 96,000 of whom are in the United Kingdom. In America, Zee TV is part of the DCI International programme stream, which is received by 7.2 million homes via cable TV. Zee TV also targets the African audience, where the channel is part of the MultiChoice digital programme stream.

44. 'StarTV Set to Double Asian Regional Programming in 1996', *TV International*, Vol. 4, No. 4, 1996, pp. 1–2.
45. Strategy described by F. Keenan, 'Murdoch's Gambit – StarTV and Indovision Attempt a Delicate Tie-up', *Far Eastern Economic Review*, 18 July 1996, p. 75.

The People's Republic of China

Developments in the Chinese television market are the result of both the country's current modernization policy and accelerating globalization in business and communication. In this vast territory with 1.2 billion inhabitants, most of them living in rural zones, the main purpose of state television is to answer the educational and entertainment needs of its viewers. Since the 1980s, it has been accessible to most of the peasant farmers in the countryside. Its audience has risen from 10 per cent in 1980 to 67 per cent in 1996. In China today there are some 240 million households with a television set and 30 million homes connected to cable TV. Together they represent more than 850 million viewers (or more than 80 per cent of the population). Colour television has penetrated up to 90 per cent of the territory in recent years, and is now received by more than 40 per cent of all households. This is considered to be one of the most important developments in Chinese television in the 1980s.

Since its creation in 1958, television has always been a state monopoly controlled by the Ministry of Radio, Television and Cinema. Chinese Central Television (CCTV) is the national network, and has a dominant position in the Chinese audiovisual industry.

CCTV offers five different channels: CCTV1 is the most popular channel on the network and reaches more than 83 per cent of the population. CCTV2 is available only in urban areas (300 million viewers). The content of this channel is more educational, economic and social. CCTV3 is a general-interest entertainment channel specializing in sport. The other channels of the major provinces manage to finance a large part of their activities through advertising, an area in which the Chinese market has exceptional potential growth. In 1995, it already stood at $900 million, with an estimated annual growth rate of 40 per cent. There are a few problems, however, in particular the difficulty of evaluating audiences accurately, and the average quality of the programmes. Chinese television has always given priority, as has India, to cultural and educational programmes. One of the central priorities for public service television in China today is to teach the rules of the 'socialist market economy' to its primarily rural audience and main target.

In addition to the national network, the regional network enables stations to broadcast to thirty-one provinces, autonomous regions and municipalities, via thirty-seven major regional broadcasters and 300 municipal channels, representing more than 700 terrestrial stations and dozens of cable-TV channels. In all, more than 25,000 to 35,000 hours of programmes are broadcast each week on nearly 800 different channels. To supply them, the Chinese television service fills part of the programmes with domestic productions and stops the gaps with imported programmes. The law on quotas limits the proportion of imported programmes and co-productions to 30 per cent of the programmes on Chinese channels.

Cable TV in China has developed on the principle of one channel per city, with the result that a network with more than 30 million subscribers has been created. In Shanghai, the largest city in China with 14 million inhabitants, more than a million households have already subscribed. In 1992, the cable-TV network comprised a dozen channels, one of which, Oriental TV, is entirely financed by advertising. Operating licences are issued by the Ministry of Radio and Television, and subscription prices are low. According to Chinese experts, the number of subscriber households to cable TV should rise from 46 million in 1996 to 100 million by 2005, or the equivalent of 25 to 30 per cent of all Chinese families. With these rising prospects, the services on offer should also diversify in order to satisfy the expectations of an increasingly fragmented audience. Other experts estimate that China may become the biggest cable-TV market in the world.[46] In a landscape

46. 'Télévision: la Chine s'ouvre timidement à la concurrence' [Television: A Timid China Lets Competition

noted for its dramatic upheavals, a major battle is going on between the audiovisual giants. The News Corp. group controlled by Rupert Murdoch seems to have succeeded in reconciling the demands of the specifications drafted by the Chinese authorities and the high hopes of the audience in terms of programmes. It is soon to set up a rival company to CCTV, through an association with a private operator in the country, to distribute satellite television programmes in China. The company is scheduled to broadcast three channels for Chinese viewers, with two new general-interest programmes and the programme stream's sports channel Star TV.[47]

India

With an indigenous population of 900 million, India would be the second largest audiovisual market in the world if the purchasing power of its population were proportional to its demographic scale. Among the major developing countries, in audiovisual terms it is still one of the most under-equipped in the world. There are some 46 million television sets in the country, and less than 10 per cent of all households have a VCR. Basically, it is the 200 million middle-class Indians who have an individual colour television set. The same classes are also hastening to buy cable-TV equipment and dish antennae. Estimates indicate there were 16 million homes with cable TV in 1996 and 7.3 million satellite dishes in 1994. The massive presence of community television sets in 600,000 rural villages gives a much larger audience access to television, even if 75 per cent of the sets sold are black and white and can receive only seven to eight channels.

As in several countries with vast territories and widescale diversity in their populations, public service television is a central vector for national integration which conditions the relations between religious and ethnic communities. The Indian audiovisual landscape has for many years been dominated by the public channel Doordarshan, which is totally financed by the government. The Indian public network reaches 85 per cent of the Indian population and covers two-thirds of the territory. Hindi and English are the two languages used on the national television service, while local and regional channels broadcast in regional languages.

With the arrival of private channels in 1993, the public network has diversified to set up six other terrestrial channels specializing in regional and national programmes. DD1 is a general-interest channel that broadcasts in English, Hindi and Urdu to nearly 30 million households, or more than 120 million viewers. DD2 is a channel specializing in feature films and is designed for young viewers. It covers nearly 8 million homes or some 30 million viewers. DD3 has been broadcasting cultural programmes since 1994. DD4 broadcasts more specifically to the southern states of India in their regional languages. Finally, DD5 and DD6 broadcast programmes destined for the states in the Gulf of Bengal and the eastern border regions, and the east and the north-east of the country.[48]

A dominant feature of Indian public television is its function as a medium for mass education. Indeed, the first schools television experiment anywhere in the world took place in India in 1961. The world's very first satellite instructional television experiment (SITE) was also launched in India in 1975 with the assistance of several partners, and of UNESCO in particular. The programmes have enabled many viewers to follow distance learning courses and even to take examinations approved by the state. The educational role attributed to television was consecrated by the

under the Door], *La Tribune Desfossés* (Paris), 18 August 1995; 'Television: China Keeps Tight Grip on Cable-TV Boom', *Financial Times* (London), 20 August 1996.

47. 'Rupert Murdoch Invests China', *Financial Times*, 19 February 1996.

48. A. Lewin, 'Inde', in Hennebelle (ed.), op. cit., pp. 416–22.

creation in 1985 of an information and in-service training programme on-screen called 'teletext'.

The opening of the Indian audiovisual market has been conditioned to a large degree by the anarchic proliferation of cable and satellite TV. The number of households with cable TV rapidly rose from 0.4 million to 16 million between 1993 and 1996. In 1995 the cable-TV network comprised twenty-eight channels broadcasting among others CNN International, Canal France International, Asian Television Network (ATN) – set up in Bombay in 1992 – Sun TV, a channel broadcasting in the Tamil language of southern India, Asianet, a channel broadcasting in the Malayalam language, also in southern India, MTV, and above all StarTV and Zee TV, both broadcasting in Hindi and both controlled by News Corp., the Rupert Murdoch group. In 1997 Murdoch created an Indian legal entity, legally distinct from Star TV, in order to launch a new digital television service known as ISkyB for direct satellite broadcasting. This will comprise four new channels and ultimately up to fifty services on seven satellite channels. Faced with this multitude of channels, a draft Bill on broadcasting, issued in 1997, placed a 49 per cent limit on foreign investment in an Indian television service. The new procedure for granting licences provides a separate accord for each type of service, depending on the broadcasting system being employed: terrestrial broadcasting, satellite, cable or direct satellite. Until such time as the Bill is passed in Parliament, the Indian Government steadfastly refuses to legalize the new Murdoch package. In recent years, political decision-makers have earnestly discussed the position of international channels: some of them are of the opinion that the incursion of cable or satellite channels may well compromise the role of television as a factor of social and material unity.

Japan

Japan is one of the most dynamic markets worldwide in the fields of telecommunications, electronics and new information and communication technology. The same drive is perceptible in the audiovisual sector, which includes the largest public channel in the world (NHK), a dozen stations that rate among the world's leading 100 enterprises in the audiovisual sector and the first use of Direct Broadcasting Satellite on Earth. In terms of broadcasting, Japanese viewers can access more than a hundred terrestrial channels and programme packages via cable and satellite. In terms of production, Japan is a leading audiovisual producer. The Japanese audiovisual environment includes a major national distributor, the public channel Nippon Hoso Kyokai (NHK), five major private channels, and approximately 100 regional stations. It is the second largest audiovisual market in the world after the United States.

NHK broadcasting corporation ranks among the top ten broadcasters worldwide. Subscriptions provide 96.3 per cent of its budget. It broadcasts all of its programmes on four channels, two of which are carried by satellite. NHK has always been at the leading edge of new technology. In 1960, it was the first station to introduce colour television, followed by DBS in 1984 and high-definition television (HDTV) in 1989. Broadly speaking, the first terrestrial channel, General TV (GTV), broadcasts general-interest programmes and news, while the second channel, Education TV (ETV), broadcasts mainly educational and cultural programmes. The channels which are carried by satellite, DBS-1 and DBS-2, specialize in cultural and sports programmes, and in news magazines. Satellite broadcasting by the public service today has to contend with competition from a third private DBS network, the Digital MultiChannel Planning Co. (DMC). The major Japanese private channels NTV, TBS, Fuji, TV Asahi and TV Tokyo are totally financed by advertising. Asahi TV, set up in 1957, is the largest of these channels. More than 95 per cent of its programmes are Japanese productions. The attempted takeover in 1996 of the channel by News Corp., when the group owned by Rupert Murdoch took a 21 per cent stake in its equity, met with strong resistance from the *Asahi* daily, which held 34 per cent in its television homonym. The Austro-American group has finally abandoned the project but with its local partner Masayoshi Son, President of Softbank, is continuing to prepare the launch of a programme stream with 150 digital channels entitled Japan Sky Broadcasting (JSkyB), scheduled for April 1998. Murdoch's offensive fits in with the group's strategy to occupy the Asian market through local alliances.

Alongside terrestrial and satellite television, cable TV is another form of broadcasting, offering a choice of more than 130 programmes, most of which are pay-TV channels. In this sector, the Japanese Government has decided to connect every household with fibre optic cables by the year 2010. As early as 1991, International Viacom and Sumitomo had begun to install a cable-TV system equipped with digital compression, thereby permitting an increase in the number of channels.

The Japanese digital television market had a rocket start in 1997. Perfect TV, the first programme stream of digital channels broadcast by satellite in Japan, which went into orbit in October 1996, already has more than 100,000 subscribers. Two other streams, Direct TV and JSkyB, will go on-air in 1997 and 1998. Finally, the traditional terrestrial channels are waiting for the new satellite BS-4 to be launched in 2000 in order to set up their own digital programme streams.

Japanese viewers are among those who spend the most time in front of their television sets: 3 hours and 25 minutes per day. Of the programmes they watch, 40 per cent are entertainment-based, 25 per cent are cultural, 20 per cent of them are news, and 13 per cent are educational. On top of this, more than 35 per cent of programmes are sponsored by advertisers. As far as interactive television is concerned, three experiments have been under way since 1994: 'PNES' (interactive video, with thirty-one cable-TV channels), 'BBC' C (teleshopping, education and electronic libraries) and a video-on-demand service, designed for the educational network.

Finally, it is worth pointing out that Japanese television is also present in the United States with TV Japan, a channel backed by NHK and controlled by Japan Airlines. It targets the 1 million Japanese residing in the United States. The sector has a similar level of presence in Europe with Japan Satellite TV, founded by MICO and ALL Nippon Airways, which broadcasts a Japanese programme for the Japanese community.[49]

Latin America and the Caribbean

General trends

Television in Latin America has been strongly marked from the 1990s onwards by two powerful trends linked to technological upheavals and to media internationalization. With the advent of digital broadcasting and the rapid rise in the number of channels, satellite reception developed at high speed with the installation of cable-TV networks and the proliferation of dish antennae. The change, which has led to strong demand for national and international programmes, raises a number of questions relating to the development of a local audiovisual industry confronted with international alliances, the risk of domination by the major national, regional or international groups, and the future of local or community public channels.

Latin America features two major audiovisual markets. The largest of these is Spanish-speaking. In demographic terms it is the second largest audiovisual market worldwide. It comprises some 333 million potential viewers, 270 million of whom are in Latin America, 39 million in Spain and 24 million in the United States. The second is Portuguese-speaking and basically concerns the 150 million viewers in Brazil. Generally speaking, a high proportion of the people

49. See IDATE, *Industrial Analyses: The World Film and Television Market*, p. 237, Montpellier, IDATE, 1994.

Audiovisual indicators and GNP for Latin America and the Caribbean, 1994 (figures in parentheses indicate an estimated total number)

Country	Households (%)				GNP/inhab. in value at parity of purchasing power
	TV	VCR	Satellite	Cable	
Argentina	97	41	N.a.	55	8 720
Brazil	85	38	4	1.5	5 400
Chile	80	23	N.a.	10	8 890
Colombia	97	21	14	3	5 330
Dominican Republic	73	12	2	5	3 760
Ecuador	(2 250 186)	30	0.1	3	4 190
El Salvador	93	31	N.a.	3	2 410
Guatemala	56	60	N.a.	46	3 440
Honduras	60	32	N.a.	11	1 940
Jamaica	95	N.a.	6	15	3 400
Mexico	85	58	N.a.	8	7 040
Panama	63	40	2	4	5 730
Peru	65	23	N.a.	1	3 610
Trinidad and Tobago	92	45	13	N.a.	8 670
Uruguay	(854 332)	41	2	8	7 710

Source: *Market and Media Facts*, 1995–96, London, Zenith Publications.

in urban communities, which represent more than 70 per cent of the population in the region, have television sets. In the large cities such as Mexico City, São Paulo, Rio de Janeiro, Buenos Aires, Lima or Bogotá, the penetration rate is as high as 90 per cent. With regard to cable television, the number of subscriber households in Latin America is estimated at 5 million, mainly located in Mexico and Argentina.

Despite the wide-ranging diversity of national sociopolitical contexts and audiovisual systems, a number of factors are common to the whole of the region: the predominance of commercial channels over public channels, and the scale of the television advertising market. Public service television in Latin America is based on a wholly different concept from that prevailing in Europe, in that although they are not controlled by the state, private television channels

are considered to serve the general interest. In the large countries of the region such as Brazil or Mexico, public television is a marginal sector. In Bolivia, Chile and Peru, local, university or community television channels express alternative points of view. In all, the average annual budget for public service stations is barely 6 per cent of the budget for commercial stations. It is estimated that of the 570 terrestrial channels currently broadcasting in the countries of Latin America and the Caribbean, 105 belong to the public service, and sixty-four of those are cultural and educational in their scope.

Relations with the nearby North American continent result in complex alliances between North American and South American communication groups. In reply to the traditional influence of channels north of the border, television groups from

Latin America have made large-scale investments in the United States targeting the 'Latino' market. The advertising market is a potentially high-return, high-growth sector with high-rise budgets.

New audiovisual landscapes

The Latin American market is dominated by two major television conglomerates, the Brazilian Rede Globo group, and the Mexican Televisa group. They both hold the high ground on their respective markets and export their *telenovelas* (soaps) and other productions all around the world, such that today they are two multimedia giants, frequently competing with the major North American groups. The Televisa channel is the leading multinational in the region, and is therefore best equipped to face the current globalization of the market. It is also the leading producer and exporter of Spanish-language programmes.[50] In 1995, it controlled 75 per cent of the Mexican market, with four major national channels and 200 regional channels. The station also owns several radios, eighty newspapers and two major football teams. In the same year, it sold off its shares in the equity of the cable-TV network CableVision in order to invest in a partnership with the Brazilian Rede Globo group and other American investors in a satellite programme package, Sky Entertainment Channel.[51] The Brazilian Rede Globo group has nine television channels. It attracts 68 per cent of the Brazilian viewership and 73 per cent of all advertising revenue. It also controls a high circulation newspaper, several magazines, and eighteen radio stations, and invests in sectors as diverse as insurance, real estate, cattle breeding, food processing and the electronics industry.[52]

Apart from Venezuela, which is similar to the Mexican and Brazilian models, the television systems in the other countries of the region are generally more decentralized. In Argentina, there are more than 1,200 cable-TV operators to fight over the cable market. Elsewhere, particularly in Central America, the television market is still rudimentary and usually confronted with practical problems which penalize local production and restrict audiences.[53]

Despite piracy – which is becoming a factor of growing concern – cable television and satellite reception are rapidly developing. Alliances between groups specialized in digital broadcasting are being set up, while operators of rival systems to cable and MMDS are honing their strategies. American investment in the region in recent years has made the market particularly buoyant. Overall investment in pay television in 1995 amounted to $684 million. The Sky Entertainment Television network is the product of a DTH (Direct-to-Home) consortium jointly controlled by the Murdoch Group News Corp., the Brazilian Rede Globo, the Mexican Televisa and the American major TCI. Since 1996 the consortium has been competing with the Galaxy Latin America multinational, controlled by the American company Hughes Electronics in partnership with the Mexican channel MVS Multivision, the Brazilian channel Televisão Abril and the Venezuelan channel Cisneros.[54]

The two alliances are battling for control of the 11 million televised Latin American households already used to a wide range of choice. The prohibitive cost of reception equipment at around $700, however, is still a prime constraint for the general introduction of digital television. It is estimated the latter will attract some 5.3 million households between now and 2005, or less than 5 per cent of the households equipped with receivers. These estimates are apparently disputed by the Sky and Galaxy broadcasters,

50.   G. Schneier-Madanes, 'Mutation et ouverture' [Change and Opening], *L'Amérique Latine et ses télévisions: du local au mondial* [Latin America and its TV stations: From Local to Global], Paris, Anthropos-Economica-INA, 1995.

51.   'L'empire mexicain de Televisa', *Le Monde supplément des médias* (Paris), 21–22 July 1996.

52.   'Fast-growth Samba', *Variety*, 2–8 October 1995.

53.   Schneier-Madanes, op. cit.

54.   'Tequila on Ice', *TV World*, May 1996, pp. 30–4.

who intend to widen the market by diversifying their range by using programmes from independent producers.[55] Faced with the alliances between operators from two continents, local players such as Clemente Serna in Mexico, and Alberto Gonzalez and Paracom in Argentina, are striving to survive in a restricted market which has become forbidding.[56]

The absence of legislation in the field of digital broadcasting in the region explains the delay in the launch of the two digital broadcasting services, Sky and Galaxy. In spite of the delays, the backers of Galaxy hope to gain more than 1.25 million subscribers in the region by year-end 1997, 40 per cent of them in Brazil – a target equalled by the resources that have been invested. The Galaxy group, for instance, has sunk the colossal sum of $500 million in the project, which should provide 144 channels, seventy-two of them in Portuguese for the Brazilian market.[57]

With the exception of Argentina, Chile and Mexico, cable TV has hardly developed at all in Latin America. In Mexico, 10 per cent of the 17 million households with television have subscribed to pay cable-TV networks. The percentage is much higher in Argentina, where 51 per cent of the 10 million televised households are connected to cable TV. The three countries mentioned above together represent 82 per cent of all cable-TV subscribers, of whom there should be 30 million by 2005.[58] Against this backdrop of forecast growth, cable-TV operators are investing in fibre optics and joining forces to face the competition from digital satellite broadcasting and the other foreign cable-TV operators. In 1995, the number of cable-TV operators in Chile rose from two to five. In Argentina, the four leading cable-TV operators are to agree on a common standard in order to check the two American majors TCI and Continental which recently arrived on the domestic market.[59] Channels specializing in feature films, music and historical documentaries seem to be meeting with considerable public success, as testified by the inroads made by

HBO Ole, CineCanal, Cartoon Network, Discovery Channel and MTV. Audiences are increasingly fragmented into multiple niche markets with diverging centres of interest.[60] The increase in the number of cable-TV channels means the expectations of an increasingly diversified audience can be met, and quashes the theory that only by providing Spanish and Portuguese programmes on the South American continent can international channels hope for success.

Brazil

With an indigenous population of approximately 160 million, Brazil is the largest market in the region. It stands out for a number of atypical features in its television environment. Its continental dimensions, the size of its cities, the large number of its isolated communes and its distinctive national language are all distinguishing features. On the economic front, in 1996 it had one of the highest gross domestic products per capita in the region: $3,620. In terms of audio-visual equipment, there are 40 million television sets and 8 million VCRs, but only 150,000 satellite dishes. In thirty-odd years, the country has been covered by powerful commercial channels making use of considerable technological resources. In 1985, Brazil was the first nation on the South American continent to have its own satellite (Brazilsat); today it is the eighth largest television advertising market and the fifth largest installed base of television sets in the world. This means Brazil does not lack appeal and is preparing to face the major technological upheavals

55. Ibid.
56. 'Latin Cable Year Outpaces the Pundits', *TV International* (London), 29 January 1996.
57. 'Regulatory Snags Hit DTH Plans in Brazil and Mexico', *TV International* (London), 22 April 1996.
58. 'Tequila on Ice', *TV World*, May 1996, pp. 30–4.
59. 'Latin Cable Year Outpaces the Pundits', *TV International*, 29 January 1996.
60. 'Competition Fragments Pan-Latin Viewing as Movie Channels Top Charts', *TV International*, 25 March 1996.

that will follow in the wake of the recent arrival of pay television via cable, DTH and MMDS technology.[61]

Emergence of large private networks. The belated development of these new resources can be explained by the supremacy of the commercial terrestrial networks which went on the air during the 1970s. With approximately 250 television stations, the Brazilian audiovisual network is one of the most highly diversified in the world. Further to the launch of the first television station in 1950, television was supposed to serve as a means of mass communication to popularize a new, modern urban lifestyle throughout the country, based on the North American model, and to overcome the inertia of regionalism. Even if the structures and the commercial rules were American, the management model was and still is patriarchal, as is demonstrated by the main television groups, with Roberto Marinho with TV Globo, Silvio Santos with Sistema Brasileiro de Televisão (SBT), Jorge Saad with TV Bandeirantes and Adolpho Bloch with TV Manchete.[62] The public service is largely dominated by the nine channels belonging to TV Globo, a group which is still the best international symbol of Brazilian audiovisual power. The network was market leader almost from the very start and is the leader in the ratings, to the point where it had virtually a market monopoly at the beginning of the 1980s. Today, some 80 per cent of the programmes watched by Brazilians are produced by this channel. In regulatory terms, operating licences and renewals, including those allocated to cable-TV operators, were granted by the executive power until the adoption of the new constitution in 1988, under which the National Assembly had to give its prior approval. By 1994, the provision had still not come into effect.

The key to the success of Globo, however, lies in its commercial policy and innovative programming. The *telenovela,* or soap opera, is still the main focus of its programme and obtains the best evening ratings. Thanks to the *novelas* and their popularity, TV Globo was able to take advantage of an under-regulated advertising market to introduce more than twelve minutes of commercial breaks per hour. In 1992, 77 per cent of all advertising revenue went to TV Globo, which had a 63 per cent share of the viewing market, while the advertising income generated by the *telenovelas* in 1994 reached some $1.1 billion, or three-quarters of all of Globo's advertising revenue.[63]

TV Globo's programming breaks down as follows: 40 per cent of airtime is taken up by *telenovelas*, against 10 per cent for TV series, 20 per cent for news magazines and feature films, most of them American, and 10 per cent for entertainment products. Fully aware of the stakes in digital broadcasting and the forthcoming commercial battles, TV Globo has refocused its strategy on becoming a multimedia conglomerate (television, radio, publishing, newspaper publishing, video publishing, cultural foundation) and has invested more than $70 million in pay television by taking an active role in the DTH project of the Sky Entertainment Channel.

The second commercial television group includes the other private channels: SBT, TV Manchete (RMT) and TV Bandeirantes (RBT). In 1992, their respective viewer ratings were 22 per cent for SBT, 9 per cent for RMT and 2 per cent for RBT. In order to access the advertising market, the other national networks have redefined their programme packages to target specific audience segments. The SBT network has a choice position as the second channel in Brazil. It was set up in 1982, and today covers 90 per cent of the country and represents another model of commercial television. Its programme package is resolutely downmarket and has no international pretensions, consisting as it does of popular shows and sensationalist newscasts. Set up in 1983, TV Manchete is one of the most recent Brazilian networks. It covers 80 per cent

61.   Vassas, 'Brésil', in Hennebelle (ed.), op. cit, pp. 42–55.
62.   Ibid.
63.   'Fast-growth Samba', *Variety*, 2–8 October 1995.

of the territory but is finding it difficult to keep its share of the viewing market. Its original aim to address the intellectual middle class has rapidly given way to the commercial logic of financial survival. TV Manchete none the less has the merit of being an area for innovative creation open to independent producers outside the Globo 'norm'. TV Bandeirantes was set up in 1967 and now covers 98 per cent of the territory. Since 1981, it has focused on sports coverage, news programmes and the broadcasting of films, half of which are European in origin.

Other channels. Three other channels, organized and operating as networks, stand out among the private terrestrial channels for the specific characteristics of the audiences they target. TV Record is the only Brazilian television controlled by an evangelist sect, the Universal Church. Since 1959 it has been based in the state of São Paulo. CNT is the second of these networks, and is a regional station located in the agricultural state of Para and in the city of São Paulo. Its programmes are deliberately popular, mostly comprising variety shows and American soap operas. Finally, the third network, Rede Brasil Sul (RBS), is an affiliate of the TV Globo group. It is particularly dynamic and is watched by the 15 million Brazilians living in the south of the country. It manages to produce 10 per cent of its programmes independently of TV Globo.

The only public television channel, Rede Brasil, has a marginal audience of 4 per cent. Its small-scale budget ($20 million to $25 million per year) is far from being commensurate with its educational and cultural ambitions. The budget is allocated by the Ministry of Education, but the channel has no economic or regulatory protection to help it resist the pull of the commercial channels, nor does it have the benefit of any licence fees. Its articles of association prevent it from receiving any advertising revenue or backing from sponsors, resulting in financial straits which are emphasized by its lack of political and administrative independence. On the other hand, its strong points include interesting news programmes and community debates. TV Cultura, an affiliate of the Rede Brasil network, is the only quality channel in Brazil that has succeeded in retaining the loyalty of its audience of students, teachers and executives.

Other opportunities are currently developing as a result of new audiovisual technology (cable, dish antenna, MMDS). Pay television has multiplied in anarchic fashion, owing to the absence of any appropriate legal framework. In 1995, a law on cable TV and MMDS was finally adopted without any licences being allocated. The two leading broadcasters are merging: NetSat, a subsidiary of the Globo group, and TV Abril (TVA), which belongs to the main publishing group in the country. Even if pay television plays only a marginal role (with only 2.5 per cent of televised households, or 1.1 million subscribers), the potential of the Brazilian market is still vast, estimated at 20 per cent of all televised households. In 1995, TVA had the highest growth rate in the world.

As far as broadcasting media are concerned, the MMDS system seems to dominate cable-TV networks.[64] Opting for cable, dish or MMDS technology largely depends on the geographical location of subscribers. The use of cable TV is still mainly reserved for urban areas, while dish antennae and MMDS are particularly suited to remote rural regions. This is why NetSat and TVA have had to review their strategies of all-DBS for the first company and all-MMDS for the second. Ultimately, control of the pay-TV market will probably remain in the hands of both firms, which will act as intermediaries between the national cable-TV operators and the broadcasters of international special-interest channels, dominated by the American networks.

The new pay-TV market is likely to put a brake

---

64. 'Brazil: Under-cabled and Unsaturated; A Market with Pay Television Potential', *TV World*, May 1996, p. 33.

on the flourishing video industry which developed during the 1980s. The latter sector is going through a twin process of concentration, both in distribution and in rental services. The market is much more lucrative for foreign producers and distributors than terrestrial television channels, which proportionally have always imported very few international programmes. At 25 per cent,[65] the piracy rate for video cassettes is one of the lowest in Latin America.

Mexico

With an indigenous population of 92 million, Mexico is the largest single-country Spanish-speaking market in the world and the second largest market in Latin America after Brazil. The NAFTA treaty has enabled the country to strengthen its economic ties with the United States: this is particularly true of the television sector, in which the large-scale alliances between the Mexican communication major Televisa and its North American partners are being multiplied all over the continent. Mexico is well equipped in audiovisual terms. More than 80 per cent of the 18.5 million Mexican households have a television set. There are 1.6 million dish homes, and some 1.8 million households subscribe to pay-TV channels (cable, DTH and MMDS).[66]

Mexican television combines all the features common to the leading television systems of Latin America: the overpowering influence of the private sector, embodied by the dominant position of Televisa and TV Azteca, the reproduction of the American TV market model and the excessive leverage of the advertising market. In 1995, television absorbed 75 per cent of all commercial investment, or $820 million.[67]

Emergence of major private networks. The first private Mexican television station started broadcasting in 1950. One year later, two other channels were set up. The alliance between the founders of these three channels resulted in the first private group in Mexican television, named Telesistema Mexicano. The network

thereafter spread over the national territory, to the whole of the American continent, including the United States. The two public television channels Channel 7 and 13 were unable to withstand the wave of privatization and were transferred at the same time as sixty-two other concessions to a private group: Télé Azteca. At present, the state controls only twenty-one regional stations and two cultural channels in Mexico.

The dominant position of Televisa dates from 1972, following the break-up of Telesistema Mexicano. The enterprise has become a very powerful multimedia multinational in Latin America, controlling 75 per cent of the Mexican television market through its four major national channels (Canal 2, Canal 5, Canal 4 and Canal 9) and its 200 television stations. It also finances several radio stations, eighty newspapers and two football teams. Like TV Globo, Televisa has become a vector for the culture industry. The production power of Televisa is considerable. In 1991, its companies produced 45,000 hours of programmes and exported more than 36,000 to fifty-two countries.[68]

Canal 2 is the main channel in the Televisa network. It broadcasts over the whole territory and has approximately 50 per cent of the national viewer ratings and of the group's advertising revenue. Its prime target is the middle classes, and above all it broadcasts soap operas, shows and news magazines. The second channel in the group is Canal 5, which is picked up by some 10 million households and has an audience share greater than 20 per cent. Canal 4 broadcasts its news programme to thirty-three local stations. Finally, the fourth and most recent channel,

65.   Vassas, op. cit, pp. 42–55.
66.   'Latin America TV at a Glance', October 1995, cited by a private adviser in 'Jornadas de cable', *Variety* (London), 13–19 November 1995.
67.   'Latin America's Prime TV Market Re-emerges from Year-long Recession', *TV International* (London), 6 May 1996, pp. 5–8.
68.   E. Sanchez Ruiz, 'Mexique', in Hennebelle (ed.), op. cit, pp. 67–70.

Canal 9, is watched by some 9 million households. In all, Televisa has an audience share outside peak hours of more than 80 per cent. Its programmes consist largely of American films and TV soap operas, especially the *telenovelas* (soaps) that it produces and distributes around the world. The principal weakness of the Televisa network is its news coverage, which is considered by observers to be very close to the political power base.

The objective of the Mexican group is to conquer the whole of the Hispanic market worldwide. Since the acquisition of Univision, the first Hispanic television station in the United States, Televisa has invested in various Spanish[69] and Latin American media companies (with a 49 per cent stake in Mega-vision in Chile, a 76 per cent stake in Canal 11 in Peru, and an alliance with ATC in Argentina). However, the remarkable headway made by TV Azteca, which is the sole competitor in the non-specialist television field, has led to losses for Televisa ($90 million in 1996), which has had to shed its assets (distribution, records, publication, etc.). In an attempt to remain in the lead in the Spanish-speaking region, the Televisa group has launched a large satellite television offensive in Latin America and Spain. In association with News Corp., the Rupert Murdoch group, the American cable operator Tele Communi-cations Inc. (TCI) and the Brazilian Globo chain, a Sky programming stream will be launched in four countries in Latin America at the end of 1997. With this project, Televisa intends to conquer the whole of the Latin American and Spanish DTH market to the detriment of cable TV, despite the fact that the latter medium has a firm foothold in Mexico, where 10 per cent of all households are subscribers to cable television.[70]

The strategy of the second-ranking private network TV Azteca consists, despite its scanty resources, in competing with Televisa by scheduling programmes bought from local or foreign producers (Brazilian and Venezuelan *telenovelas*, North American

TV series) until the group can produce its own *tele-novelas*. In 1995, its two channels (Canal 13 and 7) had a 13 per cent audience share and a 14 per cent market share in advertising revenue. A year later, the chain had increased its turnover by 93 per cent, showing profits of 788 million pesos (approx. $120 million) and even winning the TV-news battle.

Pay-TV promise. The market move towards MMDS, cable TV and DTH is far from being definitive in Mexico, given the number of the players, the size of the stakes and the financial power of the competitors. Besides the two rival regional alliances of Sky and Galaxy (in which Televisa has a stake), local operators in pay television are gaining ground in the field of cable (with CableVision, 49 per cent of whose equity was bought from Televisa by PTT Telmex and MegaCable), in MMDS (the Multivision company) and in DTH (the Mevcom and Clemente Serna radio companies). The main advantage of these national operators is their ability to offer local and national programmes that meet viewers' expectations. Most of them seek alliances with foreign operators to protect their market share and develop their networks in Latin America. Mexico, with the take-off of Televisa, and of TV Azteca, has become a power in the worldwide culture industry, but is still a virtually unexplored market in terms of pay television.

The Caribbean

The Caribbean comprises thirteen independent member states of CARICOM (Caribbean Community Secretariat) and some small territories that have yet to gain their independence. The region is populated by 6 million inhabitants. In most countries, television belongs to the state. It was in 1970 in Jamaica, during the Conference of the Commonwealth Broadcasting

69. Ibid.
70. 'À Mexico, les larmes des *telenovelas* coulent à flot', *L'Expansion* (Paris), No. 530, 1996, p. 50.

Association (CBA), that the Caribbean Broadcasting Union (CBU) was set up, to favour the exchange of programmes between radio and television in the region and to strengthen the process of cultural integration in the Caribbean. The organization today has thirty-two members in seventeen countries and territories. The private sector has only very recently made inroads, unlike the written press. Given the small size of the population, the territories and the market in the Caribbean states, the number of television channels and their financial resources are inevitably limited. The only local television production in most cases is the televised news bulletin.[71]

Caribbean television is therefore to a very high degree dependent on foreign programmes, most of them from the United States. Between 1976 and 1986, the percentage of programmes imported by the four main channels in the region rose from 78.5 to 87 per cent. The broadcasting infrastructures in several countries have developed spectacularly. Jamaica, which has a population of just under 2.5 million and a GDP per capita of $1,510, has two television stations. Trinidad and Tobago, with 1.3 million inhabitants and a GDP per capita estimated the same year of $3,720, has a similar landscape with the appearance of two new private stations. Barbados, with 300,000 inhabitants and a GDP per capita of $6,710, has the highest standard of living in the region. The island has two television stations and viewers can receive programmes from neighbouring countries by terrestrial means. The recent development of television and television production is opening up new employment prospects in the sector, but the market is naturally limited and competition intense.

The emergence of new technology (cable TV, satellite reception, dish antennae, MMDS) has produced two opposite trends: on the one hand, there is greater ease of access to the worldwide networks and to American channels, and, on the other, there are several initiatives towards alternative forms of audiovisual communication. In Kingston, the Jamaican capital, 28 per cent of households have satellite dishes, a development that has created inequality of access to information and culture. Overall, television in the Caribbean remains the privilege of an educated urban élite. This explains why the idea of satellite television common to all the countries in the region, which would enable them to have greater unity and impact, seems to be gaining currency.

Arab States

General trends

With close to 30 million households equipped with television sets and an installed base of satellite receivers estimated in 1996 at 5 million dish antennae,[72] the Arab world is a buoyant market for local, regional and international operators. Future markets include programme reception systems, pay television and new technology. The latter is increasingly arousing interest and its introduction in the region is leading to major changes in the various national audiovisual systems. Digital broadcasting by satellite or by terrestrial means has in most cases resulted in a profusion of programmes on offer, erosion of state-run monopolies of public service television, and heated competition between public television channels, pan-Arab regional television channels and international television channels of Western design. Paradoxically, however, these technological upheavals have not favoured greater general freedom in the national media, even though private stations have gone on-air in many countries.

---

71. 'Situation actuelle de la presse et des médias dans les Caraïbes anglophones' [Present State of the Press and the Media in the English-speaking Caribbean], *Le Courrier de l'ACP-UE* (Brussels*),* No. 158, July-August 1996, pp. 59–61.
72. 'Câble et satellite souffle ses dix bougies' [Cable and Satellite: Their Tenth Birthday], *Vidéo broadcast* (Paris), July 1996.

Audiovisual indicators and GNP for the Arab States, 1994 (figures in parentheses indicate an estimated total number)					
Country	**Households (%)**				**GNP/inhab. in value at parity of purchasing power**
	TV	**VCR**	**Satellite**	**Cable**	
Bahrain	(91 770)	73.0	N.a.	N.a.	13 220
Egypt	(9 400 000)	18	N.a.	0.2	3 720
Kuwait	(241 000)	85.5	N.a.	N.a.	24 730
Lebanon	100	72.0	N.a.	N.a.	N.a.
Morocco	(1 300 000)	8	3	N.a.	3 470
Oman	(279 604)	62.6	N.a.	N.a.	8 590
Qatar	(87 400)	80.8	N.a.	N.a.	19 100
Saudi Arabia	(3 021 875)	78.1	N.a.	N.a.	9 480
Tunisia	80	N.a.	3		5 020
United Arab Emirates	(375 552)	88	N.a.	N.a.	20 940

Source: *Market and Media Facts*, 1995–96, London, Zenith Publications.

The audiovisual landscape in the Arab world has a number of common features, but also has a wide-ranging diversity. In Khartoum in 1969 the radio-broadcasting organizations of twenty-one countries joined together to form the Arab States Broadcasting Union (ASBU), its purpose being to strengthen regional co-operation and enhance the exchange of programmes among member countries.

In most cases, member states have an Arab and Muslim culture in common, a variety of regional dialects, and television stations which are generally state-owned, with resulting differences in audiovisual policies and many dissimilarities both between Arab nations and within them. These differences reflect both the uneven economic development within each nation, the diversity of their political regimes and the specific nature of each audiovisual system. The result is that some television stations, such as those in the Gulf countries, have incorporated the latest digital technology in their development, while others, such as Mauritania or the Sudan, have serious difficulties in terms of equipment as well as in broadcasting.[73]

In addition, the cost of the equipment necessary for satellite reception, given the purchasing power of the countries in the region, implies that their use will mainly involve a privileged population of political leaders, business executives and social dignitaries.

Satellites are the most coveted means of broadcasting. The Arabsat network covers the whole of the Arab world and provides it with the requisite transmission and broadcasting independence. The recent launch of the new generation satellites Arabsat II and PAS-4 by the American PanAmSat group has considerably increased broadcasting capacity and the range of programme choice. Cable TV, on the other hand, is a marginal, even non-existent sector in the Arab region. This is basically due to the uneven population distribution, the geographical density of inhabited areas, and in-sufficiencies in terms of infrastructures. On the other

73. 'Middle East's Digital Pioneer Tries to Unite a Fragmented Pay-TV Market', *TV International*, 15 July 1996, p. 10.

hand, the MMDS system of multiple channel broadcasting via terrestrial networks seems to be developing in many countries, such as Saudi Arabia and Bahrain. This technique, which consists in broadcasting digital programmes via terrestrial links, may be an efficient way of increasing the number of terrestrial channels at lower cost, and may thereby encourage local initiatives.[74]

Satellite-TV channels in the Arab region basically bow to a commercial, cultural or political logic, depending on the operator and the country. Beside regional or transnational channels such as StarTV, CNN, Middle East Broadcasting Centre (MBC) or Arab Radio and Television (ART) that target the highly diverse Arab market, public operators such as Moroccan Television, TV7 Tunisia, Egyptian Space Channel, Nile TV or Algerian TV have organized satellite broadcasting networks for their respective communities in Europe and in the United States.

Regional operators

The three main regional television operators, Orbit, ART and MCME, are specialized in the satellite broadcasting of pay-TV programmes for the Arab world. Even if the Arab market is not a sector with real potential for pay television, these channels target the well-to-do households receptive to advertising messages. The success of some channels is due to their modern programme package with varied products, designed and tailored for the reality of the region.

The Orbit Satellite Television network was launched in 1993, and is the owned by the Saudi group Al-Mawaid. It is the largest and most expensive pay-TV channel in the region, and broadcasts more than thirty radio and television channels from Rome to more than twenty Arab countries. The programme package mostly comprises products in Arabic, and films recently purchased from the Disney group. In order to increase its broadcasting capacity and widen its coverage, the channel has opted for the digital satellite Intelsat. Access to Orbit programmes is

prohibitive for most Arab viewers and broadcasts are therefore limited to a somewhat select audience. The cost of the decoder is set at $10,000 and the annual subscription fee at $1,500. In 1995, the number of subscribers had barely reached 55,000, although channel backers forecast 250,000 subscribers by 1997.[75] Arab Radio and Television (ART) is another network which has been launched by the Saudi group Arab Media Corporation (AMC); from year-end 1997 it is scheduled to go on the air from Rome, with another stream of fourteen channels via the satellite PanAmSat 4.

Multichoice Middle East (MCME) is a stream of pay-TV programmes launched in 1996 by the South African group Multichoice, an ally of the other South African channel NetHold, together with Arab partners such as ART. The channel comprises the Showtime network, controlled by the American group Viacom (MTV-Europe, VH-1, Nickelodeon, Paramount, TV Land, The Movie Channel, Bloomberg Information TV) and the FirstNet network, which broadcasts five channels syndicated by the ART network. MCME targets the whole of the Arab region, from the Gulf to the Atlantic. Subscription fees accessible for the average viewer ($30 to $40) together with an aggressive programming policy are the channel's main sales arguments. The FirstNet network, which describes itself as the 'prime channel specially designed for Arab family viewing', reached 50,000 subscribers in December 1996.[76] Finally, MCME is the first pan-Arab regional pay-TV channel to join the giant American pay-TV company, Viacom.

The MBC channel is the most popular free-to-air station with Arabic audiences. It has an image of independence and professionalism owing to a worldwide network of more than fifty correspondents

74. 'Sand Castles', *TV World*, April 1996, pp. 45–8.
75. Ibid.
76. 'It's a Family Affair', *Cable and Satellite Europe* (London), 19 May 1996.

and fifteen news bureaux[77]. The channel was set up in 1991 by a relation of the Saudi royal family. It broadcasts from London and intends to operate the MMDS system via its affiliate SaraVision in a number of Arab countries, including Saudi Arabia. Despite the ban on the purchase of satellite dishes, it is estimated that more than 4.2 million Saudi households are equipped with these reception systems.[78]

MTV and StarTV are positioning themselves on the Arab market, even if they have yet to be seen as serious competitors. Their first-phase strategy consists in being present in the region and ready for the future. They are already making efforts to provide Arabic-based programmes tailored to the countries they target. Other local and free-to-air TV channels such as LBCI, Future TV and Tele Lebanon are attempting to widen their coverage beyond the limits of the region. Closer to the mind-set and culture of the Arab world, and more a part of the political fabric of the region, they may be serious competitors for the established networks.[79]

Certain national channels also have ambitions of broadcasting on an international and regional scale. Egyptian television is preparing to launch its NileSat 1 and NileSat 2 satellites in 1997. Identical projects are also planned in the United Arab Emirates with, for 1998, Dubai Satellite Channel and ETISALAT. The race is therefore still on in the region, with heated competition between the MMDS terrestrial digital networks and digital satellite broadcasting on the one hand, and between pay television and unencrypted channels on the other.[80] Control of the expanding advertising market, currently dominated by the free-to-air channel MBC, is the main issue at stake for the local and international operators.

In general, most of the satellite channels target the wealthy Gulf States such as Bahrain, the United Arab Emirates or Kuwait, countries which represent 55 per cent of the Arab TV advertising market. In 1996 MBC won more than 40 per cent of all advertising investment in the pan-Arabic market. The ART group

is increasing its market share while Orbit has only a minimal share and has to rely on subscriptions for financing. The same applies to the other channels on the Arab market, which is too limited to sustain all the international, regional and local players: only a handful will be able to survive as long as satellite television remains the privilege of a minority élite.

Challenges

The inroads made by international channels in the audiovisual landscape of the Arab world are not trouble-free, leaving producers, politicians and TV professionals often anxious about their ultimate outcome.

Politically, the Arab world is increasingly pervaded by diversified programmes with richer, more varied and often more credible news content than that provided by national channels, with the result that Arab viewers watch these less. From a cultural point of view, most of the programmes broadcast will not result in any major upheaval for Arab viewers, except in their news. The worldwide soap operas and basically Western, South American and Egyptian films are already present on national television screens.

From a legal standpoint, in spite of their continuing monopoly, national television stations are no longer the only channels to broadcast programmes; other operators even provide simultaneous translation in Arabic. The legislation pertaining to private reception is totally liberal in certain countries, inexplicit or non-existent in others, and restrictive in still others.

Confronted with these major ongoing changes, the Arab world is going to have to face up to a number of challenges. The first concerns the creation of a real

77. 'Satellite News Feed Pan-Arabic Service', *International Broadcasting* (London), September 1995, pp. 61–6.
78. 'Sand Castles', op. cit., pp. 45–8.
79. 'Middle East TV Advertising Market', *TV World* (London), April 1996, p. 46.
80. 'Sand Castles', op. cit. pp. 45–8.

public service, to serve communities, the diversity of audiences, and democracy.

The second consists in deliberate intervention in national programme production, to enhance other forms of content and types of know-how. Cultural originality, freedom of speech and artistic creation, and inclusion of linguistic and cultural diversity and artistic quality, are henceforth some of the issues on which Arab television will have to stake its fortune and future.

The third and final challenge consists in encouraging the free circulation of programmes from each Arab state in the region. It also consists in pooling the resources held by some and the know-how held by others in order to obtain an audiovisual network capable of standing up to the globalization of the media and their content. The Arab world has the human resources, the creative capacity and the means to become a player in the current upheavals.

Egypt

With an installed base estimated in 1997 at 12 million receiving sets for an indigenous population of 64 million and a per capita gross national product of $790, Egypt has the most developed national television service in the Arab world in terms of audiovisual production and broadcasting. Egyptian television began broadcasting in July 1960, spurred by a film industry with a high degree of popularity in the Arab World. It has considerably developed since within the framework of the Egyptian Radio and Television Union (ERTU), a decentralized authority of the Ministry of Information that in 1997 dominates the Egyptian audiovisual environment. The authority has eight public channels, two of which are national and six regional. Channel 1 mainly broadcasts news, films and entertainment programmes while Channel 2 provides cultural programmes and news bulletins in English and French. The two channels respectively broadcast eighteen and twenty-one hours of programmes every day. The remaining six channels,

which are also financed by advertising, cover the various regions of Egypt and broadcast specific programmes for local consumption.

A large part of Egyptian airtime is dedicated to broadcasting locally produced soap operas that are hugely successful in Egypt and throughout the Arab world. They are a substantial source of revenue, in 1995 earning more than $18 million for the ERTU. The Egyptian market is likely to thrive increasingly as Arab channels broadcast by satellite develop. Egyptian television professionals estimate their requirements to represent some 5,000 hours of programmes per year, and Egypt is the only country in the Arab world to have the infrastructures, viewership and technology needed for a real audiovisual industry to develop. The huge 'October Six' studio complex, supposedly the second-largest set in the world after the Universal studios in Hollywood, can reach a production rate estimated at over 3,000 hours of programmes per year. For many Egyptian film-makers, all-TV production is in the process of marginalizing – even annihilating – the Egyptian film industry, which is seen in the Arab world as an art form common to its cultural heritage. The film production rate, which exceeded 100 films per year in 1950, by 1997 had fallen to twenty feature films. On the other hand, the ERTU produces 3,900 hours of television programmes every year.[81]

Since 1990, the reception of foreign programmes by satellite has mainly developed in the region of central Cairo. The number of dish antennae is estimated to be 2 million. Egyptians equipped with them can receive between sixty and eighty channels, including the traditional MBC, BBC, CNN and TV5 programmes, but also those from Emirates Dubai Television, Kuwait TV, etc. Pay television is present in Cairo via Cable News Egypt (CNE), a partnership between ERTU and the South African Multichoice

81. 'Egypt Opens Its Channels', *TV World,* October 1996, pp. 79–80.

channel (Nethold group). CNE offers fourteen channels and targets a restricted audience of executives and well-to-do viewers. In order to develop the market, the government has banned the importing of decoders, thereby ousting competitors such as the Arabic channel Orbit, which broadcasts from Rome.

On its side, the ERTU is striving to make its presence felt in the world by launching its own channels by satellite. The Egyptian Space Channel since 1990 has been broadcasting programmes designed for Arab communities residing in Europe, the Maghreb and the Gulf. The Egyptian International Space channel, or Nile TV, broadcasts programmes in English and French to the non-Arabic populations in Europe and the United States. In 1997, with government backing, the ERTU intends to launch two satellites, Nilesat 1 and Nilesat 2. They will broadcast more than fifty channels, including the eight national channels and the CNE stream. It is worth noting that two training centres, the Radio and Television Institute, founded in 1971, and the professional television training centre, which was set up in 1986, provide initial and in-service training in audiovisual production techniques.

Morocco

The first trials with state television date back to March 1962, when the first channel was inaugurated to mark the coronation of the King of Morocco. Since then, the Moroccan audiovisual landscape has opened to international channels. It is organized around a public service station, the Radio Télévision Marocaine (RTM), a new, private pay-TV channel called 2 Maroc International (2M), and a host of other international programmes broadcast by satellite.

The public television channel RTM covers most of the kingdom and on average broadcasts ninety hours of programmes per week in Arabic and in French. As with television in the rest of the Arab World, foreign programme imports (from Brazil, Egypt, France, the United States, etc.) represent more

than 50 per cent of the overall programme package. As soon as the rebroadcasting of international channels first emerged and 2M became an established success, RTM strived to maintain its ratings by launching a grand modernization scheme to give its programmes a new look, with credits in computer-generated images, the recruitment of new programme presenters, etc. Sport, music and entertainment dominate a more modern, dynamic package. In this respect, for reasons of geographical proximity, the evening news bulletin has now been extended to include two further televised bulletins, in French and Spanish.[82]

The emergence of the private channel 2M in 1989 upset an audiovisual landscape which was basically a state monopoly. 2M is the first encrypted television channel to be broadcast in the Arab World, and is backed by private capital: two-thirds of the equity is held by Moroccan interests, the rest by two international private groups, the French operator TF1 and the Canadian operator Videotron. In 1996, the channel had some 300,000 subscriber households and broadcast almost twenty hours of programmes per day, four hours of which were unencrypted. The programme supply comprises mainly foreign films, modern music concerts and sport, but also local productions that do not hesitate to tackle taboo subjects. It is well-designed, with varied, well-packaged reports. On the other hand its news bulletins are presented in video form supplied by international wire services, with voice-over commentary. Channel in-house production in 1996 represented more than 30 per cent of all the programmes it broadcast. The channel is seen as giving the country a competitive edge in the worldwide image war. On the international level, one of the initial aims of the encrypted channel was to broadcast beyond the frontiers of Morocco. From 1989 to 1993, it attempted to distribute its programmes on the French cable-TV network, but obtained barely

---

82. J. Cahen, 'Maroc', in Hennebelle (ed.), op. cit., p. 301.

5,000 subscriptions on cable-TV sites in the Paris region. After this commercial failure, it set its sights on consolidating its position in neighbourhood channels with local programming better suited to the particular public's taste. In 1996, 70 per cent of 2M's capital was absorbed by the state, resulting in the unscrambling of the channel. The leading Moroccan television channel TVM, an RTM affiliate, every day transmits twelve hours of programmes via the Intelsat II satellite to an area covering the Mediterranean basin and Europe.

The opening of the market to international channels was backed by the 1992 decision of the Supreme Court, which abrogated a government decree imposing a tax of 5,000 dirhams ($650) per satellite dish installed. Since then, the installed base of dish antennae has seen high growth[83] in Morocco and in 1996 was estimated at more than 500,000. Moroccans can thus access a multitude of foreign channels including traditional stations such as MBC, CNN, TV5, the BBC, etc. The liberalization of the airwaves has heated up the competition between the foreign and national channels, with the result that the private channel 2M, for example, in 1995 posted a loss of $50 million, when the total Moroccan television advertising market was worth no more than $20 million.

83. Z. L. Adghimi, 'Les antennes paraboliques au Maroc', *Revue Tiers Monde*, Vol. 38, No. 146, 1996.

Part 3

Media and democracy

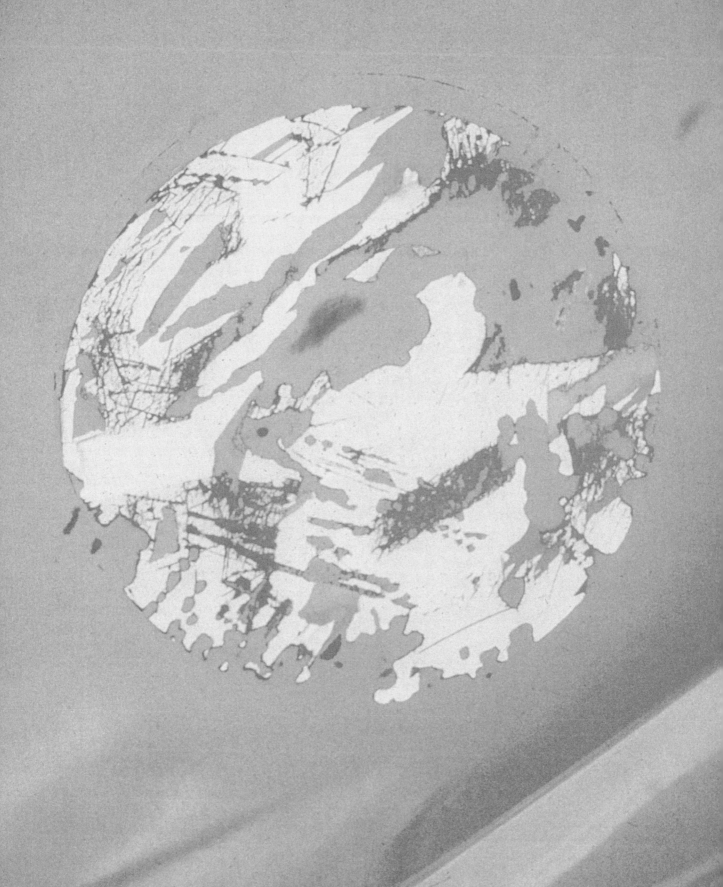

'Monochrome Abstract'
by Ernest Haas/Magnum Photos, Inc.

Chapter 12
Freedom
of information
between
legal rights
and established
powers

From the cellular telephone to digital television, from the major news agencies to the explosion of the Internet, the internationalization and multiplication of networks and information flows are ushering us into what Alvin Toffler calls 'the alchemy of communication' or the 'all-screen generation'.[1] It is another planet, where everything is becoming globalized, turned into a media event, or computerized – a trend which also, however, raises a number of issues relating to freedom of information and the exercise of democracy.

What foothold does freedom have in international law and conventions? What forms do threats to and attacks on freedom of expression take? What part can the media play in democratic progress? In what manner can concentration in a few hands represent a danger for political communication? What is the cause of the increasing growth of violence in TV programmes, video games and other media? How shall we live in the virtual age? How can people be taught to distinguish true from false? Such questions lie at the heart of the whole debate about legal rights, established power and information.

The legal foundations underpinning the free flow of information and communication

The principle of freedom of information is enshrined in the major universal and regional declarations and conventions relating to human rights. It is today the basis and criterion for the analysis and interpretation of international law relating to the media. Its history is one of slow, arduous conquests, punctuated by triumphs, resistance and occasional setbacks. Its first consecration occurred in 1789 with the French *Declaration of the Rights of Man and of the Citizen*, whose Article XI asserts that 'the free communication

---

1.　A. Toffler, *Powershift: Knowledge, Wealth and Violence at the Edge of the 21st Century*, New York, Bantam Books, 1991.

of ideas and opinions is one of the most precious rights of man', and that in consequence every citizen 'can freely speak, write and print subject to responsibility for the abuse of this freedom in the cases determined by law'.[2] Two years later, in 1791, the American Bill of Rights proclaimed a number of amendments to the Constitution of the United States, including that landmark legal provision, the First Amendment, which stipulated that 'Congress shall make no law . . . abridging the freedom of speech, or of the press'. This was a fundamental revolution, for it meant that truth had ceased to belong to any one constituted power, and pertained 'solely to the constituent parties, being immanent to individual reason' and no longer to the transcendent authority of the state. During the Second World War, the international community became alive to the way in which people's attitudes and awareness were affected by total control of the media. It was for this reason that, in 1941, President Roosevelt placed 'freedom of speech and expression everywhere in the world' in the front rank of the 'Four Freedoms'. In the years immediately following the war, defending freedom of information naturally became one of the objectives of all efforts to rebuild the international system. In 1945, the Chapultepec Act, adopted by the Inter-American Conference on problems of war and peace, proclaimed for the first time 'the freedom of international information flows'. The following year, the United Nations recognized the importance of freedoms relating to information. In 1946, the UN recalled in its resolution 59 that 'freedom of information is a fundamental human right and is the touchstone of all the freedoms to which the United Nations is consecrated'. On 10 December 1948, freedom of information was enshrined in the Universal Declaration of Human Rights, whose Article 19 is the most categorical expression thereof: 'Everyone has the right to freedom of opinion and expression; this right includes freedom . . . to seek, receive and impart information and ideas through any media and

regardless of frontiers'.[3] The Munich Declaration, adopted in 1971 by representatives of journalists' unions, adopts an identical point of view: 'The right to information, to freedom of expression and criticism is one of the fundamental rights of man.'

UNESCO's own Constitution, adopted on 16 November 1945, assigns to the Organization in its Article II, paragraph 2(a), the goal of 'advancing the mutual knowledge and understanding of peoples', in particular by means of international agreements designed 'to promote the free flow of ideas by word and image'. These principles were to be strengthened with the International Covenant on Civil and Political Rights, adopted by the United Nations General Assembly on 16 December 1966, whose Article 19 provides that: 'Everyone shall have the right to freedom of expression; this right shall include freedom to seek, receive and impart information and ideas of all kinds, regardless of frontiers, either orally, in writing or in print, in the form of art, or through any other media of his choice.'

More than ninety states have already ratified this Covenant, thereby pledging to apply its principles.[4]

2.   A now classic call for freedom of thought and information was published in 1644, namely John Milton's *Areopagitica*. Later, the philosopher John Stuart Mill put forward in his treatise *On Liberty* (1859) the idea that society does not have the right to silence a single dissident member. Quoted by V. Y. Ghébali, 'La problématique de la liberté de circulation de l'information du conflit Est-Ouest à l'après-communisme', *Le Trimestre du Monde* (Paris), 2nd quarter, 1992, p. 111.

3.   *The International Bill of Human Rights*, New York, United Nations, 1993.

4.   In order to ensure application of the principles enshrined in the Covenant, it provides for the establishment of a Human Rights Committee and stipulates in its Article 40 that 'the States Parties to the present Covenant undertake to submit reports on the measures they have adopted which give effect to the rights recognized . . . and on the progress made in the enjoyment of those rights'. Quoted by Ghébali, op. cit.

Selection of professional charters on press freedom

● THE MUNICH DECLARATION

The Declaration of Rights and Obligations of Journalists was adopted on 24 and 25 November 1971 in Munich by representatives of the journalists' unions of the six countries of the then European Community. It has since been adopted by the International Federation of Journalists (IFJ) and by most journalists' unions in Europe. The declaration, which is quintessentially a code of professional ethics, states in its Preamble: 'The right to information, to freedom of expression and criticism is one of the fundamental rights of man. All rights and duties of a journalist originate from this right of the public to be informed on events and opinions. The journalists' responsibility towards the public exceeds any other responsibility, particularly towards employers and public authorities.'

● THE DECLARATION OF CHAPULTEPEC

The Declaration of Chapultepec was adopted by some hundred professional journalists in Mexico City, at a conference organized by the Inter-American Press Association (IAPA) in March 1994. It has been signed and endorsed by the President of the United States, by a dozen Latin American Heads of State, by the Secretary-General of the United Nations and by the Director-General of UNESCO. It is in line with the Santiago (Chile) Declaration on the development of the media and democracy in Latin American and the Caribbean. In addition to recognizing the fundamental role played by freedom of expression and press freedom in all democratic societies, the declaration condemns all forms of violence and coercion against journalists. It stipulates in particular that, in a truly free society, public opinion alone has the right to reward or to condemn the work of journalists. All acts of violence directed against journalists must be 'investigated promptly' and 'punished harshly'.

● THE CHARTER FOR A FREE PRESS

The ten principles of the Charter for a Free Press were adopted in London in 1987 by journalists representing thirty-four countries and the main organizations working in the field of press freedom. The charter urges governments to:

- put an end to both direct and indirect censorship;
- prevent all discriminatory practices in regard to the independent media, particularly in regard to access to information, means of distribution and taxation;
- permit the free flow of news and the unimpeded movement of journalists and their equipment across borders;
- not restrict the practice of journalism through any licensing system;
- ensure that journalists enjoy the protection of the law and are recognized as civilians in war zones.

The charter was signed by the World Press Freedom Committee (WPFC), the International Federation of Newspaper Publishers (FIEJ), the International Press Institute (IPI), the Inter-American Press Association (IAPA), the North American National Broadcasters Association (NANBA) and the International Federation of the Periodical Press (FIPP).

Other victories for press freedom bound up with the development of the media have given rise to further international and regional declarations. All give pride of place to freedom of information as a precondition of democracy, truth as a basic duty, and respect for the human person as limit.[5] Among the many international legal instruments that establish freedom of information as a basic principle, mention may be made of Article 10 of the European Convention for the Protection of Human Rights and Fundamental Freedoms, adopted on 4 November 1950, Article 13 of the American Convention on Human Rights, adopted on 22 November 1969, and Article 9 of the African Charter on Human and Peoples' Rights, adopted on 12 July 1981. This principle was to be a driving force in the domestic legislation of the different countries.

UNESCO and communication

However, in the period immediately following the Second World War, the free flow of information would very rapidly become a Cold War issue and constitute one of the major bones of contention between states. It was interpreted in terms of two fundamentally conflicting doctrines. That of the Western democracies was based on Article 19 of the Universal Declaration of Human Rights. It advocated the dismantling of all barriers in the way of seeking, receiving and imparting information and ideas both within states and beyond their borders. For its part, the attitude of the Soviet Union and the peoples' democracies originated in Communist theory, which defined the media as educational tools operating under state control for the purpose of expediting the construction of socialism. The media had a social function, and journalists, defined as intellectual agitators and propagandists, had a mission to inform and to mould opinion. To the principle of a free and unimpeded flow of information, the Soviet Union and its allies opposed that of a controlled exchange of information, conducted on the basis of intergovernmental agreements, with due respect for sovereignty and the principle of non-interference in the domestic affairs of states.

For their part, the developing countries declared themselves to be the victims of serious inequalities in the matter of information flows between North and South, and considered the manner in which the media of the North reflected the reality of their national situations to be exaggerated, distorted and even totally false. In consequence, they called for a redressing of the balance of information flows, and hence implicitly for control over information emanating from the countries of the North.

The Communist countries' demand for controlled information exchange between East and West and the developing countries' calls for a redressing of the information flow balance between North and South were both compatible and complementary. These two groups of countries formed a united front within the international organizations concerned, first and foremost the United Nations and UNESCO, for the purpose of advocating, at the end of the 1970s, the establishment of a 'New World Information and Communication Order' (NWICO), regarded as being the counterpart of the 'New World Economic Order'.

The discussions which took place on the subject within UNESCO were extremely stormy. Tension reached a climax in the mid-1980s when the United States (1984) and the United Kingdom (1985) withdrew from the Organization. For their part, a number of international organizations representing professional media circles put all their weight into the balance in order to isolate UNESCO and to make the international community understand that the New World Information and Communication Order constituted an intolerable assault upon press freedom and the free flow of information.

5. With regard to the different charters, declarations and conventions, see D. Cornu: 'Les contenus des codes de déontologie', *Journalisme et vérité*, pp. 64 ff., Geneva, Laborde et Fides, 1994; Ghébali, op. cit.

The political changes which occurred in the USSR at the end of the 1980s, and in particular the introduction by Mikhail Gorbachev of *glasnost*, had the result of radically transforming the overall situation in regard to NWICO. With the emergence of democracy, a number of Eastern and Central European countries began to adopt the liberal conception of information whereby freedom of expression and media independence and pluralism are an essential precondition of any properly functioning democratic society.

The major upheavals which occurred in Eastern and Central Europe drove a number of developing countries as well to embark upon the path of democratic reform. Freedom of expression, and with it press freedom and pluralism, thus gained a certain amount of ground. The new information and communication technologies, in particular satellite television – which 'enters via the roof, without having to go through the censor's office' – and the Internet, have shrunk the planet to a global village, and made information available to a growing number of people on every continent. True, information flows remain largely to the advantage of the North; but an increasing number of developing countries such as Brazil, Egypt, India and Mexico are becoming in turn producers, broadcasters and operators on a regional and even a worldwide scale. Moreover, it is worth pointing out that the smaller countries of the North are themselves becoming ever more dependent upon the output of the major international, and particularly North American, corporations, in regard both to information (large international news agencies supplying texts, pictures and data) and to entertainment and fiction films. The twofold dichotomy between North and South and East and West is gradually being superseded by a new subdivision between the large, populous countries, which have a sufficiently strong domestic market to cover the costs of their national productions, and the smaller countries of the North and South alike, which are far more numerous but which, because they do not possess the necessary critical mass, are doomed to import foreign programmes in order to counterbalance the quantitative inadequacy of their domestic output. The public and private television companies of the industrialized and developing countries are indeed in danger of shortly finding themselves excluded from international deals in regard to the live broadcasting of the most popular sports events, such as the Olympic Games or the World Football Championship, since the charges for broadcasting rights are becoming, in relation to their domestic advertising market, quite prohibitive. What, then, can be said of the poorest countries of the South, in particular those of the African continent, which provide so many of today's world champions! These countries are already almost wholly dependent on the international market. In the case of some, the situation is so critical that the systematic pirating of satellite pictures and videotapes has become the sole means of survival.

Thus the disparities highlighted by the commission chaired by Sean MacBride, which served to justify the call for a new world order, the NWICO, still remain a burning issue. On the other hand, the map of these disparities has changed in relation to the situation prevailing in the 1970s and 1980s. Most Latin American and Asian countries are undoubtedly in a better position than they were twenty years ago, both in regard to media access and in terms of endogenous production.

It must not be overlooked that large sectors of their populations, notably the poorest sections, have benefited but little from this favourable trend. In the industrialized countries, while access to the media poses no special problems aside from financial constraints, the growing dependence of the small countries on the major international suppliers of texts, images and data has become an extremely worrying factor. As regards the least developed countries, their situation has worsened still further in that many have become still more impoverished, and have been left on the fringe of technological progress.

Relative access to television and volume of production for selected countries, by GDP/capita, and population size

		Access to television	Production of long films/ TV	Access and production
Large population/ high GDP	France			
	Germany			
	Italy			
	Japan			
	United Kingdom			
	United States			
Large population/ low GDP	Brazil			
	China			
	India			
	Indonesia			
	Mexico			
	Pakistan			
Small population/ high GDP	Austria			
	Denmark			
	Finland			
	Norway			
	Sweden			
	Swizerland			
Small population/ low GDP	Burundi			
	Central African Republic			
	Chad			
	Guinea			
	Haiti			
	Liberia			

Low   Medium   High

Source: Compiled from *UNESCO Statistical Yearbook 1996*, Paris, UNESCO, 1997; *Internationales Handbuch für Hörfunk und Fernsehen*, Baden-Baden/Hamburg, Hans-Bredow-Institut/Nomos Verlagsgesellschaft, 1996; *World Development Report 1996*, Washington, D.C., World Bank, 1996.

Seizing the opportunity afforded by the ending of the Cold War to move beyond the sterile discussions on the NWICO, and concerned to support the process of democratization being pursued in several regions of the world, the General Conference of UNESCO adopted, at its twenty-fifth session in November 1989 – at the very moment when the Berlin Wall was crumbling – a 'new communication strategy' aimed at meeting the needs of the burgeoning democracies and the developing countries alike. Its goals were threefold:

1. Encouraging the free flow of information, at international as well as national level.
2. Promoting the wider and better balanced dissemination of information, without any obstacle to freedom of expression.
3. Developing all the appropriate means of strengthening communication capacities in the developing countries in order to increase their participation in the communication process.

In respect of the first prong of this 'new communication strategy', UNESCO reasserted the fundamental principle of 'free flow of information' enshrined in its Constitution. In particular, it pledged to promote both freedom of expression, the cornerstone of the human rights edifice, and press freedom, itself a key component of all democratic societies. To this end, it provides assistance to intergovernmental and non-governmental organizations whose mission it is to defend these fundamental freedoms, while at the same time preserving and developing its own means of action.

In order to give concrete expression to its commitment to the democratic process in countries living through a period of transition, UNESCO, in conjunction with the United Nations Department of Public Information, has since 1991 organized a series of five Regional Seminars on Promoting Independent and Pluralistic Media (Windhoek, Namibia, 1991; Alma Ata, Kazakstan, 1992; Santiago, Chile, 1994; Sana'a, Yemen, 1996; Sofia, Bulgaria, 1997). These

workshops, which brought together in all several hundred media professionals, gave rise to the adoption of firmly worded and unambiguous 'declarations' which defined the preconditions for setting up and operating a free, independent and pluralist press. An unusual occurrence in the annals of the United Nations system, these various declarations, framed and drafted by the participants, themselves all media professionals, were later formally adopted in their entirety by the states represented at UNESCO's General Conference. In addition, the United Nations General Assembly decided, in December 1993, on UNESCO's proposal to proclaim 3 May, the anniversary of the Declaration of Windhoek, 'World Press Freedom Day'. Finally, as its most recent initiative, UNESCO established, in 1996, the UNESCO/Guillermo Cano World Press Freedom Prize, which was awarded for the first time on 3 May 1997.

In the light of the foregoing, one cannot fail to observe the developments that have occurred in the states since the end of the Cold War. Unfortunately, in so far as respect for fundamental freedoms is concerned, there is frequently a major difference between official positions, adopted 'cold' in intergovernmental forums, and the reality of the situation at grass-roots level. The fact nevertheless remains that states taken as a whole have never committed themselves so far on such sensitive issues as press freedom and the independence and pluralism of the media.

The second objective of UNESCO's 'new communication strategy' takes up one of the ultimate goals of NWICO, with this single – but major – difference: that it is no longer possible to curb or to prevent the free flow of information on the pretext that its dissemination is unbalanced. Such an argument had in fact frequently been put forward by authoritarian and totalitarian regimes, in the 1970s and 1980s, in order to justify censorship of the international news agencies, to ban the distribution of foreign newspapers on national territory and to jam electronic media broadcasts transmitted from abroad. The new strategy does not seek to weaken the strong, but rather to strengthen the weak in order to redress the balance, in so far as is possible, in the exchange of information flows. Hence the third objective of UNESCO's 'new information strategy', namely, to develop communication capacities in the developing countries.

When the General Conference of UNESCO adopted its 'new communication strategy' in November 1989, the representatives of the developing countries, somewhat at a loss after finding themselves dropped by their traditional partners among the Communist states of Eastern and Central Europe, had greatly hoped that the industrialized countries of the North, having obtained satisfaction on the free flow of information issue, would do their utmost substantially to increase their financial support for the development of communication, and in particular for the International Programme for the Development of Communication (IPDC). This hope was strengthened in February 1992 when IPDC decided to change its rules of procedure in order to be in a position to help the media, in pursuance of a recommendation formulated some months earlier on the occasion of the Windhoek seminar. As a result, projects submitted by the private sector are henceforth admissible.

In the light of the experience of recent years, it must be acknowledged that that hope has been disappointed because contributions to the IPDC Special Account have failed to increase.

It is true that, since the economic crisis which hit them in the first half of the 1990s, most of the industrialized countries have severely cut back their

Funds of the IPDC Special Account by session
Total amount of funds: US$39,466,000 (1982–97)

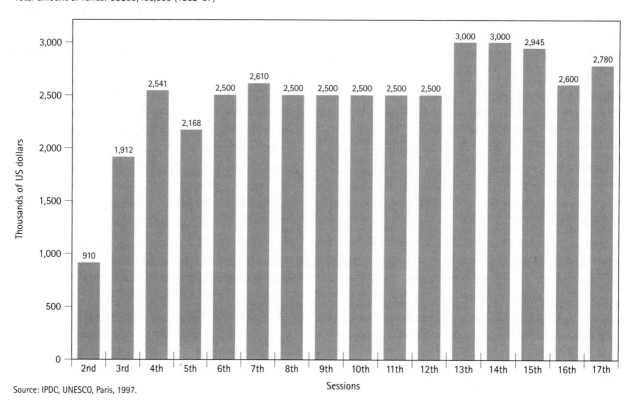

Source: IPDC, UNESCO, Paris, 1997.

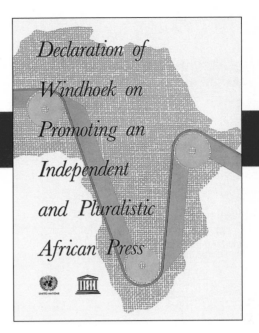

Declaration of Windhoek, 3 May 1991
endorsed by the General Conference
at its twenty-sixth session, 1991

We the participants in the United Nations/United Nations Educational, Scientific and Cultural Organization Seminar on Promoting an Independent and Pluralistic African Press, held in Windhoek, Namibia, from 29 April to 3 May 1991, *Recalling* the Universal Declaration of Human Rights, *Recalling* General Assembly resolution 59(I) of 14 December 1946 stating that freedom of information is a fundamental human right, and General Assembly resolution 45/76 A of 11 December 1990 on information in the service of humanity,

Recalling resolution 25C/104 of the General Conference of UNESCO of 1989 in which the main focus is the promotion of 'the free flow of ideas by word and image at international as well as national levels',

Noting with appreciation the statements made by the United Nations Under-Secretary-General for Public Information and the Assistant Director-General for Communication, Information and Informatics of UNESCO at the opening of the Seminar,

Expressing our sincere appreciation to the United Nations and UNESCO for organizing the Seminar,

Expressing also our sincere appreciation to all the intergovernmental, governmental and non-governmental bodies and organizations, in particular the United Nations Development Programme (UNDP), which contributed to the United Nations/UNESCO effort to organize the Seminar,

Expressing our gratitude to the Government and people of the Republic of Namibia for their kind hospitality which facilitated the success of the Seminar,

Declare that:

1. Consistent with article 19 of the Universal Declaration of Human Rights, the establishment, maintenance and fostering of an independent, pluralistic and free press is essential to the development and maintenance of democracy in a nation, and for economic development.

2. By an independent press, we mean a press independent from governmental, political or economic control or from control of materials and infrastructure essential for the production and dissemination of newspapers, magazines and periodicals.

3. By a pluralistic press, we mean the end of monopolies of any kind and the existence of the greatest possible number of newspapers, magazines and periodicals reflecting the widest possible range of opinion within the community.

4. The welcome changes that an increasing number of African States are now undergoing towards multi-party democracies provide the climate in which an independent and pluralistic press can emerge.

5. The world-wide trend towards democracy and freedom of information and expression is a fundamental contribution to the fulfilment of human aspirations.

6. In Africa today, despite the positive developments in some countries, in many countries journalists, editors and publishers are victims of repression – they are murdered, arrested, detained and censored, and are restricted by economic and political pressures such as restrictions on newsprint, licensing systems which restrict the opportunity to publish, visa restrictions which prevent the free movement of journalists, restrictions on the exchange of news and information,

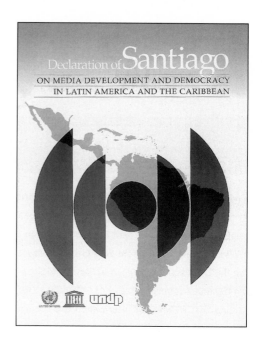

and limitations on the circulation of newspapers within countries and across national borders. In some cases, one-party states control the totality of information.

7. Today, at least 17 journalists, editors or publishers are in African prisons, and 48 African journalists were killed in the exercise of their profession between 1969 and 1990.

8. The General Assembly of the United Nations should include in the agenda of its next session an item on the declaration of censorship as a grave violation of human rights falling within the purview of the Commission on Human Rights.

9. African States should be encouraged to provide constitutional guarantees of freedom of the press and freedom of association.

10. To encourage and consolidate the positive changes taking place in Africa, and to counter the negative ones, the international community – specifically, international organizations (governmental as well as non-governmental), development agencies and professional associations – should as a matter of priority direct funding support towards the development and establishment of non-governmental newspapers, magazines and periodicals that reflect the society as a whole and the different points of view within the communities they serve.

11. All funding should aim to encourage pluralism as well as independence. As a consequence, the public media should be funded only where authorities guarantee a constitutional and effective freedom of information and expression and the independence of the press.

12. To assist in the preservation of the freedoms enumerated above, the establishment of truly independent, representative associations, syndicates or trade unions of journalists, and associations of editors and publishers, is a matter of priority in all the countries of Africa where such bodies do not now exist.

13. The national media and labour relations laws of African countries should be drafted in such a way as to ensure that such representative associations can exist and fulfil their important tasks in defence of press freedom.

14. As a sign of good faith, African Governments that have jailed journalists for their professional activities should free them immediately. Journalists who have had to leave their countries should be free to return to resume their professional activities.

15. Co-operation between publishers within Africa, and between publishers of the North and South (for example through the principle of twinning), should be encouraged and supported.

16. As a matter of urgency, the United Nations and

UNESCO, and particularly the International Programme for the Development of Communication (IPDC), should initiate detailed research, in co-operation with governmental (especially UNDP) and non-governmental donor agencies, relevant non-governmental organizations and professional associations, into the following specific areas:

(i) identification of economic barriers to the establishment of news media outlets, including restrictive import duties, tariffs and quotas for such things as newsprint, printing equipment, and typesetting and word processing machinery, and taxes on the sale of newspapers, as a prelude to their removal;

(ii) training of journalists and managers and the availability of professional training institutions and courses;

(iii) legal barriers to the recognition and effective operation of trade unions or associations of journalists, editors and publishers;

(iv) a register of available funding from development and other agencies, the conditions attaching to the release of such funds, and the methods of applying for them;

(v) the state of press freedom, country by country, in Africa.

17. In view of the importance of radio and television in the field of news and information, the United Nations and UNESCO are invited to recommend to the General Assembly and the General Conference the convening of a similar seminar of journalists and managers of radio and television services in Africa, to explore the possibility of applying similar concepts of independence and pluralism to these media.

18. The international community should contribute to the achievement and implementation of the initiatives and projects set out in the annex to this Declaration.

19. This Declaration should be presented by the Secretary-General of the United Nations to the United Nations General Assembly, and by the Director-General of UNESCO to the General Conference of UNESCO.

Declaration of the Seminar on
PROMOTING INDEPENDENT AND PLURALISTIC ARAB MEDIA

SANA'A, YEMEN
7-11 January 1996

aid budgets to developing countries. It is also true that the needs born of the transition process in the new democracies of Eastern and Central Europe have siphoned off substantial sums, frequently to the detriment of the countries of the South. However, that does not explain everything, for assistance for communication development has lagged behind both in the East European democracies currently in transition and in the developing countries of the South. This situation is all the more surprising in that, throughout the Cold War, Western countries, and first and foremost the United States, had invested billions of dollars in order to ensure their supremacy in the strategic field of communication. Those investments were far from fruitless, since it was the power of words and images that toppled the Berlin Wall. While it is understandable that, like the 'weapons of deterrence', the 'weapons of persuasion' should have suffered substantial budget cuts, it is difficult to imagine that only a few crumbs remain to consolidate the achievements of democracy in the communication field, since it is well known that the media were and are still in Europe, as in the other regions of the world, the driving force behind the transition to democracy. The scant interest shown by the industrialized countries in the development of communication and information becomes even more surprising when one considers the fact that the communication sector represents up to 10 per cent of GNP in some countries of the North. It may therefore legitimately be wondered what reasons have led the national development agencies to devote less than 1 per cent of their financial resources to date to projects relating to communication development.

The media between freedom and censorship

Satellite broadcasting, electronic printing, the explosion of the Internet and of e-mail, and the mobile telephone have resulted in a huge expansion of the potential for worldwide information flows and exchange. They have also facilitated the rapid and even instantaneous transmission of images from one region to another, transcending national borders – even though some states still endeavour to raise all kinds of barriers by operating border controls, jamming radio broadcasts and banning the possession of satellite dish aerials. All these defences are today increasingly eroded by the new progress being made by the media, the intensification of output and the higher levels of technical performance. The new communication technologies, or the new ways of optimizing the old, have become an essential dimension in all thinking about the issue. For they are capable of producing positive effects and helping to speed up the democratization process, just as they may constitute a curb upon, and a threat to, freedom of expression and democracy.

The media, allies of freedom and democracy

The media have played a key role in several countries in bringing about the democratic progress recorded throughout the world during the 1980s. Their ability to transmit, continuously and in real time, current national and international news has had the effect of both driving events along and speeding them up.[6] Examples are legion. In the Philippines, the clandestine use of video (and also of photocopying) at the time of the assassination of the opposition leader Benigno Aquino,[7] as well as the high-profile presence of foreign media during the 1986 elections, contributed in large measure to the fall of Ferdinand Marcos. Radio Veritas was occupied by the citizenry during the 'people's power' movement in order to rally

6. See on this subject Gourdault-Montagne, 'La politique étrangère et les médias' [Foreign Policy and the Media], *Le Trimestre du monde*, 3rd quarter 1992, pp. 45 ff.

7. See on this subject J. A. Lent, 'A Revolt against a Revolution: The Fight against Illegal Video', *Media Asia* (Singapore), 11 January 1984, pp. 25–30.

the population against Marcos's army. In South Africa, in Haiti and in Palestine, the pictures of apartheid, of repression and of the *intifada* prompted reactions of solidarity and support throughout the world. They enabled the international community to condemn the abuses, to defend human rights and to encourage democracy.[8]

The impact of the media can also be of paramount importance when they describe and present to peoples deprived of freedom another way of life, other political systems, other democratic values. The example of the former Communist regimes provides an excellent illustration. In the ex-German Democratic Republic, citizens could receive the radio stations and television channels of the Federal Republic of Germany. They were kept regularly informed about certain political and other events that their government preferred to cover up. That was how, in 1989, they learned of the great demonstration in Leipzig, the opening of the Hungarian borders and the first cracks that were appearing in the Berlin Wall.

After the fall of the Berlin Wall, the peoples of the neighbouring countries, who were following the events on foreign radio and television stations, decided in their turn to take to the streets. Here too, pictures invaded every sphere and played a crucial role in bearing witness to the process of liberation. They neutralized official pronouncements and undermined the authorities' position. During the same period, in Czechoslovakia, the students had installed television screens throughout the streets of Prague in order to show police brutality against the demonstrators, and to broadcast the speeches of the playwright and future President of the Republic, Vaclav Havel.[9]

In Poland, the majority of journalists found themselves on the front line with all other citizens calling for democracy. Dailies such as *Gazeta wyborcza* exerted considerable pressure on behalf of the democratization process. In Romania, television played a key role in rallying the population and helping to spread support for the liberation movement, which

was filmed, monitored and broadcast live throughout the world thanks to the famous Studio 4 of the Free Romanian Television company.[10] In striking contrast to the macabre faking of the mass grave in Timisoara, this movement established itself as a formidable force in the fight for democracy. Determined to bear witness on behalf of that revolution, citizens set up as amateur reporters to impose their video recordings by way of popular testimony in the first meetings organized by the revolution's leaders. Reaction to the events was extremely powerful, thanks to a press and television that, having thrown off their shackles, acted as catalysts in generating a genuine new awareness.

In the Federal Republic of Yugoslavia, the popular demonstrations against the authorities' refusal to accept the results of the municipal elections won by the opposition were widely and favourably reported on the Internet. Several sites made it possible to monitor in real time the evolution of the protest movement. Sites such as 'Protest 96', named after the student movement, made their voices heard throughout the world by posting reports on demonstrations, and by publishing their 'Declaration of Decency', a manifesto on behalf of respect for constitutional rights. These sites also showed photographs of demonstrations, and of graffiti observed on the walls of Belgrade. The Internet was thus instrumental in enabling the popular movement to keep up a dialogue with the outside world by receiving thousands of e-mail messages of support from all over the world.[11]

8.   J. C. Guillebaud, 'Les médias contre la démocratie' [The Media against Democracy], in D. Bougnoux (ed.), *Science de l'information et de la communication. Textes essentiels*, Paris, Éditions Larousse, 1993.

9.   According to Toffler, op. cit.

10.   D. Berindel, 'Les médias à l'épreuve de la révolution roumaine' [The Media Hurdling the Romanian Revolution], *Le Trimestre du Monde*, 3rd quarter 1992, p. 94.

11.   'En Serbie, la contestation s'installe sur Internet' [In Serbia, Dissent Spreads to the Internet], *Le Monde*, TV-Radio-Multimedia supplement (Paris), 22–23 December 1996, p. 35.

The Internet, an instrument of protest and resistance

WELCOME TO THE UNIVERSITY OF BELGRADE

THE OFFICIAL WORLD-WIDE WEB SITE

Bienvenidos al WEB Oficial
de

● NOVEDADES

- Breve Introduccion
- Historia y Logros
- Informes Internacionales
- Otros WEBs

- Documentos de Referencia
- Eventos y Actividades Especiales
- Linea de Denuncias
- Campañas Urgentes

✦ 20 Años de ABUELAS - 1977 1997

Envie su mensaje de correo electronico a:
abuelas@wamani.apc.org o a: abuelas@tournet.com.ar

Red Wamani (Home Page)

IFEX ACTION ALERT SERVICE
International Freedom of Expression Exchange Clearing House

About IFEX

The International Freedom of Expression eXchange
...linking freedom of expression groups around the world

See also: IFEX Members for addresses and links to member-organisations.

APC

Association for Progressive Communications

Global Computer Communications
for Environment, Human Rights, Development & Peace

These non-stop demonstrations, monitored continuously by the international community, drove the public authorities to confirm the opposition's victory in the capital and in several provincial cities.

In a similar context, the live broadcasting of the first trial in the history of the UN International War Crimes Tribunal has enabled international public opinion to discover the full extent of the atrocities committed in Bosnia and Herzegovina.

In other regions of the world, such as North Africa and the Near East, certain media have played and still play a key role in fostering the progress of democracy. In the Maghreb, satellite dish aerials, installed on a wide scale in the region, continue permanently to defy the public television channels operating under state control. Their unstoppable spread is breaking up monopolies and triggering off a veritable cultural and political revolution. In Algeria, the October 1988 uprising sparked a genuine democratic awakening that was immediately reflected in the emergence of a profusion of newspapers of every persuasion, and of go-getting journalists whose credo was and remains freedom of speech.

In Africa, use of the video recorder has greatly increased access to information sources and to a whole range of messages. This technology has contributed to a relative democratization of African society, which neither radio nor television had managed to achieve, for it has provided access to a greater number and variety of programmes than are offered by the traditional networks, whose coverage is limited and which generally operate under state control. Such programmes have in most cases been used to supplement or even to replace the information made available by the official media.[12]

Thus the events of the century's closing decades have provided ample proof of the close ties that exist between the media and democracy. The two are intimately linked, and develop in tandem. They demonstrate that there is no more reliable criterion for judging the quality of a democracy than press freedom and the pluralism and independence of the media.

The media: control and censorship

In most democracies, the press is perceived as both an outward sign and a guarantee of democracy. Regarded empirically as the fourth estate, it ensures that democracy functions properly, condemns abuses and clarifies the options available. Pursuing these aims, journalists enjoy certain professional rights that are supposed to guarantee their editorial independence *vis-à-vis* both the public authorities and their employers.

In practice, however, many media professionals regularly denounce the restrictions which undermine their independence – clear proof that the struggle for press independence is never over in democratic countries, even if it has lost much of its intensity.

First and foremost, journalists are concerned by the curbs placed by many governments upon the free flow of information. Access to public information sources, which is a precondition for ensuring that citizens are kept properly informed, is often limited, if not deliberately restricted. In most cases, states still impose strict regulations. For example, press coverage of military conflicts is subject to rigorous control in certain countries. There is a growing trend to limit the war correspondent's autonomy, freedom of movement and access to the front. This development has been particularly striking since the Viet Nam War in the United States, where access to information has on several occasions been channelled by the Pentagon.

---

12. On this subject see S. T. Kwame Boafo, 'Video-cassette Recorders in Ghana: Impact on Press Freedom in Sub-Saharan Africa', *New Communication Technologies: A Challenge for Press Freedom*, Paris, UNESCO, 1994 (Reports and Papers on Mass Communication, 106). The author shows how the introduction of the video-cassette recorder in Africa and in particular in Ghana is transforming the dominant communication models by reducing state control over media content to a minimum and by offering citizens a wider range of choice.

LE MATIN

LE DEVOIR DE VERITE   ISSN 111-1100 - n° **892** ven. 2-sam. 3 décembre 1994 — Prix : 10 DA – France 5 FF

Mesmar J'ha

Ce voleur qui...

Ce voleur qui, dans la nuit, rase les murs pour rentrer chez lui, c'est lui. Ce père qui recommande à ses enfants de ne pas dire dehors le méchant métier qu'il fait, c'est lui.

Ce mauvais citoyen qui traîne au palais de justice, attendant de passer devant les juges, c'est lui. Cet individu pris dans une rafle de quartier et qu'un coup de crosse propulse au fond du camion, c'est lui. C'est lui qui, le matin, quitte sa maison sans être sûr d'arriver à son travail. Et lui qui quitte le soir son travail, sans être certain d'arriver à sa maison.

Ce vagabond qui ne sait plus chez qui passer la nuit, c'est lui. C'est lui qu'on menace dans le secret d'un cabinet officiel, le témoin qui doit ravaler ce qu'il sait, ce citoyen nu et désemparé...

Cet homme qui fait le vœu de ne pas mourir égorgé, c'est lui. Ce cadavre sur lequel on recoud une tête décapitée, c'est lui. C'est lui qui ne sait rien faire de ses mains, rien d'autre que ses petits écrits, lui qui espère contre tout, parce que, n'est-ce-pas, les roses poussent bien sur les tas de fumier. Lui qui est tous ceux-là, et qui est seulement journaliste.

Saïd Mekbel

LE MATIN

LE DEVOIR DE VERITE   ISSN 111-1100 - n° **892** ven. 2-sam. 3 décembre 1994 — Prix : 10 DA – France 5 FF

'This thief who . . .

This thief who, under cover of darkness, hugs the walls as he heads homewards, that's him. This father who enjoins his children not to tell anyone what a wicked profession he practises, that's him. This bad citizen hanging round the law courts awaiting judgement, that's him. This fellow caught in a local police raid, whom a blow from a rifle butt has sent sprawling in the back of a van, that's him. He's the fellow who leaves home in the morning without being sure of getting to work, who leaves his office in the evening without knowing for certain whether he'll reach home. This vagrant who no longer knows at whose friend's home he will spend the night, that's him too. The man being threatened in the privacy of some official's office, the witness who has to choke back everything he knows, that's him too, this naked helpless citizen. This man who has vowed not to die with his throat cut, that's him. This body having its head sewn back on, that's him. He's the one who can't do anything with his hands except write little pieces, who goes on hoping against hope because roses do flourish on dungheaps, don't they? He is all this, and yet he's simply a journalist.'

Saïd Mekbel, editor of the Algiers daily *Le Matin*, published these lines in his paper on 3 December 1994, the day he was murdered.

In most cases, the culture of secrecy continues to hold sway, usually cloaked in a series of regulations, statutes and conventions that limit both the volume and the nature of the information which may be disclosed to the public. In reality, as the international monitoring organization Article 19 contends, 'governments invoke a wide variety of reasons . . . for justifying secrecy. . . . Many reasons lack justification in the sense that they are not recognized as permissible restrictions under international law, and in fact may have illegitimate aims, such as the suppression of criticism and unorthodox ideas'.[13] The French media historian and former Secretary of State for Communication, Jean-Noël Jeanneney, has pointed out that in a modern democracy 'we must beware of all

secrets, and flush out everything that is hidden in the shadows: ultimately, all curiosity is legitimate'.[14]

Thus the obligation imposed in certain cases upon journalists to reveal confidential information which they alone possess, the common tendency to confuse secrets that could jeopardize the interests of states with those that would simply harm political

13.   Quoted in *Right to Know?*, an international survey of journalists' rights and restrictions, conducted for the International Federation of Journalists and UNESCO, Brussels, January 1992.

14.   J. N. Jeanneney, 'Médias et démocratie: le su, le cru, le dit et le tu' [Media and Democracy: the Known, the Believed, the Said and the Withheld], *Communication et langage* (Paris), No. 106, p. 9.

administrations, and the repeated attempts to thwart journalists' investigative missions are all, generally speaking, detrimental to the citizen's right to information and, hence, to the public interest as a whole.

Furthermore, media professionals consider that they are not safe from threats and intimidation. Infringements of, and obstructions to, freedom of information increasingly take the form of a whole range of obstacles placed in the way of journalists: these include house searches, indictments, the forced suspension of publication, violence and even murder. The use and the interpretation made of libel actions, of requests to exercise the right of reply, of public order disturbances, provisional or emergency measures, and actions for damages are usually governed by the circumstances of the moment. The enforcement of these restrictions, which are moreover considered to be outmoded by the profession, generates a climate of insecurity and suspicion that weighs heavily upon freedom of information. Certain court rulings are experienced by journalists as intolerable infringements of their professional rights and, consequently, of the public's right to be kept informed. In the field of electronic media, the threats exercised by the courts also remain extremely powerful.[15] In the print media field, trials relating to the disclosure of documents deemed to be secret or confidential are becoming increasingly common, and are usually aimed at smaller newpapers, whose limited financial resources reduce their ability to defend themselves or to pay the fines and damages awarded against them.[16] Media professionals consider that these judgements represent a direct threat to freedom of information and investigative journalism, understood as the concern to go beyond official sources in the search for information. They face journalists with an unacceptable dilemma, since they are liable to be convicted of libel if they publish confidential information without providing proof of the facts revealed, and convicted for possession of stolen property if they hold and publish the evidence confirming their allegations.

Lawsuits are no longer brought for press offences, that is, breaches of the few prohibitions specifically established in law, but aim to put the behaviour of the media on trial. The criterion of reference is no longer that fixed by the legislature, interpreted as appropriate by the judge, but is in the last resort that of the judge himself.[17] His own values are thus imposed upon the freedom of information. In the civil courts, the judge tends to set himself up as the natural arbiter of professional ethics, a situation that journalists and legal experts find difficult to accept. For Franz Werro, a professor at the law faculty in Fribourg (Switzerland), 'if press freedom is mauled by the judges, that is because the legislator's intention is most frequently misinterpreted in the manner in which the law's provisions are applied. The practices of the courts are in great danger of deflecting the media from all critical news-reporting'.[18] Thus any exclusive coverage or disclosure bound up with the requirements of investigative journalism may be deemed by a judge to justify a court order to publish a reply, a financial investigation or even a ban on publication.

15. See Chapter 13: 'The Internet: Towards Some Form of Regulation?'

16. In France, the ruling of the Cour de Cassation of 3 April 1995 convicting the satirical newspaper *Le Canard enchaîné* for having published a facsimile of the income tax returns of the chairman of a French car manufacturing consortium which revealed a substantial rise in his salary, at a time when he was refusing to grant his striking employees any increase in their wages, was felt by French journalists to be an intolerable infringement of the freedom of information.

17. On this subject see C. F. Martin, 'Le juge et le journaliste', *Le Monde diplomatique* (Paris), September 1995, p. 28.

18. Symposium on the responsibilities of the press organized in the Société de Droit et de Législation. Report published in 'La liberté de la presse malmenée par les juges', *Le Journal de Genève* and *La Gazette de Lausanne* (Geneva), 31 October 1995, p. 15.

Threats, intimidation and censorship – the attacks and obstacles to freedom of information are on the rise throughout the world.

Photo: *Oslobodenje*

Photo: AFP

However, the Munich Declaration emphasizes the right to information by affirming that journalists may claim free access to all information sources and the right freely to investigate all events that affect public life. It adds that the secrecy of public or private affairs cannot in such cases be adduced as justification for denying journalists these rights save in exceptional circumstances and on clearly stated grounds. This trend towards freeing access to information sources from legal impediments has been enshrined, in most states of the United States of America, in the so-called 'shield laws', which shield journalists against being forced to give testimony.[19] It has also been regularly reaffirmed by regional and international courts of justice. Several recent cases have, for example, provided an opportunity to reassert the right of journalists to protect their sources. The one that attracted most attention was the ruling by the European Court of Human Rights on 27 March 1996 which condemned the United Kingdom for failure to respect journalists' rights in this respect.[20]

In countries in transition, acceptance of the principle of a press that is free, independent and openly critical of all the authorities is a relatively recent phenomenon. Theoretically, most of these countries support the principles set forth in Article 19 of the Universal Declaration of Human Rights and reiterate them in their new constitutions.

Nevertheless, such support, often solemnly proclaimed, has not solved all the problems affecting freedom of expression and the free flow of information. In many countries, particularly arbitrary forms of obstruction of and restrictions upon the freedom of information still remain. Such obstacles stem by and large from the prevailing system of media ownership and management. The majority of broadcasting networks are still state monopolies subject to strict controls. In countries with authoritarian or totalitarian regimes, the prevailing ideology leaves but little room for pluralism. The main dailies and weeklies are controlled, subsidized and administered by the state. Likewise, the co-existence of several newspapers or television channels does not necessarily constitute evidence of pluralism, in particular when their proprietors are close to the establishment. In such contexts, the public, the target audience of these media, is self-evidently not in a position to forge an enlightened and unbiased opinion of its own.

Censorship may take a variety of forms, depending on whether it is practised officially or unofficially. The ban upon satellite dishes in force in many countries, and the controls exercised on access to electronic media and the Internet, deprive citizens of alternative information sources. Moreover, various administrative measures may prove just as effective as overt censorship. These range from restrictions upon, for example, the use of newsprint and other professional materials and hardware, to more direct forms of interference: control over the printing of newspapers, monopoly on the importation of paper, right of scrutiny of newspaper circulation figures, control over the award of advertising contracts, exorbitant taxation of certain publications, etc. In order to explain the strengthening of their control over

19. The shield laws give journalists rights similar to those enjoyed by lawyers, doctors and priests in the matter of keeping information and the identity of their sources secret. These laws may also serve to prohibit carrying out searches of newspaper offices in order to discover clues in criminal cases.

20. In rendering its verdict, the European Court based itself on Article 10 of the European Convention on Human Rights, which concerns freedom of expression. The court thereby confirmed that the protection of journalists' sources is 'one of the cornerstones of the press, as is reflected in the laws and codes of ethics in force in numerous states . . . and affirmed in several international instruments on the freedoms enjoyed by journalists'. Consequently, the order of the British High Court was deemed to be 'disproportionate' and 'unnecessary in a democratic society'. Summary of an article entitled 'La Cour européenne reconnaît le droit des journalistes à protéger leurs sources', published in *Le Monde* (Paris), 29 February 1996, p. 30.

the print and broadcast media, and even to justify the censoring of news-reporting that does not serve their interests, the authorities generally put forward the same reasons: imperatives bound up with issues of national security and public order. Thus many countries grappling with terrorism and outbreaks of irrational violence have adopted public order measures that have inevitably eroded press freedom severely.

In Spain, the Bill on the secrecy of defence matters presented by the Spanish Government in June 1996, which was interpreted by media professionals as an attempt to restrict freedom of expression, was finally abandoned. The activities of the ETA continue to be publicized by Spanish news agencies and reported by the media.[21] For its part, the United Kingdom adopted on 16 September 1994, as one of its measures to deal with the Irish question, a Bill known as the 'Ulster Rule Bill' which imposed very strict controls upon news coverage of IRA activities by the BBC. For example, the BBC was not allowed to grant air time to IRA representatives. In order to circumvent this ban, the Corporation hired Irish actors to deliver the terrorists' statements. The same restriction was imposed upon the independent British television stations, which were required to sign specific agreements regarding the coverage of terrorist activities.[22] In Algeria, the Government published a decree in June 1994 relating to the reporting of security issues. That decree established a 'communication unit' to be responsible for issuing official communiqués exclusively through the Algerian news agency APS. Article 3 of the decree stipulates that 'in reporting on terrorist and subversive activities, all categories of media are required to disseminate only official communiqués'. Lastly, Article 4 provides that 'the dissemination of any information relating to security matters that is not covered in the framework of an official communiqué or a public press release shall be forbidden'. In Egypt, the law on 'crimes of publishing' authorizes journalists to be held without trial for an indefinite period in accordance with the

law instituting a state of emergency. The new law also makes provision for lengthy terms of imprisonment, should the court decide that a crime is involved, in the case of journalists found guilty of 'tendentious writings'.[23]

Freedom of information may be limited by other entities than governments (terrorist and extremist groups, the Mafia, paramilitary groups, and drug cartels). In some countries, extremist groups resort to force in order to prevent families from picking up foreign television channels that spread values alien to their own. Others launch *fatwas* against intellectuals, artists and journalists. Others still go to the extreme of murdering journalists and other media professionals. In this regard it should be pointed out that, in almost every case, inquiries into crimes committed against journalists have come to nothing, and neither those who carried them out nor those who ordered and paid for the killings have ever appeared before the courts. Concerned by this 'culture of impunity', professional organizations such as the Inter-American Press Association have set up their own committees of inquiry.

21. Miguel de Aguilera, *Bulletin of the European Institute of Communication* (Berlin), Vol. 13, No. 3, 1996.
22. 'Terrorisme et information à l'étranger' [Terrorism and Information Abroad], *La Lettre du CSA* (Conseil Supérieur de l'Audiovisuel) (Paris), October 1995, No. 73, p. 6.
23. The entire Egyptian press attacked the law on 'crimes of publishing'. The semi-official newspaper *El Akhbar* expressed the view, in a leader written by its editorialist Mostapha Amine, that the law was 'a Damocles sword which, if it does not cut our heads off, threatens to cut out our tongues'. As for the daily *El Ahram*, its editor-in-chief, Ahmed Baggat, wrote that 'the essence of democracy is to inform people about any proposed new law and to discuss it with those concerned'. – 'L'opposition et les journaux égyptiens protestent contre la loi sur la presse', *Le Monde* (Paris), 2 June 1995.

International Freedom of Expression Exchange Network (IFEX)

This initiative was launched by several professional and non-governmental organizations concerned to pool information more effectively and to enhance the impact of their interventions, which set up an electronic alert and co-ordination network to react whenever freedom of information is threatened. Operational since September 1992, the network is run by the Canadian Committee to Protect Journalists, in Toronto, with the support of UNESCO and its International Programme for the Development of Communication (IPDC).

The IFEX Network today has twenty-seven members, including the major organizations (Article 19, the Committee to Protect Journalists, the International Federation of Journalists, Index on Censorship, International Pen, Reporters Sans Frontières, World Association of Newspapers, the Media Institute for Southern Africa, the World Press Freedom Committee, the Pacific Islands News Association and the Inter-American Press Association). The network, which is a vitally important point of contact for all journalists and professional media organizations, comprised in May 1997 more than 300 subscribers in eighty countries, 160 of them located in the developing countries. This was achieved thanks in particular to the International Programme for the Development of Communication, whose aid has enabled the professional organizations of those countries to form a majority within the network.

In five years, the network has made it possible not only to improve the gathering, production and dissemination of news and information on topics relating to press freedom on an international scale but also to strengthen the development of South–South exchanges, and, finally, to set up a veritable system of alert and solidarity among all the protagonists: 1,600 alerts are issued each year, as well as a weekly press release in three languages. Joint campaigns are also conducted. A data bank has been created on the Internet which makes available the information gathered by IFEX on a World Wide Web server (http://www.ifex.org).

The media in the service of hatred

In conflict-torn countries, gaining control of the media and their use for partisan purposes constitutes a major objective of the parties in conflict. This practice may lead to a downhill spiral with ever more dangerous consequences. In the former Yugoslavia and in Rwanda, for example, newspapers, radio stations and television channels, press-ganged into the service of the various factions, have begun to launch public calls to violence, ethnic cleansing and even to genocide. The self-styled journalists working for these media no longer see their mission as being to report on events in times of crisis but as a veritable combat on the side of one or other of the parties in conflict. By resorting to the procedures of totalitarian propaganda, based on techniques of crowd manipulation, conditioning and disinformation, such media, co-opted or hijacked to serve as the tools of xenophobic and hate-filled politicians, have become vehicles or carriers of war. The authorities no longer confine themselves to censoring publications that might damage their image, but seek to orchestrate the entire system of the media in order to turn it into a political tool. It is a well-known strategy of totalitarian regimes.

In the former Yugoslavia, the media have been turned into veritable war machines putting out a mixture of crude lies and war-mongering propaganda. For nearly five years, they have sown the seeds of hatred between the Serb, Bosnian, Croat and Muslim communities. The consequences have been tragic, since they have fostered the emergence of various forms of chauvinistic and xenophobic nationalism. Be it in Serbia, in Croatia or in Bosnia and Herzegovina, most of the media have been used as instruments of war and intercommunity violence. Brought very early on under the control of the parties in power, they have embraced the most extremist causes. Their persistent rhetoric inciting to hatred and ostracism has been regularly condemned by the international community.[24]

In Rwanda, media such as the broadcasting stations Radio-Télévision Libre Mille Collines (RTLM) and Radio Rwanda, and the periodical *Kangura*, have contributed actively to campaigns inciting to racial hatred and genocide targeted against the Tutsis. Although RTLM, which was set up in April 1993, claims for itself the status of a 'free', commercial station, it was in fact financed entirely by members of the family of President Juvénal Habyarimana, who was assassinated on 6 April 1994. Installed directly opposite the presidential palace, the station became the propaganda centre of the Habyarimana clan, well known for its hostility to the Arusha peace accords of August 1993 between the government and the opposition party, the Front Patriotique Rwandais (FPR).[25]

The station succeeded in winning a wide audience thanks to live shows and musical broadcasts distinguished by a degree of professional expertise. The station's presenters gloated daily over the massacres, and the non-stop flow of their commentaries, personal messages and jokes was tinged with racial hatred directed against the Tutsi minority.[26] This process of 'ethnicization' clearly won support throughout the region of the Great Lakes. In Burundi, Radio Rutomorangingo, a pirate radio station set up by Hutu extremists, as well as both Tutsi and Hutu extremist newspapers, have enlisted in the service of ethnic hatred.

Resistance and international support

Faced with this dangerous drift by the media towards hatred-inspired campaigns of disinformation, some journalists are nevertheless striving, frequently at the cost of their personal safety, to do their job conscientiously, reporting events in an honest and unbiased manner. In Rwanda, André Sibomana, editor of the country's oldest independent newspaper, *Kinyamateka*, founded in 1933, narrowly escaped the massacres on several occasions. Having been a victim of harassment, threats and censorship, this newspaper resumed publication in December 1994, thanks to aid provided by the international community.

In the former Yugoslavia, while many journalists have thrown in their lot with the nationalists by espousing their doctrines, others have opted for a professional approach and strive first and foremost – despite the threats and obvious risks – to report the facts and to tell the truth as impartially as possible. While the former have consciously consented to take part in campaigns aimed at manipulating public opinion, for example by stirring up feelings of hatred and vengefulness, the latter have by contrast done their utmost to give a balanced and unbiased picture of the situation.

Today, the problem of the media's independence in these countries has still not been resolved, despite the efforts of the international community, and in particular of UNESCO, to create the conditions in which pluralist and independent media can develop and take an effective part in the process of reconstruction and democratization.

24. In a report published in November 1992, the UN Special Rapporteur for the region, Tadeusz Mazowiecki, denounced 'the negative role of the media in the former Yugoslavia, which puts out false and inflammatory information and stirs up the climate of hatred and mutual prejudice that fuels the conflict in Bosnia and Herzegovina'. Quoted in *Les médias de la haine*, p. 11, Paris, Éditions La Découverte, 1995.

25. V. Peronnet and F. Misser, 'Radio Machette', *Télérama* (Paris), No. 232, 29 June 1994, pp. 138–40.

26. J.-P. Chrétien (ed.), *Rwanda: les médias du génocide*, pp. 63–82, Paris, Éditions Karthala, 1995.

UNESCO in a period of conflict: the example of the former Yugoslavia

During the war years, independent journalists in the former Yugoslavia came under heavy political pressure. At a time when the independent media were fighting for survival, access to unbiased information was also becoming increasingly difficult for the public.

In December 1992, in accordance with its constitutional mandate 'to promote the free flow of ideas by word and image', UNESCO launched a pilot programme to assist independent media in conflict areas, special emphasis being given to the former Yugoslavia.

After the signing of the Dayton Peace Accords in December 1995, UNESCO renewed its support to independent media so as to pave the way for democratization and the peace process, thanks in particular to the aid supplied by several donors, and in close collaboration with other United Nations agencies and professional media organizations.

UNESCO's strategy in the former Yugoslavia was and remains threefold:

• To provide the technical and material assistance needed in order to keep the existing independent media alive and to start up new media for the promotion of pluralism in the press.

• To encourage information exchange between non-partisan media in the region and with the rest of the world.

• To foster the establishment of the conditions required to ensure press freedom.

In four years, the Organization has supplied several tonnes of newsprint to independent newspapers, delivered equipment to non-partisan electronic media and news agencies and trained journalists in most of the republics and territories of former Yugoslavia.

In 1996, UNESCO was designated 'lead agency for assistance to independent media for the reconstruction period in former Yugoslavia' by the UN Inter-Agency Appeal. As such, the Organization has lent backing in Bosnia and Herzegovina, the Federal Republic of Yugoslavia and the Republic of Croatia to eleven TV stations, ten radios, seven newspapers, three press agencies and three production companies.

The journalist: torch-bearer of democracy

Aside from the extreme cases described above, there exist throughout the world dozens of conflict situations in which the media perform a more traditional but no less essential role as 'witnesses'. Their supposed mission being to report everything that occurs in these regions and to reveal violations of the fundamental principles of humanity, the media are in a position to keep international public opinion informed and to alert it to the most horrendous situations. The journalist then becomes, as it were, a torch-bearer of democracy by reporting on what he or she has seen and learned in order to supply the citizen's basic need for information. A report on violations of the funda-mental principles of humanity, whether enshrined in the Geneva Conventions or in the human rights conventions, can in itself serve to alert public opinion and thereby constitute a major exposure of the crimes committed. In certain cases, such a report may serve to set in motion mechanisms or procedures for putting an end to those crimes.

However, in situations of armed conflict, the journalist's job is a difficult and dangerous one. Opposition groups and civil and military authorities alike generally find it in their interest to conceal certain compromising realities. Some do not then hesitate to take appropriate steps in order to curb the activities of reporters. Harassment, threats and even murder are unfortunately becoming increasingly common in dealings with journalists who get in the way too much. In this 'no-man's-land' of freedom, the reporter's sole means of protection is frequently his own experience and common sense. At present, the status of journalists on professional missions in areas of armed conflict is defined in the first Protocol Additional to the Geneva Conventions of 12 August 1949, in Article 79 relating to 'Measures of protection for journalists'. This article provides that 'journalists engaged in dangerous professional missions in areas of armed conflict shall be considered as civilians'. As such, they enjoy general protection against dangers arising from military operations, and shall not be the object of attack, acts or threats of violence (Article 51 of the first Additional Protocol).

In an effort to go beyond the legal protection afforded by international law, the efficacy of which remains wholly contingent upon the willingness or otherwise of the warring parties to comply therewith, various non-governmental organizations have taken initiatives aimed at assisting journalists on dangerous missions. For example, the International Committee of the Red Cross (ICRC), whose delegates are present in virtually all the planet's conflict areas, set up in 1985 a hotline which operates round the clock. This Geneva telephone number is available to families, newsrooms, editorial staff and professional media organizations in order to enable them to alert the ICRC whenever one or more journalists find themselves in trouble (abduction, arrest, hostage-taking, etc.) and to request its intervention on humanitarian grounds. The results obtained by the ICRC through its hotline system have by force of circumstance been extremely uneven. But the few lives which have been saved thanks to its existence amply suffice to justify it.

Chapter 13
The Internet:
towards some form
of regulation?

Throughout the world, 1995 was the year when the general public discovered the Internet: a community of 35 to 45 million users, without any structured organization or centralized management, and without any precise identification of the individual information flows. The rapid development of communications on the Internet constitutes an extraordinary collective resource for the international community. However, over the past year several governments have come to consider that the network also represents a serious threat to public order. The dissemination of offensive material – relating to paedophilia, pornography, drug trafficking, the spreading of 'negationist' or pro-Nazi doctrines, and other deviant behaviours – is highlighted by certain politicians and pressure groups who draw attention to the fact that the freedom of the Internet knows no bounds. For their part, the Internet's users consider that certain abuses and aberrations, relatively rare in proportion to the number of existing services, serve in fact as an alibi for those who wish to police freedom of expression and consequently to censor the Net. This means that politicians have their work cut out for them, all the more so in that the Internet continues to expand and to increase the number of services on offer such as radio broadcasts or, in the near future, television. In an effort to curb misuse of the network without hindering freedom of expression, states are attempting to set up concerted action bodies grouping service providers, users and representatives of civil society.

The Internet between censorship and freedom under surveillance

This vast free-communication area causes states considerable disquiet. In Germany, for example, a federal prosecutor in Munich designated 200 news-groups whose material was deemed to be actionable under German law governing the dissemination of certain forms of pornography (in particular paedo-philia). In November 1995, the Munich public

The Internet, a moral challenge to ensure better education and greater freedom of expression.
Source: P. Pailly/Eurelios

prosecutor's office ordered a search to be made of the headquarters of the on-line service CompuServe Germany, in connection with which it launched a preliminary investigation for dissemination of obscene material.[1] The American company, caught in the act of disseminating pornography, was forced to ban access to its discussion forums by its 4 million clients in nearly 140 countries, on account of the technical impracticability of restricting this measure solely to its German subscribers. Finally, in January 1997, the charges against CompuServe Germany were dismissed. On the other hand, a draft 'multimedia law' has been published whose objectives are to protect the private sphere, to create a system of certification for electronic transactions and to broaden the scope of the laws against pornography, revisionism, violent and racist literature, and incitement to prostitution in cyberspace.

In the United States, the crackdown began, in 1995, with the arrest by the FBI of several individuals charged with trafficking in child pornography on the Net. The same year, the Conservative Senator James Exon, leader of the anti-sex crusade, laid before the

American Senate a Bill relating to 'communications decency' aimed at making it an offence to transmit any 'obscene or indecent' words on computer networks. In conjunction, eleven American states passed legislation restricting use of the Internet. Most of these laws were variants of the Exon amendment, and as such they targeted pornography and indecency. At the same time, the State of Georgia adopted a law instituting penal sanctions against not only pornographic material but also other types of material such as works infringing copyright and pirated works. On 8 February 1996, President Bill Clinton signed the new Bill on the deregulation of telecommunications in the United States, and thereby gave his approval, following that of the United States Senate and Congress, to the Communications Decency Act (CDA). This law limiting the dissemination of 'indecent' or 'patently offensive' texts or images on the Internet in order to

1.   'L'Allemagne plaide l'auto contrôle' [Germany Makes a Case for Self-censorship], *Libération* (Paris), 14 June 1996, p. 29.

protect children caused an outcry in the American Cyberspace community. The American Civil Liberties Union (ACLU) and the American Library Association, assisted by associations representing computer publishing and the industry, took the matter before the Supreme Court which pronounced the Communications Decency Act unconstitutional on 26 June 1997. In its decision the court noted the particular nature of the network, being that of a public forum for the exchange of ideas and knowledge, and refuted any comparison with radio and television where the authorities may intervene if circumstances so warrant.[2]

In France, the debate began with the posting on the Internet, in January 1996, of the book *Le grand secret* by Dr Gubler on the illness of the former President of the French Republic, François Mitterrand, the sale of which had been banned. The same year, the directors of the two main French companies providing access to the Internet were charged with having disseminated paedophile materials and placed under investigation. On 18 June 1996, the law on the regulation of telecommunications was voted by the French Assembly. Two months later, an interministerial commission published its report on the Internet and proposed 'concrete measures and regulatory developments which, while strictly respecting the freedom of communication, would ensure maintenance of a satisfactory level of public order, notably in regard to young people and consumers'.[3]

Generally speaking, states recognize the economic and scientific usefulness of the Internet but continue to grapple with a question that is usually left unanswered: how to ensure that their countries benefit from the wealth of scientific knowledge and materials stored on the Internet while at the same time containing the drift towards pornography or racism. It is equally true that the discussion forums on the Internet represent a form of opposition for some states.

In order to contain such flows, the method proposed by the authorities consists either in monitoring all materials transmitted to subscribers or in banning undesirable sites. For example, in Singapore the authorities have set up programmes designed to block access to a number of Web sites and targeting in particular 'information liable to inflame political, religious or racial susceptibilities'. Other, no less repressive, methods involve using filtering software to provide personalized access: veritable instruments of censorship serving to cover up certain affairs that are politically embarrassing for the city-state.[4] Several governments are currently interested in systems of this kind. Bahrain, Saudi Arabia and the United Arab Emirates have already ordered software from American companies to enable them to block messages judged to be offensive to moral and traditional values.[5]

Regulating the Internet: mission impossible?

The adoption of this series of laws triggered off a vast protest campaign throughout the world, led by numerous organizations concerned with human rights and freedom of expression as well as associations of Internet users.

In the United States, the champions of freedom of speech rallied to protest against the Communi-

2.   'Le réseau qui n'a ni dieu, ni maître' [The Network That Has Neither God nor Master], *La Tribune Desfossés* (Paris), 20 February 1996; *The Washington Post*, quoted by *Courrier International*, 24–30 October 1996; E. Volokh, 'Speech and Spillover', in *Slate Magazine*, consulted on the Internet, 26 December 1996, on http://www.slate.com/...96-07-18/featurel.asp.; 'Justices Void Internet Indecency Law', *International Herald Tribune* (Paris), 27 June 1997.

3.   'Internet: les propositions de la mission interministérielle' [Internet: What the Interministerial Mission Proposes], *Les Echos* (Paris), 11 September 1996, p. 51.

4.   *Far Eastern Economic Review*, quoted by *Courrier international*, No. 312, 24–30 October 1996.

5.   'Internet, censure à domicile' [Internet: Censorship in the Home], *Le Monde* (Paris), 19–25 February 1996, p. 28.

cations Decency Act. Such eminently respectable bodies as the American Civil Liberties Union (ACLU) and the Electronic Frontier Foundation (EFF)[6] attacked the law on constitutional grounds, citing the First Amendment of the Constitution of the United States of 1791. At the same time, thousands of Web servers displayed their home page on a black background or ornamented with a small blue ribbon as a rallying sign of protest against the new law, and urged Internet users to inundate the White House and Congress with electronic messages of protest. The same mobilization occurred in Japan around the Japanese Internet Association, which considered that the directives of the Bill had been adopted unilaterally, and were likely to lead to self-censorship if not censorship. In France, the various court rulings also sparked off a surge of solidarity among members of the Association Française des Professionnels d'Internet (AFPI), who launched a general boycott by deciding to deprive their subscribers of all discussion forums. Moreover, the entire community of Internet users, from the Association des Utilisateurs d'Internet (AUI) to the Association Française de la Télématique Multimédia (AFTEL), including numerous academics and deputies, condemned the speed with which the law on the regulation of telecommunications was adopted. Finally, in Germany, a similar protest movement led the government to abandon all forms of repression, and to opt instead for minimal regulation by putting the onus first and foremost on the operators and content providers to practise self-censorship. The government has also stated its intention to curb the enthusiasms of certain *Länder* which are eager to extend to the Internet and on-line services the legislation in force in the broadcast media sector.

Generally speaking, the different protests converge towards the same conviction: that freedom of speech on the Net can admit of no exception. The measures taken to silence fascists of all persuasions or sexual perverts always backfire eventually, and democracy is the loser. It is better to tolerate their

abuses and aberrations, for only at this price can the freedom of all be guaranteed. Moreover, as the Net becomes ever more complex, it will become increasingly difficult to silence anyone having access to a computer. While it is true that authoritarian regimes have succeeded for several years in jamming international radio broadcasts, banning books, newspapers and satellite dishes, the use of centralized means to censor the Web is, in the view of Nicholas Negroponte, director of the Media Laboratory at MIT, doomed to failure – barring the use of terror tactics to reduce people to silence. Negroponte's conclusion is that 'there is no means of blocking access to all sites, since it is possible to move from "acceptable" pages to pages that are not, or else to use a cellular telephone to break through the barrier'.[7] Moreover, the efforts to control the Web are pathetically ineffective. This is demonstrated by the ease with which a censored site can spawn subsites. Scarcely had the Web site of Dr Gubler's unpublished (and banned) book been shut down than it became available on an increasing number of other servers, in Israel, the United States and the United Kingdom.[8] Ike Godwin, a lawyer representing the Electronic Frontier Foundation, does not deny the need for some regulation, but criticizes the legislators for having adopted only criteria applied to radio and television. 'On the Internet, material is not sent to passive consumers in their homes . . . ;

---

6. The Electronic Frontier Foundation is an American organization which has won a position for itself as an unofficial leader and mouthpiece of the Internet users' community. Only five years after its creation, the EFF is today at one and the same time a lobby, a club, a militant association, a research centre and also a 'virtual community' that is active on every front, recognized, respected and even feared.

7. *Far Eastern Economic Review*, quoted by *Courrier international*, op. cit.

8. 'La France n'interdirait pas la diffusion de contenu illégal' [France Not Opposed to Broadcasting of Illegal Content], *Le Monde* (Paris), 14 June 1996, p. 18.

National measures for regulating the Internet

● AUSTRALIA

• January 1996: Entry into force of a law on self-censorship by Internet service providers.

● CANADA

• April 1996: The Minister of Justice calls upon Canadians to express their views on the possible regulation of the portrayal of violence in the media, including on the Internet.

● CHINA

• June 1995: The Minister of Telecommunications announces that China intends to exercise control over the content of information circulated on the Internet.

• February 1996: The Bureau of Public Security makes it obligatory for Internet subscribers to register with the authorities within a period of thirty days.

● CUBA

• October 1996: Havana is connected to the Internet. Individual access is, however, controlled by a commission of the Academy of Sciences.

● EUROPEAN UNION

• October 1996: The Commission puts forward measures to ban the distribution on the Internet of pornographic material and other materials deemed to be illegal.

● GERMANY

• July 1996: The Minister for the Family, Frau Nölte, calls for a commission to be set up in order to define international criteria for monitoring the content of material distributed on the Net.

• November 1995: On the order of the German Government, CompuServe shuts down a number of Internet sites in order to combat child pornography.

• January 1996: Deutsche Telekom blocks access to certain Internet sites containing anti-Semitic material.

• January 1997: Draft 'multimedia law' on the applicability to cyberspace of the laws against pornography, racism and revisionism.

● HONG KONG

• March 1996: SuperNet, the country's leading Internet service provider, shuts down several servers containing pornographic material.

● JAPAN

• February 1996: The Ministry of Industry and Foreign Trade publishes a report on the moral principles governing the management of computer networks.

• April 1996: The Police Department sets up a unit with responsibility for computer network security.

• October 1996: The government announces its intention to legislate against offences committed on the Internet.

● MALAYSIA

• March 1996: The government announces its intention to set up a body whose task it will be to monitor the content of material available on the Net.

● PHILIPPINES

• March 1996: Censorship measures are adopted to control the content of material transmitted on the Internet.

● REPUBLIC OF KOREA

• October 1995: The government decides to institute censorship of software and video games available on computer networks.

• June 1996: The government bans access to Democratic People's Republic of Korea pages available on the Internet.

● SINGAPORE

- March 1996: The government announces a tightening of legislation on the control of material available on the Internet. (Compulsory use of filtering software, registration by Internet users with the Singapore Broadcasting Authority.)
- June 1996: The Singapore Broadcasting Authority announces that in future all Internet access providers must register with it and must ensure that no sexually explicit material is available on their networks.
- July 1996: The government imposes strict contractual obligations upon Internet access providers. All offenders are liable to lose their licences.

● SOUTH-EAST ASIA

- March 1996: The member states of the Association of South-East Asian Nations (ASEAN) announce their intention to set up a regulatory body to deal with the new technologies.

● THAILAND

- February 1996: The National Electronics and Computer Technology Center (NECTEC), the official agency responsible for new technologies, calls upon Internet access providers to monitor the content of the material circulated on their servers.

● TUNISIA

- Agence Tunisie Internet (ATI) is assigned reponsibility for operating the Internet. Any organization or company wishing to be connected must submit a request to ATI and fill out a special form for 'institutions'.

● UNITED NATIONS

- July 1995: Michael Parker Benton, British Rapporteur of the Committee on the Elimination of Racial Discrimination, proposes a draft resolution calling upon the United Nations General Assembly to canvass the views of an expert body on ways and means of controlling the misuse of global electronic communications networks in matters of incitement to racial hatred and pornography involving children. Not all the experts agree on the advisability of involving the United Nations in this matter, and it is accordingly decided to defer examination of a draft resolution to a forthcoming session.

● UNITED STATES

- February 1996: Entry into force of the Communications Decency Act (CDA). In protest, thousands of sites 'wear black' and launch the 'blue ribbon' campaign on behalf of freedom of expression on the Net.
- March 1996: The FBI secures for the first time a court authorization to put a tap on the Internet in order to track down an Argentinian hacker.
- June 1996: A Federal court in Philadelphia suspends application of the CDA. The Department of Justice appeals to the Supreme Court, which pronounces the CDA unconstitutional (26 June 1997).
- September 1996: The Governor of New York signs an order banning the circulation on the Internet of pornographic material aimed at children.

● VIET NAM

- Beginning of 1996: The launching of a public Internet service planned for early 1996 is delayed for want of any form of control or regulation.

Sources: 'Silencing the Net – The Threat to Freedom of Expression On-line,' *Human Rights Watch*, May 1996; 'Censure sur le Net, Acte II' [Censorship on the Net, Act 2], *Le Monde, supplément Télévision, Radio, Multimédia*, 19–20 May 1996; 'Internet, mode d'emploi' [Internet: Instructions for Use], *Jeune Afrique*, 18–31 December 1996; *L'événement du jeudi*, 6–12 July 1996, pp. 26–68, EFF (Electronic Frontier Foundation): http://www.eff.org/; 'L'année des contrôles', *Courrier international*, 24–30 October 1996, p. 6; http://www.FreeExpression.org; http://www.privacy.org/gilc/; http://box.hotwired.net/banned.html; http://www.surfwatch.c

what is legal in a bookshop or a library should be legal on the Internet'[9]. These different reactions in fact illustrate one of the fundamental misunderstandings that plague the Internet. It stems from the growing divergence between a community of users strongly marked by a culture that is profoundly hostile to all forms of public interference, and the public authorities, increasingly tempted to seek to monitor and even in certain cases to control the network.

By and large, the high courts have ruled in favour of the champions of freedom of expression. In June 1996, a Philadelphia Federal Court declared the Communications Decency Act (CDA) to be unconstitutional, ruling that the Act, promulgated on 8 February 1996, constituted an infringement of the First Amendment to the Constitution, which guarantees freedom of speech, and of the Fifth Amendment relating to the rights of persons involved in criminal proceedings. The court's ruling included the statement that 'the Internet has served to create the most open area of mass communication that this country – and indeed the world – has ever known. . . . Any regulation based on the content of communications, whatever its justification, would be in danger of destroying, in addition to its set target, the entire global village'.[10] In fact, the federal judges, not content with suspending the law, made a point of reasserting the higher principles incumbent upon the legislature in this matter: on the Internet as elsewhere, 'the strength of our liberty depends upon the chaos and cacophony of unfettered speech'. The judges also dwelt on the terms 'indecent' and 'patently offensive' in regard to the cultural practices of contemporary America. In their opinion, the CDA would make it illegal to transmit via the Internet the play *Angels in America*, which tackles in extremely crude terms the subject of AIDS and homosexuality, despite the fact that it is performed every night on Broadway, and that a number of teachers recommend it to their under-age pupils.[11] The Department of Justice decided to appeal to the Supreme Court. According to observers, the

Supreme Court judges will doubtless uphold the ruling of the Philadelphia Federal Court.[12]

Invoking the need to protect this same freedom, the Paris Tribunal de Grande Instance rejected the petition of the Union des Étudiants Juifs de France (UEJF), which had brought charges against nine Internet access providers for having permitted the dissemination of 'negationist' material on the network. Like his American counterparts, the French judge made a point of reiterating that 'freedom of speech is a fundamental value, of which judicial courts of law are the guardians, and which can be restricted only in specific hypothetical cases in accordance with

9.   'The Children's Protection from Violent Programming Act of 1995 S.470: An Unconstitutional Proposal to Solve a Difficult Societal Question', *People for the American Way*, document consulted on the Internet on 27 December 1996, http://www.FreeExpression.org/cpvp.htm

10.   'Federal Court Rules Communication Decency Act Unconstitutional, Groups Challenging the Law Prepare for Government Appeal to the Supreme Court'. Electronic Frontier Foundation press release: document consulted on the Internet on 12 December 1996, http://www.eff.org/pu...da-decision.statement. The weekly *Business Week* reports that, at the trial, the director of the Carnegie Library in Pittsburg, Robert Croneberger, testified to the impossibility for libraries of listing all the potentially obscene entries stored in their on-line files. The CDA was likely to lead eventually to the banning both of texts on biology (since they refer to the reproductive organs) and to the works of Shakespeare (on account of their crude language). 'La justice américaine acquitte le Net', in *Business Week*, quoted by *Courrier international*, No. 312, 24 to 30 October 1996, p. 7.

11.   'Internet Obscenity Curb Blocked', *Financial Times* (London), 13 June 1996, p. 1. '12 juin 1996. Mauvais jour pour les censeurs' [12 June 1996: A Bad Day for Censors], *Le Monde supplément Multimédia* (Paris), 16–17 June 1996, p. 29; 'The Internet is Different', *International Herald Tribune* (Paris), 18 June 1996, p. 8.

12.   The champions of the law to control pornography were outraged by the ruling. The Director-General of the National Law Center for Children, Bruce A. Taylor, stated in this connection: 'The judges allowed themselves to be overawed by technology'. Quoted in *Business Week*, op. cit.

strictly determined procedures'.[13] Finally, on 23 July 1996, the Conseil Constitutionnel quashed the provisions of the recent law regulating telecommunications, known as the 'Fillon Amendment', whereby the Conseil Supérieur de Télématique was to be given powers to issue recommendations in matters of professional ethics, infringement of which would make offenders liable to prosecution. Government measures have henceforth been limited to the obligation imposed on service providers to offer to their clients 'a technical device enabling them to restrict access to certain services or to select those services'.[14]

Court prosecutions, no less than the quashing by the high courts of the lower courts' rulings, highlight the evident difficulties experienced by states in exercising some form of regulatory control over the network. They also raise a number of questions relating to the regulations governing the liability of Internet publishers and to other threats hanging over the Net.

The first issue is bound up with the determination of the legislature to regulate the Internet and other on-line services on the basis of the same regulatory principles as those established for broadcast services. On this level, however, the content of broadcast media productions is the responsibility of editors and directors whose authorizations to broadcast may be withdrawn in the event of any failure to comply with their obligations. This is not true of the Internet, where any individual, association or firm can set up a service hosted by a server without authorization and become, at any time and on their own initiative, a transmitter or receiver of information subject to no precise borders. Nor is it the case of the forums or newsgroups offering 'banned' visual material or information, which may violate national laws with total impunity.[15]

It is here, in fact, that the Internet's true challenge lies. With its millions of interconnected computers, the network has become a gigantic global spiderweb, decentralized, and without frontiers or territorial regulations. Just as the censoring of national sites is a conceivable option, as happened in France with the Minitel, so any attempt to attack international servers is bound to prove difficult and troublesome. The list of newsgroups accessible on each computer emanates from other computers that Internauts can contact directly.

In point of fact, the access providers operate solely as retailers, and do not influence in any way the content of newsgroups, to which each user can contribute anonymously. They highlight their status as 'carriers', and claim that it is strictly impossible to control or monitor the vast volume of information disseminated daily on their servers. In the case of both the United States and Europe, we are moving towards a situation in which the access providers who have performed a purely technical function will in principle be exonerated from all responsibility. The draft 'multimedia law' in Germany illustrates this issue,

13. 'Internet: les propositions de la mission interministérielle', op. cit.

14. The text was the subject of an appeal dated 24 June 1996 to the Conseil Constitutionnel. The Conseil annulled Articles 43-2 and 43-3 on the grounds that 'the law assigned to the Conseil Supérieur de l'Audiovisuel, which is responsible to it, the task of issuing recommendations designed to ensure compliance by certain communication services with rules of professional conduct, without establishing for the determination of these recommendations, in regard to which opinions likely to have penal implications might be expressed, other limits than those, of a very general nature, resulting from Article 1 of the above-mentioned law of 30 September 1986'. 'Le contrôle d'Internet', *Le Figaro* (Paris), 23 May 1996, p. 2; 'Internet: les propositions de la mission interministérielle', *Les Echos*, op. cit. On this subject see also L. Kalogeropoulos, 'Quelques leçons des tentatives avortées de régulation d'Internet' [Drawing a Few Lessons from Failure to Control the Internet], *Les Cahiers de l'audiovisuel* (Paris), No. 9, September 1996, p. 2 ff.

15. On this subject see L. Kalogeropoulos, *Les Cahiers de l'audiovisuel*, No. 9, September 1996, pp. 68 ff.

since the Bill stipulates that access providers will be considered solely as carriers, and may not be held accountable for any actionable materials transiting through their networks unless they have been alerted thereto, and possess the 'technical capacity' to erase such data or to ban access to them.

The second problem stems from the other threats, which curiously cause less of a furore but which are just as serious as those highlighted by the champions of regulation. The rising tide of violence observed in television and other media programmes and in video games poses challenges for the public authorities which are undoubtedly more immediate and crucial than the existence of documents that, though offensive, are relatively few in number and generally not easily accessible to young people on the Internet.

Other dangers concern, no less than materials of an offensive nature, the various abuses of which consumers may be victims in their on-line commercial dealings,[16] and the possibilities of 'hijacking' or 'attacking' the servers of an enterprise or a government in order to damage its image.[17]

The increasing intrusion of all types of players, in particular the hackers, those computer pirates who won fame in the United States by gaining access to the most confidential data of the Department of Defense and the American Central Bank and who recount their feats in newsgroups christened the '2600' forums,[18] the threats of spying through interception of sensitive data circulating on the network, the deliberate destruction of software, or the transmission of viruses by the so-called 'crackers',[19] are so many new developments that represent a grave danger alike to states, business and consumers.

16. These dangers also affect the evolution of the banking profession, in particular in regard to the dematerialization of money. All financial transactions on the network are

carried out by means of 'electronic cash'. Customers create a 'cybercash wallet' or credit account on their computer's hard disk to which money is transferred from a bank account, or else pay for their purchases by credit card. Even when systems of protection such as encryption software are used, organized gangs using 'code-breakers' are able to steal the credit card and bank account numbers and use them for their own benefit. As a result, there is a whole new illicit – and galloping – economy already in operation on the network's market.

17. On this subject, see J. N. Tronc, 'Quelle régulation internationale de l'Internet?' [Which International Internet Regulation?], *Les Cahiers de l'audiovisuel* (Paris), June 1996, p. 105. To illustrate these new threats, the author cites the launching by a private individual of a server christened 'Adminet' which offers a wealth of information on the French Civil Service and on the main institutions of the French Republic. The server rapidly became one of the French Web sites most consulted throughout the world. In their reaction, which led to the temporary shutting down of some of that server's pages, the public authorities preferred to turn the server to account by merging it with the services set up by the government.

18. 2600 is a symbolic number in the hackers' world, that of the frequencies which, once transmitted in telephone exchanges, made it possible to avoid paying the bill. Hackers are the famous pioneers and mavericks of the electronic networks who have imposed upon the Internet their own code of ethics and libertarian culture. In the United States, international hackers' congresses are no longer clandestine. Certain unauthorized police operations targeted on hackers' meetings such as the 'Sun Devil' raid have been suspended. Indeed, hackers' get-togethers constitute for the CIA and the FBI a veritable pool of information as well as of talent available for recruitment. To these computer fanatics, capable of cracking the most sophisticated coding systems, must be added the 2,500 members of SCIP, the Society of Competitor Intelligence Professionals, which works in close liaison with the American secret services. (Information drawn from the proceedings of the symposium on 'Les grandes peurs informatiques de l'an 2000' organized by the Club de la Sécurité Informatique Français (CLUSIF), May 1996.)

19. The crackers' objective is to cause maximum disruption. See on this subject 'Les espions investissent le cyberespace', *La Tribune Desfossés* (Paris), 21 February 1996, p. 16.

'Netiquette' and international co-operation

How is freedom of speech, the cornerstone of every modern democracy, to be maintained while at the same time preventing the Net from becoming the Trojan horse for all abuses and threats? A wide-ranging debate has been launched throughout the world, and the strategies put forward all point in the direction of solutions of a technical, ethical and professional nature. Many countries take the view that freedom of speech and the protection of minors can be assured only through recourse to technical processes involving the use of filtering (so-called parental control) or encryption software, restrictions on which are currently being lifted.

Parental control software

Such software enables parents to select the sites which their children can access on the basis of their content. Parental control is regarded by on-line service providers as a means of escaping the responsibilities that weigh on them by shifting the onus to the users. Some forty companies and organizations, among them Microsoft, America Online,[20] Netscape and Compu-Serve, have joined forces in order to launch the Platform for Internet Content Selection (PICS). This scheme will enable each site to be labelled on the basis of a number of criteria (violence, sex, politics), with a rating system for each. It will then be for parents to 'programme' their children's computers so as to deny them access to sites regarded as undesirable.

Encryption techniques

These form part of the technologies for ensuring the security and confidentiality of information. They consist in sheltering information transmitted on the network from the prying eyes of possible industrial spies by encoding such material. In order to satisfy the concerns of enterprises as well as of ordinary

citizens wishing to safeguard the confidentiality of their exchanges on the Internet, extremely powerful encryption software has been developed. This is in fact a sensitive and complex issue which is currently giving experts and decision-makers the world over much food for thought. Governments fear that the dissemination of coding systems that are too powerful may contribute to the illegal activities of criminal or terrorist organizations. Accordingly they regard cryptography as a weapon of war which can be used only under the authorities' express control.

Computer industrialists and economic agents are contending on the other hand for the use of encryption to be liberalized. They regard this as a basic tenet for the development of electronic business and company networks constructed on the Internet. A shield for some, for others a dangerous weapon that threatens the security of states, encryption is being facilitated at present in virtually all the member countries of the Organisation for Economic Co-operation and Development (OECD). The United States is well ahead of other countries in this regard: although the debate on the issue was heated at the time of the Internet's birth, encryption software is at present freely available on the domestic market, but cannot in theory be exported. However, the first exceptions to the rule are starting to appear thanks to the authorization granted to United States firms to export encryption software for the protection of financial dealings. In France, the law of 26 July 1996 on the regulation of telecommunications has for the first time authorized the encryption of messages, provided that the keys to the codes are

20. According to the American magazine *Wired*, quoted by the French daily *La Tribune*, America Online has made the first move by recruiting 'cybercops' who are alleged to have cut off the subscriptions of a number of its members engaging in licentious exchanges. According to its chairman, the company is attempting to build a community. 'Any community is made up of good and bad members. We don't want bad ones.' – *La Tribune*, op. cit.

deposited with organizations approved by the Office of the Prime Minister. Such a custodianship principle is the subject of discussion in many OECD countries. While it is being called for by countries such as France, Germany, the United Kingdom and the United States, this principle is meeting with opposition from human rights protection groups fearful, among other things, that the principle may provide totalitarian rulers with the means of monitoring the electronic correspondence of dissidents. Broadly speaking, the OECD is in favour of liberalizing encryption. In March 1997, the organisation published seven recommendations concerning scrambling procedures regarded as essential if users are to place their trust in information and communication systems. In the Russian Federation, the situation appears to be more ambiguous, since there is a presidential decree banning encryption, while the Duma is reported to have voted in favour of total liberalization. Elsewhere, in particular in China and the Republic of Korea, encryption is strictly regulated.

Professional codes of conduct and ethics

Regulating Internet practices must be the work of the community of its users (access providers, operators, users, on-line services), whose task it is to define ethical rules that guarantee respect for the rights of the individual and the consumer. This method has the advantage of leading to a system based on voluntary participation and consensus, not one that is imposed by law. The approach ties in with an increasingly used self-regulation process known as 'Netiquette', composed of unwritten rules of conduct that are adopted by all Internet users throughout the world. Indeed it is these users, in the majority researchers, engineers and academics, who over the past fifteen years have forged the Net's code of ethics, a code that engages first and foremost the responsibility of each user. The other players, such as the access providers,

are tending increasingly to monitor the exchanges conducted in certain forums, and are reiterating their commitment to stop facilitating access to newsgroups whose names suggest that they harbour illegal documents.

The need for international co-operation

The Internet's international dimension, combined with the challenge represented by the globalization of trade, naturally makes it imperative to develop appropriate international co-operation in order in particular to ensure that the decentralization of servers does not lead to national regulations being rendered null and void. Many states envisage setting up a legal framework specific to the Internet which would be based on the adoption of an international convention to be applied by the competent authorities of each country and enshrining a minimum number of common principles that could serve as the basis for a code of conduct. That framework would include a set of ethical principles applicable to Internet services, under the joint responsibility of the publishers and host services, and, finally, governing legal co-operation between countries. Concurrently, different lines of inquiry and thinking are being pursued within international agencies such as UNESCO and the International Telecommunication Union (ITU). For its part, OECD set up in 1995 a number of workshops to think through issues relating to the information society and the Internet. The topics covered include the pricing of the network's services and the development of competition, as well as issues of professional ethics. The goal is to finalize a common charter and have it signed by states by the end of 1997. Lastly, some countries consider that international consultation should take place within the Internet's own institutions, such as the Internet Law and Policy Task Force, which can create a common descriptive lexicon for Web services in order to make them easier to use with a view to ensuring respect for the regulations governing trademarks and the permanence of electronic addresses worldwide.

In the view of many observers, an international legal framework is likely to present a number of ambiguities, particularly in the matter of agreeing at international level on the criteria for judging the reprehensible nature or otherwise of material distributed in fields bound up with different conceptions of civilization. For example, is what is possible in the European context acceptable in certain Asian and Middle Eastern countries?[21] For other observers, the idea of an additional body of universal legal norms specifically designed to protect the Internet would have the sole result of confining yet further an instrument of economic development and a tool for modernizing society in a 'legal gulag'.[22] The current debate is fuelled more by a desire to see the return of a moral order and perhaps by a fear of the future than by any coherent line of argument. According to the American association Human Rights Watch, 'horrors like negationism and paedophilia are combated not by censorship but by speech'. The same association adds: 'The battle between those who wish to impose norms and those who circumvent them is an age-old one. It is quite possible to comply with international legislation, particularly since it is wholly Utopian to think that one can control everything on the Internet. By definition, that is impossible, particularly since the legislators will find themselves grappling with a two-fold constraint: controlling information and having at their disposal an economic tool of communication'.[23] It is therefore imperative, Philippe Quéau argues, 'that all freedom-loving citizens of the world should join forces in order to prevent any restriction on the free flow of ideas and images. Even if this obliges us to exercise greater vigilance as regards the education to be given to our children. . . . Freedom of speech is indivisible. The Internet's great "short circuit" cannot be dealt with by moral repression, but only through education and the exercise of responsibility'.[24]

21. If we take as an example the installation of filtering software with the obligation for every service in the world to position itself on a scale in the moral and religious spheres, it is clear that each country could then, in accordance with its culture and domestic law, adopt measures to restrict access to certain services, using specialized filtering software. As has been seen, non-democratic countries will thus be able to require access providers on their territory to install filtering software that bars access to services deemed to be subversive, whereas in other countries some of these services could be hosted quite legally.

22. 'Internet, vers un goulag juridique?' [Internet, Towards a Legal Gulag?], *Le Monde* (Paris), 1 January 1996, p. 15.

23. The position of the Electronic Frontier Foundation largely coincides with that of the Human Rights Watch: 'We in no way approve hatred-fuelled rhetoric. However, we believe that harmful speech must be met with better arguments, and that it is wrong to impose censorship. When one right is sacrificed in order to safeguard another, both are lost.' Quoted by Y. Eudes, 'Bataille pour la liberté sur les réseaux' [The Fight for Freedom on the Networks], *Internet entre l'extase et l'effroi, Manière de voir*, supplement to *Le Monde diplomatique* (Paris), October 1996, p. 37.

24. P. Quéau, *Décence et barbarie*, Milan, Virtual, 1995.

Chapter 14
Slipping standards
in news reporting

Whereas democracy appears to be pro-gressing by leaps and bounds, the media in most industrialized countries have become the target of the harshest criticism. This criticism is levelled at a persistent drift towards sensationalism, hype and trivialization, and even a certain form of manipulation (dishonesty in the presentation of facts, lack of detachment in the reporting of information from official sources, etc.). Generally speaking, a climate of distrust has taken hold, and those whose task it is to report, disseminate and analyse the news are held in increasing suspicion. The surveys carried out in most democratic countries reveal that public opinion has little confidence in the press. The public's verdict on television is even harsher.

Economics, liberalization and the public authority

The pressures exerted by the political authorities on the media are limited in present-day democracies, and no administrative or regulatory institution appears to have the power to challenge or query freedom of speech. On the other hand, criticism has shifted to the economic sphere with the emergence of new powers largely dominated by the logic of the market, which is reflected both in the patterns of press ownership and in the way news-reporting is exploited.

With the recent easing of restrictions in the new information technology market, the worldwide liber-alization that has occurred in all telecommunications sectors and the privatization of the new economies, the planet has become an economically open space unrestricted by national borders. In order to establish themselves in the long term and to propose global package deals, companies are entering a mad race to win agreements, to conclude mergers and to engage in other transactions in order to turn themselves as rapidly as possible into giant multinationals, commer-cially and industrially spanning the whole globe.

Not only are they charged with their commercial dynamic; they also create an oligopolistic position of their own, to the point where this spills over on to the media as a whole. Such groups, embodied by communication magnates like Rupert Murdoch, Bill Gates and Steven Spielberg, are constantly expanding in order to operate on a global scale.[1] Their dynamic obeys a pure logic of planetary conquest in the multimedia sector, which obliges them to face ferocious competition in which only the most powerful survive and so become veritable power structures that frequently carry more weight than the political authorities. The liberalization, concentration and globalization of the markets have become the norms of cyberspace.[2]

The impact of such liberalization is far from negligible. As in all sectors where new arrivals seek to win a dominant position for themselves, the means of distribution are proliferating (satellite and cable, video, CD-ROM), the forms of financing are changing (subscriptions, sponsorship), and the cost of services is plummeting; finally, the range and content of the media are becoming diversified. Moreover, the capital supplied by industrialists and financiers is enabling the print and broadcast media enterprises to modernize and to develop a greater capacity to resist the offensive strategies of other multimedia groups. The arrival on the scene of the industrialists has also enabled a managerial culture to be introduced into the world of the press by rationalizing management procedures.[3]

While this phenomenon of concentration and globalization of the communications market has undoubtedly had a number of favourable consequences for the media, it is also generating real worries.

The first worry naturally stems from the global scale of the multimedia groups, which between them concentrate the entire range of the means of communication and production of images, sound and text. This phenomenon is detrimental to pluralism, and even threatens to curb the emergence of democracy. In this respect, the example of the Murdoch Group provides food for thought. Thanks to the virtual monopoly which it exercised on the distribution of

news and pictures throughout Asia, this group secured a position for itself as a real power in the region: a power largely dominated by commercial logic inasmuch as it was forced to accede to the requests of the Chinese Government to give up broadcasting the BBC news that had previously been included in the Star TV news services. For Aidan White, Secretary-General of the International Federation of Journalists, that action represents 'direct censorship operating in the very heart of Western democracy'.[4] The second cause for concern lies in the dangers of the economic power intervening in the media's affairs to restrict their autonomy.[5] In the print media, for example, journalists

1. On this subject see 'The Giants of World Telecoms', *Financial Times* (London), 2 April 1996, p. 13; 'Alliances for a Digital Future', *Financial Times* (London), 11 December 1996; 'High-flyers Seek Second Wind', *Financial Times* (London), 24 April 1996, p. 13.
2. According to the *New Scientist* (London), the National Science Foundation (NSF) has put the final touches to its project, ceding to private firms control of the Internet's 'backbone', that is, the network connecting the different elements of the Internet web. Quoted by *Courrier international*, 1 October 1995, p. 9. Moreover, according to Dan Schiller, there are four times more 'hidden networks' connected to the Internet than there are openly connected networks. In this proliferation, new closed networks are being developed which link together all the computers of a single area (firms, countries, regions) that cannot have free access to the Internet's regular users. D. Schiller, 'Les marchands du cyberespace', *Le Monde diplomatique* (Paris), May 1996, p. 19. On the same subject, see J. Robin, 'Survivre à la technologie', *Manière de voir*, op. cit. p. 83.
3. N. Coste-Cerdan and B. Schmutz, 'Les investisseurs dans les médias', *Médiapouvoirs* (Paris), No. 36, 4th quarter 1994, pp. 52–62.
4. A. White, 'L'éternel problème . . .', *Le Courrier* (Brussels), No. 158, July–August 1996, p. 40.
5. N. Coste-Cerdan and B. Schmutz, 'Les investisseurs dans les médias', *Médiapouvoirs* (Paris), No. 36, 4th quarter 1994, pp. 52–62. F. Pinto Balsemao, 'Europe: de l'économie des médias et de leur autonomie', *Médiapouvoirs* (Paris), No. 36, 4th quarter 1994, pp. 97–101.

may be subjected to pressures on the part of the shareholders. Anecdotes illustrating this type of pressure abound in the newspaper industry.[6]

The third source of anxiety is economic. It concerns transparency in the relations between firms in matters of investment and takeovers. The shifting and complex pattern of alliances, and indeed the merging and demerging of companies, makes it difficult to identify their true owners.

As a result, competition is deprived of any point of reference, and the market runs the risk of being destabilized[7]. The anxiety also stems from the commercial nature of media firms. The stakes being financial, they are led to give decisive importance to profitability. In the broadcast media sector, for example, the weight of the investors is such that channels are forced to give priority to the profit motive at the cost of programme quality, and public-sector channels feel obliged to follow suit if they do not wish to be squeezed out. The media, which historically came into their own as a counterpower or challenge to the political establishment, are increasingly tending to identify with the other, notably economic, powers. The frantic pursuit of advertising revenue frequently places them in a situation of dependence on the advertisers, who in certain cases thus become in a way the invisible proprietors. This drift leads both the print and broadcast media progressively to divest themselves of their news-reporting mission.

The increasing flood of advertising in both the traditional and the new media, which represents their principal source of revenue, has been a major development in recent years.[8] Between the economic imperatives of the press industry, which frequently coincide with those of the advertisers, and the rationale of the journalists, whose chief concern it is to report events freely and with complete independence, contradictions abound.

On all the electronic media and particularly on the Internet, advertisers are exerting increasing pressure on sites, and are even influencing their messages to a significant extent. Their advertising is progressing by giant strides, delivering an ever more varied range of increasingly attractive services.[9] Advertisements are sometimes so well designed that users find it difficult to distinguish between promotional sites and information-providing sites. There is ever more frequent confusion between the cyber equivalents of the so-called 'advertorials' and the newscasts by editors and producers operating independently of the advertisers. More and more companies are offering e-mail services free of charge to individual users on condition that they accept advertisements at the bottom of each message.

With the introduction of new technologies for newspaper printing and circulation, the development of the Internet and on-line information networks, and the explosion of digital television, new capital

6.   The French journalist J. Villeneuve, editor of the French weekly *L'Express* at the time when that news magazine was owned by Jimmy Goldsmith, provided the following testimony: 'I was given a list of companies which I was told it would be preferable for me never to mention in my magazine. The list included those that were too close to Sir Jimmy, but also those he was supposed to detest or fear, as well as those with whom he had been at odds . . .'. Quoted by N. Coste-Cerdan and B. Schmutz, 'Les investisseurs dans les médias', op. cit.

7.   P. Mounier, 'L'invisible concentration de la concentration mondiale', *Médiapouvoirs* (Paris), No. 39–40, 4th quarter 1995, pp. 75–83.

8.   P. Cramier, 'L'information entre droit et déontologie: les nouvelles frontières de la liberté' [Information between Law and Codes of Conduct: Freedom's New Frontiers], *Médiapouvoirs* (Paris), No. 39–40, pp. 170 ff.

9.   According to Jupiter Communication, a company specializing in the study of advertising on the Internet, the aggregate figure for this sector, for all advertisers, should reach US$312 million in 1996. With the anticipated expansion of the network, the market will rise to US$5 billion in the year 2000. 'La pub envahit le cyberespace' [Ads Invade Cyberspace], *Le Monde multimédia* (Paris), 20–21 October 1996, p. 32.

Communications concentration: some case-studies
(Source: *Screen Digest* (London), January 1995)

SONY SOFTWARE

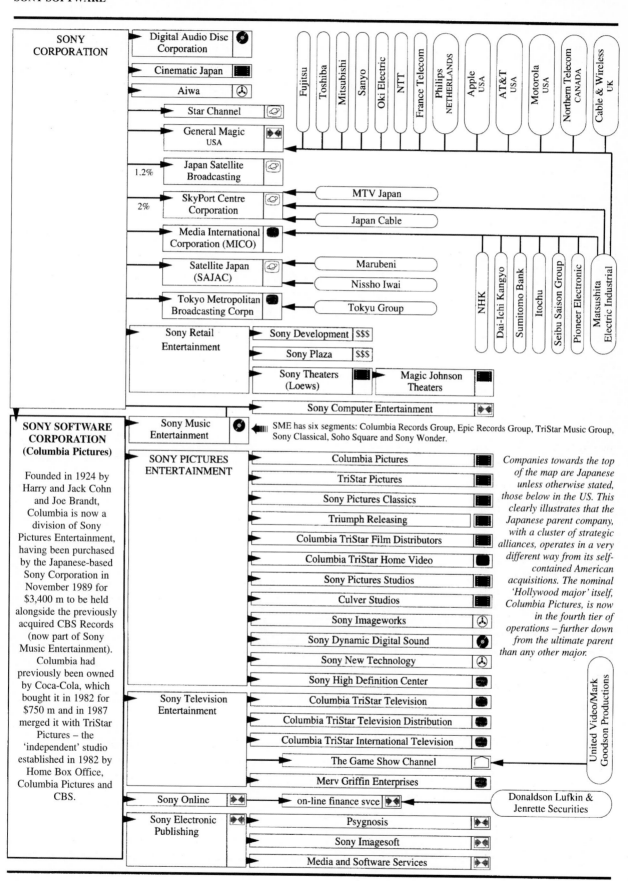

Companies towards the top of the map are Japanese unless otherwise stated, those below in the US. This clearly illustrates that the Japanese parent company, with a cluster of strategic alliances, operates in a very different way from its self-contained American acquisitions. The nominal 'Hollywood major' itself, Columbia Pictures, is now in the fourth tier of operations – further down from the ultimate parent than any other major.

SONY SOFTWARE CORPORATION (Columbia Pictures)

Founded in 1924 by Harry and Jack Cohn and Joe Brandt, Columbia is now a division of Sony Pictures Entertainment, having been purchased by the Japanese-based Sony Corporation in November 1989 for $3,400 m to be held alongside the previously acquired CBS Records (now part of Sony Music Entertainment). Columbia had previously been owned by Coca-Cola, which bought it in 1982 for $750 m and in 1987 merged it with TriStar Pictures – the 'independent' studio established in 1982 by Home Box Office, Columbia Pictures and CBS.

TIME WARNER

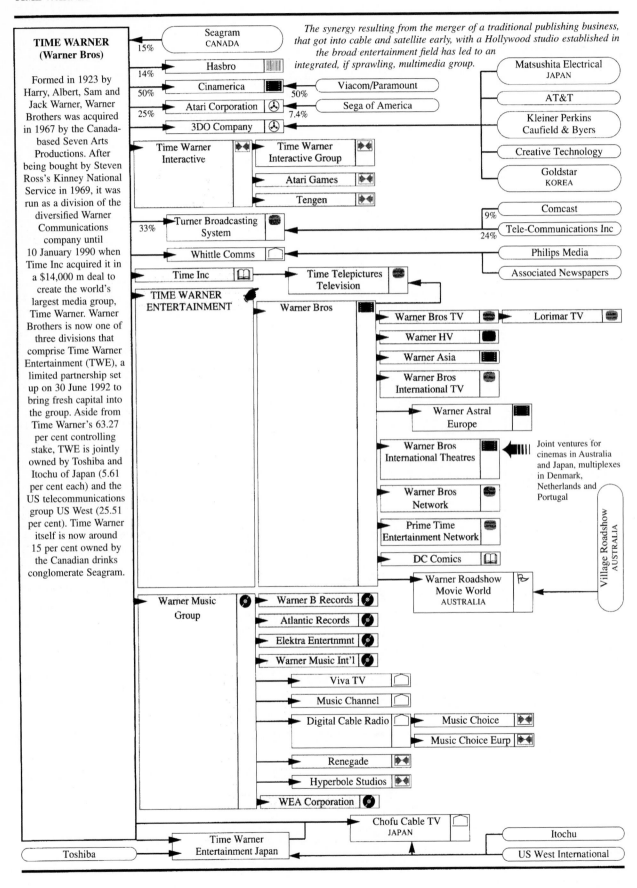

TIME WARNER (Warner Bros)

Formed in 1923 by Harry, Albert, Sam and Jack Warner, Warner Brothers was acquired in 1967 by the Canada-based Seven Arts Productions. After being bought by Steven Ross's Kinney National Service in 1969, it was run as a division of the diversified Warner Communications company until 10 January 1990 when Time Inc acquired it in a $14,000 m deal to create the world's largest media group, Time Warner. Warner Brothers is now one of three divisions that comprise Time Warner Entertainment (TWE), a limited partnership set up on 30 June 1992 to bring fresh capital into the group. Aside from Time Warner's 63.27 per cent controlling stake, TWE is jointly owned by Toshiba and Itochu of Japan (5.61 per cent each) and the US telecommunications group US West (25.51 per cent). Time Warner itself is now around 15 per cent owned by the Canadian drinks conglomerate Seagram.

The synergy resulting from the merger of a traditional publishing business, that got into cable and satellite early, with a Hollywood studio established in the broad entertainment field has led to an integrated, if sprawling, multimedia group.

Seagram CANADA — 15%
Hasbro — 14%
Cinamerica — 50% ← Viacom/Paramount 50%
Atari Corporation — 25% ← Sega of America 7.4%
3DO Company

Matsushita Electrical JAPAN
AT&T
Kleiner Perkins Caufield & Byers
Creative Technology
Goldstar KOREA

Time Warner Interactive → Time Warner Interactive Group
Atari Games
Tengen

Turner Broadcasting System — 33%
Comcast — 9%
Tele-Communications Inc — 24%

Whittle Comms
Philips Media
Associated Newspapers

Time Inc → Time Telepictures Television

TIME WARNER ENTERTAINMENT → Warner Bros

Warner Bros TV → Lorimar TV
Warner HV
Warner Asia
Warner Bros International TV
Warner Astral Europe
Warner Bros International Theatres ← Joint ventures for cinemas in Australia and Japan, multiplexes in Denmark, Netherlands and Portugal
Warner Bros Network
Prime Time Entertainment Network
DC Comics
Warner Roadshow Movie World AUSTRALIA
Village Roadshow AUSTRALIA

Warner Music Group →
Warner B Records
Atlantic Records
Elektra Entertnmnt
Warner Music Int'l
Viva TV
Music Channel
Digital Cable Radio → Music Choice / Music Choice Eurp
Renegade
Hyperbole Studios
WEA Corporation

Chofu Cable TV JAPAN
Itochu
Time Warner Entertainment Japan
Toshiba
US West International

TIME WARNER continued

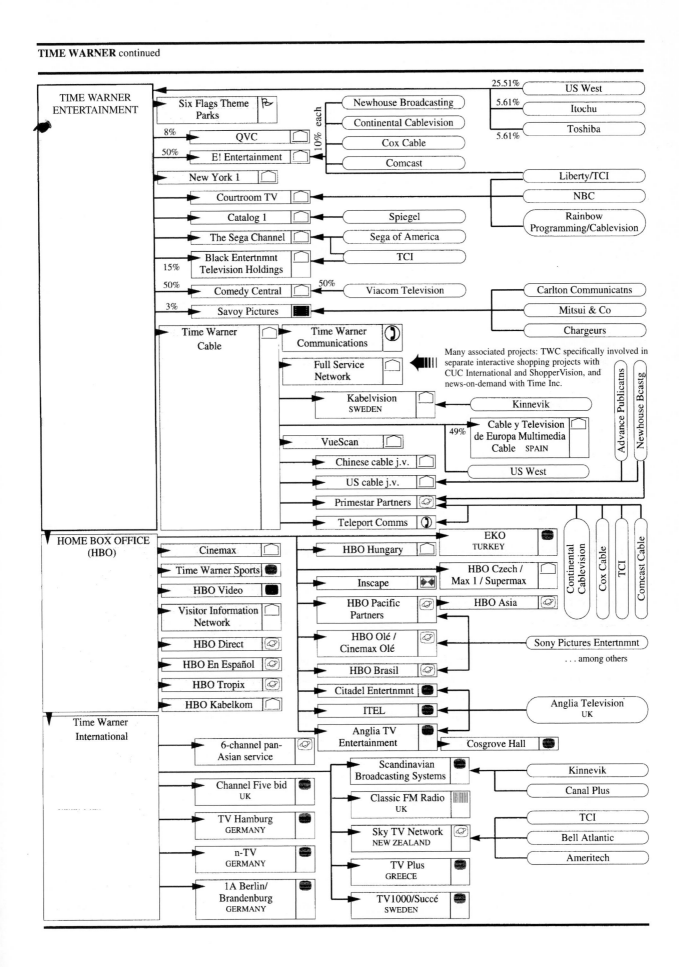

The 'Journal de Genève' to its Readers

Dear Readers,

On 5 November last, the Chairman of the Board of Directors informed you that they were looking for possible partners for the *Journal de Genève* and the *Gazette de Lausanne*. In so doing, Gilbert Coutau expressed the Board's wish to maintain the journalistic aspirations and traditions that you associate with our paper. Confident of the trust thus placed in these principles, the Editors in their turn wish to reaffirm the values they intend to uphold whatever the circumstances, in view of the fact that the title may possibly change or even disappear.

Those values are intellectual integrity, awareness of the subtlety and relativity of things, and moderation in tone. While we are not alone in possessing these, we do uphold them in our daily work. They oblige us to abide by an evidently clear rule, i.e. to give you a balanced picture from a range of viewpoints so that you may form an opinion. This approach, which is part and parcel of the information process, also helps us in our commentary, where we give pride of place to the analysis and expression of measured opinions rather than to denunciation and condemnation. Furthermore, we refuse to allow our desire to inform you to be swayed by commercial considerations.

This attitude has contributed not a little to our honourable paper's reputation for austerity over the past one hundred and seventy years. And we feel that our reputation depends above all else on our editorial freedom and the trust you place in us. For our part, we trust that you will continue to give your support to this kind of journalism, now and in time to come.

The Editors of the
Journal de Genève and the *Gazette de Lausanne*
30 November 1996

requirements will serve to intensify competition between operators and as a result make it essential to modernize the traditional media (newspapers, radio, etc.). The opening of capital to national and foreign communication groups then comes to be seen as a necessary course of action. On this hypothesis, it may fairly be wondered whether the resources available to the media will prove sufficient to enable them to withstand the influence of certain shareholders, whose interests do not always coincide with those of journalists. The dangers inherent in such conflicts of interest may well jeopardize the civic function of news-reporting, which consists in informing and enlightening citizens.

The confusion of genres

The trend towards concentration in the newspaper and broadcasting industry and the resulting competition among the media have disrupted the logic of news-gathering and news presentation. The universal adoption of all-out communication strategies in political institutions and private firms in order to upgrade a corporate image or simply to report on or promote particular activities has led to a high degree of professionalization of occupations in the communication field. This legitimate need to create a name for oneself and to assert one's presence in a context of all-round competition has had the paradoxical result of blurring the frontiers between communication, journalism and economics. Multiple forms of cross-breeding between media professionals, journalists, industrialists and politicians are becoming increasingly common. This confusion, which poses a number of threats for news-reporting, finds expression in several ways: pressures of various kinds, the 'de-professionalization' of the journalist's job, which is sometimes reduced to merely 'switching' or redirecting news items and pictures received on the networks, the standardization of news content, and the presentation of images to maximize their spectacular or sensationalist impact. These are all trends which undermine the credibility of news-reporting and create a crisis of confidence among the public, the decision-makers and even the journalists themselves.

Factors impacting on behaviour patterns and democracy

The history of political life in the West is closely bound up with communication and its media, both traditional and new. Radio, television and newspapers have always played a role in bringing politics to the people and facilitating access to political debate, which they help to broaden and clarify. However, their increasing use in political life has, since the 1980s, considerably transformed political practices, particularly at election time. The pervasiveness of certain forms of communication such as political marketing and polling, the ever more active role played by the media, the fears aroused by their new technological potential, and the controversial rhetoric of the champions of so-called 'direct democracy' all raise questions concerning the significance of politics in a modern democracy.

The first question concerns the misuse of political marketing and television in political action. In the view of many observers, elections are no longer won on the basis of a political platform representing the resultant of the demands and expectations of party activists, of which the political leaders take account. Such criteria are considered to be unduly serious, not to say downright boring, and to reflect an amateurish approach.[10] Since election candidates have begun to enlist the services of political consultants and public relations experts, the political debate has depended on advertising revenues and the ability of political leaders to project their public image. The spectacular victory won in 1959 by the Democrat John F. Kennedy over the Republican Richard Nixon transformed the nature of the relationship between television and elections. Politicians today pay far greater attention to their physical appearance, their voice and their body language when they appear on television.

Thanks to the dominant position occupied by television, political discourse is being increasingly turned into a non-stop media event. Politicians have realized that their political action will inevitably be publicized most effectively through television as the pre-eminent medium. They are increasingly aware that, thanks to television, most members of the public know politicians of national or international standing far better than they do their local member of parliament. With the help of marketing professionals, they are in turn attempting to dominate television by learning to make optimal use of its techniques and resources.[11]

The baneful impact of the media on politics is nevertheless relativized by other observers, who consider that, even if it does exist, such an impact is far from being uniform and decisive.[12] The expansion in the range of television programmes available has created a new type of viewer, one who assesses, compares and reserves judgement. In most Western countries, viewers can choose among a number of channels and thus are in a position to explore, compare and judge for themselves. This possibility of choice is perceived as a right. This does not mean that television has no impact upon an election. If it does not automatically determine a vote, it may point the undecided in a particular direction by, for example, prompting them to eliminate a candidate whose platform is presented in too arrogant or too casual a style. However, it does not wholly determine a country's political destiny. In the view of other observers, television cannot be an entity operating

10. A. M. Gingras, 'L'impact des Communications sur les pratiques politiques' [The Impact of Communications on Political Practice], *Hermès 17-18* (Paris), CNRS Éditions 1995, p. 37.
11. F. Gulielmelli, 'Television and Politics: Towards Electronic Democracy?', *Reinventing Television*, Vol. I, pp. 261-71, Turin, Association Télévision et Culture, 1995.
12. A. De Penanster, 'La dictature de la télévision est un mythe' [The Dictatorship of TV is a Myth], *Revue des deux mondes* (Paris), March 1995, p. 99.

totally outside a society's sociocultural realities and procedures. It is in fact, like all the other 'super-structures', the product of society and the environment. As Francis Balle has pointed out: 'In the final analysis, the impact of the media depends on society itself, its organization and its action. It depends on the customary networks of influence and on the position occupied in society by the various guides in whom public opinion puts its trust.'[13]

The second issue concerns the misuse or overuse of opinion polls. The omnipresence of the polling organizations was strikingly apparent during recent election campaigns, particularly in France and the United States.[14] Some have been strongly criticized and accused of incompetence, even of political manipulation. Recourse to polling techniques is a normal procedure in a democracy inasmuch as it enables a partial understanding to be gained of the fluctuations in a country's political life. However, the proliferation of polling techniques is producing a number of dangerous spin-offs. Initially a source of information, opinion polls are ultimately tending, under pressure from the marketing professionals, to create events and to become the sole spectrum for interpreting and analysing the political debate. They then tend to replace public opinion by giving the impression that they represent or even embody it. This can obviously lead to an impoverishment of the political debate, which is henceforth reduced to a confrontation between polls that frequently lack all scientific standing. This process of reduction is accentuated by many journalists who confine themselves to analysing if not presenting politics through the spectrum of the polls. This risk naturally leads the media on the one hand to lose their credibility and with them that of the journalists and, on the other, to drain political life of its essential components: discussion and its contradictions.

The third question concerns the whole controversy surrounding the concept of 'direct democracy'. Many theorists and politicians argue that the new technological advances – in particular the Internet – provide citizens for the first time with means of intervening directly, in real time and without any intermediary, in the political decision-taking process.[15] From this angle, polling techniques may be seen to represent the prehistory of electronic democracy. The champions of this theory no longer believe that the elected representatives and the media still have the possibility of acting in the interests of citizens. Direct democracy would consequently be an advantageous and attractive alternative solution.

This trend towards 'cyberdemocracy' is generating an intense in-depth debate in academic and political circles. There are the enthusiasts, like Alvin and Heidi Toffler, who contend in their book *Creating a New Civilization* that, eventually, 'technology will enable the people to shed its dependence upon pseudo-representatives who are incapable of responding to its true concerns, and to represent itself'.[16] Then there are the sceptics, who consider that direct participation by citizens in the forging of their political destiny

13. F. Balle, *Médias et société*, 7th ed., Paris, Éditions Montchrestien, 1994.

14. On this subject, see E. Sonchier and Y. Jeanneret, 'Tyrannie des sondages' [Tyranny of the Polls], *Manière de Voir* (Paris), op. cit., p. 28. According to the authors, who quote a survey conducted by the French weekly *L'Evénement du jeudi*, 655 opinion polls were published in 1994, including 119 pre-election simulation exercises, 260 individual popularity ratings, 152 political, economic and social indicators and 124 opinion polls on political parties. This corresponds to roughly two polls a day.

15. J. H. Snider, 'La démocratie on-line' [On-line Democracy], *L'Observatoire de la télévision* (Paris), March 1995; L. Scheer, 'Allons enfants de la télé' [Let's Go, TV Children], *L'Observatoire de la télévision* (Paris), March 1995. Reproduced in 'Ethique du virtuel: des images au cyberespace' [Ethics of Virtual Reality: From Images to Cyberspace], *Les cahiers de l'audiovisuel* (Paris), No. 65.

16. A. and H. Toffler, *Creating a New Civilization: The Politics of the Third Wave*, Washington, D.C., Progress and Freedom Foundation, 1994.

would foster the most demagogic forms of populism, which could become a tool to oppress minorities. Other critics discern behind such direct democracy 'a technocratic ideology . . . which considers that the electronic media have the capacity to transform the way in which politics is accepted'.[17] In fact, such a conception is based on the illusion that news and information without debate would suffice for the practice of democracy.[18] That this is indeed an illusion is pointed up by Dominique Wolton: 'If everyone tomorrow is sitting alone in front of his or her television set or interactive computer, directly in touch with all the town, departmental and regional councils, with the National Assembly and even with the Council of Europe or an international assembly, we shall be entering an era of institutionalized schizophrenia'.[19]

The fourth question relates to the ethical consequences of the development of new technologies, and in particular of virtual reality technologies. Thanks to the progress of digital techniques, images of all kinds are increasingly coming to be substituted for reality, simulating or representing it, and even themselves becoming new working, training and leisure areas. However, now that digital technology is 'virtualizing' reality, it will naturally be easier to deceive others, to 'disinform' them or to manipulate them. With totally computer-generated images produced by three-dimensional visual display software, it is possible to simulate all complex effects, in particular in the military field, and to dupe the most perceptive observer. Other dangerous trends concern the frequent use in the newspaper world of touching up and semi-reconstitution processes, to which some professionals resort when driven by cut-throat competition among the media. Thanks to the wide range of graphic and image-processing software available, manipulations are not only now perfectly feasible but easy to perform. Combining recent documents with archival material, inserting or removing well-known figures from images by means of a graphic palette, increasing or reducing the number of people present at an event or

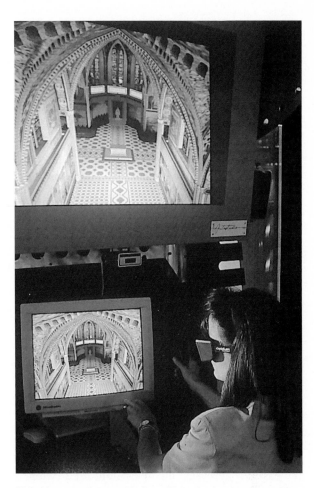

Digital images – they stand in for reality to simulate it, represent it, or even be mistaken for it. Don't be taken in!
Source: P. Pailly/Eurelios

17. J. M. Besnier, 'La démocratie au risque des technologies de l'information et de la communication', Seminar on 'Information, communication et société': 'Démocratie électronique et construction de l'opinion', Commissariat Général du Plan, European Commission DG XII, Paris, 12 December 1996.
18. Snider, op. cit., p. 107.
19. D. Wolton, 'Communication et démocratie', *Médias-pouvoirs* (Paris), No. 38, 2nd quarter 1995, p. 85.

demonstration and, finally, doctoring the sound quality of a document are today very simple operations.

Clearly, all these possibilities of introducing special effects, faking and manipulation are also available in the case of television pictures. At the symposium on 'Les manipulations de l'image et du son',[20] companies specializing in special effects presented outstanding examples of what was being accomplished in this field: a non-stop stream of computer-generated images showing prominent politicians and artists in unexpected and compromising situations – images which may entertain, but which also give cause for anxiety.[21]

Women and the media

The number of women working in the media has increased spectacularly in the past few years. More and more women are enrolling in schools of journalism, women announcers and newscasters are increasingly present on television, and women reporters have distinguished themselves in the profession, in particular since the Gulf War. Such major changes may suggest that the image of women and negative gender-based stereotyping is changing. However, we may also wonder whether this trend is real, and whether it involves all the media, in particular in terms of access to decision-making posts.

The study carried out in 1995 for UNESCO by Margaret Gallagher[22] provides answers to these questions, and seeks to elucidate the gap between the perception of an image, which implies a process of 'feminization of the media', and women's actual place in the decision-making machinery. The study endeavours to demonstrate the sexism which still exists in the world of the media on the basis of statistical comparisons by sex and by region. Appearances notwithstanding, the author notes an absence of any real power base among women media professionals, which in most cases explains the difficulty experienced by them in altering the negative stereotypes so powerfully transmitted by the media.

A presence without power

The gulf between the reality and the way in which women are perceived may be due to the fact that today they have a higher profile on television and radio, as announcers, journalists and newscasters. This fact is confirmed by Gallagher, since the number of women journalists in, for example, New Zealand rose from 18 to 45 per cent between 1984 and 1994. In 1991, women represented nearly half the profession in North European countries, and 22 per cent in a country such as Tunisia. More generally, the mean percentage of women in the different media, established in 1995 on the basis of a survey carried out in forty-three countries, is in the region of 25 per cent (37 per cent in Europe and 30 per cent in Africa), and continues to rise, even if it has barely reached 8 per cent in Japan and is increasing in the United States by only

20. During the symposium on 'Les manipulations de l'image et du son', held on 4 December 1995, the discussion organized in the workshop 'Pour être belle, l'image réelle se fait virtuelle' around the French satellite Spot revealed much about future image-processing capacities in the military context. 'The Spot satellite transmits 2,400 images a day to earth. Only 10 per cent are usable. The Army thus obtains high precision pictures, reinterpreted and analysed. It will soon be possible to produce three-dimensional pictures using stereoscopic images. The military will then be able to prepare a commando operation in virtual reality before carrying it out in the real world. But what would happen if the original data were falsified by virtual reality hackers?' This was a question raised by several participants in the discussion.

21. These trick or special effects are obtained essentially thanks to the development of powerful new hardware and their digital processes, allowing several sources of images to be combined to stunning effect, or matte painting, which is used to blank out elements or add them to a document, or again 'morphing', which enables a person or object to be transformed in spectacular fashion.

22. *An Unfinished Story: Gender Patterns in Media Employment*, Paris, UNESCO, 1995 (Reports and Papers on Mass Communication, 110).

1 per cent annually – a rate at which it will take women thirty years to catch up with their male colleagues.

However, behind a seemingly larger female presence, the world of the media in fact remains resolutely male. Women employees continue to be extremely vulnerable. They are victims of various forms of discrimination which penalize them in regard to career prospects and which marginalize their real power in decision-making terms. In terms of the division of labour, the 1990 statistics covering seventy television stations in eleven countries show that, overall, women account for 44 per cent of jobs in administration, 30 per cent in newsrooms, 4 per cent in the creative professions and 1 per cent in the technical sectors. When they are announcers and newscasters – as is the case in the majority of television stations worldwide – the nature of the programmes and programming policy are in fact determined by men.

The number of women employed in the media in general, and in particular in managerial posts and on decision-making bodies, breaks down according to a pattern that appears identical in the forty-three countries surveyed. If their numbers are undoubtedly on the increase, at the decision-making level women remain conspicuous by their absence, excluded from an exclusively male preserve. The report notes that the most senior posts in the media such as those of director-general, chief executive officer and chairman and managing director are held almost solely by men. Of the 239 organizations covered, only eight – most of them small radio stations or small-circulation periodicals, established in the main in Latin America – have a woman at their head, representing barely 3 per cent (4 per cent in Europe and 1 per cent in Africa) of the cases studied. This imbalance recurs throughout the media, since the proportion of women who secure top jobs is no more than 12 per cent in the case of television and 9 per cent in that of the press. More generally, 1 in every 1,000 women employees occupies a senior post in management, as

Women on the air

The relative exclusion of women from today's media sector is encountering pockets of resistance in many countries through either alternative media or specific productions more in line with women's expectations. New female radio stations, unlike conventional ones with their habitual programmes, are giving ordinary women a chance to speak and encouraging them to talk about their lives and difficulties.

The project started in 1995 by UNESCO in partnership with Germany to set up a radio production network for women in El Salvador is part of this new impetus. Since the project was launched, thousands of women have listened three times a week to a programme entitled *Buenos tempos* [Have a Good Time]. The broadcasters deal with subjects such as women's legal status, women's struggle in various countries, work-sharing, women's health and children's education. As a rule, they keep women informed of their rights and encourage them to take action in their communities.

The project is intended on the one hand to combat discrimination towards women, and on the other to bring about a change of behaviour in men and women. It has necessitated the training of 60 reporters and 200 trainers. The women reporters travel here and there in the country in order to record discussions with women on economic, social and cultural topics. Broadcasts then go out at five o'clock in the morning for women on night shift in the factories, and are also retransmitted by loudspeaker in the market-places.

Source: *Countdown* (Paris), No. 7, December 1996.

Women at the microphone. Community radio is a key to communication for women. In collaboration with other partners, UNESCO has launched a special 'Women Talk to Women' community radio project. Four stations are already being installed in Cameroon, India, Malawi, and Trinidad and Tobago and should be operational in 1998. Preparations for other such stations have begun in Nepal (Radio Sagarmatha) and Suriname (Radio Kono Kulibi), while eight are being set up in the Philippines under the UNESCO/DANIDA Tambuli community radio project.
Source: Louis Tabing, Tambuli Community Radio

Social education centre, Bombay, India. To provide women in all countries with the most recent learning methods, in order to fulfil, in the words of UNESCO's Constitution, 'the ideal of equality of educational opportunity without regard to race, sex or any distinctions, economic or social'.
Source: J. Bhownagary/UNESCO

In Burkina Faso, a major effort is being made to give women the right to speak up.
Source: D. Roger/UNESCO

compared with a ratio of 1 in 140 for male employees.

In reality, women's actual influence in the media depends upon their presence and the position they occupy in the media hierarchy and on their representation within internal bodies such as the board of directors and the governing board, which are generally responsible for taking all important decisions in the field of programming and management. However, women represent a very small minority within these bodies, occupying no more than 12 per cent of such posts in radio and television enterprises, and barely 9 per cent in the print media. Moreover, the study reveals that of the 120 radio and television stations surveyed, over half their boards of management are composed solely of men.

The other imbalance highlighted in the UNESCO study concerns the absence of women in posts directly associated with creative work and programme design in the different media. Technical activities are regarded as a male-only preserve. In West European radio and television companies, for example, women account for no more than approximately 5 per cent of technical staff. By contrast, a majority of the administrative staff are women, a large proportion of whom occupy junior secretarial and clerical posts which offer few career prospects in the world of the media.

'Women and the Media: Access to Expression and Decision-making' Toronto, Canada, 28 February to 3 March 1995

Under the auspices of UNESCO, an International Symposium on 'Women and the Media: Access to Expression and Decision-Making' took place in Toronto from 28 February to 3 March 1995. This was one of UNESCO's main contributions to the Fourth World Conference on Women, which was held from 4 to 15 September 1995 in Beijing (China). The symposium represented the culmination of seven regional preparatory workshops organized during 1994. It was hosted by the Canadian Government, which thereby demonstrated its fundamental commitment on behalf of women and the role which the media can play in their advancement.

The international symposium brought together some 200 media experts, journalists, researchers and representatives of international and non-governmental organizations. Participants focused on specific women's success stories, on women's access to expression and decision-making in and through the media, and on working methods for securing a more satisfactory representation of women within the media.

Thanks to their participation in the symposium, the Unit for the Promotion of the Status of Women and Gender Equality and the Secretariat of the Conference were able to obtain useful information for preparing the report on the priority topic of 'Elimination of Stereotyping in the Mass Media', which was examined by the Commission on the Status of Women at its 1996 session.

The participants drafted the Toronto Platform for Action, and formulated a number of comments on the Beijing Platform for Action with regard to the inadequate mobilization of the media on behalf of women's contribution to society.

During the discussions, the outline plan for an expert group meeting on the portrayal of women in the media and their role in this field was finalized, and possible participants were identified. The meeting of the expert group was organized by the Unit for the Promotion of the Status of Women and Gender Equality in Cambridge, Massachusetts, from 16 to 20 October 1995.

Participants were also informed about women's successes in the media sector. Particular attention was given to an example drawn from the meeting's host country: the Women's Television Network (WTN), which is the first television network whose staff is composed all but exclusively (95 per cent) of women and whose programming is focused on women's opinions and interests.

Other group discussions were geared to the persistence of gender-based stereotyping in the media and to possible measures to counter such trends. Monitoring teams have been set up in a number of countries, where they carry out their tasks at several levels, including that of decision-making. Views were exchanged on the usefulness and limitations of such self-regulatory initiatives in the matter of equality between the sexes in the media.

Organizations of women media professionals have made great strides during the past ten years. In every region, women journalists have set up professional associations; however, women's working conditions are not always in harmony with their fundamental rights (for example, in the matter of maternity leave), and no affirmative action has been taken to increase the number of women in positions of authority in the media.

Women's and men's share of selected journalism/editorial jobs: news agencies

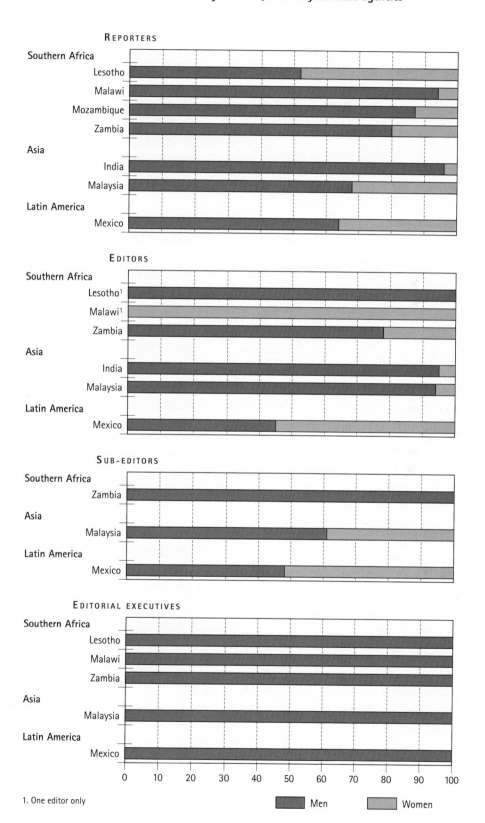

Source: *An Unfinished Story: Gender Patterns in Media Employment,* Paris, UNESCO, 1995.

Women's and men's share of jobs in main occupational categories: press
(74 organizations in 27 countries, 1993–95)

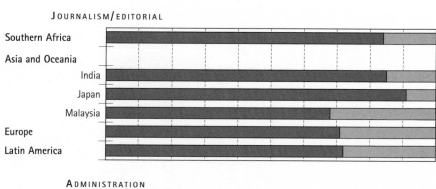

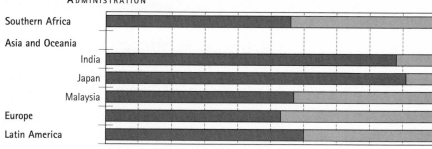

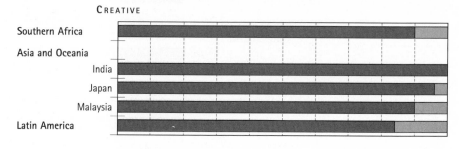

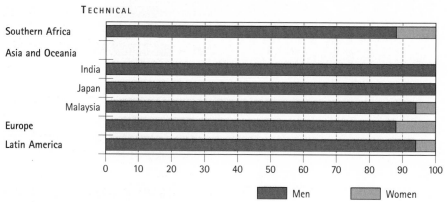

Source: *An Unfinished Story: Gender Patterns in Media Employment*, Paris, UNESCO, 1995.

**Women's and men's share of jobs in main occupational categories: broadcasting
(139 organizations in 38 countries, 1993–95)**

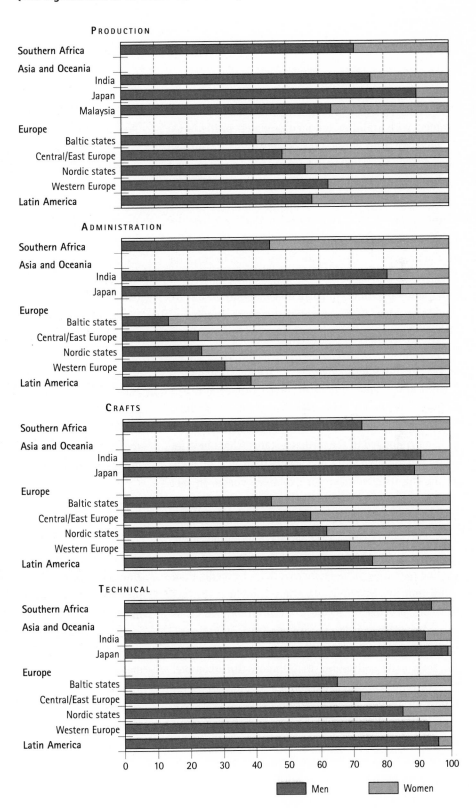

Source: *An Unfinished Story: Gender Patterns in Media Employment,* Paris, UNESCO, 1995.

Untapped skills

The study also raises the major problem of providing women with training for media-related professions. It notes that in more than eighty-three countries, women represent at least half the students enrolled in schools of journalism and communication. This figure is clear proof of women's interest in communication-related occupations. It does not, on the other hand, explain why women remain a minority in the profession. This gap between access to training and access to employment is highlighted by several international studies, in particular that carried out by the Asian Mass Communication Research and Information Centre (AMIC). Other studies confirm that men employed in the media are generally less qualified (in terms of diplomas) than their female colleagues. Hence, given equal qualifications, a woman has less opportunity than a man to find work in the media.

This discrimination undermines the status of women employed in the media, a status which in most cases remains far more precarious than that of men. In the countries studied, for example, women in fact hold only 26 per cent of the permanent full-time posts, as compared with 79 per cent of permanent part-time jobs and 44 per cent of temporary jobs. In addition, it would seem that a woman has more chance of finding part-time or temporary work in the media than a full-time job. Moreover, the study underlines the fact that the process of media concentration, which is indeed speeding up in the communications industry, usually results in more job losses for women than for their male colleagues. In Germany, for example, the rationalization programmes connected with reunification led to the abolition between 1989 and 1992 of 30 per cent of journalists' posts in the former German Democratic Republic. However, it was primarily women who paid the price for the operation, since their share of the job market fell from approximately 60 to 38 per cent of the total. Attention also needs to be drawn to the difficulties experienced by women working in the media in reconciling the obligations of family life and professional career. The increase recorded in the number of women employed has in no way altered working practices in the media, which continue to take no account of family constraints specific to women.

According to the conclusions of the UNESCO report, the persistence of such resistance is due to invisible barriers which act as a deterrent, penalizing women in a work environment adapted to male requirements and priorities. In many cases, women are discriminated against at the recruitment level simply because they are women. Prejudices and preconceived ideas concerning women's supposedly 'natural' attitudes contribute in large measure to their being denied jobs in the media. The numerical gap between women who have received high-level training and those who find work in the communications sector is to be partially explained by considerations of this kind. The solution is far from clear, even if it is self-evident that securing equality must, in this field too, be one of the goals of the feminist movement.

Changing outlooks

While there is no easy, speedy answer to the problem of ensuring equal opportunities for men and women employed in the media, the lengthiest and most uphill task consists in changing people's outlooks by adopting an employment policy based on equality. This is particularly true inasmuch as the various studies quoted by the UNESCO report reveal that women and men working in the media do not necessarily take a different approach to events or issues. Other studies drawn on show that where women constitute a numerical force to be reckoned with, they make a crucial difference by adding to the range of subjects to be dealt with, such as women's health, family and child care, harassment and rape. In regard to the last-mentioned issue, the most striking example is that of the war in Bosnia and Herzegovina where women reporters have helped to alert public opinion to the systematic recourse to rape as a weapon of war. The introduction of these new topics into the world of news-reporting is one of the means available to women journalists to place the focus on their essential difference.

The call for equality in the media does not constitute a radical feminist demand. It is a question of human rights, and as such, part and parcel of the struggle to bring about true democracy within the mass media as in societies as a whole. So long as men and women do not have opportunities to work together on an equal footing, sharing the same rights and the same responsibilities, society will suffer from a democracy deficit.

Chapter 15
The media
and violence

In recent years, violence in the media has taken on a new dimension with the multiplication of the means of transmission: digital television, cable, broadcast networks and video. Violent and aggressive programmes are today abundantly and cheaply available on the international market. This trend has become a social phenomenon on a worldwide scale. The surveys published in the national and international press indicate that public opinion throughout the world is disturbed by the omnipresence of violence on television. The study carried out in 1995 by the British Standards Council on behalf of UNESCO among regulators, broadcasters and other television observers in twenty-two countries also points up the anxiety of viewers in the great majority of those countries.[1] All have the feeling that television channels are broadcasting more and more traumatizing images in which rape, aggression and brutal killings are the norm.

Television is incriminated to an even greater extent when murders, suicides and accidents occur in the real world which involve children and young people who appear to be copying acts that have previously been seen on television or in the cinema. The recent controversies sparked off by films such as Luc Besson's *Nikita* or *Natural Born Killers* by Oliver Stone, and many more besides, have increased public anxiety and rekindled the debate on the media's impact upon youngsters.

Some of these films are shown on television, and others are available for rental, without any check being made on the customer's age. However, television is not the only medium incriminated. Video games are following the same path. Comic strips, comic books and the headlines of some of the worst offenders among the gutter press regularly display for young and adult eyes alike their non-stop stream of bloody

---

1. 'Debate at UNESCO on Television Violence', Paris, *UNESCOPress* (Paris), No. 96-10.

Young people and the media. What effect do the old and new media have on young people? What is the effect of violence on the media? At a meeting at UNESCO in Paris from 21 to 25 April 1997, more than 300 researchers and media professionals from all over the world compared the findings of their research. An encouraging fact is that children are becoming more and more active when faced with images. A consensus viewpoint is making itself heard, indicating the need to work out new approaches which take account of critical thinking and media education, not forgetting enhanced programme quality.
Source: Isopress/Sipa

murders and rapes, thereby managing only to trivialize the most horrific crimes.

Nevertheless, these media as a whole have become an important feature of the cultural environment in which most children grow up. According to generally accepted statistics, the average Swiss or French child in the 7-to-12 age bracket spends almost two-and-a-half hours a day in front of the television set. During the school holidays, this figure rises to four hours. While German youngsters watch rather less television, their American counterparts beat all records with an average four to five hours daily. American children in fact devote more time to watching television than to attending school.[2] Because television occupies so large a place both in children's leisure time and in adult households, it thus crystallizes distrust and suspicion.

The spread of violence in the media is the subject of numerous in-depth studies, symposia and discussions which bring together sociologists, jurists, psychologists and media professionals. In most cases, these studies and meetings have sparked major controversies, thus revealing how passionately people feel about the issue and how complex and difficult it is to decipher.

A never-ending but salutary debate

Generally speaking, researchers are unanimous in claiming that television exerts a considerable impact on societies. The British philosopher Karl Popper, one of the most intransigent champions of individual freedom against the abuses and interferences of the state, does not hesitate to affirm that television has become the most important power or estate of all, to the point where it now represents a real danger for democracy. He maintains that the shameless display of blood and hatred weakens our resistance to violence and undermines, in citizens' minds, the foundations of democracy. In order to circumvent this danger, Popper proposes that the root of the evil be attacked: television producers must be made aware of their

2.   'Le petit écran, grand bouc émissaire?', *Le Journal de Genève* (Geneva), Supplement, November 1995, p. 14.

responsibilities by urging compliance with a code of self-discipline inspired by medical ethics.[3] Popper thus echoes the views of those who are sincerely convinced that totally expurgated television broadcasting would constitute a form of effective antidote to violence.[4]

Other theorists argue the case for a *laissez-faire* approach. Television's cathartic effect is alleged to enable the most violent individuals to assuage their aggressive feelings by proxy or through a process of identification. On the other side, producers and broadcasters are also entering the debate. Invoking their sense of their own responsibilities, they protest against all coercive measures that would negate cultural creation and the freedom to inform. They point out, rightly, that urban violence is in the main caused by other factors, and cite in this connection unemployment, drug-taking, the collapse of parental authority and the loss of traditional values. If all such philosophical and ethical issues appear to have been properly raised, we still by contrast know nothing specific and scientifically proven about the impact of violent programmes on children. Over forty years of research and many hundreds of reports have not only failed to establish any causal link but have in most cases actually led to contradictory conclusions.[5]

Complex studies

By and large, all studies of violence carried out to date have been based on a highly empirical analysis of the amount of violence that is televised. These

3.   K. Popper and J. Condry, *La télévision: un danger pour la démocratie*, Mayenne, Éditions Anatolia, 1996.

4.   On this subject see the Report of the Chairman of the Intergovernmental Council of the International Programme for the Development of Communication, *Non-Violence, Tolerance and Television*, an international round table organized by UNESCO, IPDC and the Indian Government, New Delhi, 1 April 1994.

5.   C. Boutin, *Enfant et télévision*, Paris, Assemblée Nationale, Commission des Affaires Culturelles, 1994 (Information Report No. 1581).

UNESCO International Clearing-House on Children and Violence on the Screen

The International Clearing-House on Children and Violence on the Screen was launched by UNESCO in February 1997, in co-operation with the Nordic Information Centre for Media and Communication Research (NORDICOM) and the Swedish National Commission for UNESCO. It consists of two entities:

- A *Bureau*, to be composed of representatives of the project's partner institutions: NORDICOM, which will administer the clearing-house; the Swedish Government, the principal donor, represented by the National Commission for UNESCO; and the UNESCO Secretariat. The University of Göteborg, to which NORDICOM is attached, will also be invited to become a member of the bureau.

- A *research team*, put forward by NORDICOM.

The mission of the clearing-house – assigned to it in the spirit of the United Nations Convention on the Rights of the Child – is to gather, analyse and disseminate all information on children, young people and media violence. Its main task is to make available to all users worldwide (researchers, decision-makers, media professionals, academics, voluntary agencies and interested individuals) data of every kind on children and media violence: research findings; current research projects; children's access to and use of the mass media; training and teaching courses on these subjects; positive alternatives to media violence; measures and activities aimed at limiting violence on television, in films and in the interactive media.

The clearing-house will publish a yearbook containing scientific articles, summaries of current research projects, information on new publications, statistics, studies on legislation and constructive alternatives aimed at reducing violence. A newsletter will also be issued on more specific subjects.

studies may be broken down into three groups. The first directly incriminates television in the development of certain copy-cat reactions and attitudes of 'victimization'. In this context, fiction and reality meet in a cause-and-effect relationship directly linking television with the most appalling cases of youngsters drifting into violence. As long ago as 1985, on the occasion of its Washington conference, the American Psychological Association had acknowledged that a positive link existed between violence seen on television by children, and their aggressive behaviour. This association considers that violence has a certain fascination for children since it corresponds to an aggressive mood that is natural at that age.[6] A much more recent study carried out by four American academics on behalf of the cable television industry also concludes that violence on television has harmful effects on children's behaviour.[7]

The second group of studies points to a more subtle interaction between images of crimes and assaults and the context in which they are viewed. According to these studies, there is no factor directly linking television and aggressive or violent behaviour. On the other hand, a causal link occurs according to the child's age, sex and social background and the nature itself of the show or broadcast.[8]

The third group, led by specialists of international standing such as Professor George Gerbner (Annenberg School of Communications, Philadelphia), considers that there is only a minimal effective correlation – in the region of 5 per cent – between excessive exposure to violent programmes and behaviour of the same kind.[9] As to the theory propounded in the 1970s of an emotional liberation (catharsis) induced by the spectacle of violence on television, it has not been corroborated by later research, and has given rise to much criticism.

Thus, if there is no clear consensus on the influence of television, it is generally acknowledged that there is a wide and sometimes even conflicting range of possible responses. A young viewer may identify equally with the character perpetrating the violence and with the character subjected to it. The effects can in consequence be varied, various and contradictory, and in any case call for prudence to be exercised in interpreting the data presented.

This being so, the proliferation of studies whose conclusions echo or even contradict one another generates misgivings and some impatience among both professionals and politicians. The British Commission into the Future of Television has urged that such studies be abandoned, and that thought be focused instead on the measures needed in order to control violence more effectively.[10] For their part, television channel directors spout the same pious rhetoric in the form of self-criticism by pledging to present programmes that are cleaner, less violent and, more 'meaningful', and that carry a greater moral punch.

However, the danger appears sufficiently great for a majority of viewers worldwide to become increasingly concerned by the effects of violence, irrespective of its degree.

The political class is asserting its determination to harmonize the codes of conduct established by the profession and the public authorities. In their majority, the authorities adopt general ethical principles of law that recognize the need for professional ethical principles designed specifically for the physical, mental and moral protection of minors. Most Western countries have adopted this principle in one form or

6. B. Blin, *Television and Children*, Council of Europe, Steering Committee on Social Policy, Childhood Policies Project, December 1994.

7. 'Study Proves TV Violence is Pervasive and Harmful', *ABU News* (Singapore), Vol. 15, No. 22.

8. 'Violence et télévision', *Le Monde* (Paris), 23 February 1996, p. 18.

9. 'La puce anti-violence dans l'attente', *Le Monde* (Paris), 17 February 1996, p. 28.

10. 'Television and Children: Towards the Millennium'. *Communication Research Trends* (Canada), Vol. 10, No. 8, 1990, p. 1.

another. In some, the public authorities resort to methods of parental control, in others they encourage the adoption of rules of self-discipline and responsibility; finally, in others again, recourse to the penal code is tolerated.

Initiatives by the television companies

In order to avoid direct intervention on the part of the public authorities, media professionals prefer by and large to establish their own rules of conduct. The trend is evolving towards the principle of rating broadcasts according to a scale indicating the degree of violence.

As early as 1959, the Television Violence Act in the United States exempted the broadcast media industry for a three-year period from applying the anti-trust laws. That provision was intended to enable the networks to work out solutions to the problem of

International and national rules of conduct

● INTERNATIONAL CONVENTIONS

The protection of children has been regularly provided for in the conventions adopted by international organizations such as the United Nations and the Council of Europe.

The United Nations Convention on the Rights of the Child, adopted on 20 November 1989 by the General Assembly, recognizes in its Article 17 the child's right to receive information aimed at promoting his or her social, spiritual and moral well-being and physical and mental health. For its part, the Council of Europe has focused attention since the 1980s on the protection of minors. In 1983, the Committee of Ministers examined Recommendation 963 of the Parliamentary Assembly on cultural and educational means of reducing violence, referring to the depiction of violent scenes in television broadcasts, films and video cassettes. On 27 April 1989, the same committee adopted a recommendation concerning 'principles on the distribution of videograms having a violent, brutal or pornographic content'.

The Convention for the Protection of Human Rights and Fundamental Freedoms of the Council of Europe refers in its Article 10 to the protection of morals in order to justify certain restrictions upon the freedom of information, and the European Court of Human Rights has already tried cases of this kind. In addition, the European Convention on Transfrontier Television, adopted in Strasbourg on 15 March 1989, assigns in its Article 7 specific responsibilities to broadcasters in respect of programmes which contain pornography or give undue prominence to violence. On 3 October 1989, the EEC adopted the 'Television without Frontiers' Directive of the European Communities, which in its Article 15 bans advertising of alcoholic beverages aimed at minors, and stipulates in its Article 16 that advertising 'shall not cause moral or physical detriment to minors'. The Charter on the Portrayal of Violence on Television, adopted in January 1992 by public service broadcasting organizations which are members of the European Broadcasting Union (EBU), stipulates that programmes must not present violence as a mere means of settling conflicts.

Finally, at its meeting on 14 February 1996, the European Parliament decided to introduce a series of amendments to the 'Television without Frontiers' Directive, designed to keep check on broadcasts likely to harm the physical, mental and moral development of minors, or to disturb their psychological balance. The new provisions stipulate that states must bar television broadcasts which include scenes of gratuitous violence of a kind likely to inspire copycat attitudes and behaviour. In addition, general interest channels are required to set aside a programming slot for children, and no advertising or trailers may be included which might undermine their moral and mental integrity.

● NATIONAL RULES

Australia: This country has opted for self-regulation. Broadcasters have been urged to adopt their own code of practice for all matters relating to television programme content as listed in the Broadcasting Service Act of 1992. Private broadcasters have published their own Commercial Television Industry Code of Practice, and each public broadcaster (ABC, SBS) has established its own code. These codes have received the approval of the Australian Broadcasting Authority (ABA), a regulatory body with powers to consider viewers' complaints regarding any breaches of the ethical rules enshrined in each code, and where appropriate to punish such breaches by imposing fines. The main subjects covered by the codes are violence, sex, racial discrimination, the treatment of minorities, pluralism and the need for impartial news-reporting.

Canada: Codes of conduct applicable to the broadcast media have been a reality in Canada since the early 1980s. The first of them concerns the portrayal of sexual stereotypes on radio and television. Violence on television has given rise to the biggest effort of codification undertaken by the Canadian Radio-Television and Telecommunications Commission. In February 1993, the CRTC set up an action group against violence on television which brought together all the media professionals: producers, broadcasters, cable operators and advertisers. On 1 January 1994, private broadcasters were the first to adopt a code of ethics, which was supplemented, some months later, by an experimental national system for classifying broadcasts produced by all professionals. Compliance with these codes is regarded by the CRTC, which approved them, as one of the preconditions for awarding and renewing an operator's licence.

France: The Conseil Supérieur de l'Audiovisuel (CSA) and the television channels argue in favour of self-discipline. In November 1995, the channels pledged to establish a code of ethics. This might be included in the contract linking the CSA to private and public channels.

Germany: The basic law stipulates that the freedom to broadcast may be restricted by 'legal measures governing the protection of the young'. The outline law on the broadcast media which entered into force on 1 January 1992 prohibits, as a measure designed to protect young people, 'broadcasts depicting cruel or inhuman acts of violence, glorifying violence or undermining human dignity, as well as broadcasts that are manifestly of a nature to constitute a serious moral danger for children and young people'.

United Kingdom: The Board of Governors of the BBC has its own code, the Producers' Guidelines, established for public channel producers and programmers. The Independent Television Commission, which is responsible for regulating private channels, also has a Programme Code which sets out in detail the principles with which broadcasters must comply. The Broadcasting Act, adopted in December 1990, added a new element to this regulatory system by establishing the Broadcasting Standards Council (BSC), responsible for drafting and operating a Code of Practice which is applicable to all public and private radio and television channels.

United States of America: The Federal Communications Commission (FCC) has no powers in regard to programme content. However, it is claimed by some that regulation of the portrayal of violence would not be incompatible with the First Amendment to the United States Constitution. Since 1990 the US Congress, on the initiative of Senator P. Simon, has asked the networks to take steps to limit violence on the screen and to suspend the anti-trust laws which had hitherto barred them from adopting a common policy in respect of televised violence. That request has generally been acted upon by the channels, which have begun to take joint self-regulatory measures.

Sources: B. Blin, *Télévision et enfants*, Council of Europe, Steering Committee on Social Policy, Strasbourg, 11 December 1994; 'Télé: la non-violence sur commande', *Libération* (Paris), 15 February 1996, p. 4; F. Tome, 'Réglementation et pratique dans les différents pays européens', *Les cahiers de l'audiovisuel* (Paris), No. 7, March 1996, p. 111; H. Bourges, 'La voie de l'autorégulation', *Les cahiers de l'audiovisuel*, op. cit., p. 125; S. Jehel Cathelineau, 'La mesure de la violence', *Les cahiers de l'audiovisuel*, op. cit., p. 99.

violence together. In 1993, the initiative led the five major channels as well as fifteen cable networks to envisage a code of conduct whereby certain programmes would be preceded by warnings to parents. In February 1996, following the threats contained in the Telecommunications Bill,[11] television industry professionals agreed to operate, from January 1997, an American TV ratings system modelled on the film rating system, whose anti-violence code has been applied in the United States for the past thirty years. Six categories corresponding to each age bracket are proposed for all television programmes: TV-Y (Y for young) rated programmes are suitable for viewing by all children from age 2 to age 6. TV-Y-7 programmes are suitable for children aged 7 and over, but might frighten smaller children, who cannot yet distinguish between reality and fiction. TV-G (G for general) programmes suit all ages. The rating TV-PG indicates the need for parental guidance or monitoring on account of the programmes' rather more *risqué* or shocking content. The rating TV-14 represents a serious warning to parents of children aged under 14 in view of the programme's sophisticated subject-matter, powerful sexual content, *risqué* or indecent language, or high level of violence. The TV-M rating signifies 'mature audiences only', and is awarded to adult-only programmes that are not suitable for anyone aged under 17. Talk shows are included in the ratings system, but news and current events magazines and sport are not.

In France, the idea of regulating against violence on television resurfaced in 1989, when the Conseil Supérieur de l'Audiovisuel formulated new broadcasting rules and provided for penalties. However, it was the quantitative survey carried out by the CSA over a test week in April 1994 (registering an average of nearly ten crimes and assaults an hour in drama and fiction films shown on national channels) which led that regulatory body to establish a common system for labelling programmes jointly with the national broadcasters. Since 18 November 1996, all the major

French television channels, both public and private, have used a common identification system to warn when programmes containing scenes of violence are about to be broadcast.

In Canada, regulations on the classification of broadcasts have gradually been introduced, based on the outcome of several meetings with all the parties involved. All broadcasters have progressively worked out and adopted codes of conduct in compliance with the guidelines defined by the Canadian Radio-Television and Telecommunications Commission (CRTC). These codes provide for the establishment of a national system for rating broadcasts, and also lay down precise rules governing children's programmes, in particular cartoons. The Action Group on Violence on Television (AGVOT) has been conducting tests for a year in real-life situations on various systems for rating programmes broadcast by Canadian channels.

Blocking techniques

The anti-violence chip, the so-called V-chip, is a Canadian invention. It takes the form of a microchip which is slotted into a television set or a decoder to read the rating code assigned to each broadcast (violence, assaults, erotic scenes). Viewers can programme the chip in order to block out the signals of broadcasts whose rating exceeds the level which they consider acceptable for their families. There are several systems for blocking programmes. The two major ones are VYOU-Control, which enables the set to be automatically disconnected at certain times of the day selected by parents, and View-level Vyou Control, a

---

11.   The Telecommunications Bill adopted by the US Congress in February 1996 provided that should the television industry fail to devise a rating system within a year, the Federal Communications Commission (FCC) would impose its own guidelines. See 'Congress Backs V-Chip for TV Violence', *New York Times* (New York), 15 December 1995; 'Markey Wins on V-Chip', *Broadcasting & Cable*, 20 November 1995, p. 11.

more comprehensive system allowing parents to choose once and for all the degree of violence or sexual explicitness which they are willing to authorize in their homes without needing to check the TV schedules every day. Each broadcast will have to have a code attached to it (for example, from one to ten), readable by the chip (accessible to the parents alone, no doubt by means of an access code) which will then decide on its own whether or not to suspend or scramble the broadcast.

In Canada, the pressure exercised by the extremely powerful family associations, which were calling for concrete measures against the portrayal of violence on television, led the Canadian Radio-Television and Telecommunications Commission to establish veritable codes of conduct for the television industry which were designed to strengthen the viewer's discretionary power, thanks to the V-chip. The first trials of V-chip technology began in the autumn of 1994.[12]

In the United States, President Bill Clinton has become the champion of the V-chip, which was initially rejected by most media professionals in the name of freedom of creation and speech, but finally included in a vast programme of reform of telecommunications. In all his speeches, the US President urged that the V-chip be included in the Telecommunications Bill. The chip, which enables parents automatically to reject programmes considered to be too violent, will be installed in all sets sold in the United States. In February 1996, President Clinton brought together some thirty top executives of the television industry, from Ted Turner to Rupert Murdoch, in order to secure formal approval for an agreement which should eventually enable parents to select for their children programmes in which the level of sex and violence remains moderate.[13] The Telecommunications Bill, which was finally voted in early February 1996, made the V-chip mandatory.

One week after the United States Congress voted the V-chip provision into law, the European Parlia-

ment in Strasbourg adopted, on 13 February 1996, an amendment to the 1989 'Television without Frontiers' Directive which required all television sets sold in the future to be equipped with a technical device for filtering programmes. Given the time needed for all today's TV sets to be replaced, experts reckon that it will be twelve or thirteen years before Europe is fully equipped with this system. According to K. F. Hoppenstedt, the driving force behind the amendment, the aim is to create the possibility of voluntary, private control: 'it is for parents to decide what their children may or may not watch'.[14]

Penal measures

Many states have included in their penal codes or in the regulations governing broadcast media specific penalties for the transmission of violent programmes. In a number of countries of America, Asia and Europe, the public authorities have introduced such provisions into their legal arsenals. The courts have frequently been called upon to rule on the matter. In Germany, a father brought an action against the creators of the American cartoon *Power Rangers*, broadcast by virtually all television channels worldwide, following an assault on his son perpetrated in the manner of the 'superheroes' of that serial. In France, the mother of a teenager who was the victim of an explosion modelled upon a similar explosion featured in the MacGyver serial, also instituted legal proceedings.[15] In the United States, the film director Oliver Stone

12. K. Spicer, 'L'exemple canadien – télévision et violence', *Les cahiers de l'audiovisuel* (Paris), No. 7, March 1996, p. 121.
13. 'TV Makes History at the White House', *Broadcasting & Cable*, 4 March 1996, pp. 5–6.
14. 'La non-violence sur commande', *Libération* (Paris), 15 February 1996.
15. F. Tome, 'Réglementation et pratique dans les différents pays européens', *Les cahiers de l'audiovisuel* (Paris), No. 7, March 1996.

together with Warner Studios and the Time-Warner group had writs issued against them by a grocery-store check-out girl who had been paralysed for life after being assaulted by two youths. The two criminals, who had already committed one murder, had cited among their favourite films Stone's *Natural Born Killers*, the ultra-realistic account of a young couple's bloody spiral into violence.[16]

There is today a growing recognition throughout the world that neither the media professionals, nor the public authorities, nor the associations of parents or viewers could remain indifferent to the spread of violence on television. All concerned have come finally to a consensus on the need for self-regulation on the part of the television channels and a willingness to shoulder their responsibilities. Such rules of conduct need to be extended by other initiatives, such as an acceptance of greater responsibility by parents and by the education system and an analysis of the educational role which the media must play in this field. Training in the critical perception of visual material and the development of a discerning eye remain one of the best bulwarks against the violence portrayed in programmes of all kinds. This being so, a multimedia campaign to sensitize public opinion and help it to understand the phenomenon of violence could serve to strengthen the public's capacity to cope with the danger. Finally, priority must also be given to improving the quality of programmes, in particular those aimed at children.[17] Nevertheless, with the advent of satellite television and its programming streams, the race to attract audiences will gradually shift to other areas, more fragmented but more open to bold initiatives and creative ventures of all kinds. Contrary to what is predicted (a surfeit of news-reporting, ever more sensational and violent visual material, and so forth), viewers and young people generally could well be the great beneficiaries in the digital revolution now dawning.

16. 'Olivier Stone poursuivi devant la justice américaine pour son film *Tueurs nés*', *Le Monde* (Paris), 28–29 July 1996, p. 19.

17. C. Boutin, *Enfant et télévision*, Paris, Assemblée Nationale, Commission des Affaires Culturelles, 1994 (Information Report No. 1581).

Conclusion
An information
society at the
service of all
humanity

On the threshold of the twenty-first century, the nation-states of the world are being subjected to the direct shock of new technologies, planetary networks and globalization. At the centre of this revolution, a new cyber-galaxy is forming and creating its own space-time. Its vision is of a virtual world overreaching continents, disregarding national laws and creating new political and cultural reference points. It proposes a different culture, founded mainly on the virtual and the planetary, oriented rather to the non-linear, the multidimensional and the cross-disciplinary.[1]

Such huge transformations are without precedent in human history, and change power relationships on an international scale, eluding completely the ability of governments to understand and control them. They inspire confusion in most politicians and doubt in many observers. In truth, they have the ability both to create large-scale exclusion and to generate constraints which interfere with democratic processes, as well as to mobilize other resources for better serving civic life, collective solidarity and a feeling for shared knowledge and understanding.

Consequently, the stakes are enormous. We need to know how, on the one hand, to expand the benefits of cyberspace and its implications in the area of development and, on the other, to renew citizen participation and rethink the issues of freedom, democracy and development. Faced with these challenges, theoreticians, scientific and cultural associations and communities are taking advantage of the opportunities offered by the emerging information society, and are proposing a new form of dialogue, and new strategies centred on humankind.

1. On this theme, see P. Quéau, 'La galaxie Cyber', *Le Monde de l'éducation, de la culture et de la formation* (Paris), April 1997, and J. De Rosnay, '"La révolution informationnelle", Internet: l'extase et l'effroi', *Manière de voir* (Paris), October 1996, p. 32.

Pooling knowledge

Many researchers are now arguing in favour of the notion of 'governance', a new interactive approach to running human society. The theory no longer relies on governments and their administrative structures, but on civil society as the engine of mutual management of affairs and self-organizing.[2] Others promote the theory of 'collective intelligence', thought capable, with the help of powerful computers and computer networks, of generating a new humanism guaranteeing all persons access to knowledge.[3] A third position emphasizes 'empowerment', the concept of greater citizen participation in the management and control of media, accompanied by research on methods of self-organization, the means by which new local participants will forge global civil society.[4]

Generally speaking, all these approaches converge on the need actively to engage the new culture of cyberspace and direct its ongoing development towards shared values of justice, solidarity and development. Then a new humanism could emerge that would emphasize the citizenry and respect for civic rights, with an ethical component founded on human rights, and in particular on freedom of expression. Beyond the details and arguments specific to each approach, a central element brings together the various dialogues: the new technologies, and electronic networks in particular, are capable of modifying the workings of the worldwide market and its globalizing tendency. The organizing of society into networks, created by the various groupings and segments of the population (NGOs, cultural communities, interest groups, associations, etc.) can offset the threats and aberrations in the domain of information and communication arising from centralization of political power, abuse of power and all other forms of abuse.

This many-faceted debate contributes a new perspective on the cyberspace that is currently emerging, since it promotes communication that is interactive, non-hierarchical and of enormous scope. Thanks to this new potential, network users are no longer mere passive actors or consumers of pre-packaged services, but genuine broadcasters and receivers with greatly enhanced powers. They are in fact members of the so-called 'transnational segments', or 'virtual communities' composed of large groups of individuals sharing the same life situations, the same value systems or the same sociocultural ideas, independently of geographical proximity.

The new citizenry

This new mode of communication between and among members of civil societies has favoured the emergence of new actors on the international scene. They consist of informal groups, associative movements or non-governmental organizations which play an increasingly important role in framing national and international policies regarding the environment, human rights, the protection of minorities and the promotion of women's interests. Armed with a democratized electronic tool, these collaborative organizations have mobilized and established their own electronic networks for the exchange of information. Among the plethora of networks worldwide, the Association for Progressive Communication (APC),[5] born of the merger of sixteen national networks, has become a major actor in cyberspace, and an indispensable resource for monitoring the course of civil society on a planetary scale. The movement describes itself as a 'global communication

2.   B. Ghosh, 'Le gouvernement cède du terrain à la gouvernance' [The Government Gives Ground to Governance], *Le Journal de Genève,* 12 December 1996, p. 12.
3.   P. Lévy, *L'intelligence collective: pour une anthropologie du cyberespace*, Paris, La Découverte, 1994.
4.   C. J. Hamelink, *Trends in World Communication*, Southbound, Third World Network, 1994.
5.   APC, Global Computer Communications for Environment, Human Rights, Development and Peace, http://www.apc.org/index.html

network . . . that aims to assist organizations and activists working for peace, social justice and environmental protection'. Its mission is chiefly one of contributing aid to development by providing the tools for sharing information with several thousand organizations in 133 countries, operational in fields as widely different as ecology, human rights, feminism, the protection of minority groups, and so forth.

In 1992, these networks also contributed to the success of the major international conference known as the 'Earth Summit' (Rio de Janeiro) on environmental issues, as well as all the world summits that followed it. That instance of mobilizing global civil society illustrates a genuine revolution in the traditional view of cyberspace. Henceforth, electronic networks no longer represent just a new technology, but a deep restructuring of relations among the citizens of the world. The principal players are no longer limited to the big transnational conglomerates, or the financial groups, but include citizens as well, along with national or local associations with international aspirations. Lastly, the messages exchanged are no longer confined to commercial or financial transactions, but also include new forms of friendly, professional, cultural and educational communications. According to Pierre Lévy, these new operators, or 'virtual communities', are exploring 'new forms of public opinion'.[6] Their ambition is to institute a wider, more open public debate, one that is more mutually supportive, aimed at defending political rights and democracy. This forum has the virtue of bringing a fresh view to globalization and its contradictory currents, suggesting other modes of expressing citizens' participation. To be sure, the problem is finding new expressions for this 'citizen input'.[7] The traditional avenues for citizen representation are in place – for instance in regulatory bodies throughout the world – but today there is new emphasis on ethics and business ethics, focusing on the relationship between money, power and the media. The partisans of renewal of the idea of citizenship and community-

building are sharply focused on this range of positive, humanistic values.

The success or failure of this third path depends on the determination of world leaders to become fully aware of the emergence of these novel forms of community, and of peoples' desire to express themselves and share their views. It also depends on the ability of states to imagine a different philosophy of co-operation based on an authentic political will to promote access to the information society by poor countries. A third requirement is that civil society find a way to reorganize around the community values of justice, solidarity and sharing. These various actors have the heavy responsibility of forging an alternative strategy, faced with numerous hazards, in particular those of cultural exclusion and globalization. That is why it is crucial that an attempt be made to sketch a broader view of what is possible and desirable in the future information society, rather than allowing this society to be imposed on the world and expand according to its own principles: it must become a genuine tool for development in the service of humanity as a whole.

6. Lévy, op. cit.
7. A. Vitalis, 'Contrôle politique et démocratisation des technologies nouvelles' [Political Control and Democratization of the New Technologies], seminar on 'La Démocratie électronique', Council of Europe, Parliamentary Assembly, Palais du Luxembourg, Paris, 23–24 March 1995.

Select bibliography

ACHILLE, Y.; BUENO, J. I. *Les télévisions publiques en quête d'avenir*. Grenoble, Presses Universitaires de Grenoble, 1994.

ACHILLEAS, A. *La télévision par satellite, aspects juridiques internationaux*. Paris, Montchrestien, 1995.

BALLE, F. *Médias et société*. Paris, Montchrestien, 1995.

BARNETT, S.; MORRISON, D. *The Listener Speaks: The Radio Audience and the Future of Radio*. London, Her Majesty's Stationery Office, 1989.

BARRAT, J. *Géographie économique des médias*. Paris, Litec, 1992.

BLANC, G. (ed.). *Le télétravail au XXIᵉ siècle*. Paris, Dunod, 1995.

BOUGNOUX, D. (ed.). *Science de l'information et de la communication*. Paris, Larousse, 1993.

BOURGAULT, L. M. *Mass Media in Sub-Saharan Africa*. Indianapolis, Indiana University Press, 1995.

BOURNON Y.; CHAPUIS, J. P.; RUBY, J. L. *Pédagogie de l'audiovisuel et du multimédia*. Paris, Les Éditions d'Organisation, 1995.

BRUNNER, H. P. *Closing the Technology Gap: Technological Change in India's Computer Industry*. New Delhi/London/Thousand Oaks, Sage, 1995.

BUSTAMANTE, E.; NICOLA, G.; SALAÜN, J.-M. *Téléphone et télévision: enquête sur une convergence européenne*. Paris, CNET, 1993.

CARTIER, M. Les inforoutes, mythes et réalités. Pour passer des infrastructures aux infostructures. Montréal, September 1995. (Working copy)

CHAMOUX, J.-P. *Droit de la communication*. Paris, PUF, 1994. (Que sais-je?)

CHRETIEN, J.-P. (ed.). *Rwanda: les médias du génocide*. Paris, Karthala, 1995.

COHEN, A.; ADONI, H.; BANTZ, C.-R. *Social Conflict and Television News*. Newbury Park, Calif., Sage, 1990. (Sage Library of Social Research, 183.)

Connection, Community, Content: The Challenge of the Information Highway. Final Report of the Information Highway Advisory Council, Ottawa, Canada, 1995.

CORNU, D. *Journalisme et vérité, pour une éthique de l'information*. Geneva, Labor & Fides, 1994.

COTTERET, J.-M. *Gouverner, c'est paraître, réflexion sur la communication politique*. Paris, PUF, 1992.

Crossroads on the Information Highway: Convergence and Diversity in Communications Technologies. Queenstown, Institute for Information Studies/Aspen Institute, 1995.

DUFOUR, A. *Internet.* Paris, PUF, 1995. (Que sais-je?, 681.)

DUNN, H.-S. *Globalization, Communications and Caribbean Identity.* Kingston, Ian Randle Publishers Ltd, 1995.

Election et télévision, 25 images/secondes. Valence, 1993.

European Commission. *The Information Society and Development. Projects Supported by the European Institutions.* Brussels, 1996.

EVANS, P. *Embedded Autonomy: States and Industrial Transformation.* Princeton, N.J., Princeton University Press, 1995.

FALLENSTEIN HELLMAN, M.; JAMES, W. R. *The Multimedia Casebook, 12 Real-life Applications.* New York, Van Nostrand Reinhold, 1995.

FREUND, A. *Journalisme et mésinformation.* Paris, La Pensée Sauvage, 1991.

GARAY, R. *Cable Television: A Reference Guide to Information.* New York, Greenwood Press, 1988.

GARNHAM, N. *Capitalism and Communication.* London, Sage, 1990.

GOLDFINGER, C. *L'utile et le futile.* Paris, Odile Jacob, 1994.

GULIELMELLI, F. (ed.). *Reinventing Television.* Turin, Association Télévision et Culture, 1995.

HAARSCHER, G.; LIBOIS, B. *Les médias entre droit et pouvoir.* Brussels, Éditions de l'Université de Bruxelles, 1995.

HALLE, J. *Radio Power: Propaganda and International Broadcasting.* London, Paul Elek, 1975.

HAMELINK, C.-J. *The Politics of World Communication.* London, Sage, 1994.

HANSRA, B. S.; MATHUR, P. N. *Video in Rural Development: Production and Use.* New Delhi, Classical Publishing Company, 1992.

HENNEBELLE, G. *Les télévisions du monde.* Paris, CinémAction-Corlet, 1995.

HOWEL, W. J. *World Broadcasting in the Age of the Satellite: Comparative Systems, Policies and Issues in Mass Telecommunication.* Norwood, N.J., Ablex, 1986.

HUDSON, H. E. *Communication Satellites: Their Development and Impact.* New York, The Free Press, 1990.

INGLIS, A. F. *Satellite Technology: An Introduction.* Boston, Focal Press, 1991.

JOHNSTON, C. B. *Winning the Global TV News Game.* Boston/Oxford/Melbourne, Focal Press, 1995.

Join the October Revolution. Technology Summit. Geneva, International Telecommunication Union, 1995.

KEIRSTEAD, P. O.; KEINSTEACH, S. K. *The World of Telecommunication, Cable, and New Technologies.* Boston, Focal Press, 1990.

LACROIX, J. G.; MIÉGE, B.; TREMBLAY, G. *De la télématique aux autoroutes électroniques: le grand projet reconduit.* Montmagny (Canada), Presses de l'Université de Québec/Presses Universitaires de Grenoble, 1994.

LAWRENCE, J. *Journalists and New Technology.* Prague, International Organization of Journalists, 1988.

Le pluralisme radiophonique en Afrique de l'Ouest. Paris, L'Harmattan, 1993.

LÉVY, P. *L'intelligence collective, pour une anthropologie du cyberespace.* Paris, La Découverte, 1994.

LEWIS, P. M.; BOOTH, J. *The Invisible Medium: Public, Commercial and Community Radio.* London, Macmillan Education, 1989.

LIBOIS, L. J. *Les télécommunications, technologies, réseaux, services.* Paris, Eyrolles,1994.

MARCEAU, F. *La démocratie au XXIᵉ siècle.* Paris, J.-C. Lattès, 1996.

MARCHIPONT, J. F. *Les nouveaux réseaux de l'information. Enjeux et maîtrise de la société de l'information.* Paris, Éditions Continent Europe, 1995.

MATHIEN, M.; CONSO, C. *Les agences de presse internationales.* Paris, PUF, 1997.

MATTEI, M. G. *Televisione e interattività.* Pavia, Edizione Il Portolano, 1993.

MATTELART, T. *Le Cheval de Troie audiovisuel.* Condé-sur-Noireau, Presses Universitaires de Grenoble, 1995.

MIEGE, B. *La société conquise par la communication.* Condé-sur-Noireau, Presses Universitaires de Grenoble, 1989.

––. (ed.). *Médias et communication en Europe.* Grenoble, Presses Universitaires de Grenoble, 1990.

MIRABITO, M. *The New Communications Technologies.* Boston, Focal Press, 1994.

NEGRINE, R. *Politics and the Mass Media in Britain.* London/New York, Routledge.

NEGROPONTE, N. *Being Digital.* London, Hodder & Stoughton, 1995.

POPPER, K.; CONDRY, J. *La télévision: un danger pour la démocratie.* Mayenne (France), Editions Anatolia, 1996.

QUÉAU, P. *Décence et barbarie.* Milan, Virtual, 1995.

Répertoire des radios privées et locales en Afrique de l'Ouest. Institut Panos/ACCT, 1995.

REPORTERS SANS FRONTIÈRES. *Les médias de la haine.* Paris, Éditions La Découverte, 1995.

ROSENBERG, N. *Perspectives on Technology.* New York, Cambridge University Press, 1976.

SAILLANT, J.-M. *Passeport pour les médias de demain.* Arras, Presses Universitaires de Lille, 1994.

SANDOVAL, V. *La télévision interactive.* Paris, Hermès.

——. *Les autoroutes de l'information.* Paris, Hermès, 1995.

SCHEER, L. *La démocratie virtuelle.* Paris, Flammarion, 1994.

SCHNEIER-MADANES, G. (ed.). *L'Amérique latine et ses télévisions: du local au mondial.* Paris, Anthropos-Economica/Institut National de l'Audiovisuel, 1995.

THÉRY, G. *Les autoroutes de l'information. Rapport au Premier ministre.* Paris, 1994. (Official reports.)

TOFFLER, A. *Powershift: Knowledge, Wealth and Violence at the Edge of the 21st Century.* New York, Bartam Books, 1990.

TOFFLER, A.; TOFFLER, H. *Creating a New Civilization: The Politics of the Third Wave.* Washington, D.C., Progress and Freedom Foundation, 1994.

TRUXAL, J.-G. *The Age of Electronic Messages.* Cambridge, Mass., MIT Press, 1994.

TUDESQ, A.-J. *L'Afrique noire et ses télévisions.* Paris, Anthropos/INA, 1992.

——. *Feuilles d'Afrique, étude de la presse de l'Afrique subsaharienne.* Tallence, Éditions de la Maison des Sciences de l'Homme d'Aquitaine, 1995.

World Press Trends, FIEJ, 1996.

Reports consulted

African Telecommunication Indicators 1996. Geneva, International Telecommunication Union, 1996.

Green Paper: Copyright and Related Rights in the Information Society. Brussels, Commission of the European Communities, 1995.

International UNESCO Symposium on Copyright and Communication in the Information Society. Madrid, 11–14 March, 1996.

Our Creative Diversity. Report of the World Commission on Culture and Development. Paris, UNESCO, 1995.

Technology Revolution Study: Communications and Knowledge-based Technologies for Sustainable Human Development. New York, UNDP, 1996.

World Communication Report. Paris, UNESCO, 1989.

World Education Report. Paris, UNESCO, 1995.

World Telecommunication Development Report. Geneva, International Telecommunications Union, 1995.

Principal newspapers and periodicals consulted

01 informatique (Paris)

ABU News (Kuala Lumpur)

Al Ahram Hebdo (Cairo)

Broadcasting & Cable (New York)

Broadcasting & Cable's TV International (New York)

Business Week (New York)

Cable & Satellite Europe (London)

Combroad (London)

Communication et langages (Paris)

Communication et stratégies (Paris)

Communications International (London)

Compte à rebours (Paris, UNESCO)

Computers in Africa (London)

Development Policy Review (Newbury Park, Calif.)

Diffusion. Quarterly Journal of the European Broadcasting Union (Geneva)

Dossiers de l'audiovisuel (Paris)

The Economist (London)

Far Eastern Economic Review (Hong Kong)

Financial Times (London)

Futuribles (Paris)

Hermès (annual review) (Paris)

Industrial Property and Copyright: Monthly Review of the World Intellectual Property Organization (Geneva)

Information Technology for Development (Bombay)

International Broadcast Engineer (London)

International Broadcasting (London)

International Herald Tribune (Paris)

Iris (Strasbourg)

ITU News (Geneva)

Jeune Afrique (Paris)

Keio Communication Review (Tokyo)

The Khaleej Times (Dubai)

L'Expansion (Paris)

La Tribune (Paris)

Le Communicateur (Paris)

Le Courrier (Brussels)

Le Figaro (Paris)

Le Journal de Genève (Geneva)

Le Monde (Paris)

Le Monde diplomatique (Paris)

Le Monde informatique (Paris)

Le Nouvel Observateur (Paris)

Le Point (Paris)

Le Trimestre du Monde: revue trimestrielle (Paris)

Les Cahiers de l'audiovisuel: revue trimestrielle (Paris)

Les Cahiers du cinéma (Paris)

Les Echos (Paris)

Media Studies Journal (New York)

Media, Culture & Society (London)
Médiaspouvoirs: revue trimestrielle (Paris)
Middle East Communications (London)
Modern Asian Studies (London)
New York Times (New York)
Quaderni (Paris)
Revue Tiers Monde (Paris)
Science et vie (Paris)
Sequentia (Strasbourg)
Telos (quarterly review) (Madrid)
Terminal (Paris)
The Times of India (Bombay)
Transition (Washington)
TV World (London)
Variety (London)
Vidéo broadcast: revue mensuelle (Paris)
The Wall Street Journal (New York)
World Development (New York)

Acronyms and abbreviations used in the text

ABA	Australian Broadcasting Authority
ABC	American Broadcasting Corporation
ABU	Asia Broadcasting Union
ACCT	Agency for Cultural and Technical Co-operation
ACLU	American Civil Liberties Union
ADAC	German Automobile Club
ADSL	Asymmetrical Digital Subscriber Loop
AFP	Agence France Presse
AFPI	Association Française des Professionnels d'Internet
AFTEL	Association Française de la Télématique Multimédia
AG/UFA	University Film Association
AGVOT	Action Group on Violence on Television
AIDS	Acquired Immune Deficiency Syndrome
AIR	All India Radio
AISI	African Information Society Initiative
AITV	International Television Agency
ALER	Latin American Association for Education by Radio
ALL	Nippon Airways
AMARC	World Association of Community Radio Broadcasting
AMC	Arab Media Corporation
AMD	Advanced Micro Devices
AMIC	Asian Mass Communication Research and Information Centre
AMRC (or CDMA)	Multiple access by code distribution
AOL	America Online
APC	Association for Progressive Communication
APS	Algérie Presse Service
ARD	Allgemeine Deutsche Rundfunkanstalten (das Erste Programm)
ARPA	Advanced Research Projects Agency
ART	Arab Radio and Television
ART	Autorité de Régulation des Télécommunications
ASBU	Arab States Broadcasting Union
ASEAN	Association of South-East Asian Nations
AT&T	American Telegraph & Telephone
ATC	Annuaire Télématique de Communication
ATI	Agence Tunisie Internet
ATN	Asian Television Network
AUI	Association des Utilisateurs d'Internet
BBC	British Broadcasting Corporation
BITNET	Because It's Time Network
BOP-TV	Buy Our Products Television
BSB	British Satellite Broadcasting
BSC	Broadcasting Standards Council
BSKYB	British Sky Broadcasting
BT	British Telecom
BTITV	British Telecom Interaction Television
CAAMA	Central Australian Aboriginal Media Association
CANA	Caribbean News Agency
CARICOM	Caribbean Community Secretariat

CBA	Commonwealth Broadcasting Association
CBC	Canadian Broadcasting Corporation
CBS	Columbia Broadcasting System
CBU	Caribbean Broadcasting Union
CBU	Contrôle Bibliographique Universel
CCTV	Chinese Central Television
CD	Compact Disc
CD-I	Compact Disc – Interactive
CD-ROM	Compact Disc – Read-Only Memory
CDA	Communications Decency Act
CEDEP	Centro de Educación Popular
CEO	Chief Executive Officer
CERT	Compagnie Européenne de Radiodiffusion et Télédiffusion
CFI	Canal France International
CIA	Central Intelligence Agency
CIS	Commonwealth of Independent States
CITED	Copyright in Transmitted Electronic Documents
CLT	Compagnie Luxembourgeoise de Télédiffusion
CLUSIF	Club de la Sécurité Informatique Français
CMC	Computer Maintenance Corporation
CNBC	Consumer News and Business Cable Network
CNDP	Centre National de Documentation Pédagogique
CNE	Cable News Egypt
CNN	Cable News Network
CNNI	Cable News Network International
CNRS	National Centre for Scientific Research (France)
CNRT	Polish Broadcasting and Television Council
CNT	National Technical Commission
COFDM	Coded Orthogonal Frequenced Dated Multiplexing
CPU	Commonwealth Press Union
CRDI	International Development Research Centre
CREN	Corporation for Research and Educational Networking
CRTC	Canadian Radio-Television and Telecommunications Commission
CSA	Conseil Supérieur de l'Audiovisuel
CSNET	Computer Science Research Network
CTN	Cable Television Network
CTQC	Canada Quebec Television Consortium
CTV	Cable Television
DAB	Digital Audio Broadcasting
DANIDA	Danish International Development Agency
DBS	Direct Broadcast Satellite
DCI	International Common Documentation
DD1	First Development Decade
DEA	Digital Equipment Australia
DEC	Digital Equipment Company
DEI	Digital Electronics Incorporated
DFH	Dong Fang Hong
DLF	Deutschland Funk
DMC	Digital Multichannel Planning Company
DMX	Digital Music Express
DOD	Department of Defense
DOJ	Department of Justice
DPA	Die Deutsche Presse-Agentur GmbH.
DRRI	Digital Radio Research Inc.
DTH	Direct to Home
DVD	Digital Versatile Disc
DVD-R	Direct-View Device
DW	Deutsche Welle
E-mail	Electronic Mail
EARN	European Academic Research Network
EBN	European Business News
EBU	European Broadcasting Union
ECA	Economic Commission of the United Nations for Africa
EEC	European Economic Community
EFE	EFE Press Agency (Spain)
EFF	Electronic Frontier Foundation
EGP	Experimental Geodetic Payload
ENIAC	Electronic Numerical Integrator and Computer
ERTU	Egyptian Radio and Television Union
ESPN	Entertainment and Sports Programming Network
ESPRIT	European Strategic Programme for Research and Development
ETA	Euzkadi Ta Azkatasuna
ETI SALAT	Education and Training Institute
ETSI	European Telecommunications Standards Institute
ETV	Education TV
EUNET	Electronic University Network
FAO	Food and Agriculture Organization (of the United Nations)
FBI	Federal Bureau of Investigation
FCC	Federal Communication Commission
FESPACO	Pan-Africain Cinema Festival
FIEJ	International Federation of Newspaper Publishers
FIPP	International Federation of the Periodical Press
FM	Frequency Modulation
FPR	Front Patriotique Rwandais
G7	Group of 7
GATT	General Agreement on Tariffs and Trade
GII	Global Information Infrastructure
GMPCS	Global Mobile Personal Communication by Satellite
GSM	Global Standard for Mobile Communications
GTV	General TV
HAAC	High Authority for Audiovisual and Communication
HBO	Home Box Office
HDTV	High-Definition Television
IAB	International Association of Broadcasting
IAPA	Inter-American Press Association
IBA	Independent Broadcasting Authority
IBC	International Book Committee
IBM	International Business Machines

ICCB	Internet Configuration Control Board
ICL	International Computers Limited
ICO	International Cultural Organization
ICRC	Comité International de la Croix Rouge
IDATE	Institut de l'Audiovisuel et des Télécommunications en Europe
IDC	International Data Corporation
IEC	International Electronics Commission
IEE	Institute of Electrical Engineers
IFA	Internationale Funkausstellung
IFEX	International Freedom of Express Exchange Network
IFJ	International Federation of Journalists
IFRB	International Frequency Registration Board
ILO	International Labour Organisation
IMC	Independent Media Commission
INA	French National Audiovisual Institute
INWG	International Network Working Group
IP	Internet Protocol
IPDC	International Programme for the Development of Communication
IPI	International Press Institute
IRA	Irish Republican Army
IRS	Information Retrieval Service
ISAD	Information Society and Development
ISDN	Integrated Service Digital Network
ISKYB	India Sky Broadcasting
ISO	International Standards Organization
ISOC	Internet Society
ISRO	Indian Space Research Organization
IT	Information Technology
ITC	Independent Television Commission
ITU	International Telecommunications Union
ITU-R	International Radio Consultative Committee
JSKYB	Japan Sky Broadcasting
KANU	Kenya African National Union
KBC	Kenya Broadcasting Corporation
KCOMNET	Kenya Community Media Network
KIMC	Kenya Institute of Mass Communication
KTN	Kenya Television Network
LRNT	Research Laboratory on New Technologies
M&As	Mergers and Acquisitions
MBC	Middle East Broadcasting Centre
MBS	Mutual Broadcasting System
MCA	MCA Telecommunications
MCI	Metropolitan Communications Incorporated
MCM	Monte Carlo Music
MCME	Multichoice Middle East
MFH	Multichoice Future Holding
MICO	Micronized Coal-in-Oil
MIME	Multipurpose International Mail Extension
MIT	Massachusetts Institute of Technology
MITI	Ministry of International Trade and Industry
MMDS	Multipoint Multichannel Distribution Service
MOST	UNESCO's 'Management of Social Transformations' programme
MPT	Ministry of Post and Telecommunications
MSN	Manhattan Street Network
MTV	Music Television
MVS	Multiple Virtual Storage
NAFTA	North American Free-Trade Agreement
NANBA	North American National Broadcasters Association
NB	National Broadcasting
NBC	National Broadcasting Company
NC	Network Computer
NCP	Network Control Protocol
NCRF	National Community Radio Forum
NEC	National Engineering Consortium Incorporated
NECTEC	National Electronics and Computer Technology Center
NGO	Non-Governmental Organization
NHK	Nippon Hoso Kyokai
NICAM	Digital stereophonic sound system
NII	National Information Infrastructure
NIRS	National Indigenous Radio Service
NORDICOM	Nordic Information Centre for Media and Communication Research
NREN	National Research and Education Network
NRK	Norsk Rikskringkasting
NSF	National Science Foundation
NSFNET	National Science Foundation Network
NTT	Nippon Telephone and Telegraph
NTV	Nachrichten TV
NVOD	Near Video on Demand
NWICO	New World Information and Communication Order
NYC-SVG	National Youth Council of Saint Vincent and the Grenadines
OANA	Organization of Asia Pacific News Agencies
OECD	Organisation for Economic Co-operation and Development
OFTEL	Office of Telecommunications
OLPED	Observatory on Press Freedom, Ethics and a Professional Code of Conduct
OMRI	Open Media Research Institute
OMSYC	Communication Networks Observatory
ORSTOM	Overseas Office of Scientific Technical Research
ORT	Russian public TV station
PANA	Pan-African News Agency
PBS	Public Broadcasting System
PC	Personal Computer
PEC	Programme Exchange Centre
PEM	Processor Element Memory
PIBA	Pacific Islands Broadcasting Association
PICS	Platform for International Content Selection
POP	Point of Purchase

PPP	Point-to-Point Protocol
PTT	Postes, Télécommunications et Télédiffusion (France)
PUG	Prestel Users Group
Radio TSF	Radio Télégraphie sans Fil (wireless)
RAITNET	Regional Arab Information Technology Network
RAM	Random Access Memory
RAMAC	Random Access Method of Accounting Control
RAND	Research and Development
RARE	Réseaux Associés pour la Recherche Européenne
RBS	Rede Brasil Sul
RBT	Reliability Maintainability Trade-off
RCTI	Recherche de Corrélation de Topologie – Information
RDI	Research, Development and Innovation
RDS	Radio Data System
RFC	Resources for Communication
RFI	Radio France Internationale
RFM	Radio Frequency Modulation
RMT	Remote Batch Terminal
RMTK	Russian Television of Moscow
RTBF	Belgian Radio and Television (broadcasting in French)
RTL	Radio-Télévision du Luxembourg
RTLM	Radio-Télévision Libre Mille Collines
RTM	Radio-Télévision Marocaine
RTR	Rossia Television
RTV	Reuters Television
RTV	Romanian Radio-Television Network
SABC	South African Broadcasting Corporation
SBA	Singapore Broadcasting Authority
SBS	Scandinavian Broadcasting System
SBT	Sistema Brasileiro de Televisão
SCIP	Society of Competitor Intelligence Professionals
SCT	Computerized Telecommunication System
SEP	Newspaper Publishers' Society
SES	Société Européenne de Satellite
SITE	Satellite Instructional Television Experiment
SMTP	Simple Mail Transfer Protocol
SNG	Satellite Newsgathering
SNMP	Simple Network Management Protocol
SOFIRAD	Financial broadcasting society
SOHO	Small Office Home Office
SPA	Software Publishers Association
SSR	Swiss Radio Broadcasting Authority
STB	Singapore Telephone Board
SUN RPC	SUN Regional Processing Center
TBS	Turner Broadcasting System
TCI	Tele Communications Inc.
TCP	Transmission Control Protocol
TCPIP	Transmit Control Protocol Internet Protocol
TCS	Tata Consulting Services

TNB	Télévision Nationale du Burkina
TNT	Turner Network Television
TPS	Télévision par Satellite
TSF	Television Without Frontiers
TSN	Tape Serial Number
TVA	TV Abril
TVM	Télévision du Maroc
UBI	Universality, Bi-directionality, Interactivity
UCLA	University of California at Los Angeles
UEJF	Union des Etudiants Juifs de France
UER	European Radio-Television Union
UN	United Nations Organization
UNB	United News of Bangladesh
UNCTAD	United Nations Conference on Trade and Development
UNDA	International Catholic Association for Radio and Television
UNDP	United Nations Development Programme
UNESCO	United Nations Educational, Scientific and Cultural Organization
UNIX	Universal Inter-Active Executive (IBM)
UP ITN	Independent Television News
UPI	United Press International
UQAM	University of Quebec at Montreal
URTNA	Union of National Radio and Television Organizations of Africa
USSB	United States Satellite Broadcasting
UUCP	Unix to Unix Copy
VCR	Video-cassette Recorder
VDT	Video Dial-Tone
VOA	Voice of America
VOD	Video on Demand
VOK	Voice of Kenya
WIPO	World Intellectual Property Organization
WPFC	World Press Freedom Committee
WT	Windows Terminal
WTN	Women's Television Network
WTN	Worldwide Television News
WTO	World Trade Organization
YTV	Yokohama Television

ADSL (Asymmetric Digital Subscriber Line): Technique developed by telecommunications operators in order to transmit digitized video signals via the copper, twisted-pair telephone network, hence its widespread name Video Dial-Tone (VDT).

Analog: Conventional method of converting an oscillation such as that produced by a sound into an electrical signal. Audiovisual signals were most commonly stored in analog form before the advent of *digital*[1] technology.

ATM (Asynchronous Transfer Mode): Technique for assembling and transmitting signals via high-speed multi-service telecommunications networks which has become the most widespread technique for encoding and transmitting all types of services (data, voice, video) in packet mode, in particular on the *Internet*. It is the basic packet switching technique used by the information highways, since it enables the optimized use of very high-speed *broadband* channels (45 Mbps and higher).

Audience ratings: Technique designed to measure the proportion of viewers watching a programme or channel over a given period of time. The surveys are usually made with an audiometer installed in each of the homes forming the panel, or representative sample of the various sections of the population in terms of socioprofessional category, age, sex, type of home, etc. The information is automatically collected overnight and fed to a computer database; the latter estimates the share of viewing time allotted to a channel and thus its rank in the local audiovisual landscape.

1.　Terms in italics are themselves defined elsewhere in the Glossary.

Baud: The term is an abbreviation of Baudot, the name of its inventor, and refers to a unit of transmission speed for data in a telecommunications network. One baud corresponds to one *bit* per second.

Binary: Refers to the fact that all computer languages and the messages they convey ultimately comprise a simple series of 0s and 1s, or any other dual form of mutually exclusive, elementary components.

Bit: Contraction of 'binary digit'; refers to the smallest element of information transmitted in *binary* digital mode (i.e. 0 or 1). In the fields of information technology and *digital* tele-communications, the unit of measurement for transmission speeds is the *bit* per second, or bps.

Broadband: Refers to a telecommunication link or network capable of transporting a large quantity of information at high frequencies. The term is generally used to designate data speeds greater than 1 million bits per second (Mbps).

Byte: The encoded unit representing one alphanumeric character in a page of text. Each byte comprises eight *binary* digits with a value of '1' or '0'. A byte can therefore have 256 different combinations. The capacity of the primary storage or RAM of a computer is expressed in bytes (b). The multiples of a byte are kilobytes (Kb), or 1,024 bytes; megabytes (Mb) or 1,024 Kb; gigabytes (Gb), or 1,024 Mb. The megabyte (Mb) is the most widespread unit for quantifying the capacity of a *hard disk* or primary storage unit of a microcomputer.

Cable: Physical medium used to transmit signals in electrical form (copper coaxial cable), or as light (*fibre optic* cable) to carry radio and/or television

programmes, and other services. Cable transmission is an alternative to the transmission of signals through the atmosphere in electromagnetic form (e.g. a radio signal).

C–band and **KU–band:** *Frequency* bands allocated to *satellite* transmission.

Compact disc: Invented by Philips in 1973 to store *digital* audio data, compact discs have become an essential peripheral for most new communication media. They are capable of storing every type of information in every format, including text, graphics, still or moving pictures and computer data. The support has been upgraded several times. Its various configurations include the CD-ROM (Compact Disc – Read-Only Memory), which is used as a computer peripheral to store alphanumeric data, the CD-I (Compact Disc – Interactive), a support for multimedia applications for television use, the CD Photo, used to store photographic data that can then be displayed on a microcomputer or television, and finally the DVD (Digital Video Disc), which is destined to replace all other existing data carriers.

Computer-generated image: Image created using computer *software*. The *technology* is used in television and film productions. Several sequences of films such as 'Jurassic Park', 'The Mask', or 'True Lies' have been produced using 3-D (three-dimensional) computer images.

Cracker: Networked computer users who are both deft and dangerous. They pirate supposedly foolproof or protected computer systems, not for fun as *hackers* do, but to destroy or defraud.

Cyber: Concept referring to all forms of thought or activity connected with new information and communication *technology*, and with planetary communication networks in particular.

Cyber-café: Public place where users can purchase food and drink, in return for which they have access to the *Internet*.

Cyberspace: Concept invented in 1984 by the author William Gibson in his science fiction novel 'Neuromancer'. The term defines a new form of *virtual* space in which the whole world is connected via *cable* systems, *satellites*, and global networks such as the *Internet* or the forthcoming *information highways*.

DAB (Digital Audio Broadcasting): New system of *digital* transmission for radio programmes. It has the advantage of being immune to transmission noise or interference, and of enabling the simultaneous supply of several programmes and/or services of all kinds and sources. It provides radio listeners with audio quality equivalent to that of a *compact disc*. The system also makes it possible to transmit data connected with the programme. This means that on their radio receivers, listeners will also be able to read the title of a song or musical work, a biography of the performers, and the dates and venues of their current tour.

Data bank: A stock of computerized information relating to a specific field of know-how or knowledge, organized to enable remote access by telecommunications networks. Electronic data banks have done away with paper files and microfilm.

Decoder: Device required for the *encryption* and decryption of data (such as video or textual messages), also permitting the purchase of programmes at will, via *pay-per-view* (PPV).

Deregulation: Complete or partial removal of the rules restricting competition in a given economic sector (telecommunications, banking, air transport, etc.).

Digital: Refers to all the operations involving the encoding of data, audio and video information in *digital* form in order to process it by computerized means and use it for *multimedia* applications in particular. Digital information is by definition discrete, unlike its *analog* counterpart. Another major advantage is that digital information can be duplicated an infinite number of times without any loss in quality in relation to the original.

Digital Data Compression: Technique used to reduce the size of a file containing the data for still or moving pictures, in order to minimize the time required to transmit it. The two most widespread data compression standards are *MPEG* for moving pictures and *JPEG* for still pictures. Applied to the transmission of audio or video signals, compression *technology* enables the transport of a greater number of programmes on a given channel. Instead of the single programme that can be transported on a given *analog* channel, using digital data compression, eight or even ten programmes can be transported on the same channel.

Dish antenna or aerial: Antenna of parabolic shape used for the reception of signals transmitted by satellite. Dish antennae enable a maximum amount of the energy received to be concentrated in a single point, the focus of the dish. The quality of the signal received depends on the output power of the satellite, the dimension of the dish and the quality of its peripheral equipment. The latest technological breakthroughs now make it possible to have a receiving signal of good quality with medium-size dishes (40 to 80 cm in diameter) and satellites of medium power.

Electronic commerce: Refers to all the commercial activities involving the electronic transmission of data via *e-mail*, Electronic Funds Transfer (EFT) and Electronic Data Interchange (EDI).

Electronic trading: Designed to replace banknotes and cheques by computerized means, using magnetic or microprocessor cards.

E-mail: Refers to the transmission of messages and data from computer to computer by remote users. The latter can send messages or files containing audio or video data to correspondents on the other side of the world, who can pick them up later at will. As with any other form of mail service, users need an address as their identity card.

Encryption: In the field of broadcasting, the term refers to a video encoding technique. Unscrambled reception of the picture is only accessible to subscribers with a *decoder.* In information technology, data encryption is performed with algorithms that code messages in such a manner that they can be interpreted only by users with a computer. Encryption forms part of the security and confidentiality technologies used to protect the data transmitted on networks.

Fee-paying: Method of direct financing in the form of subscriptions paid by viewers to watch scrambled channels transmitted either by terrestrial means or by satellite or *cable* networks. Fee-paying is developing around the world based on the North American model, in which subscribers pay a fee to receive a certain number of programmes, just as they do for their electricity, water or telephone services.

Fibre optics: See optical fibre.

Frequency: The number of vibrations in an electromagnetic wave over a given period of time. For the purposes of radio transmission, frequency is expressed in hertz, a unit of measurement corresponding to a frequency of one vibration per second. In practical use, radio transmission takes place at frequencies of at least kilohertz level (kHz), or multiples of 1,000 vibrations per second, but also in megahertz (MHz) or multiples of 1 million vibrations per second, as in the case of frequency modulation (FM) radio.

Geostationary orbit: In order for *dish antennae* to be permanently directed towards a given satellite, the latter must remain immobile in relation to the Earth's surface. To do so, the rotation of the satellite around the planet must be at the same angular speed as that of the rotation of the Earth in relation to the same axis. The orbit must therefore be situated in an equatorial plane passing through the centre of the Earth and perpendicular to its axis. Given that they are in geostationary orbit, only three satellites are needed to cover the entire surface of the Earth with the signals they transmit.

Globalization: Concept originating in Anglo-Saxon countries which refers to the increasingly worldwide nature of industrial production and trade, caused by the rapid development of new information and communication technology, and the instant, planetary transmission of their content.

Gopher: Network navigation service or, more generally, a search tool designed to facilitate and accelerate the retrieval of information from one computer server to another, by selecting options on a menu. Named after the mascot of the University of Minnesota (United States).

Graphic interface: Screen display based on graphics designed to facilitate the use of a computer. With the launch of the Macintosh and its celebrated icons in 1984, the American manufacturer Apple was the first company to develop a humanized form of computing similar to the user's own sense of intuition. This concept formed one of the major breakthroughs in microcomputing. Since then, *technology* and techniques have slowly faded into the background, giving way to more user-friendly, *interactive* processes, thereby helping to close the gap between users and computers.

GSM (Global System for Mobile Telecommunications): A cellular *digital* radiocommunication system set up by the ETSI (European Telecommunications Standards Institute) and adopted worldwide on the 900 MHz waveband following agreement between operators around the planet.

Hacker: Computer expert or enthusiast, capable of secretly penetrating the supposedly foolproof computer programs of large firms or institutions. The hacker can thereby gain access to confidential information.

Hard disk: High-capacity storage unit on computers. Hard disks are used to store *software* systems and computer data. Without them, a computer would have no *memory*, and would lose its autonomy of operation. The breakthroughs that have been made in terms of the miniaturization of hard disks and their storage capacity are phenomenal.

Hardware/software: The former term refers to everything connected with the material forms of computer *technology*. Software refers to computer programs and their applications in every field of activity.

HDTV (High-Definition Television): *Analog* form of television *broadcasting* enabling the number of sweep lines to be doubled (from 625 lines to 1,250 in Europe, and from 525 lines to 1,125 in Japan and the United States), in order to transmit cinema-quality sound and pictures on screens which have been expanded from a 4/3 width-height ratio to 16/9. The various attempts to develop HDTV systems, such as the MUSE-HIVISION broadcasting standards developed since 1966 by the Japanese company NHK, and the D2 Mac-Pac followed by the HD Mac standard developed by the leading European industrials, have now been abandoned in favour of all-digital television.

Home or home page: The first page which is displayed on-screen when one accesses a service or an application on the *Internet*.

House automation: The use of new *technology* in managing the home (remote control of household appliances, safety automation, power management and communications). Home automation is slowly being integrated into the design of 'intelligent' buildings in industrialized countries.

HTML (Hypertext Mark-up Language): Computer language which defines the syntax of pages on the *World Wide Web* (WWW). This means a document has a constant form, no matter what computer is used to access it, and enables documents to be connected by links. HTML is interpreted by WWW customer *software* such as Mosaic or Netscape.

Hypertext: Concept invented by the American computer expert Ted Nelson in 1965, giving *interactive*, non-linear access to data of all sorts. The term refers to the logic underlying the links created within a text or image displayed on the screen of a computer terminal, and enables instant migration from one file or data server to another by clicking to select a given text or image with a computer mouse.

Information society: A form of modern society that is currently developing, created by the new information and communication technologies and the convergence between them. The mutation has led to a modern industrial revolution based on information, knowledge and know-how, providing new potential for human intelligence, and changing the ways in which people live and work together. Production in 'paperless' or immaterial form in particular is becoming a decisive factor in the new 'added value' form of economy. According to its promoters, the information society should enable each and every citizen to access some form of intellectual creativity and attain a high level of productivity.

Information superhighway and highway: Global, high-speed network capable of routing a series of *interactive* services to subscribers, such as *teleshopping*, distance learning, data bank accession, *pay-per-view* television, visiophoning, and other new services. The highways are seen as a technological, economic and cultural revolution, comparable in industrial circles to the major civil engineering undertakings of the nineteenth century.

Integrated Service Digital Network: A digital telecommunications network with a broad *passband* enabling a series of signals of widely differing types to be transmitted simultaneously. This makes possible the integration of basic services such as telephony, remote computing, visiophoning and data transfer.

Intellectual property: Copyright or patent protecting the product of human thought, such as new ideas, inventions, written texts, films, etc.

Interactivity: System of information transmission for the exchange of messages between a user and a computer or other type of audiovisual medium. When applied to television, the system enables viewers to access services such as *pay-per-view* television, distance learning, telemedicine, *teleshopping* and *video on demand*, and to intervene in the programmes that are being broadcast (playing games, downloading them, choosing a different camera shot, etc.).

Internaut: User of the resources available on the *Internet*.

Internet: Global communication network formed by the interconnection of all the IP (Internet Protocol) networks in the world. The Internet is the largest computer network on the planet, linking more than 130 countries. The network provides an extremely extensive range of services, the best known of which are the *World Wide Web*, the multimedia part of the Internet, *newsgroups*, *e-mail* services, etc. The development of the services on the Web is determined by three factors: the processing power and speed of the multimedia computers connected to it, the throughput capacity of the transmission channel (telephone line or *cable* network) they use, and the *data compression* rate possible for the source documents. These three factors will enable multimedia products to be dispatched via the Internet. The predecessor of the Internet was the Arpanet network developed during the 1960s by the US Defense Department.

Intranet: Private network using *Internet* techniques, principally designed for use inside companies.

ISO (International Standards Organisation): Defines the technical standards for international use in various fields, particularly in information technology and telecommunications.

JPEG (Joint Photographic Expert Group): Standard used for the *data compression* of still pictures (photographs).

Laser (Light Amplification by Stimulated Emission of Radiation): *Technology* for the transmission of a luminous signal with considerable energy, in the order of kW/mm^2.

LEO: Low Earth Orbit satellite (780 km).

Memory: Device used to store, file and retrieve computer data. A standard distinction is made between two types of memory: the primary storage or RAM (for Random Access Memory), whose contents can be modified or written, and Read-Only Memory (ROM), the contents of which, as its name implies, can only be read.

Microprocessor: Concept based on the term 'process', referring to a small-scale electronic circuit with a surface area of a few square centimetres containing several million transistors. In the field of information technology, microprocessors form the heart of a computer. They process and route data. The faster the flow of data, the better the performance of the computer. The processing power of the microprocessor, expressed in megahertz, defines the computing speed of the machine.

MMDS (Microwave Multichannel Distribution System): Also known as a 'microwave cable' or 'wireless cable'. Permits the multiple distribution of television channels in microwave form, transmitted either in *analog* or in *digital* mode. It is used as a complement to cable networks, particularly in areas where the installation of a cable network would not be worth while.

Modem: Contraction of modulator-demodulator. Device which converts *digital* signals into *analog* form, and vice versa. In information technology, it refers to a device which converts the signals conveyed by telephone lines (i.e. in analog form) into digital signals that can be processed by a computer, and vice versa. This peripheral enables the computer to be connected with the outside world, to dialogue with another computer or to access a *data bank*.

MPEG (Moving Picture Expert Group): A standard, named after the international group of experts who defined it, for the data compression and formatting of moving pictures. There are two versions of the standard: MPEG 1, designed for low-definition images (of VHS quality), has already been defined, for throughputs of up to 1.5 Mbps. The MPEG 2 standard, which was finalized in 1995, is a variable throughput standard designed to obtain a quality of image which is closer to the level expected by professionals in the imaging industry.

Multimedia: Communication technique designed to combine the information conveyed by different media (texts, graphics, photographic, video and audio data) on a single support medium in *digital* form, thereby making it easy to store, copy or transmit without any loss in quality. The resulting combined programme can be simultaneously and *interactively* transmitted on a single support medium.

Netiquette: Contraction of Inter*net* and *etiquette*. The notion refers to the set of rules, common sense and courtesy that govern the behaviour of *Internauts*.

News agency: Company that gathers, collates and processes information of all kinds – wires, texts, photographs, illustrations and filmed documents – in order to distribute and transmit it in return for payment, most frequently in subscription form, to the business companies and various media, such as daily newspapers, weeklies, radio stations and television networks, which form its customer base.

Newsgroup: Specialized *on-line* discussion groups in which ideas, opinions and points of view on a wide variety of subjects are exchanged, often on a store-and-forward basis using bulletin boards.

Off-line: Refers to an independent service or application, i.e. which is not connected to a network or other computerized system.

On-line: Refers to a system in direct contact with another, such as access in *real time* to data via a computerized network. *Interactive* access, or simply browsing for information, are both possible.

Optic fibre: Technical medium for transmission comprising a thin tube of glass fibre capable of routing vast quantities of information transmitted at the speed of light by laser pulses. Despite their extremely small diameter (from 5 to 80 microns), fibre-optic cables can transmit much more information than coaxial *cables* or copper wire. They also have the advantage of being able to propagate light waves over extremely long distances.

Passband: Width of the *frequency* band used to transmit a signal on a communication network. The unit of measurement for bandwidth is the megahertz, and its transmission capacity is expressed in *bits* per second, or bps. The wider the bandwidth, the greater the 'fluidity' of the information transported. The quality of the signal transmitted and received, and therefore the quantity of data which can be transmitted, depend on these characteristics. Voice data are generally transmitted on narrow bandwidths, whereas multimedia applications require wide bands. When referring to the information highways, the term *broadband* is often used.

Password: Private, secret code that a computer user enters during the access procedure to a communication network.

Pay-per-view: Television service in which payment is made on the basis of the programmes watched.

Photographic typesetting: Printing process using typesetters, no longer to produce type lines made of lead, but transparent positive or negative films.

Photojournalism: Form of journalism in which greater emphasis is placed on photographic pictures than written material as a source of information.

Pixel: The smallest unit, or picture element, of the image on a television or computer screen.

Plug and play: Refers to the possibility of immediately connecting and using a computer and its main functions without having to go through a series of frequently complicated assembly and installation procedures.

Programming stream: A series of television programmes broadcast by satellite and marketed in group form.

Radio beam: System of terrestrial transmission based on the propagation of electromagnetic waves. The frequencies of these waves are extremely high. The waves are concentrated into a narrow beam and propagated in a straight line. Their transmission requires a large number of relays to account for abrupt changes in terrain. The hertz is the unit of measurement of *frequency* corresponding to one oscillatory cycle per second (from the name of its inventor, Hertz).

Radio broadcasting: Technique consisting in the transmission through space of a modulated carrier. Sound signals, for instance, are transformed into electrical signals that are modulated in relation to the original sound and then broadcast. On reception, the electrical signals are converted back into sound and then amplified into a loudspeaker. There are basically two modulation processes: amplitude modulation (AM), and frequency modulation (FM).

Real time: Refers to the immediate processing of computer data, thereby enabling *interactive* applications.

Regulatory authority: Institution generally free of any administrative or political allegiance, whose assignment is to ensure the independence of communication resources, to oversee changes in the audiovisual landscape and to enforce the rule of pluralism.

Remote typesetting: Preparation of texts using computers and telecommunications networks to transmit type.

Satellites: Broadcasting based on radio waves can make use of networks of terrestrial transmitters, but can also use satellites. There are two main families of satellite: telecommunications satellites, and direct-broadcast satellites, although the differences between the two are increasingly small. Telecommunications satellites make use of point-to-point satellite links (with very low power output, transmitting signals between a limited number of stations) and distribution satellites (which are more powerful, and transmit data and telephone traffic as well as television channels). Direct-broadcast satellites are used for the individual reception of programmes via parabolic antennae with a diameter of 60 cm, based on the use of simple, inexpensive *technology*. Combined satellites transmit telephone communications or data traffic, and live television programmes.

Standard: In television, refers to the PAL, SECAM and NTSC systems for encoding the information required for the transmission and reception of colour television and video pictures. The PAL process (for Phase Alternating Line) is a German standard invented in 1962 by Walter Bruch at the Telefunken company. It is used throughout Europe except for France and the countries of the former Soviet Union and in Central and Eastern Europe. The system is based on a screen sweep of 625 lines, 25 images of which are broadcast every second

(50 Hz). The SECAM process (from 'séquentiel à mémoire') is a French standard created in 1953 by Henri de France and is based on the transmission of 25 images each with 625 lines. It is mainly used in Eastern Europe and in Africa with various technical differences. The NTSC process (National Television System Committee) is an image encoding system defined in 1954 which is used mainly in Canada, Japan, South America and the United States. It is based on screen sweeps of 525 lines (60 Hz).

TCP/IP (Transmission Control Protocol/Internet Protocol): Designates the family of protocols used in the Internet architecture.

Technological convergence: The merging of telecommunications, audiovisual and computer technologies.

Technology: Concept that has replaced 'techniques', and refers to a set of tools and equipment used in crafts and industry. By extrapolation, it also refers to the advanced techniques, material resources and structural organizations which implement the latest scientific discoveries and their applications. In the field of communication, it designates an array of new equipment used to create, produce, manage and disseminate data (text, video, audio). This involves everything related to telecommunications, the audiovisual sector and computer systems, and includes both the material media and the use of their content by means of *software* systems and programs.

Telecommuting: Working at home or remote from the workplace using computerized tools and/or telecommunications, involving the transmission of the data needed for carrying out the requisite work.

Telematics: Contraction of *tele-* and infor*matics*. Refers to all the computerized services providing users with transparent, interactive access. Telematics makes use of information technology, telecommunications and *interactivity*.

Teleshopping: Modern form of mail ordering made possible by interactive television, enabling viewers to remote-access product catalogues, place their orders in *real time* and pay for their purchases direct if their terminals are equipped with an *electronic money* system.

Television broadcasting: The transmission of television signals to cover a given territory. There are three main technical means of broadcasting: radio networks, *cable* networks and *satellites*. Broadcasting using radio waves consists in transmitting signals as modulated electromagnetic waves. Historically, radio networks were the first means of broadcasting radio and then television programmes. Cable networks have developed mainly in the industrialized countries as a complement to terrestrial broadcasting. Satellites are the ideal medium for the broadcasting of new channels and the transmission of national and international programmes. A distinction is generally drawn between two types of satellite: telecommunication satellites and direct-broadcast satellites.

Universal service: Form of public service designed to contend with competition, mainly in the field of telecommunications. A universal service guarantees by law that every citizen shall have the same right of access to telephone services and other basic facilities.

Videoconference: A meeting between people physically situated at different locations linked by telecommunications systems enabling the transmission in real time of video and sound. Because the pictures are transmitted simultaneously in both directions, videoconferencing is a

telecommunications service that requires networks with high transmission capacity (*broadband*).

Video memory: Refers to the VRAM (for Video RAM) memory device in which images to be displayed on-screen are stored. The greater the storage capacity, the faster the images are displayed, and the better their definition, as long as the performance of the screen is equally high.

Video on demand: Service enabling consumers to rent video programmes from a catalogue which they have accessed remote.

Virtual reality: Concept related to the new techniques of simulation, designed to make the world generated in three dimensions by a computer appear to be real. Three words are characteristic of virtual reality: immersion, interaction and navigation. They refer respectively to the notion that the viewer is no longer in front of the image but inside it, and is capable not only of interacting with his or her immediate environment, but of navigating through it. Flight simulators, the first of which was produced by General Electric in 1958, are a good example of virtual reality.

Voice recognition: The capacity of a system to understand and respond to a command voiced by a user. Ultimately, the technique is designed to enable computer users to do away with keyboards.

World Wide Web (WWW, 3W): Hypermedia[2] system enabling the display of electronic documents interconnected by *hypertext* links. Developed by Tim Bertners-Lee of the CERN (Conseil Européen de Recherche Nucléaire) in Geneva, the system permits

---

2.   *Hypertext* software that enables the user to combine text and graphics with audio and video on a computer.

the design of 'home pages' or 'welcome screens' for use on the *Internet* which guide users as they navigate through the network to read or find documents. Web pages of this kind can be accessed and consulted just as one would a vast indexed dictionary.

Wireless communication: Stationary, portable or otherwise mobile communication device based on radio waves.